WITHDRAWN

Higher Education Research

Also available from Bloomsbury

Reflective Teaching in Higher Education, Paul Ashwin

Higher Education Research

The Developing Field

Malcolm Tight

BLOOMSBURY ACADEMIC

LONDON • NEW YORK • OXFORD • NEW DELHI • SYDNEY

BLOOMSBURY ACADEMIC
Bloomsbury Publishing Plc
50 Bedford Square, London, WC1B 3DP, UK
1385 Broadway, New York, NY 10018, USA

BLOOMSBURY, BLOOMSBURY ACADEMIC and the Diana logo are trademarks
of Bloomsbury Publishing Plc

First published in Great Britain 2019

Cover design by Anna Berzovan

ISBN: HB: 978-1-4742-8373-1
PB: 978-1-4742-8374-8
ePDF: 978-1-4742-8375-5
eBook: 978-1-4742-8376-2

Typeset by Deanta Global Publishing Services, Chennai, India

To find out more about our authors and books visit www.bloomsbury.com
and sign up for our newsletters.

Contents

Chapter 1
Introduction

As higher education has expanded – as measured by the number of students enrolled, the number of universities and colleges enrolling them, the number and size of research grants obtained, and numerous other indices – so the interest in researching higher education has grown (though with something of a time lag built in). In part, this growing interest in higher education research is simply a function of the size of the higher education enterprise, but it also relates to the increasing concern to ensure that value is obtained for the money and time invested in higher education (historically, much of the former has been public, but, with the arrival of mass higher education, it is becoming increasingly private).

In the UK, for example, at present over 4 per cent of the population are enrolled in higher education and nearly 1 per cent work in it in some capacity (www.hesa.ac.uk), so one in twenty of the population are 'directly involved'. Higher education is 'big business', and most universities – many now the size of small towns – are the major employer and traffic hub in their localities. All of this activity is hard to ignore, so it is a natural focus for research. This focus is only made stronger because most of the researchers involved themselves work within higher education.

The aim of this book is to provide an analytical and critical overview of how the field of higher education research has developed worldwide, its current state and future prospects. Or, to put it another way, what have we learnt about the theory and practice of higher education, and what requires further study? This book should, therefore, be of considerable interest to anyone working in or concerned by higher education at the present time, and should serve as a record of where we were at the time of publication.

What this book contains

As well as this introductory chapter and a concluding chapter (Chapter 11), the book has been organized in terms of nine main chapters. The first of these, the next chapter (Chapter 2), focuses on research designs and frameworks. It discusses, with examples, the range of research methodologies, methods, designs and theoretical frameworks that have been applied to the study of higher education. This provides a methodological and theoretical overview for what follows.

The next eight chapters make up the substantive part of the book. Between them, these set out to cover the entire field of higher education research organized in terms of eight themes or topic areas. These focus successively on:

- Teaching and learning (Chapter 3)
- Course design (Chapter 4)
- The student experience (Chapter 5)
- Quality (Chapter 6)
- System policy (Chapter 7)
- Institutional management (Chapter 8)
- Academic work (Chapter 9)
- Knowledge and research (Chapter 10)

Chapter 3 deals with research into how students learn and how they are taught; while Chapter 4 examines research on the higher education curriculum, its organization and assessment; and Chapter 5 discusses research on students' access to and exit from higher education, and their broader life experience while they are studying.

Chapter 6 focuses on research that has evaluated the quality of teaching, research and other aspects of higher education; while Chapter 7 is concerned with research on all other aspects of higher education policy, at national and international levels. Chapter 8 examines research on how higher education institutions are organized, managed and governed; Chapter 9 considers research on the roles of those who work in academe; and Chapter 10 focuses on research on academic disciplines and the research process.

This organization was developed from research I have been conducting into the field over the last two decades; more details of this are provided in the next section of this chapter. While there are inevitably some overlaps between the eight themes (cross-references are provided between chapters where appropriate), and there are, of course, other ways in which the discussion could have been organized, this structure has proved sufficiently robust and has been adopted and/or adapted by a number of other researchers.

Each of the eight core chapters is organized in the same way, and in two main sections. The first of these sections provides an overview of the development of research on the topic in question and its current status. The second section then examines three research designs or frameworks that have become influential and/or prominent for researching the topic. Of course, other research designs or frameworks might have been chosen for detailed discussion; but the ones I have selected should give a good idea of the state of higher education research, theme by theme.

The final, concluding chapter draws together what we have learnt from several decades of higher education research, and sets out to identify where further research is particularly needed.

How the book was compiled

This book is research based; it is a guide to the research that has been done rather than a manual on how to do research (though it should be useful in suggesting what needs to be researched now, and how this might be done). Indeed, it is based on a great deal of research, both my own in putting it together and the far greater volume of other people's research that I have drawn upon in doing so.

In essence, the strategy adopted in compiling the book has been to identify, read, categorize and analyse as much as possible of the higher education research that has been published. This is a technique that goes beyond the standard literature review, taking the form of what has been termed a meta-analysis or a systematic review (see, for example, Cooper 2010; Hunter and Schmidt 2004; Lipsey and Wilson 2001; Littell, Corcoran and Pillai 2008). The former term is generally used when the analysis is quantitative, the latter when it is primarily qualitative; both, but particularly the latter, are employed in this book.

The research for this book was, therefore, no small task, so I have had to place some limitations on it. The most important of these has been to focus on research outputs produced in the English language (which, as well as being my own, is also the dominant academic language globally). While this has inevitably led to a greater focus on higher education research in the United States, United Kingdom, Australia and other major English-speaking nations, a substantial amount of higher education research by researchers based in non-English-speaking countries, notably in continental Europe and East Asia, has also been published in the English language, particularly in the most recent decades.

The other major limitations have had to do with ease of access and recency. In terms of access I have focused principally on those research outputs that were most readily available: that is, those published as articles in what are, arguably, the leading higher education journals internationally, and are available online. Books, reports and other forms of publication have also been considered. In terms of recency, while I have sought to track research trends back to their origins, there is inevitably an over-emphasis on more recent publications. This is partly a function of there being many more research papers published today than there were seventy years ago – on higher education as on almost any other subject – and partly to do with the greater difficulty of identifying and accessing older publications.

The research which led to this book began with the comprehensive examination of the articles published in fifteen journals focusing on higher education research in the years 2000 and 2010. The fifteen journals were: *Assessment and Evaluation in Higher Education, Higher Education, Higher Education Management and Policy, Higher Education Policy, Higher Education Quarterly, Higher Education Research and Development, Innovative Higher Education, Journal of College Student Development, Journal of Higher Education, Journal of Higher Education Policy and Management, Research in Higher Education, Review of Higher Education, Studies in Higher Education, Teaching in Higher Education, Tertiary Education and*

Management. These journals were chosen as representing the best-quality specialist journals in the field internationally, based in the United States, the United Kingdom, Australasia and continental Europe.

Following this initial analysis of 388 articles published in 2000, and 567 published in 2010, the work spread outwards to other dates, other journals and other forms of publication, and backwards to track the historical development of the research literature. Each publication analysed has been considered in terms of the themes and issues covered, the methods and/or methodologies employed to examine these issues, the broader research designs adopted, the theoretical frameworks employed (if any), the level at which the analysis was pitched (anything from an individual student or academic to the whole world), and the characteristics of the researchers/authors involved.

Considerable use has been made of databases and search engines, most notably Scopus and Google Scholar, both to chart the trends in publication on particular themes (all searches referred to in the book were checked on 1 October 2017, before the book was handed over to the publisher) and to identify further publications of potential interest. Interestingly, while the trends in publication are typically of increasing numbers year by year, in some cases publication rates have dropped as fashions in research and nomenclature have changed (i.e. sometimes much the same topic continues to be researched, but it is given a different label).

The 2000 and 2010 analyses were published in two books (Tight 2003, 2012a). Other publications have examined, in a more focused way, the application of particular research designs (Tight 2016a), methods or methodologies (Tight 2013), and theoretical frameworks (Tight 2004, 2014a,c,d, 2015a,b,c, 2016b, forthcoming a, b), comparative trends (Tight 2007, 2014b), levels of analysis (Tight 2012c), journal publication patterns (Tight 2012b, 2018, forthcoming a), citation patterns (Tight 2006, 2008, 2009b), and the historical development of research (Tight 2009a, 2015d,e) in higher education.

How to use this book

While this book has been designed and written as (at least an attempt at) a comprehensive synopsis of the entire field of higher education research, there are a number of ways in which it might be read and used. As a whole, it should form a reliable guide for those engaged or interested in the field of higher education research, as students or researchers. Those interested in particular areas of the field, such as teaching and learning or academic work, might choose to devote their attention to specific chapters; while those interested in the use of specific theoretical frameworks or research designs, such as phenomenography or communities of practice, in higher education research may focus down on particular sections, using the contents pages or index to navigate their way through the book.

Whichever way you use the book, however, there should be plenty here to engage your interest. The extensive references provided should enable you to track down key researchers and publications, and follow up your interests as thoroughly as you wish.

Chapter 2
Research Designs and Frameworks

Introduction

This chapter provides an overview of the range of research methods, methodologies, designs and theoretical frameworks that have been applied to higher education research. It is organized in four main sections:

- the terminology of methods, methodologies, designs, frameworks and so on is discussed, and the distinctions between them, and their usage in this book, are clarified;
- the range of methodologies and methods used within higher education research are identified, and their relative prevalence and application to different topics are discussed;
- the major theoretical frameworks employed within higher education research are examined, together with their origins and usage; and
- the overall research designs that have been adopted in higher education research are identified and explained.

This chapter, which ends with some conclusions, is intended to serve as a reference point for the discussion in the chapters that follow.

Terminology: Research methodologies, methods, frameworks and designs

The terminology used in discussing and categorizing research can be both complex and confusing. Hence, it makes sense at the beginning to try and make some useful distinctions, and set out how the terminology will be used in this book. We will discuss methodology and method first, then theoretical frameworks and finally research design.

Methodology and method

Definitions of the terms 'method' and 'methodology' may be found in most research textbooks. Thus, Punch (1998, p. 3) defines methods as 'the techniques or procedures used to gather and analyse data related to some research question or hypothesis', and methodology as 'the strategy, plan of action, process or design lying behind the choice and use of particular methods and linking the choice and use of methods to the desired outcomes'. Cohen, Manion and Morrison (2007, p. 47), to take a second example, put it slightly differently:

> By methods, we mean that range of approaches used in educational research to gather data which are to be used as a basis for inference and interpretation, for explanation and prediction. ... If methods refer to techniques and procedures used in the process of data-gathering, the aim of methodology then is to describe approaches to, kinds and paradigms of research.

While these distinctions are helpful, they are perhaps not as clear cut as they might be, as is suggested, for example, by Cohen, Manion and Morrison's use of the term 'approaches' in their definitions of both methodologies and methods. Nevertheless, the distinction between the overall plan for data collection and analysis (methodology) and the specific techniques used (methods) is fairly clear. In practice, though, some researchers – in higher education as in other fields – use these terms fairly interchangeably and/or in overlapping ways. In recognition of this, the compound term method/ologies will be employed in places in this book.

Some researchers – again in higher education as in other fields – are also not always explicit about their methods or methodology. In some cases, this may be because they are simply unaware of them, or do not consider them of importance: they just 'do' the research and then write it up. In part, it may also be because the article format in which research is most commonly published offers only a limited amount of space, although many journals do require (or expect) that authors are explicit about methods and methodology.

Theoretical frameworks

Like all key terms, our understanding of what constitutes theory is contested. Nevertheless, two recent definitions of theory provided by social/educational researchers suggest a good deal of common ground:

> The idea of theory, or the ability to explain and understand the findings of research within a conceptual framework that makes 'sense' of the data, is the mark of a mature discipline whose aim is the systematic study of particular phenomena. (May 2001, p. 29)

> Theory denotes any coherent description and explanation of observed phenomena which provides a testable, verifiable or falsifiable, representation of social relationships. (Kettley 2010, p. 9)

If the articulation and application of theory is, as May argues, a key characteristic of a mature discipline, it is an aspect that higher education researchers are steadily coming to terms with. Previous analysis (Tight 2004) indicated that much published higher education research showed little or no engagement with theory. Yet, as Maassen and Stensaker (2005, p. 223) have stated, 'It is vital to search for and use robust and rich theories in our common development of the field of higher education studies.' The position, however, appears to be improving, particularly if we examine articles published more recently in the higher quality journals (Tight 2012a, 2014a).

The apparent reluctance, on the part of at least some researchers, to engage with theory is likely partly due – as the quotation from May suggests – to the relative immaturity of higher education research as a field. A rather more important factor in this respect, however, has to do with the emphasis placed in much higher education research (and in educational research generally; e.g. Adams, Cochrane and Dunne 2012a; Pring 2005) on the improvement of practice. Hence the role of theory in educational research has been hotly debated (e.g. Ball 1995; Biesta, Allan and Edwards 2011; Carr 2006). Yet, theoretical development and practical improvement may go hand in hand and be mutually supportive.

In focusing on the place of theory in research, some looseness in language has also to be acknowledged. A multiplicity of more or less analogous terms are in common usage alongside theory, including, for example, concept, idea, framework and model (thus, two of these terms are used by May in his quoted account of theory). Underlying this looseness of language, however, is a good deal of variability in the way the term 'theory' is used:

> Theory has a multitude of meanings, not all of which can be easily reconciled, making it a concept open to wide appropriation. For example, theory can simply mean an idea about a social configuration, or it can mean an intellectual formula that enables one to structure experience (or data, in terms of research); sometimes it is used broadly and is synonymous with philosophy, or it is used specifically as an interpretative description of experience. Theorizing can be an expansive business, in that it can be thought of as an act that generates new ways of thinking about the way the world is configured, and may be generalized and transferred to a multitude of new concepts in the expectation that it will throw light on them. (Adams, Cochrane and Dunne 2012b, p. 1)

Others would make different, if perhaps analogous, distinctions between, for example, high- and low-level theories, or between grand and everyday or common-sense theories.

While we may, therefore, accept that theories are attempts at explanation, we may also ask, when examining their usage in research, what sort of theory is being articulated.

Research designs

What, then, is a research design, and how does it differ from methodology and theory? I am using this term to refer to the overarching approach (that word again, I'm afraid) taken towards a particular research project. As such, a research design typically encompasses distinctive methodological *and* theoretical positions or viewpoints (even if these are not recognized and articulated). Research designs are, therefore, set above both methodology and theory in the research hierarchy.

The relationships between research design, methodology and theory – as these terms are being employed here – may readily be illustrated in the context of phenomenography (discussed further in Chapter 3). Phenomenographers adopt a particular (albeit with some variations) methodological strategy for data collection and analysis. This typically involves the use of interviews, the data from which is then treated collectively for the purposes of analysis, such that the focus is on the variations in understanding across the whole sample. In terms of theoretical framework, phenomenographers operate with the underlying assumption that, for any given phenomenon of interest, there are only a limited number of ways of perceiving, understanding or experiencing it.

Phenomenographers, therefore, have firm (if, inevitably, somewhat varied) ideas about how phenomenography should be practised (i.e. a methodology). They also have firm ideas about the pattern of what they are likely to find through their research (i.e. a theoretical framework). Taking these characteristics together, therefore, we may refer to phenomenography as a research design.

That said, however, we must recognize that phenomenographers themselves characterize phenomenography in a wide variety of ways (Collier-Reed and Ingerman 2013). Indeed, in the remainder of this chapter, phenomenography will be further discussed in terms of its contribution to both methodology and theory.

Methodology and method in higher education research

Higher education research, broadly speaking, makes use of much the same range of methods and methodologies that are applied in the social sciences generally, but with the occasional addition or development of its own. Thus, an analysis carried out of the 567 articles published in 15 leading international higher education journals in 2010 (Tight 2012a, p. 26) identified 7 main groups of methods or methodologies:

- documentary analysis, where the focus is on the examination of one or more documents (either textual or audio–visual in nature);
- interviews, with one or more individuals or groups (including focus groups);
- surveys and multivariate analyses, ranging from simple questionnaires to the use of highly sophisticated mathematical or statistical techniques;
- conceptual analysis, where the focus is on advancing understanding of one or more concepts;
- phenomenography, exploring people's understanding of a particular phenomenon or phenomena of interest;

- critical/feminist perspectives, setting out to challenge existing structures and understandings; and

- auto/biographical and observational studies, where the focus is on, in the former case, the experience of a particular individual, or, in the latter case, watching and keeping notes of events of particular interest.

Other groupings are, of course, possible and, as their descriptions make clear, a finer grained categorization would also be possible, if more unwieldy.

Naturally enough, some of these method/ological categories proved to be much more popular among higher education researchers than others: the first three categories, after all, are the main method/ologies used throughout social science research. Thus, the most popular method/ologies in use in the sample of articles examined were surveys and multivariate analyses (43.6 per cent of articles), documentary analysis (26.5 per cent) and interviews (21.0 per cent).

By comparison, there were relatively few examples of articles based on auto/biographical and observational studies (4.2 per cent), conceptual analysis (3.7 per cent) or phenomenography (1.1 per cent). There were no examples of articles taking critical or feminist perspectives in the database of articles examined (such articles do exist, but are probably more likely to be published in different sorts of journals, even if their focus is on higher education). These four categories are clearly, then, relatively unpopular or what might be termed niche methodological approaches; each, however, has its strong advocates.

There were some interesting variations in the use of method/ologies in terms of the different topics or themes being researched. The most popular method/ology overall, surveys and multivariate analyses, was the most popular approach taken for five of the eight themes identified: teaching and learning, course design, the student experience, quality and academic work. Documentary analysis was the most popular method/ology for the remaining three themes: system policy, institutional management, knowledge and research. Interviews were widely used to research course design, the student experience and academic work.

The more specialist (or less widely used) method/ologies were heavily concentrated in just two of the eight themes. Both conceptual analysis and auto/biographical and observational studies were chiefly employed to research course design, while phenomenography was mainly used to research either teaching and learning or course design.

Theoretical frameworks in higher education research

Table 2.1 identifies some of the theoretical frameworks that have been used, and are still being used, in higher education research (see also Tight 2012a, p. 198–9). It is not, of course, comprehensive, but lists some of the most popular and/or influential

Table 2.1 Theoretical frameworks in higher education research

Theme	Theoretical frameworks considered in this book	Other theoretical frameworks
Teaching and learning	Phenomenography; teaching and learning approaches; the scholarship of teaching and learning	Concept mapping; ways of knowing; motivation
Course design	Academic literacies; activity systems; threshold concepts	Problem-based learning; generic skills; service learning
The student experience	The first-year experience; student retention and engagement; the transition to work	Transition to higher education; actor–network theory; social inclusion
Quality	Quality assurance/management; the student as consumer or customer; ranking and league tables	Student satisfaction; quality assessment; total quality management
System policy	Human and social capital; globalization and internationalization; massification	Marketization; privatization; stakeholder theory
Institutional management	Managerialism and collegiality; institutional mission and diversity; academic drift and institutional isomorphism	Governance; institutional space; the third mission
Academic work	Academic tribes and territories; academic identities; communities of practice	Professional development; well-being; academic writing
Knowledge and research	The research/teaching nexus; interdisciplinarity; professional and vocational disciplines	Modes of knowledge; idea of the university; classification and framing

frameworks. The table is organized in terms of the eight thematic areas identified, but some of the theoretical frameworks identified could have been listed under more than one of these. Thus, the communities of practice theoretical framework is relevant to the student experience as well as to academic work; while the student as consumer or customer framework is important to institutional management as well as to quality.

While the second column of Table 2.1 lists the twenty-four theoretical frameworks that are discussed in detail in the following eight chapters (three per chapter, though some of these involve a pair of linked frameworks), the third and final column identifies three alternative frameworks for each chapter, from among many other possibilities, that might have been considered instead or as well. In the end, the choice as to which frameworks to focus on in this book was partly to do with how widely or frequently they had been used in higher education research, and partly down to personal preference.

It has to be acknowledged that most of these theoretical frameworks would only qualify as low-level theories; that is, they are essentially labels for the area of interest (e.g. the first-year experience, interdisciplinarity) that is being researched and theorized about. Thus, researchers focusing on the first-year experience, for example, will construct their understanding of this topic in particular ways, steadily building up both a body of knowledge and a theoretical framework.

Pre-existing, and typically higher-level, theories are less frequently applied in higher education research, and, when they are, they almost invariably come from other established disciplines. Human capital (discussed in Chapter 7), with its origins in economics, and activity systems (discussed in Chapter 4), stemming from Soviet psychology, are examples of this.

Theoretical frameworks from other disciplines have, nevertheless, been widely applied in higher education research, simply because many of those studying higher education have come from or remain based in those disciplines. In addition to economics and psychology, these contributory disciplines include sociology (e.g. actor–network theory), business and management (e.g. stakeholder theory), linguistics (e.g. academic literacies, discussed in Chapter 4) and biology (e.g. diversity, discussed in Chapter 8).

Research designs in higher education research

If you have read this chapter from the beginning, you will have realized by now that some frameworks can be viewed and used – by different researchers at different times, or by the same researcher at the same time – as method, theory and design. This is, perhaps, most clearly the case with phenomenography, which was identified earlier as a research design which embodied particular methodological and theoretical approaches.

Phenomenography has a good claim to be recognized as the most innovative development – in terms of method, theory and/or design – so far within the higher education research field. It was developed by researchers whose main interest was in higher education, though they also had interests in, and applied phenomenography to, other levels of education as well. Phenomenography has been influential, even though it has been little used beyond higher education/education, and remains a minority interest within higher education research.

What other overarching research designs are there in use within higher education research? Looking through the examples of theoretical frameworks identified in Table 2.1, teaching and learning approaches are another obvious example, partly because of their close link to phenomenography. Advocates of teaching and learning approaches (which are discussed in more detail in Chapter 3) argue that there are a limited number of approaches that can be adopted to teaching and learning, and that some of these are more preferable in given situations; indeed, for learning approaches, just two, deep and surface, are commonly recognized. That is their theoretical framework.

Researchers into teaching and learning approaches also have particular ways of researching these approaches, that is, a methodology. Actually, there are two main, and somewhat opposed, methodologies in use. One of these is phenomenography, a qualitative approach. The other methodology is quantitative, involving the development, validation and use of survey instruments to measure individuals' learning or teaching approaches.

Threshold concepts (discussed further in Chapter 4) are a third example worth discussion. If perhaps not yet a full-fledged research design, as there is no standard or agreed method for researching them (beyond the all-too-common use of interviews and surveys), they are, like phenomenography, unusual as a framework for having been developed essentially within higher education research. Threshold concepts researchers believe that, within a given discipline, there are particular concepts which are problematic for many learners, but which are essential for them to learn if they are to proceed further.

A case might also be made for those who research activity systems in higher education, or the development and influence of human and social capital, as having an overarching research design underlying their work. In both of these cases, however, the theory and method come from outside higher education research, and are simply applied in a fairly straightforward way within it.

Finally, a case could certainly be made for grounded theory as a research design which, although it originates outside higher education research, has been applied as an overarching research design within it. This was not listed in Table 2.1, because it is such a generic approach that it could have been placed in many, perhaps, all, of the rows. While it is debatable whether grounded theory is either grounded or a theory (see Thomas and James 2006), grounded theorists (e.g. Charmaz 2006; Strauss and Corbin 1990) believe in developing theory inductively through data collection and analysis, proceeding iteratively through repeated episodes of data collection and analysis, and revising their theories as they proceed. Grounded theory has had a huge influence in higher education research, and social research in general, and its principles inform much qualitative research, even when the researchers are unaware of it.

Conclusions

It is clear, then, that a wide range of methods and methodologies, theoretical frameworks and research designs have been applied within higher education research. Most of these have come from outside higher education research – from contributory disciplines – and then have been applied within it. There are, however, also many examples of theories, in particular, being developed within higher education research, usually through theorizing about topics of interest, and there are also a few examples of overarching research designs that have been, or are being, developed within higher education research.

Higher education research is a relatively new, and multidisciplinary field, but, as the rest of this book will show, one that is developing rapidly and holds great promise for the future.

Chapter 3
Research on Teaching and Learning

Introduction

For many of those working outside higher education, and for quite a few of those working within it, teaching and learning may appear to be the core function of higher education: students enrol to learn higher-level knowledge and skills, while professors and lecturers are employed to teach them that. Research into teaching and learning, with the express aim of finding ways in which to improve them, should, therefore, be at the forefront of higher education research.

Research into teaching and learning is, indeed, a major part of higher education research, but by no means the entirety, or even the majority, of it. Research itself is also a major function of higher education (research into research is considered in Chapter 10), while the operation of higher education institutions, and the policies under which they operate, are major foci for research as well (examined in Chapters 6 to 9).

Teaching and learning, broadly conceived, is a wide and diverse field for research, and so it has been divided up into three parts, considered in this and the next two chapters, for the purposes of this book. Chapter 4 focuses on research on course design, that is, the ways in which the educational experience is planned, structured and delivered by those responsible for it. Chapter 5 examines research on the student experience, that is, the entirety of the individual's experience while they are a student, including not only their study experience but also their social, family and work experience, plus their experience of entering and moving on from higher education.

In this chapter, we examine research on teaching and learning in higher education more narrowly conceived, that is, focusing directly on studies of how lecturers teach and how students learn, and the relationship between these practices.

Following an overview of trends in researching teaching and learning, three popular research designs and frameworks are considered in more detail: phenomenography, teaching and learning approaches and the scholarship of teaching and learning.

Research trends

A series of bibliographic searches were carried out, using Google Scholar and Scopus, of the number of published articles with different combinations of the words 'teaching', 'learning', 'higher' and 'education' in their titles. By focusing on the titles of articles, the searches have excluded a lot of articles which would still be relevant but didn't use the chosen terms in their titles, but should, nevertheless, have identified the most relevant.

A number of interesting trends were identified. First, it is clear that articles focusing on learning or teaching in higher education are increasingly popular: while, according to Google Scholar (which has a wider coverage than Scopus), around 10 a year were published in the 1970s, this rose to 20 per year in the 1980s, 100 per year by the end of the 1990s, and over 1,000 per year in the 2010s. Though this impressive increase is partly due to the increasing number of higher education researchers, and the growing number of outlets for them to publish in, it demonstrates the significance of this field within higher education research.

Second, it appears that articles focusing on learning and higher education are roughly twice as common as those focusing on teaching and higher education; though, interestingly, the former only became more common than the latter after the mid-1990s. This confirms a shift in emphasis from a focus on what was done to the student (i.e. teaching) to what one wanted the student to do (i.e. learning). Third, however, articles with both 'learning' and 'teaching' and 'higher education' in their titles make up a significant grouping: teaching and learning remain almost inseparable in higher education researchers' thinking; two sides of the same coin.

A more detailed analysis of the returns from Scopus for publications with 'learning', 'teaching', 'higher' and 'education' in their titles reveals the following. Most of the 389 documents identified were journal articles (213), conference papers (70), book chapters (46) or books (18) – the conventional outputs for academic research – with the remainder (42) made up of reviews, editorials and so on. Not surprisingly, most were produced by authors based in English-speaking countries, with the United Kingdom (100), Australia (66) and the United States (45) accounting for the majority; but some other countries, such as Spain (31), Canada (13), China (13), Portugal (13) and South Africa (13), were also well represented. The relatively low position occupied by US-based authors (in third instead of their more usual first place) is unusual, and most likely a function of the greater popularity of different terminology in that country.

Most of the articles identified by Scopus were published in higher education or education journals, with *Studies in Higher Education* (13), *Journal of Geography in Higher Education* (10), *Higher Education* (8), *British Journal of Educational Technology* (7), *Higher Education Research and Development* (7) and *Innovations in Education and Teaching International* (7) – all journals based outside of the United States – the most popular.

In terms of the topics researched in teaching and learning, a number of foci may be recognized, some of which are of long standing while others have developed more recently. They may be researched with a focus on a particular discipline, department or course, or generically across the university, college or system.

Among longstanding concerns, two stand out. One is the continuing interest in what makes for effective or excellent teaching and learning (e.g. Ford 1981;

Ramsden 1987, 1993). The other, since the mid-1970s in particular, is the concern with understanding better how students and lecturers conceive of learning and teaching, and how they then behave as a consequence (e.g. Dahlgren and Marton 1978; Kember 2001; Nicholls 2005; Van Rossum 1988). The two concerns are, of course, linked, as the findings from the latter feed into the former.

The first of these concerns has latterly become bound up with policy, in particular with demands to ensure and/or improve the quality of teaching and learning (e.g. Pennington and O'Neil 1994; Sharp 1995; see also Chapter 6). Such demands have led to training being provided to new lecturers, and to calls for more engagement in pedagogical research, as through the scholarship of teaching and learning movement (which is discussed in detail later in this chapter). The second concern has driven the research into teaching and learning approaches (also discussed in detail later in this chapter), and related attempts to develop theoretical frameworks that could be of practical use.

More recent research concerns within teaching and learning include, most obviously, the role of technology and how it may be employed to improve teaching and learning (e.g. De Freitas, Morgan and Gibson 2015; Lofstrom and Nevgi 2007; Miller, Martineau and Clark 2000; Price and Kirkwood 2014; Steeples et al. 1996). Other more recent interests – such as the nature and use of learning spaces (e.g. Savin-Baden, McFarland and Savin-Baden 2008) and the development of learning communities (e.g. Ward and Selvester 2012) – have attracted less attention, but may prove to be long-term.

One other aspect of the literature on learning and teaching in higher education which demands recognition is the continuing production of edited volumes focusing on the topic (e.g. Ashwin 2005; Brandenburg and Wilson 2013; Groccia, Alsudairi and Buskis 2012; Hartley, Woods and Pill 2005; Leisyte and Wilkesmann 2016; Tennant, McMullen and Krezynski 2009). These both distil the findings of recent research on the topic and offer practical guidance, particularly for lecturers.

Research designs and frameworks

In this section, three research designs or frameworks which have been influential in recent decades for researching teaching and learning in higher education are examined in more detail: phenomenography, teaching and learning approaches and the scholarship of teaching and learning. The first two of these are closely linked, with teaching and learning approaches being a popular framework for thinking about how we teach and learn (and how we should), and phenomenography being one research design for examining this. The scholarship of teaching and learning, by comparison, may be thought of as a movement for encouraging greater attention to be paid to teaching and learning, as opposed to research (see also the discussion of the research/teaching nexus in Chapter 10).

As indicated in Chapter 2, and as is true for each of the following seven chapters, these are not, of course, the only research designs or frameworks to be applied to teaching and learning in higher education. Indeed, in one case, phenomenography, their application is not confined to teaching and learning, or to higher education. Yet they have been, and are, arguably, among the most influential ways of thinking about teaching and learning in higher education.

Phenomenography

Phenomenography is an innovative research design, which aims at identifying and interrogating the range of different ways in which people perceive or experience specific phenomena (in this case typically learning, teaching or aspects thereof). Phenomenographers adopt a particular methodological strategy for data collection and analysis. This typically involves the use of interviews as a method for collecting data on the phenomenon of current interest; though other forms of data, such as written responses, may also be used. All of the data collected is then treated collectively for the purposes of analysis, such that the focus is on the variations in understanding across the whole sample, rather than on the characteristics of individuals' responses.

In terms of theoretical framework, phenomenographers operate with the underlying assumption that, for any given phenomenon of interest, there are only a limited number of ways of perceiving, understanding or experiencing it. Typically, the number identified is relatively small – for example, only four or five variants are commonly found – and, as with most forms of qualitative research, these are identified on the basis of a relatively small number of interviews (twenty or fewer are typical). Most commonly – and, it would seem, most satisfactorily – the various ways of experiencing the phenomenon identified can be organized in a hierarchy, with each higher level encompassing those below it, and the highest level representing the most advanced or developed way of experiencing the phenomena.

While only a small proportion of higher education researchers have ever used phenomenography (Tight 2012a), it is an important niche research design within this field, particularly for research into teaching and learning. It also appears to be one of the few research designs to have been substantially created and developed within higher education research (Tight 2014c), which makes it of added significance to the field. The qualifying term 'substantially' is used here because the originators of phenomenography have also researched other levels or areas of education using this design, and others have applied it outside education altogether (notably in nursing and other health care fields).

Phenomenography was developed and practised for some years before it was named and designated as a distinct research design. Its origins lie in research on 'approaches to learning' (i.e. the different ways in which students conceive of and go about their learning; teaching and learning approaches are discussed in detail in the next section) carried out at Goteborg University in Sweden in the 1970s by Marton, Svensson, Dahlgren, Saljo and others (Dahlgren and Marton 1978; Fransson 1977; Marton and Saljo 1976a,b; Svensson 1977).

An early external review of the work at Goteborg clearly positioned it as a distinctive response to existing research approaches:

> The perspective of the Goteborg group is a reaction to the naturalism of traditional research on learning. Their aim is to describe the 'world as perceived' – a phenomenological aim. Marton contrasts this with the aim of traditional research – to describe the world 'as it is'. (Gibbs, Morgan and Taylor 1982, p. 139)

This made it, for phenomenographers, a 'second order' perspective.

The first use of the term 'phenomenography' in print by the originators of this new research strategy did not come until 1981:

> The kind of research we wish to argue for is complementary to other kinds of research. It is research which aims at description, analysis and understanding of experiences … . Such an approach points to a relatively distinct field of inquiry which we would like to label *phenomenography*. (Marton 1981, p. 180; emphasis in original)

Marton notes elsewhere (1986, p. 28), however, that the term was in use from 1979.

It is a characteristic of specialist terms, such as phenomenography, that they often turn out to have been used before, either in related or different contexts (Tight 2014d, 2015c), with the supposed 'originators' being unaware of this. Not surprisingly, given the longer history of the related term 'phenomenology', this was the case for phenomenography (Dahlin 2007; Needleman 1963; Sonnemann 1954/1999). Marton has, though, unlike Svensson (1997), consistently rejected the idea of any link between phenomenography and phenomenology.

Marton (1986) defined phenomenography in the following fashion:

> Phenomenography is a research method for mapping the qualitatively different ways in which people experience, conceptualize, perceive and understand various aspects of, and phenomena in, the world around them. (p. 31)

At the heart of this approach were the conceptions that people had regarding the phenomena of interest; or, as Marton and Pong (2005) later put it, conceptions were the units of description in phenomenography. Marton's view of phenomenography has, naturally enough, developed over the years (see, for example, Bowden and Marton 1998; Marton 1988, 2000; Marton and Booth 1997).

Bowden offers guidance on how many interviews – if, as usual, the study is interview based – should be carried out in a given phenomenographic project, stressing the importance of seeking variation in conceptions:

> You need to interview enough people to ensure sufficient variation in ways of seeing, but not so many that make it difficult to manage the data … . In practice, most phenomenographers find that between 20 and 30 subjects meet the two criteria. (2005, p. 17)

This does not sound greatly different from standard qualitative research practice. Greater issues arise, however, when it comes to the analysis of the collected data, particularly as some phenomenographers insist on the importance of 'bracketing out' all prior knowledge of the concept under consideration throughout the process (cf. classical versions of grounded theory), so as to reduce bias and help the researcher to focus on the data (Ashworth and Lucas 2000).

Concerns remain, however, about whether, in undertaking phenomenographic analysis, the researcher is 'consciously interpreting the data, choosing and discarding data, and thereby constructing the relationship', rather than 'looking into the transcripts to discover the particular ways in which people understand the phenomenon' (Walsh 2000, p. 20). Such concerns have led to an increasing focus on clarifying and tightening up the processes involved in doing phenomenography. As Akerlind notes, 'It is only recently that epistemological and ontological assumptions, a theoretical basis and specification of methodological requirements underlying the approach have been more clearly developed' (2005b, p. 321).

At the same time, it has become more and more obvious that there are considerable variations in practice among phenomenographers, concerning, for example, 'how much of each transcript is considered at one time … the emphasis placed on analytic collaboration with other researchers; variation in ways of practically managing the large amount of data involved; the degree to which the logical structure of the outcome space [i.e. the results] is seen as needing to emerge as directly as possible from the data versus more explicitly reflecting the professional judgement of the researcher' (Akerlind 2005b, p. 332). These differences are also apparent in the prefixes now used by many phenomenographers, including developmental, empirical and pure phenomenography.

The search for variation has always been at the heart of phenomenography, leading to the development of variation theory (Marton and Trigwell 2000; Pang and Marton 2003; Rovio-Johansson 2013). Once identified, the strategic use of variation in teaching then becomes a key method for encouraging effective learning: 'Phenomenographic research, in identifying the limited number of qualitatively different ways in which something is experienced, acts as a source of data with which to develop awareness of variation' (Prosser and Trigwell 1997, p. 51). More recently, Akerlind, McKenzie and Lupton (2014) have proposed a curriculum design method based on phenomenography, variation theory and threshold concepts theory (the last of these is discussed in Chapter 4).

Phenomenography, while remaining a minority interest, has been fairly widely applied or discussed within higher education research. A search through Google Scholar found a total of over 15,000 academic publications that mentioned either or both of the terms 'phenomenography' or 'phenomenographic', of which 520 used one of the terms in their titles. Interest and publishing about phenomenography has expanded decade by decade since the 1970s, and particularly most recently, such that over 90 per cent of the articles mentioning 'phenomenography' or 'phenomenographic' have been published since 2000.

The interest in phenomenography has been global – at least within the Western developed world – but has also been particularly intense in certain countries. Thus, as well as in Sweden, the country where phenomenography was first developed, the authors of articles focusing on phenomenography as applied to higher education research have been based in Belgium (Koenen, Dochy and Berghmans 2015), Canada (Ebenezer and Erickson 1996), Fiji (Mugler and Landbeck 1997), Finland (Kinnunen and Simon 2012), Hong Kong (Pang and Marton 2003), Hungary (Toth and Lundanyi 2007), Israel (Austerlitz 2007), the Netherlands (Vermunt 1996), New Zealand (Brown et al. 2016), Rwanda (Bamwesiga, Fejes and Dahlgren 2014), South Africa (Linder and Marshall 2003), Taiwan (Yang and Chen 2002), Turkey (Kilinc and Aydin 2013), the United Kingdom (Alsop and Tompsett 2006) and the United States (Felix 2009).

Overall, however, over half of all the refereed journal articles identified that applied phenomenography in higher education research have been authored by researchers based in either Sweden or Australia, with the latter now having overtaken the former in terms of numbers of outputs. Australia-based authors such as Akerlind, Bowden, Prosser and Trigwell have added substantially to the literature on phenomenography initiated by Marton and his colleagues in Sweden. By comparison, researchers in the United Kingdom, the United States and elsewhere have only engaged to a lesser degree.

The concepts examined in these studies have gone far beyond the initial interest in teaching and learning (e.g. Marton, Dall'Alba and Beaty 1993; Prosser 1993; Prosser and Trigwell 1999). Thus, phenomenographic studies have addressed the varied understandings within higher education of academic development (Akerlind 2005a), environmental conceptions (Pherali 2011), feedback (McLean, Bond and Nicholson 2015), grade descriptors (Tan and Prosser 2004), information literacy (Boon, Johnston and Webber 2007), internationalization (Ojo and Booth 2009; discussed in Chapter 7), the literature review (Bruce 1994), reading (Macmillan 2014), research (Brew 2001), the research/teaching nexus (Prosser et al. 2008; discussed in Chapter 10), study support (Hallett 2013), sustainable development (Kilinc and Aydin 2013), understanding (Marton 1992) and using the internet (Roberts 2003).

Phenomenography has also been applied across the academy, within and/or to disciplines as varied as accounting (Rovio-Johansson 2013) business studies (Lamb, Sandberg and Liesch 2011), chemistry (Lybeck et al. 1988), computing (Bruce, Pham and Stoodley 2004), design (Austerlitz 2007), economics (Dahlgren 1989), environment (Loughland, Reid and Petocz 2002), geography (Bradbeer, Healey and Kneale 2004), healthcare/nursing (Barnard, McCosker and Gerber 1999), information systems/technology (Rose, Le Heron and Sofat 2005), languages (Anderberg et al. 2008), mathematics (Crawford et al. 1994, 1998), music (Reid 2001), physics (Ingerman and Booth 2003), science (Dall'Alba et al. 1989), sociology (Ashwin, Abbas and McLean 2014) and statistics (Reid and Petocz 2002).

In addition to phenomenology, phenomenography has been linked to other research designs, including activity theory (Hallett 2014; discussed in Chapter 4), contextual analysis (Svensson 2016), ethnography (Austerlitz 2007), evaluation (Jones and Asensio 2001) and grounded theory (Kinnunen and Simon 2012). Similarly, in addition to threshold concepts and variation theory, it has been linked to other theories, such as knowledge space theory (Toth and Ludanyi 2007). And, perhaps most interestingly, it has been applied to the analysis of other forms of data than the near-universal interviews, including, for example, gestures (Herbert and Pierce 2013).

The bulk of the higher education research that has employed phenomenography has been concerned not just with better understanding how students and academics think about and approach teaching and learning (or other topics), but also with applying these findings to improve practice (Booth 1997). This was evident from the start, even before the term phenomenography was employed, in Marton and Saljo's (1976a,b) early work on deep and surface learning approaches, which continues to be used widely in academic development activities. It is also apparent in the more recent development of variation theory, and its application in improving learning through the variation of teaching. Trigwell, Prosser and Ginns (2005) have even gone so far as to identify what they term phenomenographic pedagogy.

It should not be surprising to learn that a research design that has been the subject of development and application for over four decades has also come in for some critique, by phenomenographers at least as much as non-phenomenographers. The earliest published critiques, from the 1990s, came mainly from non-phenomenographers, and tended to question whether phenomenography was achieving anything new (e.g. Taylor 1993).

Webb (1997) made a joint critique of the notions of deep and surface learning (discussed further in the next section) and of phenomenography, 'the associated methodology and theory of knowledge' as he termed it (p. 195). He was particularly critical of the tendency of phenomenographers to identify hierarchical arrangements of conceptions, with the most highly developed of these identified as the 'correct' one towards which teachers should be working to develop their students. Kember (1997) echoed some of Webb's concerns in raising the question of the accuracy of the categorizations identified by phenomenographers. More recently, Alsop and Tompsett (2006) have doubted the long-term validity of the categorizations arrived at.

The tone of most critical discussions has, however, been accepting of phenomenography as a research design, while seeking to improve its practice and impact (e.g. Francis 1993; Richardson 1999). Phenomenographers themselves have become centrally involved in these debates, with Saljo (1997), one of the pioneers of the approach, expressing some doubts in later years, notably about the collective analytical approach ignoring the individual.

Meyer and Shanahan (2002) – like Kember (1997) – focused on the categories of description identified by phenomenography, exploring whether they could also be measured quantitatively. Picking up on earlier work by Dahlgren and Marton (1976) on students' conceptions of price, they tried to replicate these findings through surveys, with limited success. Alsop and Tompset (2006) raise the related issue, common to much qualitative research because of its typically small-scale nature, of the generalizability of phenomenographic results.

Sandberg (1997) tackles this issue from the perspective of reliability. In particular he is concerned by the use of inter-judge reliability, whereby the interpretation of the data produced by one researcher is shared and checked by one or more others, so as to minimize researcher bias. Cope (2004) disagrees, arguing that phenomenographic research can satisfy the demands of validity and reliability if certain standards are explicitly adopted and demonstrated. This will involve careful design of interview questions, taking care not to influence or bias the interviewee, adopting the analytical framework of a structure of awareness (i.e. how the interviewee is aware of the phenomenon in question), controlling and checking the researcher's interpretations, presenting results in a manner to enable scrutiny, and establishing inter-judge communicability (his term for inter-judge reliability). Collier-Reed, Ingerman and Berglund (2009) focus on the related issue of the trustworthiness of phenomenographic research.

Clearly, then, as a research design, phenomenography remains both very much alive and the subject of ongoing debate and further development.

Teaching and learning approaches

The framework of teaching and learning approaches – initially the focus was on learning approaches – was first developed in the 1970s. It was described over twenty-five years ago as 'one of the most influential concepts to have emerged from research into teaching and learning in higher education during the last 15 years' (Ramsden 1992, p. 39). Teaching and learning approaches are an interesting example of an idea that developed in three places – Sweden, Australia and the UK – almost simultaneously (Ashwin 2009; Case and Marshall 2009; Ertl et al. 2008). Not surprisingly, those responsible had somewhat different 'takes' on the idea, using different methodologies to get at their data and applying different terminologies to what they found.

The initial Swedish research was carried out at Goteborg University in the 1970s by Marton and others (Dahlgren and Marton 1978; Fransson 1977; Marton, Dall'Alba and Beaty 1993; Marton and Saljo 1976a,b, 1984; Svensson 1977). It was closely associated with the development of a new research design, phenomenography (see Cassidy 2004; Tight 2016a, and the preceding section), which involved the use, typically, of interviews to identify the range of conceptions of a particular phenomenon (in this case, learning) held by a group of people (in this case, students). It led to the fundamental distinction between deep and surface learning conceptions, where deep learning was characterized by the desire to master or fully understand a given topic, while surface learning was concerned with knowing enough to pass the associated assessment.

The Australian research was carried out by Biggs and colleagues (e.g. Biggs 1976, 1979; Biggs and Collis 1982), and was based on the development of survey instruments and student responses to them. This led to the creation of the Structure of the Observed Learning Outcome (SOLO) taxonomy, which identified five levels of learning – pre-structural, uni-structural, multi-structural, relational and extended abstract – involving the ability to increasingly question what one was learning and understanding.

The UK research largely stemmed from the work of Entwistle and his collaborators at Lancaster University and elsewhere (Entwistle 1984, 1988; Entwistle and Marton 1984; Entwistle, Hanley and Hounsell 1979). Like the Australian research, it was concerned with the development of scales to measure students' study methods and motivations, and came to draw upon both the Swedish and Australian research, and on earlier British research by Pask (1976) and others. This led to the identification of a third orientation to learning in addition to the deep and surface approaches, termed the 'achieving' or 'strategic' orientation, in which the student mixed the two former strategies with the aim of gaining the best result possible.

As the researchers became more aware of each other's research, and began to exchange ideas and collaborate, their different terminologies were ironed out, such that conceptions, orientations or approaches to learning or studying became generally known as learning approaches, and differentiated from related but different notions such as learning styles. At the same time, the definition of what was meant by approaches to learning became clearer:

> Students' approaches to learning are defined as incorporating both the way
> they go about their study (strategy) and their reasons for adopting that strategy
> (intention) ... students' learning approaches are related to their perception of their
> situation and to their prior learning experiences. (Prosser and Trigwell 1999, p. 83)

Research into the learning approaches of students in higher education has been popular, and increasingly widespread, in recent years. Thus, a search through Google Scholar for articles with the phrases 'approaches to learning' or 'learning approaches' in their titles found 1,262 of the former and 2,808 of the latter. While not all of these relate to higher education – some relate to other levels of education, and others, particularly in the case of the latter, more generic, term, relate to machine learning – the majority do. Only 222 in total with the term 'approaches to learning' in their titles had been published by 2000. Since then the numbers have mushroomed, with 25 articles published in 2000, 86 in 2010 and 104 (the peak to date) in 2013.

Research into learning and teaching approaches has occupied academics across the world. As well as the originating locations of Australia, Sweden and the UK, English language publications focusing on this topic have been published by authors based in countries as dispersed and diverse as Bangladesh (Islam and Shafiq 2016), Belgium (Baeten et al. 2010), Canada (Bouckenooghe et al. 2016), China (Yin, Lu and Wang 2014), Denmark (Herrmann, Bager-Elsborg and Parpala 2016), Finland (Varunki, Katajavuori and Postareff 2017), Nepal (Dhalin and Regmi 1997), Norway (Saele et al. 2016), Pakistan (Ullah et al. 2016), Portugal (Pedrosa-de-Jesus and Silva Lopes 2011), Singapore (Ling, Ng and Leung 2011), South Africa (Case and Gunstone 2003), Taiwan (Shen et al. 2016), Turkey (Kirkgoz 2013) and the United Arab Emirates (McLaughlin and Durrant 2016). Interestingly, however, this area of research has been mostly ignored in North America (but see Schmeck and Geisler-Brenstein 1989).

As well as having a global reach, research on learning and teaching approaches has been carried out in a wide range of disciplinary contexts, including accounting

(Everaert, Opdecam and Maussen 2017), chemistry (Almeida et al. 2011), earth sciences (Shen et al. 2016), economics (Johnston 2001), education (Gordon and Debus 2002), engineering (Ling, Ng and Leung 2011), information systems (Cope and Staehr 2005), mathematics (Crawford et al. 1998), medicine (Clarke 1986), psychology (Lonka and Lindblom-Ylanne 1996), pharmacy (Varunki, Katajavuori and Postareff 2017) and teacher education (Baeten, Struyven and Dochy 2013).

This interest also extends to different forms of provision, both within and beyond higher education. Thus, there is a considerable literature on learning and teaching approaches in distance education and e-learning (e.g. Ellis, Ginns and Piggott 2009; Gonzalez 2012; Harper and Kember 1986; Morgan, Taylor and Gibbs 1982; Richardson, Morgan and Woodley 1999). Other forms of higher learning (e.g. problem-based learning: Sadlo and Richardson 2003), types of students (e.g. mature students: Sadler-Smith 1996) and levels of learning (e.g. secondary education: Van Bragt et al. 2007) have similarly been researched using the framework of learning and teaching approaches.

Research into learning approaches has taken a number of different tacks. One key emphasis, which dates back to the earliest Australian and British research, has been the development and application of inventories to measure learning approaches. These have adopted a bewildering variety of names and acronyms, including the Approaches to Studying Inventory (ASI), Approaches to Teaching Inventory (ATI), Course Experience Questionnaire (CEQ), Experiences of Teaching and Learning Questionnaire (ETLQ), Inventory of Learning Styles (ILS), Learning and Studying Questionnaire (LSQ), Learning Process Questionnaire (LPQ) and Study Process Questionnaire (SPQ) (Kember, Biggs and Leung 2004; Prosser and Trigwell 2006; Ramsden and Entwistle 1981; Richardson 2000; Trigwell and Prosser 2004).

Some have questioned what these inventories actually measure (e.g. Biggs 1993), while others have reviewed what this line of research has achieved. Thus, Entwistle and McCune (2004) compare seven instruments: ASI, SPQ, Inventory of Learning Processes - Revised (ILP-R), Learning and Study Strategies Inventory (LASSI), ILS, Motivated Strategies for Learning Questionnaire (MSLQ) and Approaches to Learning and Studying Inventory (ALSI). They note:

> The ILP and MSLQ both had strong roots in the mainstream psychological literature, and the MSLQ has kept quite close to those origins by defining many tightly focused concepts that retain their psychological meaning and nomenclature. Although the SPQ and the ASI both acknowledged links to the psychological literature, they were guided strongly by conceptualizations drawn from educational research. Both these inventories, along with the ILS, also grouped subscales into broader composites derived from factor analyses, and having distinctive meanings. (p. 338)

A second major interest has concerned the relationship between learning approaches and other factors or variables, typically using one of the inventories discussed in combination with others. These variables have included assessment (Scouller 1998); the 'big five' personality traits (Chamorro-Premuzic and Furnham 2009); conceptions and self-efficacy (Tsai et al. 2016); course and discipline (Ohrstedt and Lindfors 2016); learner identities and self-efficacy (Herrmann, Bager-Elsborg and McCune 2016); questioning approaches (Pedrosa-de-Jesus and Silva Lopes 2011); self-regulated learning and cognitive strategies (Heikkila and Lonka 2006); the teaching–learning environment (Struyven et al. 2006); and workload and task complexity (Kyndt et al. 2011). These studies are almost wholly quantitative in nature.

Two particular sets of relations have attracted a good deal of attention. Thus, unsurprisingly, the link between learning approaches and academic achievement has been a major concern, with committed researchers keen to be able to demonstrate that the adoption of a deep learning approach was associated with better results (see, for example, Beckwith 1991; Diseth 2007; McLean 2001; Valadas, Almeida and Araujo 2016). Other researchers have been equally interested in unravelling the linkages and differences between learning approaches, learning styles, learning strategies and similar constructs (Ramsden 1985; Richardson 2011; Van Rossum and Schenk 1984; Vermunt and Vermetten 2004).

A third major research interest has focused on how to encourage students to adopt deep approaches to learning (Asikainen and Gijbels 2017; Baeten et al. 2010; Entwistle and Tait 1990; Varunki, Katajavuori and Postareff 2017; Vermetten, Vermunt and Lodewijks 1999). It is in this context that the link between learning approaches and teaching approaches has, of course, come to the fore (Campbell et al. 2001; Kember and Kwan 2000; Lindblom-Ylanne et al. 2006; Norton et al. 2005; Prosser and Trigwell 1997). Biggs (1999) refers to this link as 'constructive alignment'. This research interest has also led to the publication of a number of guidance manuals (e.g. Entwistle 1988; Ramsden 1992).

As with all conceptualizations that have been around for a few decades, learning and teaching approaches have attracted their share of criticism. One recurring criticism is that the notion of teaching and learning approaches oversimplifies the situation or ignores certain factors. After all, categorizing all learning approaches as either deep or surface, with a third possibility of their being strategic sandwiched somewhere in between, could hardly be simpler. For Malcolm and Zukas (2001), this amounts to what they term the 'psychologization' of higher education pedagogy:

> Dominant psychological approaches to teaching and learning are identified as promoting a limited conceptualisation of pedagogy as an educational 'transaction' between individual learners and teachers, and an asocial construction of the learner. Certain approaches to the interrelationship of theory, research and practice are criticised for their reduction of pedagogic theory to a set of professional rules for practice, and for their contribution to the isolation of pedagogic theory from the rich literature of higher education policy and purpose. (p. 33)

For Ashworth and Greasley (2009), the problem with learning approaches is their focus on the mental orientation of the student, ignoring other important aspects:

> The Gothenburg research on approaches to studying focuses primarily on the mental orientation with which learning material is approached. The meaning for the student of the learning material itself (including such things as its difficulty or interest, or the fatefulness or otherwise of success or failure in learning it) is not sought. (p. 562)

Another doubt regarding learning approaches has concerned the cultural transference of the idea; as indicated, however, it has been widely applied internationally. Richardson (1994), in a survey of the published literature up until that time, came to the conclusion that the differences were mainly in the nature of surface learning in different cultures. A particular manifestation of this criticism has been the discussion of the so-called Chinese paradox; the recognition that, in Confucian heritage countries, extensive memorization (which in the West would be regarded as surface learning) is still widely practised and highly regarded in education, as such students achieve good results (Kember and Gow 1990). Kember, for example, argues:

> It is clear that common mis-perceptions of the learning approaches and preferences of Asian students have resulted in the adoption of didactic teaching methods and assessment and examinations which test recall. If the academics concerned realise that Asian students are capable of more active forms of learning and benefit from curricula which demand higher forms of learning, the performance could be better still. (2000, p. 117)

A more comprehensive critique has been advanced by Haggis (2003, 2009):

> Questions remain about the possibility of manipulating the relationships between conceptions/perceptions/approaches and outcomes/grades, as many studies continue to report that students are mainly resistant to attempts to change the way they approach their learning … . Despite research results continually showing that (a) changing approaches is extremely difficult, and (b) a surface approach can lead to very successful learning in terms of results, further research and theorising continues to focus on how environments can be changed in order to increase deep approaches. (2003, pp. 92–3)

In essence, Haggis is arguing that the learning approaches research project is misconceived and failing; she concludes that the academic literacies approach (discussed in detail in Chapter 4) has more to offer. Case (2015), though less critical, suggests that a critical realist approach might be more useful.

Other critiques have also been far reaching; thus, referring to Biggs's model, Howie and Bagnall argue that 'there are significant problems with the model in the areas of supporting evidence, imprecise conceptualization, ambiguous language, circularity, and a lack of definition of the underlying structure of deep and surface approaches to learning' (2013, p. 389). Tormey's (2014) critique is based upon the framework being too simplistic yet trying to do too many things:

> The approaches to learning framework is dogged by a number of difficulties: a framework that is simple enough to be a powerful metaphor may be too simple to adequately account for learning in different contexts; empirical claims that are strong enough to motivate action from teachers may be too strong to be sustainable in light of evidence; and a model that is tried and trusted has perhaps imposed blinkers that make useful alternative conceptualisations invisible. (p. 8)

Clearly, the idea of teaching and learning approaches has been, and continues to be, popular. It has had an impact across disciplines and in many parts of the world, and provides one of the underpinnings for the training and development of teachers in higher education (as well as for the associated emerging 'profession' of educational or academic development). The latter point may, of course, be one of the main reasons for its continuing popularity.

In research terms, its main achievements have arguably been to enable the assessment or measurement of how students are going about their learning, and suggest how teachers might respond, if and as necessary, to try and improve this. It has helped in giving greater attention to the teaching function in higher education. On the other hand, however, it does offer only a simplistic and limited framework, one which is, again arguably, in need of further development or replacement.

The scholarship of teaching and learning

The scholarship of teaching and learning is a movement as much as it is an idea or a framework, and may be closely linked to discussion around the research/teaching nexus (i.e. the relationship between the research and teaching functions of higher education; see Chapter 10). It developed partly as a reaction to quantitative studies, chiefly American, which found no strong relationship between research and teaching (e.g. Feldman 1987; Hattie and Marsh 1996). This had policy consequences, with an increasing de-coupling of funding for and oversight of research and teaching. In such an environment, the fear was that the research function would assume increasing prominence, particularly in the leading universities, resulting in a perceived need to re-emphasize the importance of teaching and learning.

While this is, of course, a longstanding debate, it was given a renewed edge in the last decades of the twentieth century through the development of the notion of, initially, the scholarship of teaching. The founding father of this movement was an American scholar, Boyer (1990; see also Boyer Commission on Educating Undergraduates in the Research University 1998; Rice 1991), whose starting position was that

> the most important obligation now confronting the nation's colleges and universities is to break out of the tired old teaching versus research debate and define, in more creative ways, what it means to be a scholar. It's time to recognize the full range of faculty talent and the great diversity of functions higher education must perform. (1990, p. xii)

Boyer went on to identify four forms of scholarship – the scholarship of discovery (i.e. research as commonly understood), the scholarship of integration (i.e. synthesis, often interdisciplinary in nature, of which this book is an example), the scholarship of application (i.e. applied research) and the scholarship of teaching (i.e. involving pedagogical learning and research) – each of which he saw as crucial to the life of the university.

Since Boyer's report was published, the scholarship of teaching – typically now broadened out as the scholarship of teaching and learning, recognizing explicitly the importance of students as well as teachers (Boshier and Huang 2008) – has taken on a life of its own. Numerous authored and edited books have been published by Boyer's co-workers at the Carnegie Foundation for the Advancement of Teaching and others (e.g. Glassick, Huber and Maeroff 1997; Huber and Morreale 2002; Hutchings, Huber and Ciccone 2011; McKinney 2013; Murray 2008).

There is an international society (the International Society for the Scholarship of Teaching and Learning, founded in 2004), which organizes an annual conference. The first specialist journal, the *Journal of Scholarship of Teaching and Learning*, started operations in 2001. It was followed by the *International Journal for the Scholarship of Teaching and Learning* in 2007, and a range of other national or disciplinary journals focused on the topic.

Not surprisingly, there are different interpretations of the scholarship of teaching and learning, and these have also developed over time. Thus, Kreber and Cranton (2000) identify three successive perspectives on what was then known as the scholarship of teaching: one valuing research on teaching and learning, a second emphasizing excellence in teaching, and a third involving the application of educational theory and research.

A relatively early definition, incorporating at least two of these perspectives, is offered by two of Boyer's co-workers, Hutchings and Shulman:

> A scholarship of teaching is not synonymous with excellent teaching. It requires a kind of 'going meta', in which faculty frame and systematically investigate questions related to student learning – the conditions under which it occurs, what it looks like, how to deepen it, and so forth – and do so with an eye not only to improving their own classroom but to advancing practice beyond it. (1999, p. 13)

Over a decade later, Hutchings and two co-authors came up with a more extended account:

> The scholarship of teaching and learning encompasses a broad set of practices that engage teachers in looking closely and critically at student learning for the purpose of improving their own courses and programs. It is perhaps best understood as an approach that marries scholarly inquiry to any of the intellectual tasks that comprise the work of teaching – designing a course, facilitating classroom activities, trying out new pedagogical ideas, advising, writing student learning outcomes, evaluating programs. When activities like these are undertaken with serious questions about student learning in mind, one enters the territory of the scholarship of teaching and learning. (Hutchings, Huber and Ciccone 2011, p. 7)

Clearly, the key elements remain much the same: questioning, criticality, adopting what we might call a 'researcherly' attitude towards teaching and learning practice. The scholarship of teaching and learning involves being an informed, reflecting and inquiring teacher, whose focus is on the improvement of their teaching so as to improve their students' learning, and on sharing their practices widely with others so as to advance the status and practice of teaching and learning in their discipline and in higher education in general.

The number of academic publications focusing on the scholarship of teaching and learning has increased significantly over the last three decades, as shown by searches carried out using two popular databases, Scopus and Google Scholar, for publications with the words 'scholarship of teaching' in their titles. The term 'scholarship of teaching' was used rather than the more contemporary 'scholarship of teaching and learning' because the former search would also identify examples of the latter. The focus was limited to article titles only, rather than abstracts, keywords or the complete text, as this would identify those items most strongly focusing on the topic.

Scopus and Google Scholar have different coverages, with the latter recording around three times as many articles as the former. Before 1990 there were only a handful of articles published with 'scholarship of teaching' in their titles, and they did not use that exact phrase: rather they were focused on some other aspect of the relationship between teaching and scholarship. From 1990 onwards, following the publication of the Boyer Report, several articles were published each year with a specific focus on the scholarship of teaching (and learning), as this is understood today. This figure rose to over fifty a year, taking the Google Scholar data, from 2007 onwards, with a peak to date of seventy-four articles published in 2011.

This growth is, of course, a function not only of the increasing interest in the topic, but also of the increase in the number of journals and other outlets interested in publishing articles on the topic. Significantly, research and writing on this topic is popular both in North America and in the rest of the world (the more common pattern is for North America and the rest of the world to have different foci of interest, or at least to use different labels for the same focus: see Shahjahan and Kezar 2013; Tight 2014b).

Research on the scholarship of teaching and learning is now an established feature of higher education research. While perhaps not truly global, this interest is particularly strong – naturally enough, given that the review focused on English language outputs – across the English-speaking world. Thus, articles have been published by authors based in Australia (e.g. Bennett et al. 2016; Brew and Ginns 2008), Canada (Boshier 2009), Ireland (O'Sullivan 2011), Malaysia (Harland, Hussain and Bakar 2014), New Zealand (Haigh, Gossman and Jiao 2011), Singapore (Geertsema 2016), South Africa (Leibowitz and Bozalek 2016), Sweden (Martensson, Roxa and Olsson 2011), Trinidad and Tobago (Blair 2014), the United Kingdom (Craig 2014, Healey 2000) and the United States (e.g. Cottrell and Jones 2003; Willingham-McLain 2015).

It is also notable that the interest in the scholarship of teaching and learning is genuinely cross-disciplinary (Huber and Morreale 2002). Thus, the research for this chapter identified examples of writing from academics in accounting (Lucas 2011), communication (McCroskey, Richmond and McCroskey 2002), dentistry (Lanning et al. 2014), economics (Horspool and Lange 2012), education (Pelliccione and Raison 2009), engineering (Nilsson 2013), geography (Healey 2003), history (Booth 2004), hospitality (La Lopa 2013), law (Greaves 2015), librarianship (Mitchell and Mitchell 2015), management (Frost and Fukami 1997), mathematics (Bennett and

Dewar 2012), nursing (Oermann 2014), occupational therapy (Hammel et al. 2015), pharmacy (Peeters, Beltyukova and Martin 2013), philosophy (Riordan 2008), political science (Craig 2014), psychology (Gurung et al. 2008), science (Rowland and Myatt 2014), social work (Grise-Owens, Owens and Miller 2016), sociology (Paino et al. 2012), textiles (Meyer and Kadolph 2005) and theology (Killen and Gallagher 2013).

Not surprisingly, a major concern of this literature is with 'how to do' the scholarship of teaching and learning (Fanghanel 2013). The suggestions made have included academic development (Hubball and Burt 2006), action learning (Albers 2008), collaborative scholarship (Weaver et al. 2013), collaborative self-study (Louie et al. 2003), design-based research (Sharma and McShane 2008), e-portfolios (Pelliccione and Raison 2009), e-teaching/learning (Benson and Brack 2009), expert teachers (Yair 2008), institutional research (Shreeve 2011), international writing groups (Marquis, Healey and Vine 2016), lesson study (Wood and Cajkler 2017), peer partnership (Barnard et al. 2011), practice research (Hatch 2009), reflection (Cranton 2011, Kreber 2005), reward (Roxa, Olsson and Martensson 2008), using theory (Hutchings and Huber 2008) and shared practice (Kahn et al. 2013). Others (e.g. Bartsch 2013a,b; Kanuka 2011) have focused on how to research the scholarship of teaching and learning.

The claims made by proponents about the scholarship of teaching and learning can be quite far reaching; for example:

> Using a transformative learning and critical theory lens to view the Scholarship of Teaching and Learning takes us to an emancipatory Scholarship of Teaching and Learning in which the assumptions, beliefs, norms and values of the discipline, the institution, the community and the state are directly and critically questioned. Such an approach has the potential to yield a deep shift in perspective on teaching and learning at both an individual level and a social level. (Cranton 2011, p. 85)

Another enthusiast, Kreber (2013, 2015), takes the discussion further in arguing that the scholarship of teaching and learning is not just an evidence-based but a virtues-based practice. She also views the evidence-based aspect of the scholarship of teaching and learning as incorporating two types of evidence: 'Evidence of the internal ethical consistency between our strategies and desired ends and evidence of the effectiveness of these strategies in achieving these ends' (2015, p. 578). Leibowitz and Bozalek (2016), writing in the South African context, go even further in linking the scholarship of teaching and learning with a social justice approach.

Ultimately, however, the primary and most immediate reason for engaging in the scholarship of teaching and learning remains, of course, the desire to improve student learning and the student experience more generally. In this context, therefore, it is reassuring that there is evidence that this actually occurs (Horspool and Lange 2012; Trigwell 2013). For example, an Australian study was able to conclude that 'there is a significant relationship, at the faculty level, between engaging in the scholarship of teaching and learning, and changes in students' course experiences' (Brew and Ginns 2008, p. 543).

Set against these expansive and positive views of the practice of the scholarship of teaching and learning, however, there are also less positive accounts, particularly regarding the (relative) lack of rewards for those engaging in such scholarship when compared with conventional research (e.g. Henderson and Buchanan 2007; Mathison 2015). Much of the drive to engage with the scholarship of teaching and learning continues to rest, therefore, with the individual academic and their motivation.

Not surprisingly, the scholarship of teaching and learning (now frequently abbreviated as SoTL) has been subject to a number of critiques. Here, for example, is one proponent identifying a number of issues or 'impediments':

> First, there is a persistent tendency to use scholarship of teaching as a synonym for other activities. Second, Boyer's definition was conceptually confused. Third, it is difficult to operationalize … . Fourth, much discourse concerning SoTL is anti-intellectual and located in a narrow neoliberalism. Fifth, there is an uncritical and almost quaint reliance on peer review as the mechanism to detect scholarship.
> (Boshier 2009, pp. 12–13)

In an earlier article, Boshier and Huang (2008) argue that the scholarship of teaching and learning is marginalized in most institutions of higher education, and that part of the problem is the subsidiary position that learning takes in relation to teaching.

Recent discipline-based surveys of the state of the scholarship of teaching and learning also raise concerns. Gurung et al. (2008) report on the findings of an American survey of psychology departments:

> Despite our optimistic expectations, the survey respondents failed to report a prevailing sentiment of support for the 'systematic, literature-based inquiry into processes and outcomes involved in teaching and learning' either among members of psychology departments or among the institutions that house them. (p. 257)

Hamann, Pollock and Wilson (2009) took a different approach, analysing the articles published in three US-based political science journals that focused on the scholarship of teaching and learning. They found that such articles were disproportionately authored by women and/or junior faculty, which could be interpreted positively – as they do – as indicating a healthy future for research in this area, or negatively as suggesting that it was of less interest to senior or established members of politics departments.

In a similar study, Paino et al. (2012) looked at the articles published in another US-based journal, *Teaching Sociology*, over the period between 2000 and 2009. While they found an increase in the volume of relevant research being published in that journal, and an increasing sophistication in the approaches taken, they noted that relatively little of this research was externally funded and questioned 'just how institutionalized and accepted SoTL has really become' (p. 103).

In another American study, Henderson and Buchanan (2007) examined who was being published in a range of pedagogical and research-oriented journals across the disciplines for the period between 1997 and 2004. They also examined editorial board membership. Their main conclusion was that research and publishing on the scholarship of teaching and learning had become 'a special niche for faculty at comprehensive universities' (p. 523); that is, universities that were not research intensive.

Moving away from the United States, a New Zealand study (Haigh, Gossman and Jiao 2011) undertook a stocktake of the scholarship of teaching and learning in three universities. Their findings, while suggestive of growth, also revealed that there was a long way to go: 'While the data indicated quite variable publication patterns between the three universities during the period 2000 to 2005 … the proportion of SoTL publications to research publications overall is relatively low for this period (3.6%)' (p. 14). In an Australian context, Bennett et al. (2016) argue for the pivotal role of academic development staff in maintaining and developing the scholarship of teaching and learning. But the limited response elsewhere does not bode well.

It may be, of course, that the scholarship of teaching and learning is simply a current (and temporary) manifestation, and labelling, of an ongoing concern regarding the quality of teaching and learning in our universities and colleges.

Conclusions

Clearly, research on teaching and learning in higher education is in a reasonably healthy state. The overall trends in research publications are upwards. A specific research design, phenomenography, has been developed largely to study this area, and has proved resilient over the last four decades. The theoretical framework of teaching and learning approaches, studied in part using phenomenography and in part using survey instruments, has become not just popular, but endemic, in thinking outside of North America. And the scholarship of teaching and learning movement, originating in the United States, has provided an example of a framework which has been applied both worldwide and across disciplines.

While other designs and frameworks – for example, concept mapping, student motivation and ways of knowing – could have been considered, this would have added emphasis to this conclusion. That said, however, none of these designs or framework is without its critics, and there is evidence of continuing widespread disinterest (rather than opposition) in the findings and application of pedagogical research.

Chapter 4
Research on Course Design

Introduction

Course design concerns how what is taught (and learnt) in higher education is planned, organized, delivered, assessed and evaluated. It is a more contemporary take on what used to be termed the curriculum or the syllabus, implying rather more in the way of conscious engagement.

As higher education has grown from a craft into big business, and student numbers and class sizes have got larger, course design has become increasingly important. While there are still clear craft elements to teaching in higher education – for example, many lecturers are largely left to their own devices to decide how to deliver the courses they are responsible for (at least until something goes noticeably wrong) – the need to deliver a good (enough) product has become paramount.

Course design and its various component elements are, therefore, much more widely discussed and reviewed within universities and colleges than hitherto. Departments, schools and faculties spend more time considering how to deliver their courses, examining how well they were received, and then debating whether they could be delivered in a different, and hopefully better, way. The borderline between informal and internal evaluation and a research project leading to publication is a fine one, and many of the former slip over into the latter in the form of small-scale evaluative case studies. Indeed, of the eight themes into which higher education research has been divided in this book, course design is arguably the most widely researched (Tight 2012a).

The following section reviews trends in research into course design. Three theoretical frameworks for researching course design – academic literacies, activity systems and threshold concepts – are then examined in detail, before some conclusions on this research field are offered.

Research trends

A search using Scopus for articles with the words 'course', 'design', 'higher' and 'education' in their titles, abstracts or keywords gave a good indication of the changing popularity of research writing with course design in higher education as a key interest. While only a handful of such articles were being published each year in the 1970s, and hardly any before then, the numbers had risen to over 100 each year by 2000 and over 500 each year by 2010. Clearly, then, this is a growth area of research interest.

Early writing on course design reflects the emerging significance of it as a topic. Thus, Clift and Imrie (1980) focus on the growing importance of course evaluation:

> Institutions of higher education are now realising the need for the continuing evaluation of the learning experience which is provided for their students. This awareness has resulted in the establishment of research and advisory units within tertiary institutions. (p. 78)

However, they note the failure of many evaluation efforts due to poor communication between the educational researchers and those responsible for planning and delivering the courses, and make some suggestions for improving this state of affairs.

O'Neil and Jackson (1983) discuss the problems associated with course teams or groups of lecturers charged with developing or revising programmes of study, notably the scope for disagreement and for individuals simply to focus on their specialist interests. They advocate the use of nominal group technique as a means for overcoming these problems.

Liow, Betts and Lit (1993) explore the relationship between educational objectives and teaching methods, comparing the views of staff and students. They conclude that '(1) the choice of teaching method should be linked closely to educational objectives; and (2) project work and tutorials are more likely to meet the important objectives than lectures' (p. 65). In other words, if educational objectives are the driver, more unusual teaching methods might need to be developed and emphasized.

Contemporary research on course design has mushroomed, and, in doing so, helped to support an interest in an increasing variety of designs for learning, including blended learning (Chen and Liang 2011; Lai, Lam and Lim 2016), collaborative learning (Kali, Levin-Peled and Dori 2009) and inquiry-based learning (Justice et al. 2007). In practice, of course, the differences between these different approaches may not be that great, and the overlaps considerable. Thus, Jones and Bennett (2016) argue that online and offline learning – that is, the basic components of blended learning – share a good deal in common. Interestingly, they also offer a definition of course design: 'The creation of context-sensitive learning habitats that cater to the differing needs of blended and online-only students, within a single pedagogical ecosystem' (p. 1).

Other ideas which have been explored in terms of their impact on course design include constructive alignment (Maffei et al. 2016), the flipped classroom (Boeve et al. 2016; McNally et al. 2017), interdisciplinarity (Mavor and Traynor 2001; interdisciplinarity is discussed further in Chapter 10) and teaching technology (Marshall and Meacham 2007), as well as the implications of internationalization (Luxon and Peelo 2009; internationalization is discussed further in Chapter 7).

While there has undoubtedly been a great deal of progress over the last forty years and more in our understanding of course design, it would be false to claim that everything has improved. For example, Zundans-Fraser and Bains (2016), in examining the process used for course design and review in one Australian institution, come to a rather critical conclusion:

> Analysis … demonstrated a chasm between the documents supporting the process of course design and review, the requirements … for information submitted … for the approval of a course and the work that occurred in the process of course design and review … the policy document, supporting document and minutes did not direct a Course Director to use a theoretical base or incorporate a design framework. (p. 851)

Many would still recognize these kinds of issues in their own institutions.

Research designs and frameworks

Of the various research designs and theoretical frameworks that have been applied to researching course design in higher education, we will examine three contrasting examples in some detail: academic literacies, activity systems and threshold concepts. The three examples chosen are indeed contrasting; with academic literacies, a theory deriving from linguistics, offering a framework for understanding how students become acculturated to the disciplines they are studying; activity systems, a theory deriving from Soviet psychology, providing a way for thinking about the relations between, in this instance, students, courses, academics and institutions; and threshold concepts, developed within higher education research itself, suggesting the need to identify (but not necessarily providing a way of identifying) 'troublesome' knowledge.

Academic literacies

The academic literacies framework has been described as 'the way that students learn, or fail to learn, through the processes involved in their interaction with texts and writing' (Haggis 2003, p. 101). Its usage is not confined solely to academic texts and writing, however, but may be extended to cover the way in which students engage with a discipline or area of study, and how academics help to facilitate this. The academic literacies framework has its origins outside of higher education research, in new literacy studies in linguistics (Barton 1994; Ivanic 1998; Street 1984).

The academic literacies framework came to prominence in the 1990s, with US- and UK-based researchers at the forefront of the development. Its proponents rejected the earlier models of study skills and academic socialization as accounting for student learning (Lea and Street 2006):

> The ... model ... of academic literacies ... suggests a more complex and contested interpretation in which the processes of student writing and tutor feedback are defined through implicit assumptions about what constitutes valid knowledge within a particular context, and the relationships of authority that exist around the communication of these assumptions. The nature of this authority and the claims associated with it can be identified through both formal, linguistic features of the writing involved and in the social and institutional relationships associated with it. (Lea and Street 1998, p. 170)

Thus, the context for study – the course, programme, discipline, department and/or institution – is critical, and the practices and authorities associated with that context have to be identified, communicated with and understood by the student if they are to progress successfully (cf. threshold concepts, discussed later in this chapter).

The idea of academic literacies challenges

> the belief that literacy is concerned with the acquisition of a particular set of cognitive skills, which once acquired can be put to use unproblematically in any new context. ... It takes as its starting point the position that literacy is not a unitary concept; reading and writing – literacies – are cultural and social practices, and vary depending upon the particular context in which they occur. The more recent work ... has been concerned to build on these frameworks through research into the particular contexts of higher education and the apparent gaps between tutors' and students' understanding of writing for assessment. ... The research undertaken in the field tends to be qualitative in nature and of an ethnographic type, adopting language-based methodologies drawn from social linguistics. These methodologies have enabled researchers to look in depth at students' and tutors' interpretation of student writing in higher education. (Lea 2004, p. 740)

Like many popular theoretical frameworks, however, the academic literacies framework has come to be interpreted and applied in differing ways:

> There is considerable fluidity – and at times confusion – in meanings attached to the use of the phrase ... the phrase is increasingly used to signify courses intended to enable student writers to meet the demands of writing in the university. ... This instrumental focus is strongly echoed in research which considers specific courses or teaching initiatives in relation to student achievement or students' acquisition of required linguistic, rhetorical or cognitive structures ... there is a tendency ... to use the phrase referentially: that is as referring to reading/writing/texts in academic contexts, rather than as indexing a critical field of inquiry with specific theoretical and ideological historical roots and interests. (Lillis and Scott 2007, pp. 6–7)

Bibliometric searches using Google Scholar and Scopus show that, while only a handful of articles focusing on academic literacies (i.e. with the term in their titles) were being published each year in the 1990s, and hardly any before then, by the

2010s the figure was between 50 and 100 each year. These searches also indicate that the singular form, 'academic literacy', is more commonly used than 'academic literacies'.

Academic literacies research in higher education is fairly widespread globally. Examples have been identified from, for example, Australia (Matthews, Simon and Kelly 2016), Chile (Marinkovich et al. 2016), Hong Kong (Braine 2002), Ireland (Sheridan 2011), Israel (Ferenz 2005), New Zealand (Adams et al. 2016), Norway (Jonsmoen and Greek 2017), South Africa (Amos and Fischer 1998), Spain (Guzman-Simon, Garcia-Jimenez and Lopez-Cobo 2017), Sweden (Bergman 2016), the United Kingdom (Pearson 2017) and the United States (Hedgcock and Lee 2017). The theoretical framework provided by academic literacies has been applied to a wide range of disciplines, including art and design (Melles and Lockhart 2012), business studies (Shrestha 2017), engineering (Archer 2008a,b), health sciences (Rose et al. 2008), pharmacy (Scouller et al. 2008), social work (Goldingay et al. 2016) and sociology (Black and Rechter 2013).

The academic literacies framework has also been applied to a wide range of teaching and learning contexts, including second language learners (Ferenz 2005) and international students (Newman, Trenchs-Parera and Pujol 2003). It has been utilized to research online learning (Goodfellow 2005), in connection with information literacy (Adams et al. 2016; Guzman-Simon, Garcia-Jimenez and Lopez-Cobo 2017), and at doctoral level and beyond (Koutsantoni 2006; Tardy 2005). In a study of first-year doctoral students, for example, Seloni (2012, p. 47) concluded that 'socializing into the practices of academic discourse is a complex and multi-layered process in which students collaboratively construct meaning and engage in interactive dialogues outside of their classrooms in order to learn how to become legitimate participants in their academic disciplines'.

The usefulness of an approach using the academic literacies framework has been favourably contrasted with the more common generic or key skills training:

> The effectiveness and persuasiveness of a research text is reified and legitimated through social and linguistic convention (some of which are disciplinary), specific kinds of genre, rhetorical practices and cultural norms. Effective research writing can be considerably enhanced by structured introductions to and engagements with specific cultural writing contexts, including reflection on research purposes and cultural norms, and the textual move patterns, language choices and rhetorical strategies with which they are expressed. Support of the writing cycle is also important. Without this, students can take considerable time and many wrong turns in clarifying the purpose and conventions appropriate within different research writing contexts, and the meanings they want to convey within them. (Bastalich, Behrend and Bloomfield 2014, p. 381)

This implies, of course, the need to discuss and explain academic literacies at a disciplinary, department or course level.

A good deal of research into academic literacies has, therefore, been concerned with how to embed them within the curriculum (e.g. Benzie, Pryce and Smith

2017; Bergman 2016; Fouche, van Dyk and Butler 2017; Jacobs 2005; Murray and Nallaya 2016); which is why they have been considered in this chapter rather than the previous one. Typically, these studies have taken the form of small-scale evaluations, examining the experience on a particular course or programme. Others have focused on how academic literacy might be tested for (Cliff 2015; Rambiritch 2015).

As an example, Tribble and Wingate (2013) report on an institution-wide, genre-based initiative which has put together disciplinary databanks of sample academic texts, together with grading and feedback, and commentary from academics, to serve as the basis for writing courses. They argue that 'although it requires time and resources to develop these kind of writing courses within disciplines, the proposed approach offers a realistic and sustainable way of providing focused, discipline-specific writing instruction to students across all levels in higher education' (p. 318).

The academic literacies framework has been widely linked to, and compared with, other theoretical ones. Given its origins in linguistics, many of these assessments have concerned its role in linguistic research, notably concerning English for specific and/or academic purposes (McGrath and Kaufhold 2016; Turner 2012; Wingate and Tribble 2012). One such comparison, for example, was with systemic functional linguistics (Coffin and Donahue 2012, p. 64):

> Although these approaches both draw from ethnographic and sociocultural traditions, they have tended to focus on different aspects of EAP [English for academic purposes]. SFL [systemic functional linguistics] as a theory of language has employed linguistic analysis to establish the nature of disciplinary discourses and ways of encouraging students to engage in these discourses; research and pedagogy have concentrated on texts, language in use and the language system. Academic Literacies as a research paradigm has maintained a strong commitment to ethnographic investigation and to critiquing dominant academic and institutional practices; methods have concentrated on identifying practices, student identities, and conflicts that individual language users experience in university writing.

Within the field of higher education research, other comparisons have been made, some of them to other frameworks considered elsewhere in this book, such as approaches to learning research (Haggis 2003; 2009; see Chapter 3) and communities of practice (Hirst et al. 2004; see Chapter 9). It has also been suggested that acquiring academic literacy is a threshold practice (Gourlay 2009; see the later section in this chapter). Others have linked academic literacies to critical thinking (Hammer and Green 2011), knowledge structures research (Paxton and Frith 2014), Bernstein's work (Tapp 2015) and student voice research (Paxton 2012).

Activity systems

Cultural historical activity theory (CHAT), or activity systems theory as it is also widely known, has been applied within higher education research (and within other areas of research) for the last few decades. While it may not be the most popular or widespread theoretical framework in use for examining course design, it is an interesting example deriving from Soviet psychological research.

There are varied accounts available regarding the origins and development of activity systems theory, but most summarize it in terms of a series of succeeding generations of research, typically three in number (e.g. Axel 1997; Cole and Engeström 1993; Engeström 2001; Nussbaumer 2012; Roth and Lee 2007). These authors agree in identifying Vygotsky (Vygotsky 1978) as the key initial thinker in the 1920s Soviet Union:

> Instead of focusing on the direct impact of stimulus on response, Vygotsky devised a new approach: the concept of mediation, the first generation of this theory. He maintained that human beings as agents react to and act upon mediating objects of the environment such as tools, signs, and instruments leading to an outcome. (Nussbaumer 2012, p. 38)

According to Roth and Lee (2007, p. 189):

> Vygotsky … created what is referred to as first-generation activity theory. It was substantially developed by two of his students, Aleksandr Luria and A. N. Leont'ev, to incorporate societal, cultural, and historical dimensions into an explication of human mental functioning, leading to what constituted second-generation activity theory.

The third generation is usually associated with the Finnish researcher Engeström:

> Engeström further detailed activity systems to include networks of interacting systems to deal with tensions and contradictions that encourage collective learning through change. This latter model, known as third generation CHAT, may be seen as applying to large systems, evolving into institutions and organizations. (Nussbaumer 2012, p. 39)

Engeström himself summarizes the developments as follows:

> The first generation, centered around Vygotsky, created the idea of mediation. This idea was crystallized in Vygotsky's famous triangular model in which the conditioned direct connection between stimulus (S) and response (R) was transcended by 'a complex, mediated act'. … The limitation of the first generation was that the unit of analysis remained individually focused. This was overcome by the second generation, centered around Leont'ev. In his famous example of 'primeval collective hunt' Leont'ev explicated the crucial difference between an individual action and a collective activity. However, Leont'ev never graphically expanded Vygotsky's original model into a model of a collective activity system. … The third generation of activity theory needs to develop conceptual tools to understand dialogue, multiple perspectives, and networks on interacting activity systems. … In this mode of research, the basic model is expanded to include minimally two interacting activity systems. (2001, pp. 134–6)

Engeström continues, making the cultural and historical aspects of the theory clear:

> In its current shape, activity theory may be summarized with the help of five principles. The first principle is that a collective, artifact-mediated and object-oriented activity system, seen in its network relations to other activity systems, is taken as the prime unit of analysis. ... The second principle is the multi-voicedness of activity systems. ... The third principle is historicity. Activity systems take shape and get transformed over lengthy periods of time. ... The fourth principle is the central role of contradictions as sources of change and development. ... The fifth principle proclaims the possibility of expansive transformations in activity systems. (Engeström 2001, pp. 136–7)

Engeström also developed Vygotsky's triangular model, which he typically portrays as four triangles within a larger triangle, with the six apexes – labelled as subject, object, instrument, rules, community and division of labour – as the organizing principles.

Roth (2007a,b) stresses the importance of emotion, motivation and identity in helping to develop third generation CHAT, while Sannino (Sannino 2011; Sannino and Sutter 2011) emphasizes the role of intervention. Alongside Engeström, the other Western academic most associated with the dissemination outside of the Soviet Union/Russia of the ideas behind CHAT is the American Cole (Cole and Engeström 1993; Lecusay, Rossen and Cole 2008): 'CHAT penetrated Anglo-Saxon academia rather late; historians may come to identify in Michael Cole the single most influential person for acquainting Western scholars to this tradition, both through his writings and through the mediating role of his Laboratory for Comparative Human Cognition at the University of California, San Diego' (Roth and Lee 2007, p. 190).

In a recent article, Foot (2014, p. 330) helpfully articulates the importance of the terminology of CHAT:

> There is significance in each word in the label *cultural-historical activity theory*. *Cultural* points to the premise that humans are enculturated, and everything people do is shaped by and draws upon their cultural values and resources. The term *historical* is used together with cultural to indicate that since cultures are grounded in histories and evolve over time, therefore analyses of what people do at any point in time must be viewed in light of the historical trajectories in which their actions take place. The term *activity* refers to what people do together and is modified by both cultural and historical to convey its situatedness. *Theory* is used in this label to denote a conceptual framework for understanding and explaining human activity. (emphases in original)

Foot also presents her own synopsis of the ideas that lie at the heart of CHAT: 'CHAT centers on three core ideas: (1) humans act collectively, learn by doing, and communicate in and via their actions; (2) humans make, employ, and adapt tools of all kinds to learn and communicate; and (3) community is central to the process of making and interpreting meaning – and thus to all forms of learning, communicating, and acting' (ibid.).

This interpretation, with different emphases from those of Engeström, draws CHAT closer to the idea of communities of practice (see Chapter 9), a framework with which it is often compared and/or contrasted. Thus, like all theoretical frameworks of any age, and hence value, CHAT has both developed and, to some extent, diversified, leading Holzman (2006, p. 1) to argue that 'there is no unified theory of activity theory, but a set of articulations that more often than not overlap rather than separate'.

A Scopus search for articles with the words 'cultural', 'historical', 'activity' and 'theory' in their titles, abstracts or keywords suggests that a current total of around 100 are being published each year. We need only go back twenty years, however, to find a mere handful of such articles being published each year, so the interest is clearly a recent phenomenon. Not all of these articles focused on higher education, of course, though many did.

Most were authored by researchers in the social sciences, psychology or the arts and humanities. The majority were produced by researchers based in the main English-speaking countries of the United States, the United Kingdom, Canada and Australia, though Finland-based authors (Finland being Engeström's homeland) were the fourth most prolific. There have been several special issues of journals produced which have focused wholly on CHAT (e.g. Roth and Lee 2009; Somekh and Nissen 2011; Williams, Davis and Black 2007).

A related search using Google Scholar identified all articles with the exact phrase 'cultural historical activity theory' somewhere in their text. This is not such a focused search as the Scopus one, as many of these articles may have just mentioned the term in passing, but it does give a better idea of the breadth of interest. It showed that, at the present time, about ten times as many articles – several hundred a year – mention the theory as focus upon it.

Academics researching and writing about CHAT have been based or interested in a variety of disciplinary or skill areas, including art and design education (Addison 2014), clinical education (Varpio, Aschenbrener and Bates 2017), creative writing (DiSarro 2014; Russell 1997), mathematics education (Roth 2012), occupational therapy (Toth-Cohen 2008), science education (Saka, Southerland and Brooks 2009), social work (Fire and Casstevens 2013), teacher education (Kim 2012) and teaching English as a foreign language (Lilley and Hardman 2017). Some have been concerned with particular types or levels of higher education, such as open/distance learning (Joo 2014) and professional doctorates (Simpson and Sommer 2016).

The particular topics that have been explored with the assistance of CHAT have also been wide ranging. They have included, for example, academic development (Saroyan 2014), classroom education (Nussbaumer 2012), educational change (Lee 2011), entrepreneurial activity (Holt 2008), the learning of professionals working with marginal groups (Daniels 2004), learning outcomes (Addison 2014), peer coaching (Lofthouse and Leat 2013), undergraduate research mentoring (Schwartz 2012) and whiteness (Leonardo and Manning 2017).

In addition to the major English-speaking nations of the United States, the United Kingdom, Canada and Australia, and the homeland of one of the theory's major contemporary exponents, Finland, research on CHAT has been carried out in a wide range of countries worldwide. These have included, for example, Italy (Morselli, Costa and Margiotta 2014), Mexico (Montoro 2016), New Zealand (Berg et al. 2016), the Philippines (Morales 2017), Russia (Mironenko 2013), Singapore (Lee 2011), South Africa (Lautenbach 2014) and South Korea (Joo 2014).

Some authors have sought to make links between CHAT and other theorists (e.g. Dewey: Miettinen 2006), or theories or approaches, such as action research (Wells 2011), complexity science (McMurtry 2006), critical realism (Nunez 2013) and visual techniques (O'Brien et al. 2012). Lecusay, Rossen and Cole (2008) discuss the relation between CHAT and another of Vygotsky's key ideas, the zone of proximal development.

Three linked aspects of CHAT that have attracted particular attention as it has developed are the role of contradictions, the importance of expansive learning and the use of change laboratories. Engeström noted that 'the idea of internal contradictions as the driving force of change and development in activity systems … began to gain its due status as a guiding principle of theoretical work and empirical research' (2015, p. xv) after activity theory was taken up in Western countries from the 1970s onwards.

On expansive learning, Engeström and Sannino argue:

> The theory of expansive learning puts the primacy on communities as learners, on transformation and creation of culture, on horizontal movement and hybridization, and on the formation of theoretical concepts. … The theory … focuses on learning processes in which the very subject of learning is transformed from isolated individuals to collectives and networks. Initially individuals begin to question the existing order and logic of their activity. As more actors join in, a collaborative analysis and modeling of the zone of proximal development are initiated and carried out. Eventually the learning effort of implementing a new model of the activity encompasses all members and elements of the collective activity system. (2010, pp. 2, 5–6)

They review research into expansive learning as transformation of the object, as movement in the zone of proximal development, as cycles of learning actions, as boundary crossing and network building, and as distributed and discontinuous movement, concluding that

> research based on or inspired by the theory of expansive learning has reached a transitional phase. The multiplicity and diversity of research applications indicates that the theory has opened up a rich set of novel research questions and topics. However, the different applications are often not very well aware of one another and there are too few examples of cumulative creation of knowledge that would build on previous studies. It is time to move from a mainly inspirational to a more systematic mode of research on expansive learning. (ibid., p. 16)

The change laboratory is presented as a practical methodology for using activity theory to change practices:

> In the mid-1990s, researchers … at the University of Helsinki developed a new intervention toolkit under the generic name of Change Laboratory. Variations of this

toolkit have been used in a large number of intervention studies in settings ranging from post offices and factories to schools, hospitals, and newsrooms. ... A Change Laboratory is typically conducted in an activity system that is facing a major transformation. ... Working practitioners and managers of the unit, together with a small group of interventionist-researchers, conduct five to ten successive Change Laboratory sessions, often with follow-up sessions after some months. ... Critical incidents, troubles, and problems in the work practice are recorded and brought into Change Laboratory sessions to serve as first stimuli. This 'mirror material' is used to stimulate involvement, analysis, and collaborative design efforts among the participants ... interventionists typically introduce conceptual tools such as the triangular models of activity systems as a second stimulus. ... The participants are challenged to use the mediating second stimulus as an instrument in the design of a new concept for the activity they are trying to transform. (ibid., p. 15)

Within higher education settings, Montoro (2016) used the change laboratory methodology as an aide to foreign language learning in Mexico, while Morselli, Costa and Margiotta (2014) apply it in entrepreneurship education in Australia and Italy.

Cultural historical activity theory has not been as widely critiqued as might be expected, perhaps because it is not the easiest theory to engage with and might, therefore, be purposefully ignored or overlooked. Where there has been criticism, it is often positively formulated with a view to modify and/or improve the theory: for example Blunden (2007) on how the theory handles individual agency, and Stetsenko and Arievitch (2004) on the place of the self.

In a similar way, Langemeyer and Roth (2006) claim that activity theory is over-psychologized and under-socialized:

An error in Engeström's theory does not only consist of a lack of comprehending the subjective and intersubjective plane of human activity but also in a missed articulation of societal contradictions. By referring to the concept of an 'inner contradiction' (cf. a 'double-bind' situation), Engeström tends to psychologize the societal level of human practice. He tends to identify societal, social and individual dimensions (like the motive and the object of activity) instead of comprehending the dialectical interrelation *and distinction* of societal, social and psychic processes. (Langemeyer and Roth 2006, p. 38)

This is one reason why communities of practice (discussed in Chapter 9) appears to be rather more popular in higher education research, though it might equally be criticized for being under-psychologized.

Rather more forcefully, Nunez (2013; see also Nunez 2014) argues for the integration of activity theory within critical realism:

Critical realism provides a new ontology by which to ground activity theory and the conceptual means to transcend its problems ... a proto-explanatory critique has introduced basic critical realism in practice; i.e. it has exemplified how a non-Humean ontology and the philosophy of critical naturalism allows us to deal with such unsolved dualisms of activity theory, resolving macro-aporias [doubts] of (1) individualism and collectivism, (2) reification versus voluntarism (or society versus the individual), (3) naturalism versus anti-naturalism (or the problem of positivism versus hermeneutics), and the micro-aporias of (4) body–mind dualism versus reductionism and (5) causes versus reasons … the philosophical system of critical realism … is able to resolve dualisms and arrive at a more complete and explanatorily adequate account of reality. (2013, pp. 162–3)

As that explanation indicates, however, such a strategy might make activity theory even less accessible to most higher education researchers, who tend to be much more focused on improving practice.

Bligh and Flood (2017), who carried out an analysis of fifty-nine articles they identified as applying activity theory in higher education research, argue that most application of the theory is fairly conservative and lacking in ambition:

Activity theory is typically *chosen* for its perceived empirical utility: because the 'context' of the researched phenomenon is obviously important, or because particular activity-theoretical concepts (like contradiction) are intuitively applicable. Activity theory is typically *used* for the *abstraction* and *explanation* of phenomena – to highlight particular aspects and name them or their relationships – and for. *contextualising* those phenomena. The theory is *valorised* for apprehending the dynamics of complex situations and for identifying contradictions (the two being intertwined). Conversely, activity theory is rarely chosen to directly challenge prior conceptualisation of the research object, or because of interest in the theory per se. It is used infrequently to establish investigative *paradigms* or *hypotheses*; very rarely to calibrate *norms* for researched practices; and never for *predictive* purposes. (p. 148, emphases in original)

More needs to be done, therefore, both to make the theory more accessible and to extend its applications.

Threshold concepts

Beaty (2006), in the foreword to one of a number of edited volumes on threshold concepts that have been produced in the last decade, traces the origins of this theory to a series of UK research and development projects undertaken in the 2000s. Meyer and Land (2003) are cited as the first published source, and they attribute the original idea to Meyer, who was drawing on Perkins's (1999) idea of troublesome knowledge.

Since then, Meyer and Land together (Meyer and Land 2005, 2006a,b,c), as well as individually (Land 2011, 2012) and with other authors (Baillie, Bowden and Meyer 2013; Land et al. 2005; Land, Meyer and Flanagan 2016; Land, Meyer and Smith 2008; Meyer, Land and Baillie 2010; Meyer, Ward and Latreille 2009; Shanahan, Foster and Meyer 2006), have produced a succession of publications on the topic.

Of course, neither Meyer nor Land were the first to match the words 'threshold' and 'concepts' together; researchers and practitioners in different disciplines have long recognized the existence of various kinds of concepts, some of which they have termed 'threshold concepts'. The oldest use of the term found in a Google Scholar search dated to 1950, and was in an article on 'Auditory Masking and Fatigue' in the *Journal of the Acoustical Society of America* (Rosenblith 1950). The earliest use found in a title dates to 1976, in an article on 'Dose-Response Relationship and Threshold Concepts' in the *Annals of the New York Academy of Sciences*. Clearly, as these titles indicate, threshold concepts have been used in specific ways in a variety of disciplinary contexts.

There has been a steady growth in the use of the term 'threshold concepts' from the 1950s to the present day. Much of the most recent expansion is down to the work of Meyer and Land, and its impact upon others. Thus, according to a Scopus search, 84 per cent of the articles mentioning threshold concepts and 73 per cent of the articles using this term in their titles (314 out of 431) date from 2000 or later. Most of these articles, particularly those using the term in their titles, are concerned with the application of threshold concepts as a theoretical framework to researching learning and teaching in higher education.

Meyer and Land, in one of their earlier works on the topic, define threshold concepts in the following fashion: 'A threshold concept can be considered as akin to a portal, opening up a new and previously inaccessible way of thinking about something' (2006b, p. 3). In other words, it is a concept that, once grasped and fully comprehended, enables the individual to move on significantly in their thinking. The idea of a threshold concept is usually immediately linked to that of troublesome knowledge: 'A threshold concept can of itself inherently represent … *troublesome knowledge* – knowledge that is 'alien', or counter-intuitive or even intellectually absurd at face value' (ibid., p. 4).

Meyer and Land give many examples in their publications of what may be considered as threshold concepts: for example *complex number* and *limit* in pure mathematics, *signification* and *deconstruction* in literary and cultural studies, and *opportunity cost* in economics. Acknowledging that many types of concepts are recognized in the different disciplines, they distinguish threshold concepts from core concepts, which do 'not necessarily lead to a qualitatively different view of subject matter' (ibid., p. 6).

A series of characteristics of, or criteria for distinguishing, threshold concepts have been mapped out:

A threshold concept … is likely to be: *transformative*, in that, once understood, its potential effect on student learning and behavior is to occasion a significant shift in the perception of a subject, or part thereof. … Probably *irreversible*, in that the change of perception occasioned by acquisition of a threshold concept is unlikely to be forgotten, or will be unlearned only by considerable effort … *integrative*, that is it exposes the previously hidden interrelatedness of something. … Possibly often (though not necessarily always) *bounded* in that any conceptual space will have terminal frontiers, bordering with thresholds into new conceptual areas. Potentially (though not necessarily) *troublesome*. (ibid., pp. 7–8, emphases in original)

Threshold concepts are also linked to the related idea of liminality, the condition of being between different states, in this case moving from a lack of understanding to an understanding of the concept in question. Meyer, in particular, has also made considerable efforts to link the developing ideas around threshold concepts to other elements of learning theory, including metalearning activity (Meyer, Ward and Latreille 2009, Ward and Meyer 2010), and capability and variation theory (Baillie, Bowden and Meyer 2013; variation theory is discussed in the context of phenomenography in Chapter 3).

The idea of threshold concepts has undoubtedly had a significant impact upon the higher education research community over the last decade: 'There is now substantial evidence for threshold concepts in the disciplines, drawn from over 150 scholarly papers in 80 disciplinary or subject contexts from authors in the higher education sectors of many countries' (Land 2011, p. 177).

Threshold concepts have been applied in a wide range of disciplines and fields, including accounting (Lucas and Mladenovic 2007), biochemistry (Green et al. 2017), biological sciences (Ross et al. 2010), business/management (Wright and Gilmore 2012), computer science (Boustedt et al. 2007), creative writing (Adsit 2017), dental education (Kinchin et al. 2011), disability theology (Duke and Mudge 2016), diversity training (Winkler 2017), economics (Davies and Mangan 2007), engineering (Holloway, Alpay and Bull 2010), English language teaching (Skinner 2017), geography (Srivastava 2013), health care (Clouder 2005), history (Adler-Kassner, Majewski and Koshnick 2012), information literacy (Hosier 2017), law (Wimshurst 2011), leisure studies (Harris 2017), literature (Wisker 2007), mathematics (Scheja and Pettersson 2010), nurse education (Stacey and Stickley 2012), occupational therapy (Nicola-Richmond, Pepin and Larkin 2016), politics (Korosteleva 2010), psychology (Picione and Freda 2016), social work (Morgan 2012), statistics (MacDougall 2010), sustainability education (Barrett et al. 2017) and translation studies (Meister 2017).

As well as specific disciplinary applications, the framework of threshold concepts has been applied to more generic higher education concerns, such as academic writing and literacies (Gourlay 2009; see also the discussion of academic literacies earlier in this chapter), doctoral research (Kiley and Wisker 2009), information literacy and librarianship (Hofer, Townsend and Brunetti 2012) and sustainability (Sandri 2013). It has also been applied in thinking about interdisciplinarity (see Chapter 10) and cross-disciplinarity (see, for example, Carmichael 2012, who also links it to tribes and territories research; see Chapter 9), and to other levels of education (Long 2009).

One of the earliest published critiques of threshold concepts theory was especially thorough and hard-hitting. Rowbottom begins by questioning: 'How can we empirically determine if there are such threshold concepts?' (2007, p. 264). He argues that 'Meyer and Land not only fail to specify what is essential to a threshold concept, but also neglect to explain what they understand a concept to be' (ibid.). Rowbottom considers different views of the nature of concepts, and their relation to abilities, and concludes 'that so-called "threshold concepts" are not as easy to spot as anyone has previously thought, even if there are such things' (p. 268).

In a more recent analysis, Walker (2013) begins by noting that 'it appears that a Threshold Concept could be viewed as both a "product" (something developed in the mind of the learner) and a "process" (as a transformative journey with distinct stages)' (p. 248). He goes on to identify a number of limitations:

> Firstly, and perhaps most importantly, is it a theory which explains empirical observations, or is it a concept incorporating and representing several abstract ideas? Secondly ... the relative paucity of empirical work would seem to grant considerable scope for innovation. Third, despite the intuitive nature of TCs [threshold concepts] how exactly are they defined? ... Fourth, and finally, despite some significant conceptual overlaps, none of the literature on TCs refers to Schema Theories of Learning. (pp. 250–1)

Walker argues that 'several powerful synergies exist between schema theories of learning and threshold concepts' (p. 252), which he then illustrates through an empirical study making use of the technique of semantic networks.

Barradell (2013) focuses on the problems in the identification of threshold concepts, and offers transactional curriculum inquiry, involving dialogue between teachers, students and educational designers, as a means of doing this. Nicola-Richmond et al. (2018) take this further in considering whether, and how, threshold crossing might be measured. Quinlan et al. (2013) focus on problems with methodology, concluding that 'it would be useful to bring together researchers who have been developing complementary research methodologies, to compare and contrast these approaches and to develop more rigorous methodological protocols for the research' (p. 12).

These issues and critiques may be both extended and added to. Are all of these researchers identifying the same sort of thing as concepts, or are these supposed threshold concepts just a collection of different aspects of learning in disciplines in higher education that particular teachers have found difficult to get across? To take just another three examples, Kinchin et al. (2011) identify the recording of a complete dental jaw registration (a process) as an example of a threshold concept in dental education, Sandri (2013) discusses systems thinking (recognizing and appreciating the interrelatedness of many factors) in learning for sustainability, and Wisker and Savin-Baden (2009) consider the problems experienced by academics and research students in writing (a very generic process).

This sense of threshold concepts theory being used by a range of researchers to explore a huge diversity of problems is further accentuated if we note the different terminologies being used to identify concepts. Meyer and Land themselves distinguish threshold concepts from core concepts. Davies and Mangan (2007) distinguish between basic, discipline and procedural concepts, all of which can be threshold concepts.

Conclusions

As an area for higher education research, course design is clearly complementary to teaching and learning, the subject of the previous chapter. While the focus in teaching and learning research is on the direct experience and understanding of teaching and learning by the participants involved, course design research is more about the planning that goes into organizing, delivering and evaluating a course.

The three theoretical frameworks discussed in some detail in this chapter are each both interesting and revealing in their own ways. Two – academic literacies and activity systems – have been brought into higher education research from outside, from linguistics and psychology respectively; while the third – threshold concepts – has been developed in higher education research.

Activity systems theory has been in development for around a century, but has only been taken up outside the former Soviet Union in the last few decades. Academic literacies have been around and applied in higher education research for a few decades, while threshold concepts is a very recent development, essentially confined to the present century.

Each may be seen in relation to other theoretical frameworks, including those discussed elsewhere in this book. Thus, the academic literacies approach may be viewed as a rival to teaching and learning approaches (discussed in Chapter 3), while activity systems may be compared to communities of practice (discussed in Chapter 9). Academic literacy has also been proposed as a threshold concept.

Chapter 5
Research on the Student Experience

Introduction

What is meant today by the term 'the student experience' – that is, the entirety of the individual's experience while they are a student, including not only their study experience but also their social, family and work experience – is a relatively recent understanding, going back little more than two or three decades. Prior to then, when the term 'the student experience' was used, it was typically applied much more narrowly to mean just the study experience.

Until recently, much less attention was paid to the broader student experience, as it is now commonly understood, with the exception of those small elite groups of young school-leavers who were able to study full-time in residential colleges. For such privileged groups, living and studying in a small community of students and academics was seen as the ideal, as it still is in Oxford, Cambridge and other similar universities (Tight 2011).

The more recent, broader interest in the student experience is, in essence, due to a transformation in the way that students are seen by the universities and colleges they study in or with; which is itself related to a change in the way governments, parents, employers and other stakeholders view higher education. Students are increasingly seen as customers of higher education institutions (a perspective discussed in more detail in Chapter 6), with the latter being responsible both for preparing the former for subsequent employment and ensuring they receive a well-rounded and satisfying experience while they do so.

This change in perspective has, naturally enough, generated a growing research interest in the broader student experience, the focus of this chapter.

Research trends

A search using Google Scholar for articles with the exact phrase 'student experience' in their titles showed that, prior to the mid-1990s, there was only a small amount of published research focused on this theme. Further exploration indicated that most of this actually dealt with the study experience more narrowly construed, and was usually confined to medicine and health. For example, in 1955 Mills wrote about 'broadening the student experience in mental hygiene and abnormal psychology', by which he meant introducing more practical elements into the curriculum.

Interest in the student experience, more broadly conceived, began to take off about two decades ago. While only a handful of articles focusing on the topic were being published each year at the beginning of the 1990s, this had risen to around 20 per year by the beginning of the 2000s, and to over 100 per year by the 2010s. Books focused on the issue also began to be published (e.g. Haselgrove 1994; Shah, Nair and Richardson 2016).

A number of sub-themes are evident within this literature, including

- assessing and enhancing the student experience
- the early/first-year student experience
- the international student experience
- the minority ethnic student experience
- the doctoral student experience

We will consider four of these, and more minor sub-themes, in turn here. The first-year experience, which has become a major research interest – because of its perceived criticality in both getting students off to a good start and retaining them to continue and complete their studies – is discussed in more detail in the next section as a research framework.

Assessing and enhancing the student experience

The major reason underlying the growing interest in researching the student experience is the realization that, in an increasingly competitive higher education sector, higher education institutions, departments and academics need to be aware of, and responsive to, their students' feelings and situations. Hence the emphasis on, first, assessing the student experience (this is also discussed in Chapter 6 in the context of quality), and then doing what can be done to enhance it where necessary.

The danger that the ways in which the student experience was measured might lead to standardization, and hence limitation, in what universities and colleges then provided for their students was recognized relatively early:

> Once established, survey instruments can set standards and expectations about the nature of teaching and the student experience by virtue of the type of questions asked, or just as important, questions not asked. Universities are inevitably tempted to comply with, or at least drift towards, these implicit definitions. (McInnis 1997, p. 65)

This has led some to propose much more bespoke ways of assessing the student experience, even where institutions already (or are effectively compelled to) make use of standardized instruments:

> The lesson learned in this study is that the process of searching for outcome measures itself is an institutional 'soul-searching' process, in which the college community has to revisit and/or redefine its institutional mission and goals constantly … that so many taxonomies can be used for assessing college outcomes clearly shows that there can be as many ways of defining excellence in higher education. (Cheng 2001, p. 536)

The research clearly shows that dissatisfaction with the quality of the student experience is one of the major reasons for students dropping out or failing to complete their higher education courses (Yorke 2000, 2013; see also the discussion of student retention later in this chapter). Even if not all dissatisfied students discontinue their studies, they all present at least potential problems to the institutions they are studying with. Keeping tabs on the quality of the student experience is, therefore, a major concern for higher education institutions across the world (e.g. Buultjens and Robinson 2011; Shah and Richardson 2015; Staddon and Standish 2012; Tucker 2013).

The international student experience

The particular concern with the international student experience relates to the growth in studying abroad in recent years, and the importance of international student numbers to higher education sectors in countries such as the United States, the United Kingdom and Australia. Difficulties with language and initial adjustment, and in integrating with the home student and local communities, are among the issues highlighted by the research. This might involve dealing with instances of racism (Brown and Jones 2013) or, in the case of Saudi students studying outside of their country, mixed sex classrooms (Alhazmi and Nyland 2013).

Thus, Tian and Lowe (2009), in a study of the experience of Chinese students in the UK, illustrate how this can be about anything other than genuine internationalization:

> Rather than the increase of international students on British campuses enhancing cultural awareness and offering opportunities for intercultural communication, it too easily leads to withdrawal into national enclaves with reinforced notions of cultural separation. Our data show Chinese respondents were in fact homogenised, 'foreignised' and 'otherised' in the 'internationalising' communities both in and off campus. (p. 673)

This view has been challenged, however, by others (e.g. Rose-Redwood and Rose-Redwood 2013), with Montgomery and McDowell (2009; see also Montgomery 2010) arguing that international students show considerable facility in developing and using supportive international communities of practice, so that it is probably the home students who are missing out more:

> International students' somewhat superficial relationships with UK students do not appear to contribute much to the development of their global perspective, but this should not be seen as a deficit against the background of the gains from their international group … in view of the strength and value of the international network … the success of international students' experience at university is not predicated on social and cultural contact with UK students. However, in terms of the experience of the UK students who live and study in a parallel community, there may be a missed opportunity to develop an international perspective through more profound social contact with the international student group. (p. 465)

Most likely, of course, the experience varies considerably among the international student body. In a quantitative Australian study, for example, Russell, Rosenthal and Thomson (2010) identified three main types of adaptation: positive and connected (the majority), unconnected and stressed, and distressed and risk-taking. Taking a more positive approach, Mak and Kennedy (2012) explore how increasing academics' intercultural awareness and modifying the curriculum can contribute to improving the international student experience.

More recently, research has reflected the increase in the number of international students studying in non-Western countries, such as China (Ding 2016) and Hong Kong (Ladegaard 2017).

The minority ethnic student experience

Research on the minority ethnic student experience shares similarities with that into the international student experience, in that the focus is on a (diverse) group of students perceived as different from the norm, and on whether and how they adjust and fit into the majority student experience. This sub-theme is particularly strong in the United States, where research into the black student experience is of long standing, with research into Hispanic students also becoming prominent more recently. Indeed, in the United States there are a number of established journals devoted to this theme, including the *Journal of Negro Education* and the *Journal of Hispanic Higher Education*. In countries like the United States, Canada, Australia and New Zealand, there is also a growing body of research on students from indigenous or native communities.

For example, Jones, Catellanos and Cole (2002) examined the experience of different ethnic minority student groups at a predominantly white university in the United States, focusing on the role of cross-cultural centres. Guiffrida and Douthit (2010) carried out a similar study, but focused particularly on the experience of black students and the role of counsellors in aiding their transition. They concluded that 'school and college counselors who understand the sociocultural challenges that

Black college students face in their transitions … can provide an invaluable means of support and advocacy for these students to facilitate their academic success' (p. 317). Simmons et al. (2013) apply relational dialectics theory to study the relationship between African American students and their universities, suggesting that a transformative model may be needed to really improve matters.

Other researchers have focused on the experience of other kinds of minority student, such as those with autism (Cox et al. 2017) and those from lower socio-economic groups (Finnegan and Merrill 2017; Jury et al. 2017).

The doctoral student experience

While much of the research on the student experience has focused at the undergraduate level, and understandably so as this accounts for the great majority of students in higher education, others have examined the postgraduate student experience, at both masters (e.g. Steele 2015) and doctoral levels (e.g. Gardner and Gopaul 2012; Mantai 2017; Stubb, Pyhältö and Lonka 2014). For the latter, Gardner and Gopaul looked at the experience of the part-time doctoral student, while Stubb, Pyhältö and Lonka considered the different conceptions of research held by doctoral students and how these might impact upon the research experience.

Other minor sub-themes

Other researchers have focused on specific aspects of the student experience. Thus, Ainley (2008) has stressed that there is not one (undergraduate) student experience, but a wide variety of student experiences, depending significantly on factors such as the student's socio-economic background and the type of higher education institution attended. Sabri (2011) offers a similar argument, in her case based on a critical discourse analysis of selected UK higher education policy texts. She concludes:

> 'The student experience' discourse does consign experience to a vacuum, and in doing so it advances three false promises. First, it promotes the illusion that students' educational experiences and chances of attainment are unconstrained by class, ethnicity, gender, race, religion, sexual orientation, or responsibility for dependents. Second, it ignores the ways in which students' experiences are intimately connected to the quality and strength of their relationships with academics, with other higher education workers, and with each other. Third, it elides the reality that their experiences differ because they take place in a range of very different higher education institutions. (p. 664)

Koenig-Lewis et al. (2015) examined how the student experience, both academic and social, is recalled by university alumni, and how this relates to their loyalty. Others have explored the student experience in relation to, for example, assessment

(Bevitt 2015), finance (Curtis and Klapper 2005), academic literacy (Scouller et al. 2008), extracurricular activities (Stuart et al. 2011) and the student voice (Yannuzzi and Martin 2014). Thorpe and Godwin (2006), Cutajar (2017), Shapiro et al. (2017) and others have researched the experience of students studying online. Mann (2001) argues that the student experience may be one of alienation rather than engagement.

Research designs and frameworks

The three frameworks for researching the student experience in higher education which will be discussed in detail in this section – the first-year experience, student retention and engagement, and the transition to work – are all both important and popular. It should be stressed, therefore, as the previous section indicated, that other frameworks or foci also exist.

In some cases, these alternative foci are more specialist, as in the examples of the international or ethnic minority student experience. In other cases, they represent an alternative way of looking at what is much the same field. For example, there is a considerable literature on the processes involved in accessing higher education (or the transition to higher education) – that is, choosing courses and institutions, applying, the institutional selection process and so on – which both predates and prefigures many of the issues now considered in the first-year experience literature.

The first-year experience

Interest in the first-year experience is closely linked to that in student retention and engagement, the subject of the next section. This interest recognizes the importance of making students' initial impressions of their course and institution as good as they can be, thus encouraging their close and continuing integration and engagement:

> Students come to higher education to learn and ... it is within the first year curriculum that students must be inspired, supported, and realise their sense of belonging; not only for early engagement and retention, but also as foundational for later year learning success and a lifetime of professional practice. (Kift 2009, p. 1)

What is provided for students in their first year, and especially in the first part of that first year, is critical for their future higher education and beyond.

A bibliographic search using Google Scholar and Scopus was undertaken to identify trends in the publication of articles focusing on the first-year experience. It showed a steady build-up of research interest in this topic, such that, by the 2010s, over fifty articles were being published each year that included the phrase 'first year experience' in their titles, with about four times as many mentioning it in their abstract.

There is a journal focusing on the topic, the US-based *Journal of the First-Year Experience and Students in Transition*, and there used to be a second one, the Australia-based *International Journal of the First Year in Higher Education*, between 2010 and 2015 (Creagh 2015), but this was folded into another journal.

Interest in the first-year experience is not just confined to the United States and Australia, but is also prevalent, though to a lesser extent, in the United Kingdom. Examples of research focusing on the first-year experience can be found from other developed countries, such as Germany (Trautwein and Bosse 2016), Hong Kong (Evans 2016) and Japan (Fryer 2017). Research has also focused on less obvious subjects, such as engineering (Holmegaard, Madsen and Ulrikssen 2016) and STEM (i.e. science, technology, engineering and mathematics) subjects in general (Ulrikssen, Holmegaard and Madsen 2016). A number of national reports have been funded and produced on the topic, notably in Australia (e.g. James, Krause and Jennings 2010, Kift 2009, McInnis 2001, Nelson et al. 2011, Yorke and Longden 2008).

Overall, as a result of all of this research and interest, it has been claimed, in the Australian context, that

> good progress has been made in improving the transition to university and the quality of the educational experience for first year students. The investment in high quality transition programs and in monitoring and responding to the needs and experiences of first year students is yielding dividends. The emphasis of the higher education sector on the first year must intensify as the student population grows and diversifies. (James, Krause and Jennings 2010, p. 4)

There have been hundreds of studies carried out at an institutional level, with the aim of establishing the best approach to adopt to improve the first-year experience. To give just one example, Trotter and Roberts (2006) studied courses in one university with high or low student retention rates to make recommendations on what the latter might do to improve matters. They concluded that

> in order to enhance the early student experience it is essential that senior management overtly shape, support and monitor appropriate coordinated policies and actions. Institutions should involve all departments in … enrichment programmes. They should coordinate, facilitate and encourage the development of links with local schools and colleges at institutional, departmental and programme levels. Staff development workshops on induction should include a particular emphasis on activities designed to help students integrate. Personal tutorial systems should be adequately resourced, with an agenda of activities that can be followed in personal tutor meetings. (p. 383)

Other studies of the first-year experience have focused on a diverse array of factors, characteristics and/or strategies that may impact on the satisfactoriness of the student experience. These affect students, staff and the institutions they work in.

Thus, from the students' perspective, researchers have emphasized the importance of cultivating a sense of community among students (Townley et al. 2013), or a sense of belonging (Kane, Chalcraft and Volpe 2014), and have discussed the need for academic and social integration (Nevill and Rhodes 2004). Academic support has been highlighted as a key role (Penn-Edwards and Donnison 2011), while the criticality of regular faculty–student interaction has been stressed (Delaney 2008). Social support has also been identified as a key factor in the student experience (Wilcox, Winn and Fauvie-Gauld 2005), and the role of social networking in this has been explored (Nalbone et al. 2016).

Other researchers have examined the first-year experience of particular kinds or types of students. These have included those who were the first in their family to study at the higher education level (O'Shea 2015), those from particular ethnic backgrounds (Hernandez 2002) and international students studying abroad (Yan and Sendall 2016). The health behaviours of first-year students have also been the subject of research (Gibson et al. 2016), as have their reflections on the first-year experience at a later date (Hailikari, Kordts-Freudinger and Postareff 2016).

From the staff or faculty perspective, research has stressed the importance of maintaining and developing staff collegiality in ensuring a good first-year student experience (Wojcieszek et al. 2014). It has also explored beliefs about teaching and learning (Brownlee et al. 2009), and assessment (Goos, Gannaway and Hughes 2011), and identified the need for changes in teaching and learning strategies (Coertjens et al. 2017), and the overall curriculum (Ulrikssen, Holmegaard and Madsen 2016). This might entail the development and use of specific first-year experience courses (Jamelske 2009, Turner et al. 2017).

Particular advocates have gone so far as to coin the term 'transition pedagogy' to cover the approaches involved, with this being defined as 'a guiding philosophy for intentional first year curriculum design and support that carefully scaffolds and supports the first year learning experience for contemporary heterogeneous cohorts' (Kift 2015, p. 54).

Perhaps unsurprisingly, the focus on the first-year experience appears to have produced relatively little in the way of critique, though it has raised a number of issues. Predominant among these is the realization that there is no simple, single answer to the question of how to make the first-year experience as good as possible:

> The issue of the first year experience of undergraduate students is one which is enduring. While we make adjustments and changes to meet the needs and expectations of the present generation of university students, these needs and expectations are continually changing. We will never get the first year experience right. We need to continue to monitor how our students are experiencing our first year programs and continue to change and develop them. (Pitkethly and Prosser 2001, p. 198)

Looked at more broadly, this conclusion applies not just to the first year, but to each year of the higher education experience, and it also differs from institution to institution: 'Ultimately, as this research demonstrates, there is no "one size fits all" solution to attrition, and responses must be differentiated by year of study and university' (Willcoxson, Cotter and Joy 2011, p. 349).

Part of a critique of the research focus on the first year would be, therefore, that it ignores or underplays the importance of subsequent years, particularly, perhaps, the final year of study, when students are preparing to graduate and either engage in further study or start their professional career (see the later section on the transition to work). Another element of this critique would be that the research on the first-year experience is funded and supported because of its criticality to the 'neo-liberal' agenda of retaining as many students in higher education as possible, and keeping them as satisfied as possible:

> Much of the focus on student transitions to university has been driven by the requirement to prevent student attrition and thus has sought to improve retention and progression rates. This managerial focus has resulted in a great deal of research on how to better support students during their first weeks and months at university. In contrast, our research has shown the complexity of the transitions students continue to make beyond their entry point to the university by offering a longitudinal analysis of the connections between learning, participation in practice and identity across the lifetime of a student's degree programme. What emerges most powerfully from the analysis presented here is that students coming into the university from a background in further education colleges had to work hard to make sense of their new academic community; over time they came to know and understand how it worked. (Christie et al. 2016, pp. 487–8)

The first-year experience debate illustrates well, therefore, the tensions between the general and the specific, between the desire to provide a good overall experience for all students and the extreme difficulty – in a mass higher education system – of recognizing and treating every student as an individual.

Student retention and engagement

Institutions of higher education and individual academics have long been concerned with trying to ensure that students, once enrolled, remain and successfully complete their studies, and that they get as much out of them as they can. These two related concerns are encapsulated in the concepts of student retention and student engagement.

Student retention is the older of the two concerns, at least in research terms, and was formerly also known by other, more negative, synonyms, such as student withdrawal, attrition and dropout. Student engagement, through which the student is involved in the higher education experience as deeply as possible, though a more recent concern (cf. the changing meanings of the student experience), represents one obvious response to the problem of student retention. In other words, the more engaged a student is, the less likely they are to voluntarily leave higher education before they have completed their studies.

Tinto, one of the key (American, as most of them have been) researchers to have studied student retention, traces the research interest back to the 1960s, and notes how the underlying assumptions have changed since then:

> When the issue of student retention first appeared on the higher educational radar screen, now some 40 years ago, student attrition was typically viewed through the lens of psychology. Student retention or the lack thereof was seen as the reflection of individual attributes, skills, and motivation. Students who did not stay were thought to be less able, less motivated, and less willing to defer the benefits that college graduation was believed to bestow. Students failed, not institutions. This is what we now refer to as blaming the victim. This view of retention began to change in the 1970s. As part of a broader change in how we understood the relationship between individuals and society, our view of student retention shifted to take account of the role of the environment, in particular the institution, in student decisions to stay or leave. (Tinto 2006, p. 2)

Indeed, in the 1960s, students who dropped out, or thought about doing so, might find themselves regarded as being mentally ill (Ryle 1969). The more nuanced interpretation recognized by Tinto, accepting that the university or college itself had a major role to play in ensuring high rates of student retention, reflected, of course, the recognition that – with funding increasingly coming directly from, or following, the student – it was financially desirable to keep dropout rates as low as possible (Astin 1975; Spady 1970, 1971; Tinto 1975).

Research into student engagement got underway about twenty years after the earliest student retention research, with early work undertaken by Pace (1984) and Astin in California, and then Kuh in Indiana (see Chen, Lattuca and Hamilton 2008, Gasiewski et al. 2012).

Wolf-Wendel, Ward and Kinzie (2009) link the idea of engagement to the related terms 'involvement' and 'integration'. They argue that student engagement has two facets, reflecting the extent to which the student engages and the efforts made by the higher education institution to engage them:

> The concept of student engagement represents two key components. The first is the amount of time and effort students put into their studies and other activities that lead to the experiences and outcomes that constitute student success. The second is how institutions of higher education allocate their human and other resources and organize learning opportunities and services to encourage students to participate in and benefit from such activities. (pp. 412–3)

Ideas around student retention and student engagement, which can be seen as different ways of addressing the same issue, have developed at different rates and times. Bibliographic searches were carried out using Google Scholar and Scopus, recording the numbers of times the exact words 'student retention' and 'student engagement' appeared in the titles of articles over time. While Google Scholar records roughly twice as many examples as Scopus, the trends for both are very similar.

The term 'student retention' appeared in article titles 20 to 30 times a year during the 1990s, rising to 50 to 100 times a year by 2008, since when the numbers have again increased, reaching a maximum (to date) of 96 articles in 2014 (according to Scopus) or 173 articles in 2016 (according to Google Scholar). 'Student engagement', by contrast, is a more recent interest, with no appearances in article titles before 1970, and very few articles before the 2000s (many of which were about school rather than higher education). Yet, 'student engagement' overtook 'student retention' in popularity in 2005, and has mushroomed since, with 349 (Scopus) or 745 (Google Scholar) articles produced in 2016.

Nearly two-thirds, 64 per cent, of the articles identified by Scopus with 'student retention' in their titles were authored by people located in the United States, with a further 13 per cent by authors in the United Kingdom, Australia or Canada. Despite this concentration, interest in the topic is also apparent in other, non-English-speaking, nations, for example Columbia (Mendoza, Suarez and Bustamente 2016) and Norway (Hovdhaugen, Frolich and Aamodt 2013). There is a specialist journal, the *Journal of College Student Retention*, devoted to the field, and a number of literature reviews (e.g. Bowles and Brindle 2017; Cameron et al. 2011; Zepke and Leach 2005) have been published. Several books have also been produced summarizing the research in this field (e.g. Crosling, Thomas and Heagney 2008; Pascarella and Terenzini 1991, 2005; Seidman 2012).

Interest in student retention among higher education researchers dates back to before the mid-1960s start date suggested by Tinto (e.g. Hanna 1930 (who also referred to it as 'student elimination'); Scales 1960). Following the initial recognition of, in some cases, the relatively high proportions of students who were not successfully completing their courses, attention turned to understanding and explaining the phenomenon, and then working out what could be done to improve matters.

A great deal of work, particularly in the United States, has now been devoted to modelling and predicting student retention, on a course, institution and national level. Among the earlier researchers, Astin (1975), Tinto (1975, 1993, 2012) and Bean (1980; Bean and Metzner 1985) have been particularly influential. Interestingly, Tinto, following Spady (1970, 1971), based his model on Durkheim's theory of suicide, while Bean adapted a model of employee turnover in work organizations. Cabrera, Nora and Castenada (1993) sought to combine elements of both of these models.

Tinto's model appears to have had the greatest impact, and there have been many follow-up studies which have applied, modified or re-assessed it (e.g. Braxton, Milem and Sullivan 2000; Kerby 2015; Pascarella and Terenzini 1980). There have also been similar studies following up Bean's work (e.g. Johnson et al. 2014). Others have applied alternative multivariate models in analysing student retention (e.g. DeShields, Kara and Kaynak 2005; Dey and Astin 1993). Understanding what causes retention or dropout – or at least what these phenomena are related to – and hence being able to better predict which students are likely to persist and which may need additional support remains a key interest (e.g. Forsman et al. 2014; Reason 2009; Wild and Ebbers 2002).

Many studies have focused on the retention of particular kinds of students, including black students (e.g. Kobrak 1992), Hispanic students (e.g. Oseguera, Locks and Vega

2009), American Indian students (e.g. Shotton, Oosahwe and Cintron 2007), disabled students (e.g. Kilpatrick et al. 2016), nontraditional students (i.e. non-campus, part-time and mature students: e.g. Roberts 2011; Thomas 2011), distance/open/online students (e.g. Simpson 2013) and higher degree students (e.g. Pearson 2012). Others have examined the relation between student retention and aspects of higher education institutions, such as quality improvement (e.g. Peterson, Kovel-Jarboe and Schwartz 1997) or institutional image (e.g. Angulo-Ruiz and Pergelova 2013).

An overriding concern of the research literature on student retention has, of course, been on what to do about it (e.g. Ackerman and Schibrowsky 2007; Campbell and Campbell 1997; Singell and Waddell 2010). The suggestions or recommendations made have been many and varied, from relationship marketing to mentoring to identifying at-risk students. A common theme that has been emerging, however, is that the response should not be about helping students to better adapt to the higher education institution they are studying at or with, but about the institution adapting to the students it admits:

> Central to the emerging discourse is the idea that students should maintain their identity in their culture of origin, retain their social networks outside the institution, have their cultural capital valued by the institution and experience learning that fits with their preferences. Content, teaching methods and assessment, for example, should reflect the diversity of people enrolled in the course. This requires significant adaptation by institutional cultures. (Zepke and Leach 2005, p. 54)

The research literature on student engagement is less dominated by US-based authors than that on student retention, according to Scopus, with only 45 per cent of authors from the United States. However, both Australia-based and UK-based authors account for another 12 per cent each, with Canada contributing 4 per cent and New Zealand, 2 per cent, meaning that these five Anglophone nations together account for three-quarters, 75 per cent, of the English language publications on the topic. Nevertheless, interest in student engagement is widespread globally, for example in China (Zhang, Gan and Cham 2007), Denmark (Herrmann 2013), Italy (Gilardi and Guglielmetti 2011), Korea (Choi and Ree 2014), South Africa (Wawrzynski, Heck and Remley 2012), Taiwan (Hsieh 2014) and Thailand (Hallinger and Lu 2013).

A number of literature reviews have been published (e.g. Trowler and Trowler 2010, Wimpenny and Savin-Baden 2013, Zepke and Leach 2010), as well as a handbook (Christenson, Reschly and Wylie 2012). Authors have also sought to categorize the literature and the approaches adopted. Thus, Zepke (2015) identifies

> a two-strand student engagement research programme that focuses both on identifying and measuring classroom engagement behaviours and on facilitating academic and social integration of students with study and the institution. The former is often associated with quantitative survey research; the latter with qualitative case studies, narratives and action research. Both strands research quality and successful learning (and teaching) in a constructivist, learning-focused framework. (p. 1314)

By comparison, Pittaway (2012) identifies five elements in an 'engagement framework' – personal, academic, intellectual, social and professional engagement – depending on which aspect of engagement is in focus. Kahu (2013), however, only identifies four

> dominant research perspectives on student engagement: the behavioural perspective, which foregrounds student behaviour and institutional practice; the psychological perspective, which clearly defines engagement as an individual psycho-social process; the socio-cultural perspective, which highlights the critical role of the socio-political context; and, finally, the holistic perspective, which takes a broader view of engagement. (p. 758)

These clearly overlap, to an extent, with those identified by Pittaway, with the final, holistic, perspective having some similarities with the emancipatory approach favoured by Zepke.

As Zepke points out, one major focus for research into student engagement has been the development of instruments designed to measure it, thus allowing institutional performances to be compared and benchmarked nationally. The first such instrument to be developed was the National Survey of Student Engagement (NSSE; Kuh 2003) in the United States, which is also used in Canada. Australian researchers modified and added to the NSSE to create the Australian Survey of Student Engagement (AUSSE; Coates 2010; Krause and Coates 2008), which is also used in New Zealand. In the UK, however, the National Student Survey (NSS) doesn't cover student engagement at present, though there have been separate developments in that direction recently (Yorke 2016).

As in the case of student retention, another direction for student engagement research has been to examine the experience of different student groups, including ethnic groups (e.g. Greene, Marti and McClenney 2008), nontraditional students (e.g. Wyatt 2011), international students (e.g. Zhao, Kuh and Carini 2005) and online/distance learners (e.g. Robinson and Hullinger 2008). Others have focused on variations in the institutional approach taken with regards to engagement in terms of institutional missions (e.g. Kezar and Kinzie 2006; Pike and Kuh 2005), and on variation in student engagement by year of study (e.g. Soria and Stebleton 2012) or discipline (e.g. Leach 2016; Pike, Smart and Ethington 2012).

For example, in terms of the latter, Leach found, using AUSSE data, that

> there were many significant differences between disciplines on the six student engagement scales. Some of these differences may result from assumptions within the AUSSE and ways of thinking and practising within disciplines. … AUSSE results may be best used at discipline or programme level. (2016, p. 784)

A related research approach has been to examine how the student body as a whole varies in its engagement. Hu and McCormick (2012), for example, concluded that

> distinctive student groups exist on American campuses with respect to their patterns of engagement in educationally purposeful activities … seven distinctive patterns

of engagement, each accounting for 10–17% of the student population ... those distinct patterns of engagement correspond to different patterns of learning and development in the first year of college, and different rates of persistence to the second year. (p. 751)

The problem, then, for those wishing to use this information to promote student engagement patterns which are associated with greater levels of learning, development and persistence is how to do it. We know that a greater level of

student engagement in educationally purposeful activities is positively related to academic outcomes as represented by first-year student grades and by persistence between the first and second year of college ... engagement has a compensatory effect on first-year grades and persistence to the second year of college at the same institution. (Kuh et al. 2008, p. 555)

Conversely, however, the evidence also suggests that levels of student engagement have not been increasing:

The purpose of this study was to determine whether student engagement in three good educational practices (cooperation with peers, active learning, faculty-student interaction) increased between 1983 and 1997 in response to the calls to improve the quality of undergraduate education in the United States. The data source was 73,050 students who completed the College Student Experiences Questionnaire. The results from multiple regression and effect size analyses showed that the frequency of involvement in these good practices did not change over time. (Koljatic and Kuh 2001, p. 351)

Unsurprisingly, therefore – and, again, as with student retention – there is a growing literature on how to improve student engagement (e.g. Kearney 2013, Umbach and Wawrzynski 2005, Zhao and Kuh 2004). The suggestions range from using active and collaborative learning approaches, including self and peer assessment, to getting academic staff to interact more with students, to offering support programmes for those students deemed to be at risk. As an example of this genre, Price and Tovar (2014) identify four suggestions:

- Requiring students to work together on projects during class.
- Encouraging students to work with classmates outside of class to prepare class assignments.
- Creating opportunities for students to tutor each other, either voluntary or paid.
- Committing faculty time for students to discuss ideas from readings or classes with instructors outside of class. (p. 778)

Student retention research has, of course, been subject to critique right from its inception. In the early days there was debate over which was the most appropriate model – Tinto, Bean or some combination or alternative – and whether their underlying theoretical frameworks were appropriate. Then there were arguments that student retention might not always be a 'good thing'; in some cases a student dropping out might be a positive decision, or the least worst decision in the circumstances; while in other cases what was classified as dropout might actually be a student transferring to a different institution or course (Hovdhaugen, Frolich and Aamodt 2013).

Other sorts of critique might also be envisaged. For example, it is clear that – in a mass higher education system – students are an increasingly heterogeneous group. Therefore, the idea that, rather than expecting students to prepare for and adapt to higher education institutions as they are, it is the responsibility of each institution to adapt and support each student on an individual basis (Zepke and Leach 2005) runs into major practical problems. With class sizes for many first-year undergraduate courses in excess of 100, it is simply not possible to give each student individual attention in any meaningful way, so a lower percentage retention rate is to be expected.

Then there is, of course, the neo-liberal critique that student retention has predominantly financial drivers. In other words, it is not so much about doing what is best for the student, but about ensuring that the institution receives the highest number and proportion of student fees possible.

Research into student engagement has also been criticized from a variety of perspectives. For a start, there has been the criticism – common to many popular concepts – that the meaning of the term is unclear or varied: 'Despite … widespread enthusiasm for the concept of student engagement, there is very little consensus as to its meaning or how we might measure the success of student engagement initiatives' (Baron and Corbin 2012, p. 761). Then there is the argument, also regularly advanced, that student engagement is under-theorized (Kahn 2014).

Other researchers have argued that student engagement research is lacking in other ways. Thus, Carini, Kuh and Klein (2006) note that student engagement only explains a small part of learning outcomes, so focusing upon it risks ignoring the bigger picture:

> Learning outcomes stem from a variety of sources, of which student engagement is only one. Indeed, the positive relationships between engagement and outcomes described in this paper are relatively small in magnitude. A large portion – and in some cases a majority – of the variance in key outcomes remains to be explained by yet undiscovered factors. (p. 23)

Hagel, Carr and Devlin (2012) argue that the instruments commonly used for measuring student engagement, in this case, the AUSSE, are partial in their coverage:

> By borrowing its student engagement scales from the USA, Australia has adopted a conception of student engagement and a measurement instrument that fails to capture some important aspects of engagement. There are contextual differences between the higher education systems of the two countries that raise questions about how well the scales apply to undergraduate students currently attending Australian universities. (p. 484)

In a similar vein, Gourlay (2015) reasons that, as with many initiatives that focus on measurement, it is the readily measurable that gets attention rather than the deeper, underlying elements: 'Mainstream conceptions of student engagement emphasise practices which are observable, verbal, communal and indicative of "participation" ... private, silent, unobserved and solitary practices may be pathologised or rendered invisible – or in a sense unknowable – as a result, despite being central to student engagement' (p. 410). Others have given a name to some of these missing, and often less positive elements – disengagement, alienation and/or burnout (Case 2008; Mann 2001; Stoeber et al. 2011) – and urged that further research be carried out into them.

Student retention and student engagement are clearly closely related frameworks: two sides of the same coin, cause and effect (or, rather, effect and cause, respectively), or whatever other analogy or metaphor you prefer. But they are also what might be called succeeding frameworks, illustrative of the tendency for established frameworks for research to be overtaken and partially supplanted by more recent entrants to the research field. They demonstrate how related, indeed competing, frameworks can occupy much the same research territory with relatively little overlap in terms of researcher membership or enterprise.

Transition to work

While higher education's teaching function is not solely concerned with the preparation of 'work-ready graduates', the transition to work (or, increasingly, further study) is a critical part of the student experience. It is also an aspect that has been much researched, as higher education institutions, employers, governments and other stakeholders are keen to keep tabs on how well the transition is taking place.

One thing which this research has clearly established is that 'the transition from university to work is a complex phenomenon, with many intervening factors' (Biggeri, Bini and Grilli 2001, p. 303). This has been shown both in large-scale, primarily quantitative, national studies (e.g. Biggeri, Bini and Grilli 2001; Finnie 2004; Gartell 2012; Pozzoli 2009) and small-scale, typically interview based and limited to a single institution or course, qualitative studies (e.g. Jungert 2013). There have also been a growing number of comparative international studies (e.g. Leuze 2011; Noelke, Gebel and Kogan 2012; Schomburg and Teichler 2006).

Research into the transition to work has adopted a wide variety of perspectives, from exploring the overall environment within which transition takes place, to the role of higher education institutions in smoothing the path, to the experience of particular types of students.

Taking the overall environment first, researchers have noted the increasing vocationalization of higher education (Brint et al. 2005; see also the discussion of professional and vocational disciplines in Chapter 10). Through this an increasing proportion of courses are specifically geared to the demands and requirements of specific professions or careers (e.g. in accounting, hospitality or social work), and a declining proportion offer a broad liberal education or a qualification in the pure sciences. Thus, Giret (2011), in the French context, concludes that vocationalization has improved the transition to work process:

> Vocational bachelor training facilitates transition from university to the labour market, even when controlling for student characteristics ... vocational training at university level helped to reduce the professional downgrading and increase the wages of university leavers three years after graduation. In addition, the vocational bachelor graduates benefited from the stronger institutional links between universities and employers to find their job. (p. 254)

Others have noted, however, that the recent economic recession has not helped matters (Aronson, Callahan and Davis 2015).

Turning to the institutional role, some researchers have stressed the impact of higher education institutional stratification on the transition to work (e.g. Leuze 2011; Noelke, Gebel and Kogan 2012). That is, in systems which have a marked status hierarchy of institutions, this explains a significant part of the transition process, with graduates of higher status universities and colleges enjoying a much smoother transition, typically to more financially rewarding jobs and careers.

Others have stressed the general importance of the institutional support role (e.g. Wendlandt and Rochlen 2008; Wright 2001), as manifested in the activities of careers advisory staff. This may involve the use of particular techniques for developing links with, or appealing to, employers, such as the use of internships or placements (e.g. Daniel and Daniel 2013; Gallagher 2015), or emphasis on the development of employability in the curriculum (e.g. Okay-Somerville and Scholarios 2015; Stiwne and Jungert 2010).

Researchers who have focused on the impact of the transition to work on students have examined, for example, changes in their well-being (Buhl 2007), the role of learning and fit (Grosemans, Coertjens and Kyndt 2017), professional identity formation (Nyström 2009), and their work-related goals or values (Dietrich, Jokisaari and Nurmi 2012; Sortheix et al. 2013). In the context of the latter, Schomburg (2007) reported on an international survey of 36,000 graduates, arguing that monetary return was by no means the only factor of importance in employment decisions:

> Graduates in Europe and Japan are not only at the top of the education pyramid in their countries, they also have high expectations regarding employment conditions and professional work. The character or content of work, the possibilities of using acquired knowledge and skills, challenging work tasks, and chances to work independently are amongst the most important work orientations of young graduates in Europe and Japan. Income and career advancement, which are often the focus of indicators of professional success, seemed to be less important when graduates were asked. (p. 55)

Others have looked at the experience of particular groups of students, such as those from minority ethnic backgrounds (e.g. Brekke 2007) or lower socio-economic groups (e.g. Opheim 2007). Reflecting the increasing globalization of higher education, the transition to work of foreign-born graduates and international students has also been researched (e.g. Anderson, McGrath and Butcher 2014; Popadiuk and Arthur 2014).

Criticism of research and thinking on the transition to work have chiefly focused on how practices could be improved and on what more research needs to be done. Dahlgren et al. (2007), for example, have criticized the continuing focus, in many institutions, on the discipline rather than the profession, with preparation for employment largely confined to the final year of the degree programme rather than being implicit throughout:

> Professional programmes in higher education as well as classical liberal arts studies still seem to provide students with a discipline-based identity. In cases where notions of a professional role are developed, this seems to be accomplished during the later, sometimes more applied, elements of the programme. (p. 314)

In a similar fashion, Guile (2009) identifies the need for a broader view of the transition and higher education's role in it, with a focus on the development of vocational practice rather than qualification itself: 'The transition from education to work should no longer be conceived as the accumulation of qualifications and, instead, should be re-thought as the development of vocational practice ... re-thinking transition as the development of vocational practice presupposes the replacement of routinised with a more multifaceted conception of vocational practice in UK educational policy' (p. 776). Others would, of course, disagree with this view, arguing that higher education was as much about preparation for life and a role in society, as it was about the transition to work.

Holden and Hamblett (2007) have noted that, while the transition from higher education to work may be smooth and cohesive for some, for others it is unsatisfactory and fragmented. In part, of course, this is down to contemporary economic uncertainty (Lechner, Tomasik and Silbereisen 2016), but there are also regularly expressed concerns that, in a period of mass higher education, many graduates may be over-educated or mismatched to the jobs they come to occupy (e.g. Iammarino and Marinelli 2015, Storen and Wiers-Jenssen 2016; see also the discussion of human and social capital in Chapter 7).

A more far-reaching contemporary critique is that the idea of a transition to work as a one-off event or phase is out of date, with recurrent transitions now likely to occur, going in different directions: 'Transitions from education to work (and from work to education) can take place several times and occur at different points in an individual's life cycle' (Alves and Korhonen 2016, p. 676).

Conclusions

Research on the student experience has, as we have seen, been largely driven by pragmatic demands. Researchers and their funders have wanted to know how to improve the student experience and the transition of graduates to work, and how to increase student retention by encouraging student engagement. This is, of course, perfectly understandable.

Yet, it does mean that we lack a more in-depth understanding of the varieties of the student experience: what it actually feels like to be a student, the day-to-day, week-to-week, month-to-month experience. We may remember, to some degree, what it felt like when we were students, but the higher education environment has changed greatly in the last twenty, thirty or forty years.

Such an understanding may not, of course, be so immediately useful in terms of improving institutional practices, but it is likely to have both longer-term and unanticipated benefits. It would most probably involve more in-depth and longitudinal studies, both qualitative and quantitative; and it would also most likely involve the direct participation of students themselves in the research. If such research could be undertaken, we would end up with a much fuller and more rounded idea of what it feels like, and means, to be a student at the present time.

Chapter 6
Research on Quality

Introduction

While it is not the most popular topic for research into higher education, quality accounts for a respectable – and slightly growing – proportion of the articles published in higher education journals (Tight 2003, 2012a). Indeed, there is a journal, *Quality in Higher Education*, which specializes in this topic, and a generic education journal, *Quality Assurance in Education*, which regularly carries articles focusing on higher education.

The age of *Quality in Higher Education* – it was founded in 1995 – gives some indication of the recency of the interest in researching quality in higher education. Like the growing popularity of research into higher education in general, this interest largely stems from the massification (as a theme for research this is discussed further in Chapter 7) of higher education systems. This expansion in provision was associated with a concern on the part of stakeholders, notably governments, regarding the maintenance and improvement of standards. National and international quality agencies were set up to review provision and practice.

This growing interest immediately led to research into what was meant by quality in higher education, how it might be measured or assessed, and into the practices and impact of those now responsible for maintaining and improving it.

Research trends

A bibliographic search using Scopus for publications with the words 'quality', 'higher' and 'education' in their titles identified a total of around 1,400. Having these words in their titles is taken as a clear indication of the publication's focus on quality in higher education; which is not, of course, to say that other publications did not pay the topic any attention. The body of research and writing on quality in higher education has grown over the years. While there were hardly any publications with 'quality', 'higher' and 'education' in their titles before 1970, and only a handful were published each year in the 1980s, the pace of publication then picked up, such that there are now over 100 publications specializing on this topic published each year.

Most of the earliest publications were American and dealt with particular aspects or examples of quality. Thus, Russell (1958) described the work of a federal agency, the Veterans Administration, in assessing the quality of the counselling provided to war veteran students in universities and colleges; while Barnard (1960) discussed what he referred to as a 'crisis' in higher education, brought about by growing enrolments, over whether the emphasis in provision should be on economy or quality (which has proved to be a recurring theme over the years).

These trends and foci continued into the 1970s. Thus, Morgan, Kearney and Regens (1976) examined the issue of how to assess, or rank, quality among graduate institutions of higher education in the United States, while Knoke and Isaac (1976) looked at how sociopolitical attitudes were affected by the quality of people's higher education experience there. There was also, however, evidence of American researchers looking outwards, particularly to the developing higher education systems of South-East Asia: Danskin (1979) offered a comparative analysis of quality and quantity in higher education in Thailand and the Philippines, while Thomas (1973) looked at the role of consortia in ensuring quality in Indonesian higher education.

By the 1980s, a strong concern with quality was developing in Western Europe and Australasia, both then areas experiencing the expansion to mass higher education. For example, in the UK, Barnett (1987) considered the role of the Council for National Academic Awards in maintaining quality in non-university higher education, Cuthbert (1988) looked at the relationship between management and quality, while Wright (1989) examined the role of professional power in determining conceptions of quality. In the rest of Europe, Maassen (1987) reviewed quality control procedures in the Netherlands, while Neave (1988) presented an overview of recent trends in Western Europe, linking quality concerns to efficiency and enterprise.

Moodie (1988) compared the debates over quality in higher education in the United Kingdom and the United States, noting that while, in the former there was much concern with value for money, in the latter equity and the nature of liberal education featured strongly. There was continuing interest in quality issues in North America (e.g. Peterson and Stakenas 1981), with Tan (1986) providing a critical review of the existing research literature on quality. Interest in these issues was also spreading worldwide: for example, to Venezuela (Salcedo 1988).

The 1990s, however, were when the research interest in quality in higher education really took off, stimulated and supported in part by the development of specialist journals such as *Quality in Higher Education* and *Quality Assurance in Education*, as well as more generic journals such as *Total Quality Management* that were not solely concerned with education or higher education.

Many articles addressed the current state of play in particular countries, such as the Netherlands (e.g. Segers and Dochy 1996) or Australia (e.g. Vidovich and Porter 1999). There were more comparative studies, with developments in countries within Europe being a particular focus (e.g. Maassen 1997; Neave 1994; de Weert 1990), but also a continuation of comparisons between practices in the United States and countries in South-East Asia, such as Malaysia (Kanji, Tambi and Wallace 1999). A few articles went beyond this, with van Vught and Westerheijden (1994), for example, putting forward a general model of quality assessment.

Other research focused below the national and international levels, examining the impact of quality regimes on higher education institutions (e.g. Billing 1998;

Frederiks, Westerheijden and Weusthof 1994). Specific concerns included the question of how quality could or should be measured (e.g. Gatfield, Barker and Graham 1999; Li and Kaye 1998; Ramsden 1991), and the use of performance indicators (e.g. Patrick and Stanley 1998). Other researchers considered the impact of quality measures on student learning (Horsburgh 1999) and the perceptions of employers (e.g. Joseph and Joseph 1997).

A particular focus of research and writing was on the application of established systems of quality assessment or management to higher education (this topic is discussed in more detail in a later section in this chapter). Most typically, these systems had already been developed and applied in commercial or industrial settings.

The 2000s saw a continuation of many of these concerns. Nationally focused studies continued to be popular, but covering a wider range of countries, including, for example, Australia (Vidovich 2002), Germany (Bornmann, Mittag and Daniel 2006), Malaysia (Sohail, Rajadurai and Rahman 2003), New Zealand (Meade and Woodhouse 2000), Norway (Welle-Strand 2000), South Africa (Fourie and Alt 2000), Sweden (Nilsson and Wahlen 2000), the United Kingdom (Hoecht 2006) and the United States (Grant, Mergen and Widrick 2002).

Comparative studies continued to focus on Europe (e.g. Haug 2003; Tomusk 2000) and East Asia (e.g. Mok 2000) as before, but also more broadly (e.g. Billing 2004; Dill 2000). Reflecting the developing global patterns of higher education, particular articles examined the transferability of quality assurance (Billing and Thomas 2000), the demands of cross-border higher education (Stella 2006) and the impacts of internationalization (van Damme 2001; this is considered in more detail in Chapter 7).

Concern over how quality was conceptualized or modelled was still evident (e.g. Srikanthan and Dalrymple 2007; Yorke 2000), and this clearly linked to how it was measured. This was reflected in the interest in instruments imported from industry, such as SERVPERF and SERVQUAL (e.g. Abdullah 2006; Tan and Kek 2004), in the focus on service quality (e.g. Clewes 2003; Quinn et al. 2009) and in the development of survey instruments specific to higher education to measure students' perceptions (e.g. Coffey and Gibbs 2001; Ginns, Prosser and Barrie 2007). The latter interest increasingly began to extend from the assessment of quality to the positioning of higher education institutions, departments and individual academics assessed in 'league tables' (e.g. Marginson and van der Wende 2007; Hendel and Stolz 2008; this topic is discussed further later in this chapter).

Other researchers examined the relationships between quality in higher education and other issues of contemporary importance, including student engagement (Coates 2005), generic skills (De La Harpe, Radloff and Wyber 2000) and employability (Morley 2001).

The last few years have seen much the same concerns remain in focus. Studies continue to be published on the quality concerns of, and practices adopted in, countries throughout the world, for example, Argentina (Coria, Deluca and Martinez 2010), Italy (Pompili 2010), Kenya (Odhiambo 2011) and Taiwan (Hou 2012). The interest in comparing trends within Europe remains strong (e.g. Burquel and van

Vught 2010) and has been extended further to examine members of the Organisation for Economic Cooperation and Development (OECD; see Bernhard 2012). Increasing attention appears to be being given to the quality issues and concerns involved in transnational higher education (e.g. Pyvis 2011; Stensaker and Maassen 2015).

The conceptualization of quality remains an issue (e.g. Filippakou 2011; Krause 2012), as do the models through which it is enacted in higher education, where both service quality (e.g. Jain, Sinha and Sahney 2011) and total quality management (e.g. Asif et al. 2013) remain in the forefront. Interest also continues in the ways in which quality may be measured (e.g. Law and Meyer 2010; Sun and Richardson 2012). Other researchers have examined quality in higher education in relation to performance evaluation (Sarrico et al. 2010) and as a political process (Skolnik 2010).

Research designs and frameworks

Three popular frameworks for researching quality in higher education will be considered in this section: quality assurance/management; the student as consumer or customer; and ranking and league tables. The first of these frameworks offers a more detailed examination of some of the general issues identified in the previous section. The second and third discuss research into two of the major unexpected consequences of the massification of higher education and the concern with quality: the changing way in which students are viewed and view themselves, and the repackaging of the quantitative institutional data produced by quality assessment.

Quality assurance/management

Concerns about the standards of higher education, particularly teaching in higher education, are of long standing. Students, their parents, schools and future employers, as well as governments as policymakers and funders – in other words, the full range of stakeholders, as they are termed today – have always had an interest in the standard of university and college teaching. With the massification of provision and participation, this concern has understandably become stronger, and for the last few decades has been re-badged as a concern with quality.

Here we discuss two related responses to this contemporary concern, quality assurance and quality management. These may be seen as different positions along a spectrum of increasing concern and response, with quality management further along the spectrum than quality assurance. Some, though, would argue that the latter is simply a subset of the former (Manatos, Sarrico and Rosa 2017), while others use the terms interchangeably. There are also other variant terms in use, such as 'quality control' and 'quality enhancement', but here the focus is on the research literatures examining quality assurance and quality management.

Rhoades and Sporn (2002) date the idea of quality assurance in the United States back to the formation of the oldest of the six accrediting bodies: 'The New England Association of Schools and Colleges, founded in 1885; the Middle States Association of Colleges and Schools, founded in 1887; and the North Central Association of Colleges and Schools' (p. 359). The advent of quality management, a direct transfer from business and commerce, was much more recent:

> Quality management came to U.S. higher education in 1991 in the form of variations of Total Quality Management. ... A 1995 American Council on Education survey found that 65% of campuses reported TQM/CQI [total quality management/ continuous quality improvement] activity. In addition, El-Khawas found that from 1988–1995 the proportion of institutions involved in assessment rose from 55 to 94%. (Rhoades and Sporn 2002, p. 361)

American universities, which experienced mass participation earlier than elsewhere, had, however, engaged with strategic management practices since at least the 1960s.

In Europe, the application of quality assurance practices, through the use of external examining, dates back even further than in the United States, 'perhaps as long as the history of the universities themselves' (Warren Piper 1994, p. 21). A fuller engagement with quality assurance and management came rather later; from

> the mid-1980s, quality control mechanisms like independent quality audit standards and units were being created in the United Kingdom and in the Netherlands ... the discussion of quality assurance was related to limitations of public expenditures and demands for greater accountability in higher education. It also was related to governmental policies introducing more self-regulation into higher education. The aim was to enlarge institutional autonomy and improve institutional performance. (Rhoades and Sporn 2002, p. 363)

Rhoades and Sporn identify somewhat different causes for the adoption of quality management practices in the United States and Europe:

> These practices emerged in the U.S. through both mimetic and coercive processes of isomorphism, in which higher education was influenced by private sector and state government practices. In Europe the same mechanisms operated through different structures: multinational business was a source of mimetic isomorphism (e.g., TQM); and national government, with New Public Management, was a source of coercive isomorphism. Those were supplemented by the influence of U.S. academics effected through professional mechanisms – normative isomorphism. (2002, pp. 382–3)

Williams (1993) dates the adoption of the particular doctrine of total quality management within higher education as being virtually simultaneous in the United States and the United Kingdom: 'It seems to have occurred spontaneously in a number of organizations in the United States and the United Kingdom in response to growing financial pressures on higher education institutions that, during the 1980s, increasingly found themselves being required to behave like commercial enterprises in a fiercely competitive market' (p. 229). While total quality management has been the most common system assessed or promoted in higher education (Owlia and Aspinwall 1996; Willis and Taylor 1999), others have also been investigated and applied, including ISO 9000 (Lundquist 1997) and continuous quality improvement (Hogg and Hogg 1995).

Just as there is disagreement over what quality means when applied to higher education, so there is variation in the use of the terms 'quality assurance' and 'quality management':

> Management and quality in higher education are each broad and slippery concepts. Statements about quality, management and the relationship between them need to be examined carefully to establish their context, purpose, frame of reference, authorship, and the criteria and yardsticks which are being used. (Cuthbert 1988, p. 67)

In part, of course, as Manatos, Sarrico and Rosa (2017, p. 159) argue, this is due to a resistance on the part of academics to being 'managed':

> There seems to be an aversion to the word 'management' in much of the literature dealing with higher education (HE). As a consequence, even when the literature on public services addresses QM [quality management], it tends to use a different terminology. HE in particular habitually refers to QM as 'quality assurance', which is rather odd for QM research, as it reduces the scope of QM to its assurance component.

Research and writing on quality assurance and management in higher education has been widespread and extensive. Steinhardt et al. (2016) identified 1,610 articles on these topics published in the period between 1996 and 2013. Their analysis identified four clusters of publications, and confirmed an overarching tension between focusing on management or on education:

> Two distinct strands of research on the quality assurance of teaching and learning became evident and emphasized an antagonistic tension in the research. First, the management strand in the Quality-Management-Cluster and Student-Evaluation-of-Teaching-Cluster comprises all aspects of quality assurance. This management strand is in tension with the education strand of research prevalent in the Assessment-Cluster and Quality-Cluster. Especially in the Quality-Cluster, the management and steering logic of quality assurance are criticized. (pp. 13–14)

Research on quality assurance has focused on many countries, including Australia (Harman 2001; Shah, Lewis and Fitzgerald 2011), China (Huang 2014), Colombia (Rubaii and Bandeira 2016), Croatia (Currie, Krbec and Higgins 2005), Ecuador (Rubaii and Bandeira 2016), Egypt (Schomaker 2015), Ethiopia (Semela 2011), Finland (Ala-Vähälä 2016), Germany (Bornmann, Mittag and Daniel 2006), Ghana (Ansah 2015), Greece (Stamoulas 2006), Hong Kong (Mok 2000), Italy (Barnabè and Riccaboni 2007), Japan (Yonezawa 2002), Kenya (Odhiambo 2014), the Netherlands (Enders and Westerheijden 2014), Oman (Carroll et al. 2009), Russia (Motova and Pykkö 2012), Singapore (Mok 2000), South Africa (Luckett 2007), Taiwan (Hou et al. 2015), the United Kingdom (Brown 2013, Hodson and Thomas 2003) and the United States (Welsh and Dey 2002). As well as the obvious cases for English language publications – Australia, the United Kingdom and the United States – this includes examples from all six continents, and a particularly strong representation from Europe.

Other studies have examined Europe as a whole (Damian, Grifoll and Rigbers 2015; Gvaramadze 2008; Hendel and Lewis 2005), as well as other continents or regions, such as Latin America (Lamarra 2009), Scandinavia (Schmidt 2017), South-East Asia (Umemiya 2008), the West Indies (Gift and Bell-Hutchinson 2007), developing countries as a whole (Lim 1999) and OECD member countries (Bernhard 2012). There have also been a number of comparative studies, examining the experience of two or more countries (e.g. Rhoades and Sporn 2002; Yokoyama 2010), and studies of international quality assurance agencies (e.g. Blackmur 2008; Brady and Bates 2016).

Billing (2004), in synthesizing comparative studies of quality assurance, detects the existence of a common or general model, incorporating both developmental (e.g. quality enhancement, contributing to planning) and judgemental (e.g. accreditation, public accountability) elements, while recognizing forces of both divergence and convergence:

> A 'general model' of external QA [quality assurance] does not completely apply in all countries, but ... most elements of it do apply in most countries. ... In each country, there may be specific additions of elements or omissions from the model, but more usually there are modifications or extensions of elements rather than their omission. These variations are determined by practicalities, the size of the HE [higher education] sector, the rigidity/flexibility of the legal expression of QA (or the absence of enshrinement in law), and the stage of development. (p. 133)

Research on quality management in higher education appears to be less widespread than that on quality assurance (Tari and Dick 2016). Nevertheless, examples may be identified from Australia (Holt et al. 2013), Greece (Papadimitriou 2011), Hungary (Csizmadia, Enders and Westerheijden 2008), India (Sahney 2016), Iran (Aminbeidokhti, Jamshidi and Hoseini 2016), Ireland (O'Mahony and Garavan 2012), the Netherlands (Kleijnen et al. 2011), Pakistan (Asif et al. 2013), Saudi Arabia (Noaman et al. 2017), Slovakia (Hrn iar and Madzík 2017), the United Kingdom (Kanji, Malek and Tambi 1999, Sutcliffe and Pollock 1992) and the United States (Burgar 1994; Grant, Mergen and Widrick 2002). Tellingly, perhaps, most of those identified from the United Kingdom and the United States focus on total quality management.

A lot of this research, however, consists of single institution case studies, with only limited engagement with theory. Thus, a study of nineteen articles on the topic published in *Quality in Higher Education* concluded that

> quality-management approaches can be described as quite heterogeneous; either by studying or reporting from a single case study, advocating the possible transferability of the findings from one institution or setting to another. Very few studies try to

build their analytical and theoretical frameworks on extensive literature reviews, close examination of research in the field or by developing or building upon more established theories or perspectives. (Pratasavitskaya and Stensaker 2010, p. 46)

In comparing the practice of quality assurance and quality management in higher education, there is a sense in which academics are generally prepared (even if grudgingly) to accept quality assurance, with the promise it offers of recognizing and improving what they do, while resisting quality management as something alien being imposed upon them by others:

> The 'total' integration of QM [quality management] in HEIs [higher education institutions] does not yet seem to be a reality. It appears that the QM field is still often treated as a separated field, run by a separate department within HEIs, and is not yet an integrated part of the organisation. (Manatos, Sarrico and Rosa 2017, p. 171)

Unsurprisingly, both quality assurance and, in particular, quality management, have been the subject of regular and sustained critique. One common criticism of quality assurance is that the results do not justify the considerable investment of time and effort in the process (Leiber, Stensaker and Harvey 2015). Thus,

> studies of academic staff perceptions about the impact of quality assurance in universities indicate that it has had little or no impact on curriculum, teaching quality or student learning. At worst, quality assurance has served only to increase the time and cost associated with bureaucratic requirements within universities and diverted attention away from the core processes of teaching and learning. (Houston and Paewai 2013, p. 262)

A related criticism is that the process also largely ignores the actual or potential impact on students, and on whether quality assessment leads to them engaging more in their learning:

> Determinations about the quality of university education are often made without information about whether students are engaging with the kinds of practices that are likely to generate productive learning and about whether institutions are providing the kinds of conditions that, based on many years of education research, seem likely to stimulate such engagement. Despite its value, information about what students are actually doing at university is largely ignored in discussions about the quality of university education. (Coates 2005, 35)

The reason for this lack of impact may be that quality assurance processes have, until now, largely focused on accountability and efficiency, rather than on the enhancement of provision (Brady and Bates 2016); though others (e.g. Filippakou and Tapper 2008; Gvaramadze 2008) have detected progress in that respect.

Another concern has been that quality assurance procedures are standardized – 'one size fits all' – and often ignore institutional diversity, typically by focusing on the characteristics of elite universities (Skolnik 2016). Similar problems occur internationally in cross-border higher education, where the quality assurance practices of the providing institution, typically from a Western country, are seen as taking precedence (Lim 2010; Ramirez 2014).

Finally, an underlying criticism of quality assurance is that it is an element of managerialism (which is discussed further in Chapter 8):

> QA [quality assurance] regimes continue to spread and occupy a central place in governance approaches to the regulation of higher education around the world … however, QA regimes are not benign managerial instruments – they must be understood as part of a broader series of agendas associated with neo-liberal policy prescriptions that valorize market rationality. Of itself, this is not a new observation. It is, however, not an observation that is frequently made and typically not in the context of university administrators who, in adopting such practices and ideational approaches to the management of research, teaching and funding activities are transforming university operating environments. The sense in which these practices enhance quality in terms of standards of academic excellence, scholastic rigour or the academic achievements of students and their learning, however, is typically a matter of conviction rather than evidence based policy determination. (Jarvis 2014, p. 164)

Much the same criticisms may be made, of course, and perhaps even more so, of quality management. For some, this is because of a dissonance between the principles of quality management and how they are put into practice:

> With a few exceptions of those academics who appreciated the clarity and high standards of control, nearly all respondents feared and dreaded the consequences of increased emphasis on quality assurance. … The general opinion is that quality management in its current shape and character does not suit the individual academic, neither their teaching nor their research. While the respondents are not so much against the general idea of quality management (or performance management and measurement), they dislike the manner [in which] it is being carried out. (Teelken and Lomas 2009, p. 272)

In the specific case of total quality management, the resistance from academics has been both stronger and continuing:

> The adoption of TQM practices into universities continues to be slow and controversial among the academic community. Some academics view TQM as a new management fad that does not have universal application, while others see it as a major paradigm shift. (Cruickshank 2003, p. 1164)

The explicit adoption of quality assurance and quality management techniques within higher education are, perhaps, the clearest example of a direct transfer of practice from business and commerce. They also represent another example of higher education practice and research that has rapidly spread worldwide from its original uptake in the United States and other English-speaking countries. It is no surprise, therefore, that they have been widely critiqued as an example of spreading managerialism (see also Chapter 8).

The student as consumer or customer

With the massification of higher education participation, policymakers in many countries have had to find ways of spreading the costs of provision. This typically leads to a shift in the responsibility of funding for higher education away from the state and towards the students themselves. Understandably, in such circumstances, students become even more concerned about the quality of what they are paying for.

These developments have arguably led to a change in both the way students think of themselves and in the way they are perceived by universities and colleges, and those who work for them. The student is no longer (just) a learner, the argument goes, but is now also, and perhaps primarily, a customer of the institution they are registered with, as well as a consumer of the higher education experience. As such, their satisfaction becomes of paramount importance for all concerned. Not surprisingly, many academics and academic managers – more comfortable with the traditional student/lecturer and student/university relationships, in which the student is definitely in the subsidiary position – reject this view as overly simplistic or just plain wrong.

The notions of *the student as customer* and *the student as consumer* are clearly closely related. They involve an analogy between universities and colleges and other types of organizations, particularly those in the private sector. The argument is that, just as we are customers of a car manufacturer when we purchase a new car, or consumers of fast food when we visit the local takeaway – with all that this implies in terms of expectations and obligations – so students, having paid their fees, are customers of universities and consumers of the education and other services they provide.

In the UK context, McCulloch explains *the student as consumer* metaphor as follows:

> The university acts as the provider of products and services, in the form of programmes of study and support for the pursuit of those programmes, and the student acts as a consumer of those products and that support. The notion of the student as consumer has driven much change within universities, not only within academic areas where 'quality', and its maintenance and enhancement, have dominated agendas over the same period, but also in areas such as student support and institutional marketing. (2009, 171–2)

The notion of *the student as customer* conveys a similar, but slightly differing, image to that of *the student as consumer*. It is a somewhat more active and engaged image, implying more in terms of choice and continuity.

Research into the student as customer or consumer has developed into a distinctive niche in the last three decades. Bibliographic searches using Scopus demonstrate that, while articles focusing on student satisfaction are relatively common, with over one hundred a year being published since 2010, those examining the student as a customer or consumer are rarer, only reaching double figures annually in the last decade.

Articles focusing on the student as customer or consumer are, however, fairly widespread, though largely limited to countries where students are responsible for paying at least a significant portion of their fees. Thus, as well as the obvious source nations of Australia (e.g. Pitman 2016; White 2007), the United Kingdom (e.g. Budd 2016; Tomlinson 2016; Woodall, Hiller and Resnick 2014) and the United States (e.g. Delucchi and Korgen 2002; Gates, Heffernan and Sudore 2015), there have been articles authored by academics based in Estonia (e.g. Koris et al. 2015), Finland (Vuori 2013), Germany (Budd 2016), the Netherlands (Moerkerke 2015), Norway (Svensson and Wood 2007), Portugal (Tavares and Cardoso 2013), Sweden (Modell 2005) and Thailand (Watjatrakul 2014), as well as some journal special issues (e.g. Chalcraft, Hilton and Hughes 2015) and books (e.g. Molesworth, Scullion and Nixon 2011). The prominence of the Nordic nations in this list is noteworthy.

The idea of the student as customer or consumer has, unsurprisingly, attracted considerable critique. Some of this has got little further than outright rejection:

> The college experience should be focused on the pursuit of learning, not customer satisfaction. That pursuit is hindered when professors become purveyors and the students become buyers. Now that unabashed consumerism has infiltrated the college experience – from extravagant dining options to elaborate dormitory living – it may seem inevitable that classrooms across campus will subscribe to the pervasive customer consciousness. Nevertheless, those loyal to the cause of learning must resist that pull. (Hubbell 2015, p. 89)

Others have offered both a more reasoned critique and an alternative solution. Thus, McMillan and Cheney, having noted the prevalence in the use of the student as consumer metaphor in the United States, criticize it on the grounds that it

> (a) suggests undue distance between the student and the educational process; (b) highlights the promotional activities of professors and promotes the entertainment model of classroom learning; (c) inappropriately compartmentalizes the educational experience as a product rather than a process; and (d) reinforces individualism at the expense of community. (1996, 1)

They offer 'critical engagement' as an alternative descriptor for the teaching/learning process.

In addition to McMillan and Cheney's reservations, the metaphor may also be criticized both as an inadequate summary of the complexity of the student experience, and for encouraging particular forms of undesirable behaviour. Thus, it portrays the student as a relatively passive recipient of what the university has to offer, rather than the active, engaged, indeed self-directed, individual which most academics would wish to deal with.

When we consider the teaching/learning interaction, which is arguably at the core of the student experience, this metaphor suggests an approach close to that which Freire (1972, 1974) critiqued as the 'banking' method, whereby students' minds are seen as 'empty vessels' to be filled up with the wisdom imparted by their teachers. It would seem, therefore, to encourage the much derided surface learning, rather than the desired deep learning that has been emphasized in the student learning literature for the last four decades (Marton et al. 2005; see the discussion of teaching and learning approaches in Chapter 3).

Kaye et al. (2006) examine the impact of the student as consumer metaphor from a legal perspective, comparing the situation in the United Kingdom and the United States. Somewhat reassuringly, they find that it had not made much of an inroad in this sense, but, nevertheless, they urge higher education institutions to draft appropriate contracts with their students regarding their mutual expectations so as to safeguard against future challenges.

Another approach has been to examine students' behaviour. Based on interviews with sixty first-year students in the Porto area of Portugal, Tavares and Cardoso conclude that 'although students seem to behave as rational consumers when they decide to enrol in higher education, that behaviour was not so evident regarding the choice of HEI [higher education institution] and seemed to be absent from the study programme choice' (2013, p. 307).

However, in an English study, Bunce, Baird and Jones came to rather different conclusions. They found that students vary in the extent to which they adopt a consumer orientation, and, which may cause particular concern, that this was also related to their academic performance:

> The analysis revealed that consumer orientation mediated traditional relationships between learner identity, grade goal and academic performance, and found that a higher consumer orientation was associated with lower academic performance. Furthermore, responsibility for paying tuition fees and studying a Science, Technology, Engineering and Mathematics subject were associated with a higher consumer orientation and subsequently lower academic performance. (2016, p. 1)

The notion of the student as customer has also been widely critiqued (Sharrock 2000), partly because of its actual or anticipated consequences:

> Viewing the student as a customer rather than as a 'worker' or 'apprentice' is argued to have created several problems ... with market forces leading to the substitution of purchased commodities for 'production for self', the role of the student in actively participating in the learning process is threatened. Several trends, including grade inflation, shortened contact hours, and the redefinition of study time are offered as evidence that the non-salable components of higher education are declining in importance. (George 2007, p. 965)

Lomas takes a longer-term perspective in arguing that

> the difficulty of regarding students as customers is based on the view that the professional service in higher education cannot be fully evaluated until some while after it has been provided. The student is only able to reflect fully upon the benefits of the knowledge and skills acquired and the attitudes that have been developed after a number of years when there has been sufficient opportunity to realize what they have learnt in a workplace setting. (2007, 35)

He reports on an interview-based study of British academics' attitudes, finding that 'lecturers are antipathetic towards this notion of the student as a customer … on the grounds that higher education is not like other forms of service provision' (42).

As with the idea of the student as consumer, studies of students suggest that they tend not to see themselves as customers either: 'This study suggests that entering students do not express a customer orientation towards their education' (Saunders 2015, p. 24). Others, however, particularly those working in university marketing departments, see these rejections and critiques as overly defensive and poorly informed:

> The student-as-customer concept is largely valueless in higher education if we have in mind a simplistic notion of the customer as exemplified in a straightforward, low-involvement purchase of a consumer good. However, marketing theory and practice have much more complex conceptions of the customer, particularly where the exchange process is lengthy and involving, concerns an intangible service with uncertain outcomes, and involves the customer in the production process. (Eagle and Brennan 2007, p. 56)

In short, there is undeniably an element of a customer relationship in higher education institutions' dealings with their students, but it is a rather more complex relationship than that involved in purchasing fast food or a new car (Guilbault 2016).

An alternative approach to rejecting or critiquing the idea of the student as a consumer or customer has been to come up with other metaphors. There appear to be two main competing metaphors under offer at the present time: the student as client and the student as a labour contributor or co-producer.

Bailey prefers the metaphor of the student as client, which implies an analogy between academics and other professionals such as accountants and lawyers. He argues that this metaphor has a number of advantages, suggesting both 'a greater level of professionalism' and 'a qualitatively more substantial relationship' (2000, pp. 355–6). In addition,

> clients are more actively involved in the creation and enactment of the service. … A greater degree of respect is afforded both the professional and the client in a professional/client relationship. (pp. 356–7)

The idea of the student as client is not, however, without its problems. The most significant of these is that it implies a much closer, indeed individualized, relationship between academics and students. While this may be an attractive ideal, and it may still be realized in some elite institutions, it is not really feasible in most contemporary universities, with first-year undergraduate courses frequently now accommodating hundreds of students, and often being delivered by research students.

Halbesleben et al. (2003, p. 257) introduce the idea of seeing the student as a labour contributor to, rather than a customer of, their education. They argue that

> viewing students as … labor contributors to their education offers a more complete insight into their role in the classroom. The student labor contribution metaphor,

based on theories of performance and research on customer labor contributions, offers a plausible framework for managing the role of the student in the classroom.

This metaphor moves us away from the image of the student as a relatively passive recipient, recognizing higher education as work, to which all concerned – institution, academic and student – have to contribute in a joint or shared enterprise.

Halbesleben and Wheeler (2009) explored how groups of business students identified with a series of metaphors or models: student as customer, employee, co-producer (analogous to the idea of the student as labour contributor) and/or junior partner. They found that

> students tended to have lower identification with the student-as-customer or student-as-employee models ... students held similar identifications with the student-as-coproducer and student-as-junior partner models ... the student-as-customer and student-as-employee orientations were associated with lower satisfaction. ... The student-as-coproducer and student-as-junior partner models were associated with higher satisfaction. (pp. 186–7)

Co-production 'conceptualizes service delivery as both an arrangement and a process, wherein citizens and governments share "conjoint responsibility" in producing public services' (Marschall 2004, 232). This, McCulloch (2009) argues, sees 'the student, lecturers and others who support the learning process as being engaged in a cooperative enterprise, which is focused on knowledge, its production, dissemination and application, and on the development of learners rather than merely skilled technicians' (p. 181).

Cuthbert (2010) also prefers the idea of the student as co-producer, arguing that this takes us beyond narrower conceptions of both the student as customer and of the university's marketing role:

> We need to see that the student may only be a true customer for a limited and peripheral part of the university's offering. For the most part it will be more productive to see the student in other roles, as member, client, person, and most of all as learner. But we can extend the idea of student as learner by bringing together modern marketing thinking with modern scholarship of teaching and learning, to see the student as a co-producer of learning and knowledge with other students, staff and perhaps others outside the university. (p. 22)

Like all metaphors, however, that of the student as co-producer simplifies and standardizes the idea it is being related to, in this case the student experience. Similarly to the student as client metaphor, it is also rather unrealistic, in implying that all students have the capacity and the desire to engage in the co-production of knowledge.

These debates over the student's role, and the implications of using different metaphors to summarize this, could arguably, however, be missing the key point. The role of the higher education institution and its employees is to provide a good quality learning experience for its students, taking care to involve them in decisions over the approach to be taken. As D'Eon and Harris (2000) argue, in the context of medical education,

> we need to take a more student-centered approach and involve students appropriately in identifying and solving problems with their education. As faculty we need to be less paternalistic and defensive of a system that needs overhauling. We need to work within an ethical model built on mutual trust, a fiduciary [trusting] model. Such trust, of course, must be earned, placing responsibilities on both faculty and students. ... But we as faculty control the system and so must take the lead. Whether we call students our customers, our clients, or our knowledge workers – or simply our students – we must not be afraid of involving them more in shaping their education. (p. 1176)

Ranking and league tables

The ranking of higher education institutions and their component departments or schools in terms of their performance on a variety of indices (chiefly to do with research, teaching and facilities provided), and the subsequent use of these rankings to produce league tables displaying their performance in relation to other institutions, is a relatively recent phenomenon. While the American and Canadian systems were ahead of others in developing and using such metrics, their widespread application and acceptance in other national systems, and their extension to provide international comparisons, is largely a phenomenon of the twenty-first century.

Two main factors may be identified as being behind the development of university rankings and league tables. The first of these was the increasing concern of governments and their agencies, as the main funders of higher education, with measuring and ensuring the quality of the provision they were funding. This led to the adoption and refinement of performance indicators: for example, entry qualifications and graduation rates of students, staff/student ratios, and numbers of research publications produced by staff (Ball and Wilkinson 1994). Minimum or desired performance levels could then be set, institutional performances could be compared with each other (benchmarking) and tracked over time, and action could be taken when performance was deemed to be unsatisfactory or sub-standard.

Second, and unsurprisingly given the public availability of the developing performance indicators, the media, and in particular quality newspapers, came to play an increasingly influential role: for example, the *Times* and the *Times Higher Education Supplement* in the UK (Jobbins 2002). Their targets were potential students, their families and advisers, who could readily be persuaded to buy special editions (which would evolve into annual guides) to guide them on which universities and colleges were better rated for particular subjects. University rankings and league tables quickly then took on a life of their own, seeming to provide essential and supposedly objective information on relative performance.

The application of university ranking methodologies has become widespread, initially in Western developed economies, and more recently across the globe in systems that were attempting to emulate or catch up with them. Examples of the former include Anglophone nations such as Australia (Williams and Van Dyke 2008), Canada (Proulx 2007) and the United States (Meredith 2004), as well as other developed countries such as Germany (Federkeil 2002), Japan (Ishikawa 2009, Yonezawa et al. 2002) and Spain (Robinson-Garcia et al. 2014).

Other East Asian countries have also become involved, including China (Yang and Welch 2012), Hong Kong (Mok 2005) and South Korea (Byun, Jon and Kim 2013). Some Latin American countries have engaged as well (Ordorika and Lloyd 2015), though Brazil is seen as somewhat of an exception (Alperin 2013). Even in Europe, however, some nations, such as the Nordic countries (Elken, Hovdhaugen and Stensaker 2016), have largely stood apart from paying much attention to these developments.

According to a bibliographic search using Scopus, the number of articles focusing on university ranking (i.e. with the words 'university' and 'ranking' in the title) did not reach double figures per year until the mid-2000s, but subsequently rose to around 40 per year in the 2010s. The United States was the origin of the largest number of these articles (50 out of the total 415), followed by Spain (41) and the United Kingdom (33).

Many researchers have analysed and compared different ranking systems, sometimes suggesting improvements or adaptations (e.g. Fowles, Frederickson and Koppell 2016; Huang 2012; Moed 2017; Usher and Savino 2007). Others have focused on the workings of particular ranking systems, such as the Shanghai Jiao Tong University's *Academic Ranking of World Universities* (Jeremic et al. 2011; Liu and Cheng 2005) or Universitas 21 (Millot 2015), which is unusual in ranking whole systems rather than individual institutions.

Such researchers have found that, over time, the ranking systems employed, and the results they generate, have become increasingly similar. This appears to be the case whether national or international ranking systems are being compared. In the former case, for example, Dill and Soo (2005) compared selected league tables compiled annually in four major English-speaking nations, concluding: 'Our review of the five leading commercial university league tables from Australia, Canada, the UK, and the US suggests that the definitions of academic quality used in these tables are converging' (p. 525).

In the latter case, Aguillo et al. (2010) compared five international ranking systems, including those produced by the Shanghai Jiao Tong University, the *Times Higher Education Supplement*/Quacquarelli Symonds Ltd (these two have since separated, with each now producing their own rankings), Webometrics (in Spain), the Higher Education Evaluation and Accreditation Council in Taiwan, and the University of Leiden (for Europe only). They concluded that 'there are reasonable similarities between the rankings, even though each applies a different methodology' (p. 243).

As well as evaluating their overall influence, both globally and in specific countries, researchers have also been concerned to assess the impact of university rankings and league tables on student behaviour (their primary intended target), on higher education institutions (seeking to better position themselves in the rankings), and on policymakers and policy.

Research on the impact of university rankings on student behaviour originated in the United States, but has since spread to the United Kingdom and other countries. The US research has had a particular focus on the impact of the *US News and World Report* rankings. This has shown that ranking does impact upon student behaviour, but in a limited and qualified fashion. For example, in an early analysis, Monks and Ehrenberg (1999, p. 49) found that 'an increase in a selective private institution's U.S. News rank (a move to a less favorable ranking) leads the institution to accept a greater percentage of its applicants (an increase in its admit rate) … a smaller percentage of its admitted pool of applicants then matriculates (a decrease in its yield); and … its resulting entering class is of lower quality' (p. 49).

Similarly, Bowman and Bastedo (2009) concluded that

improvements in college rankings can influence admissions outcomes, but these effects occur primarily for universities ranked in the top 25 and for institutions moving onto the front page. For other types of elite institutions, increases in alternative measures of prestige (e.g., tuition costs and instructional expenditures) contribute to substantial improvements in admissions outcomes. Thus, it seems that college rankings play a role in some students' decision-making processes, but other indicators of reputation and prestige also exert considerable influence for some students. (p. 434)

Finally, Luca and Smith (2013) indicate that much depends upon how the ranking data is presented, in a conventional league table format or alphabetically:

When explicit rankings of colleges are published in *U.S. News*, a one-rank improvement leads to a 1-percentage-point increase in the number of applications to that college … the response to the information represented in rankings depends on the way in which that information is presented. Rankings have no effect on application decisions when colleges are listed alphabetically. (p. 58)

In the UK, researchers have examined the impact of a variety of league tables. Thus, both Gunn and Hill (2008) and Soo (2013) focused on the *Sunday Times* rankings, while Chevalier and Jia (2016) looked at the *Guardian* rankings, and Broecke (2015) examined both of these and those produced by the *Times Higher Education Supplement* and the Shanghai Jiao Tong University. Others have looked at the impact of the original data which forms part of the ranking methodologies, such as the NSS results (Gibbons et al. 2015), or at thematic league tables, such as those focusing on employability (Christie 2017) and sustainability (Jones 2015).

These studies tend to find that league tables do have an impact on student behaviour – that is, on students' decisions to apply for particular degree courses at particular universities – but that this impact is modest. For example, Broecke (2015, p. 137) found that

> when their rank worsens, universities are found to experience small but statistically significant reductions in the number of applications received as well as in the average tariff score of applicants and accepted applicants. Although the effects found are stronger for certain types of students and institutions, they tend to be modest overall, and suggest that other factors play a more important role in attracting applicants to universities.

Similarly, Chevalier and Jia (2016, p. 600) concluded that

> a one standard deviation change in the subject-level ranking score of an institution is associated with, on average, a 4.3 per cent increase in application numbers per faculty. This effect is particularly pronounced among faculties with the best scores, and overseas applicants.

By contrast, however, Soo (2013, p. 188) argued that the impact was not on application behaviour but on reputation:

> The Sunday Times rankings have a positive and statistically significant impact on academic and head teacher perceptions of university quality, but not on student applications. There is evidence that academic and head teacher perceptions, and especially student applications, are persistent over time, thus suggesting that reputational factors play an important role in influencing perceptions and applications.

Similar studies have been carried out in other countries, including Germany (Horstschraer 2012).

It is not just students and their advisers, however, who have been impacted by the increasing availability and popularity of university league tables. Universities themselves, as well as their funders and other stakeholders, have also been effected: 'It is … clear that while universities, policymakers and stakeholders criticize and lampoon league tables and rankings, few can afford to ignore them – and most have incorporated them in some fashion into their strategic thinking if not their planning' (Hazelkorn 2008, p. 213).

For universities, and particularly their leaders, the most obvious response to league tables involves using them in their publicity, assuming that they reflect well on the institution concerned. A more insidious impact involves the identification of those elements that go to make up the rankings on which the institution's score could be readily improved upon, and taking the appropriate action.

For policymakers, particularly in countries whose universities do not rank highly in the international league tables, a recent response has been to seek to create their own world-class universities (Deem, Mok and Lucas 2008; Hou, Morse and Chiang 2012; Rodriguez-Pomeda and Casani 2016; Schmoch, Fardoun and Mashat 2016), by channelling available resources into one university or a select number of institutions. The recency of this interest is confirmed by a bibliographic search, with only a handful of articles published with the words 'world', 'class' and 'university' in their title before the 2010s, though interest is increasing, with twenty such articles published in 2016 alone.

In a relatively early analysis, Mohrman et al. (2008) identify eight key qualities that define a world-class university, or, as they referred to it, the emerging global model (EGM) of the research university:

(1) EGM universities see their mission as transcending the boundaries of the nation-state … . (2) EGM institutions are increasingly more research intensive with the use of scientific methods in disciplines outside the sciences. (3) Faculty members … are… shifting from traditional independent patterns of inquiry to becoming members of team-oriented, cross-disciplinary, and international partnerships … . (4) … Universities are going beyond government support and student contributions to diversify their financial base … . (5) New relationships are being created among universities, governments, and corporations to advance economic development and to produce knowledge for the social good. (6) … universities are adopting worldwide recruitment strategies for students, faculty, and administrators. (7) EGM institutions require greater internal complexity directed toward research … . (8) Universities participate with international non-governmental organizations and multi-governmental organizations in support of collaborative research, student and faculty mobility, and validation of international stature. (p. 7)

Not surprisingly, the increasingly widespread use of university rankings and league tables has attracted considerable criticism from within higher education. Early critics appeared offended by the implicit comparison between universities and sports teams, stressing 'the inappropriateness of the "league table mentality." Higher education institutions are not football teams, they have differing institutional missions and operate in different environments' (Ball and Wilkinson 1994, p. 426).

Another early criticism, and one that has been regularly repeated, is that ranking methodologies are overly simplistic, reducing huge diversity (e.g. among the departments or schools that make up a university, which will inevitably be of variable quality) and complexity down to a single index. Thus, Berry (1999, p. 9) comments:

The Times league table in particular presents an untroubled picture of a simple, ordered world, in which a *pot pourri* of data is concocted to string British universities along a single continuum of 'quality', on which all the old universities rank above all the new. This picture is hard to sustain as affording a stable, reliable and valid view of the relative quality of British universities.

More recently, Tofallis (2012, p. 14) has argued that

a single figure cannot possibly represent all the activities that take place in any large organisation. It is more preferable by far to have a number of separate scores for each activity or function. … This would replace the single overall score by a performance profile, which would make it easier to see where the strengths and weaknesses lie.

Goglio (2016, p. 223) makes a similar point in noting that

> the 'one size fits all' approach is not the most appropriate one when dealing with university rankings. Rather, the field may better benefit from a plurality of university rankings, each one serving different (but equally important) functions and answering di erent demand niches.

In addition to the overall simplicity of the idea of university ranking, others have noted the importance of the choice of the indicators of performance, which are then combined to give an overall score: 'The choice of indicators is a non-arbitrary process that should be guided by, among other things, a knowledge of the strengths and limitations of the indicators being considered as well as their validity, reliability, and comparability for the schools or programmes to be ranked' (Clarke 2002, p. 457). In practice, however, the selection of indicators has been governed more by pragmatic considerations of what is readily available or easily measurable.

When indicators have been selected, and measurements collected, the issue of their relative weighting – so that they can be combined into a single index – is also crucial: 'The construction of a league table … requires that arbitrary weighting be assigned to the various measures, that diversity of mission is ignored and that inputs and outputs are treated in an identical manner' (Turner 2005, p. 370). Turner recommends the use of data envelopment analysis – a complex multivariate technique – to overcome these problems, allowing institutions with similar missions to benchmark themselves against each other.

More recently, in addition to summarizing the problems with ranking and league tables (Bougnol and Dula 2015), researchers have gone further to critique their outcomes and impact. At the core of these critiques is the argument that, because of the way they are compiled, the published league tables largely reflect the established reputations of the institutions included rather than their actual performance (Kehm 2014; Li et al. 2011). Thus, Safon (2013), in a multivariate analysis of the Shanghai Jiao Tong University and *Times Higher Education* rankings, finds that they

> are based on a common underlying factor. … As expected, certain variables are significantly correlated to the potential X factor obtained from the factor analysis. Out of these variables, and coinciding with certain previous literature, reputation turns out to be the most likely candidate for putting a name to the X factor. The final analysis focuses on the search for an underlying university profile for the rankings analyzed, the so-called X entity. Using multivariable regressions, we obtain a university profile that explains a large part of Factor 1, which implies an explanatory power that is greater than that of the individual candidates. These results support the existence of an underlying entity profile, characterized by institutions with a high reputation, from the U.S. or other English-speaking

countries, oriented towards research, that are active in hard sciences, and have extensive budgets. (Safon 2013, pp. 237–8)

A more general critique sees rankings and league tables as simply part of a broader trend towards 'quantified control', one in which some academics and academic managers are complicit:

> Whereas once metrics were simply part of auditing process and, as such, functioned to ensure accountability they have, in more recent times, taken on another role, and now function as part of a process of, what has been called 'quantified control'. In essence academic metric assemblages are at the cusp of being transformed from a set of measures able to mimic market processes to ones that are able to enact market processes … these metrics function as a form of measure able to translate different forms of value. Academic value is, essentially, becoming monetized. (Burrows 2012, p. 368)

As such, university rankings work as a tool for the powerful, simultaneously serving 'the purposes of states and leading postsecondary institutions, and hence the purposes of those social groups and economic interests best able to influence both' (Pusser and Marginson 2013, p. 562). Or, as Erkkila (2014, p. 97) puts it, 'There is a sense of economist reductionism in the development, as higher education is only valued for its economic potential.'

In this environment, it is not surprising that some authors have urged academics and universities to play a greater role in the development of ranking systems: 'It is vital that rankings systems are crafted so as to serve the purposes of higher education, rather than purposes being reshaped as an unintended consequence of rankings' (Marginson and van der Wende 2007, p. 326). Tapper and Filippakou (2009, p. 64) argue that 'the central research focus should be upon understanding what institutions value and how they sustain, adjust or abandon those values in the context of pressures for change'. Amsler and Bolsmann (2012, p. 295) go further in lamenting 'the absence of critical public debate about the practice of ranking or the drive for "world-class" status amongst universities'.

More positively, Salmi and Saroyan (2007, pp. 58–60) offer guidance for improving ranking systems: 'Be clear about what the ranking actually measures. … Use a range of indicators and multiple measures rather than a single, weighted ranking … compare similar programmes or institutions. … At the institutional level, use rankings for strategic planning and quality improvement purposes. … At the government level use rankings to stimulate a culture of quality. … Use rankings as one instrument available to inform students, families and employers, and to fuel public debates.'

Despite all of this criticism, it is abundantly clear that university rankings and league tables have become an established feature in national and international thinking about higher education. Understandably, therefore, this development has become an important focus for higher education research, designed both to understand what is going on, and to improve and diversify the methodologies being used so as to better reflect the nature of higher education and higher education institutions.

Conclusions

In an extensive analysis of the American research literature on quality in higher education available some thirty years ago, Tan (1986) concluded that, while much useful research had been done,

> four critical issues remain yet to be resolved. First, no one is certain what reputational studies are measuring – reputation or quality? … The use of objective variables in the assessment of quality … has met with limited success. The main problem has been the assumption by many researchers that faculty research productivity is the major indicator of quality. … Third, no one is certain what the definition of quality should be. … Finally, even though most studies have been successful at identifying a variety of correlates of quality, none has adequately examined the relationship between quality and the educational development of students. (pp. 259–60)

In short, much more needed to be done to produce credible results that might then lead to the production of consistent improvements in quality in higher education, with all that this might entail.

Writing twenty-four years later, Harvey and Williams (2010a, b), in two editorials summarizing the output of the journal *Quality in Higher Education* over its first 15 years – some 320 articles all told – concluded that, while quality assurance in higher education had become a global phenomenon, there was little evidence that externally mandated quality assurance initiatives were having the desired effects within higher education institutions. They also argued that, while quality assurance initiatives had made the workings of higher education institutions clearer to those outside, academics remained largely indifferent to them, except to the extent that they were forced to engage.

Harvey and William's conclusions can be read as being even more negative in tone than Tan's. While Tan was largely focused on the practicalities of researching quality in higher education – what it was, how to measure it, what is was related to and so on – Harvey and Williams could be read as casting doubts over whether all the efforts at engaging in quality assurance in higher education are achieving anything tangible, suggesting that they are only continuing because of the demands of external agencies, with academics largely indifferent to the work.

What, then, does the current analysis have to add to these conclusions? First, and perhaps most significantly, it confirms the continuing and growing importance of quality in higher education, and of research into it. It indicates that this is virtually a global concern, at least among the developed nations and those aspiring to be like them. And it shows that there are currently only a limited number of ways of 'doing' quality in higher education, which have been adopted and transferred largely without question from their sources in North America and Europe. Hence, there is also a considerable interest in comparing the state of quality in higher education, and what is being done with the aim of improving it, in different countries. This interest is particularly strong where there is close economic linkage between neighbouring countries, as in Europe and East Asia.

Second – and this is where the debates over quality in higher education link to broader and longer-lasting debates about the purposes of (higher) education and its relationship with work and other aspects of life – there is clearly an underlying issue about whether higher education is a commodity, and can, therefore, be assessed and/or improved using the same strategies and instruments used in other businesses. If this view is accepted, then the student is a customer of higher education, but also, when we view their subsequent employers as customers, its product. If we do not accept this rather reductionist view, then concerns over quality in higher education need to be addressed in other ways.

Third, confirming previous analyses, and largely because of this continuing tension over the purposes of higher education, there is no – indeed, there cannot be – general consensus over what quality in higher education is or even might be. Hence, quality can be sought, claimed and/or critiqued in numerous ways, some of them opposed to each other. Because we are not clear about what to measure in order to assess quality, we end up measuring everything (or, at least, everything that appears relatively straightforward to measure).

Fourth, measurement is doubly problematic, because not only are we not sure what to measure, but, when we do measure something, we are not sure we have really measured what we want to measure. We have to doubt whether the number of published outputs produced by an academic, or even the number of citations these outputs have received, is an accurate measure of their quality. And these doubts are only increased when we come to more subjective measures, such as students' expressed views on the quality of their teaching and learning experience.

What might the implications of these rather disquieting conclusions be? Clearly, they may all be traced to the reasons why we became so interested in quality in higher education: the enormous growth in participation and the size of higher education institutions and systems, coupled with the need of those funding this activity to be reassured that their money was being well spent. With that came all of the bureaucracy – of assessment and accreditation, paper work and record keeping, ranking and league tables, compliance and deference; the entire 'quality industry' within higher education – with which we are now struggling.

While it has to be doubted whether we can ever now rid ourselves of all of this, we clearly do need to find better, more creative and less time-consuming, ways of convincing governments, their agencies and the general public that we are doing a reasonable job and can be trusted. That should be the priority for research into quality in higher education in the future.

Chapter 7
Research on System Policy

Introduction

Research into higher education policy has long been popular, and much of it has been critical in nature. In part, this is because almost everyone working in higher education has an opinion about current policies – whether operating at the institutional, national or international level – and many are keen to express them publicly, either verbally or in writing. In part, it is also because system policy is a very broad field for study, extending into areas considered separately in this book, most notably quality (discussed in Chapter 6), but also some aspects of institutional management (discussed in Chapter 8).

Previous analysis of research into system policy showed that it chiefly employed documentary and multivariate analysis, of varying levels of sophistication, and emphasized larger scales of analysis (institutions or nations) than were typical in other areas of higher education research. This is one of the areas of higher education research that remains dominated by men, including significant numbers of senior higher education managers. The main focus for research into this topic is on changing policy and funding arrangements, and their consequences for practice (Tight 2003; 2012a).

Research trends

A search using Scopus identified 1,003 articles with the words 'higher', 'education' and 'policy' in their titles, which might reasonably be expected (as a check confirmed) to be focused on higher education policy. The earliest dated from 1965; by the 1990s up to 10 were being published each year, a figure which had risen to over 100 per year most recently. Of the total, 238 (24 per cent) were produced by authors based in the United States, 158 (16 per cent) in the United Kingdom, 74 (7 per cent) in Australia, 32 (3 per cent) in Germany, 26 (3 per cent) in Brazil and 25 (2 per cent) in both Canada and South Africa.

Of course, articles focusing on some aspect of higher education will not all include the words 'higher', 'education' and 'policy' in their titles, so we may conclude that a healthy number are being produced each year, with their authorship spread throughout the English-speaking world and beyond.

As some of their titles suggest, a number of higher education journals specialize in policy issues. These include *Higher Education Policy* and the *Journal of Higher Education Policy and Management*, *Research Policy* and also *Higher Education Management and Policy*, though this discontinued publication in 2014. However, other higher education journals with a more generic focus also publish significant numbers of articles on this theme, including *Higher Education*, *Higher Education Quarterly* and *Research in Higher Education*.

Perennially popular issues within system policy research include funding issues and arrangements (e.g. Delaney and Doyle 2014; Nkrumah-Young, Huisman and Powell 2008; Sav 2000; Toutkoushian and Shafiq 2010), internationalization (e.g. de Haan 2014; Horta 2010; McLellan 2008; Yang 2000; this topic is discussed in more detail in a following section), research policy and funding (e.g. Caraca; Conceicao and Heitor 2000; Lepori and Kyvik 2010; Warshaw and Hearn 2014) and changing national policies (e.g. Callender 2014; Freeman 2014; Lo 2017).

Other issues have become popular research themes for a period, most notably, perhaps, the impact of the Bologna process (e.g. Dobbins and Knill 2009; Kehm, Michelsen and Vabo 2010) and widening participation/equity (e.g. Coates and Krause 2005; Greenbank 2008). Neo-liberalism is also currently a popular topic (Morrison 2017; Rosser 2016), as is student finance (e.g. Ahier 2000).

Yet other issues persist but are seldom very popular, including, for example, accountability (e.g. Bogue and Johnson 2010; McLendon, Hearn and Deaton 2006), international development (e.g. Collins and Rhoads 2010), the relation between policy and institutional performance (e.g. Martinez and Nilson 2006) and the role of the private sector (e.g. Amaral and Teixeira 2000).

The most noticeable development in research and writing on higher education policy over the last few decades has probably been the move away from single nation policy analyses – though these remain popular (e.g. Goedegebuure et al. 1993; Klein and Schwartzman 1993; Gounko and Smale 2007; Menahem 2008) – towards both international/comparative analyses (e.g. Larrechea and Castro 2009; Luitjen-Lub, Van der Wende and Huisman 2005; Watson 2009) and more specialist policy analyses (e.g. Pelkonen, Teräväinen and Waltari 2008). The former has been driven by factors such as the increasing involvement of bodies like the European Union (EU) and the OECD in higher education (Saarinen 2008), as well as by the increasing internationalization of higher education.

Research designs and frameworks

The three frameworks for research considered in this section – human and social capital, globalization and internationalization, and massification – are arguably among the most influential, perhaps the most influential, in higher education research and practice. Human capital theory – the idea that investing in education brings economic and financial returns – can be seen as the greatest influence on higher education policy in the post-war period, social capital being its more recent and somewhat 'softer' partner. Massification is the result of the belief in human capital, bringing its own consequences. Globalization and internationalization may be seen as closely related to massification, or indeed as a major element of it, as national higher education systems expand to collaborate and compete with each other.

Human and social capital

The theory of human capital has arguably been the most influential theory relating to higher education policy (indeed, education policy in general), nationally and internationally, over the last fifty years or more:

> Human capital theory is the most influential economic theory of education, setting the framework of government education policies since the early 1960s. After a period of eclipse, there was a major revival of human capital theory after 1985 – in more free market guise than before – led by the Organisation for Economic Co-operation and Development. (Marginson 1993, p. 31)

The importance and value of human capital, and the role of higher education in developing it, has also gained widespread acceptance among researchers (e.g. Douglass 2010), particularly those concerned with evaluating government policies (often, of course, funded by governments or their agencies).

The related, or spinoff, idea of social capital has attracted more recent attention, again among both academics and politicians (e.g. Gewirtz et al. 2005), though it has also attracted plenty of criticism:

> Social capital has become a buzzword among political and academic elites, though the term remains relatively unfamiliar to the general public. (Halpern 2005, p. 1)

> 'Social capital' is one of those elusive terms that provide 'think tanks', academics, journalists, politicians and policy-makers with a way to speak as if something meaningful is under discussion. (Law and Mooney 2006, p. 127)

What, then, do these theories or ideas mean, how do they relate to each other, and how have they been explored in higher education research?

The contemporary theory of human capital was developed and articulated by economists in the early 1960s, and is particularly associated with the work of Schultz (1961) and Becker (1962, 1964). It builds, however, on the work of earlier economists, including Adam Smith, John Stuart Mill, Alfred Marshall and Karl Marx (Baptiste 2001).

Historians of human capital identify a series of phases in its development and acceptance: (i) 'the 1960s [with] ... public investment in human capital, dominated by claims about a link between education and economic growth' (Marginson 1993, p. 40); (ii) a subsequent period of abandonment, when alternative frameworks, like the screening hypothesis (which argues that employers use qualifications as a screening device when shortlisting potential employees), were put forward; (iii) the current phase, from the mid-1980s onwards, with renewed policy commitment, but an emphasis on private rather than public investment, and acknowledgement of the role of the screening hypothesis and of technology.

Becker (1964, p. 1) defined human capital to include

> activities that influence future monetary and psychic income by increasing the resources in people. These activities are called investments in human capital. The many forms of such investments include schooling, on-the-job training, medical care, migration, and searching for information about prices and incomes ... all these investments improve skills, knowledge, or health, and thereby raise money or psychic incomes.

However, as Baptiste (2001, p. 189) points out, 'The contemporary version of human capital theory differs from its predecessors in three important respects: (a) it incorporates technology as a factor that mediates the relationship between human capital and productivity, (b) it integrates elements of the screening hypothesis, and (c) it advocates private over public investment in education.'

The enormous influence that human capital theory has had on economic and educational thinking is easily demonstrated:

> Since 1971, five Nobel prizes have been awarded to scholars in, or affiliated with, the field of human capital theory. The Nobel distinction belongs to Theodore W. Schultz and Gary S. Becker, the two most pronounced scholars of human capital theory; Milton Friedman and Simon Kuznets ... and Robert M. Solow. (Sweetland 1996, p. 342)

Turning to social capital, there are many recent overviews of the uses of, and of research into, this topic (e.g. Adler and Kwon 2002; Andriani and Christoforou 2016; Castle 2002; Coradini 2010; Field 2008; Fine 2001, 2010; Halpern 2005; Lin 2001; Vorhaus 2014; Woolcock 2010). Its usage is not as longstanding as that of human capital, though it has links to both well-known social theorists, such as Bourdieu, Dewey and Marx (again), and lesser-known writers (e.g. Hanifan 1916): 'The term *social capital* itself turns out to have been independently invented at least six times over the twentieth century, each time to call attention to the ways in which our lives are made more productive by social ties' (Putnam 2000, p. 19).

As Putnam, one of the leading contemporary social capital researchers, states, 'The core idea of social capital theory is that social networks have value' (2000, pp. 18–19). There are many, slightly differing, definitions of the term in the literature; for example,

> social networks, the reciprocities that arise from them, and the value of these for achieving mutual goals. (Schuller, Baron and Field 2000, p. 1)

the goodwill available to individuals or groups. Its source lies in the structure and content of the actor's social relations. Its effects flow from the information, influence, and solidarity it makes available to the actor. (Adler and Kwon 2002, p. 23)

Portes (2000) identifies two key meanings of the term, as an attribute of either individuals or collectivities. Another distinction commonly made is between types of social capital: 'Of all the dimensions along which forms of social capital vary, perhaps the most important is the distinction between *bridging* (or inclusive) and *bonding* (or exclusive)' (Putnam 2000, p. 22). Different components of social capital may also be identified:

> Most forms, be they kinship, work-based or interest-based, can be seen to have three basic components. They consist of a *network*; a cluster of *norms, values and expectancies* that are shared by group members; and *sanctions* – punishments and rewards – that help to maintain the norms and network. (Halpern 2005, p. 10)

In other words, three dimensions of social capital may be identified: level (individual, group, community, nation, etc.), type and components.

Not surprisingly, writers on human and social capital have expended considerable energy on making clear the distinctions and links between the two terms. For example:

> Just as physical capital is created by changes in materials to form tools that facilitate production, human capital is created by changes in persons that bring about skills and capabilities that make them able to act in new ways. Social capital, however, comes about through changes in the relations among persons that facilitate action. (Coleman 1988, p. S100)

Others have identified further or different kinds of capital:

> Capital can present itself in three fundamental guises: as *economic capital*, which is immediately and directly convertible into money and may be institutionalized in the form of property rights; as *cultural capital*, which is convertible, on certain conditions, into economic capital and may be institutionalized in the form of educational qualifications; and as *social capital*, made up of social obligations ('connections'), which is convertible, in certain conditions, into economic capital and may be institutionalised in the form of a title of nobility. (Bourdieu 1986, p. 243)

What Bourdieu refers to as cultural capital is clearly close to what others term human capital. Political, religious and other kinds of capital have also been discussed.

The relative popularity of human and social capital as research topics, both in general and in relation to higher education, may be readily illustrated through a bibliographic search using the Scopus database for articles with the words 'human capital' or 'social capital' in their title, abstract or keywords, as well as the number of articles with those words and 'higher education'. There are substantial numbers of articles currently being published with a focus on human or social capital. Since 2003 there have been more than 1,000 such articles published each year on each of these topics (note that there will be some overlap and double-counting), and, since 2012, more than 3,000 articles each year. The growth in publication rates is impressive, with the number of publications focusing on social capital having recently overtaken those focusing on human capital.

Of course, not all of those articles will relate directly to higher education, though many of them will. Searching for the numbers of articles with 'human capital' or 'social capital' and 'higher education' in their titles, abstracts or keywords, indicates that up to about one-tenth of the articles previously identified qualify. This currently amounts to around 200 to 300 a year in each case: these are still impressive quantities. An analysis of these articles reveals that the majority are by authors based in the social sciences, economics, business or medicine. Most are also located in the major English-speaking countries of the United States, the United Kingdom, Australia and Canada, but the concepts have been widely applied in other countries as well; for example, in Italy (Lovaglio, Vacca and Verzillo 2016) and Spain (Daza 2016).

Human capital remains a major focus for research across the social sciences, particularly in the business, economics and education disciplines. Much research looks at the measurement of human capital and its relationship with economic health. For example, 'there seems to be a significant correlation between the endowment of human capital of European regions and their economic performance over the last few years … the relationship between human capital and economic growth tends to be clearer for winning and losing regions, than for those catching up and falling behind' (Rodriguez-Pose and Vilalta-Bufi 2005, p. 560).

One problem, however, is that research into human capital has become too diverse and widespread. Thus, in the editorial introduction to a collection of papers on human capital research, Nyberg and Wright note:

> (1) the gulf across HC [human capital] research domains is substantive … there is not a common language among … researchers; (2) with no common language, it is extremely challenging to appreciate areas where research interests overlap, and this challenge is exacerbated when researchers focus on theoretical issues; and (3) even brilliant scholars who are open-minded and intellectually curious can sometimes struggle to move beyond the bounds of research that has long engulfed their talents and focus. (2015, p. 288)

Social capital has, so to speak, come out of the shadow of human capital, and now appears to enjoy greater popularity – both among researchers and policymakers (e.g. at the World Bank; see Bebbington et al. 2004) – as a seemingly softer and more malleable concept. The concept now has considerable empirical support; thus, Huang, van den Brink and Groot (2009, p. 460), on the basis of a meta-analysis of existing research, concluded that 'education is a strong and robust correlate of individual social capital'. Similarly, Kwon and Adler (2014, p. 419) argue that 'it is difficult to avoid the impression that the basic thesis – that social ties can be efficacious in providing information, influence, and solidarity – is no longer in dispute'. Foley and Edwards (1999, p. 163) also provide support for the theory:

> The notion of social capital provides a useful heuristic for capturing the ways in which social resources are created and made available to individuals and groups. And properly operationalized, it is more than a heuristic. … Recent research has shown how interpersonal relations and institutional context may affect outcomes as diverse as individual exploitation of their own human capital, juvenile delinquency, and the success of communities in attracting resources for economic development … other work has shown to what extent economic and political context may shape the level and kind of social capital a community may enjoy.

Part of the attraction of social capital over human capital is that the former does not have an overwhelmingly economic focus; though, arguably, that is always present and only slightly in the background. For example, one UK study found that higher education participation was linked to other factors than the desire for a better paid job:

> Economic and sociological explanations of participation in HE [higher education] are frequently portrayed as oppositional. The evidence presented in this study suggests that it is more appropriate to regard each theoretical standpoint as offering part of the story. Using evidence from students in their final year of compulsory schooling in English schools we have found an intention to go to university positively associated with: (a) parental education; (b) cultural capital; and (c) expectations of graduate premium. (Davies et al. 2014, p. 820)

Other researchers have looked in more detail into the relations between higher education and social capital. Thus, Salaran (2010) examines research productivity in higher education, concluding that 'social capital as an asset rooted in relationships has actual and potential benefits for individuals and institutions' (p. 147). Thompson, Conaway and Dolan (2015) consider the development of undergraduates' social, cultural and human capital, and Wells (2008) looks at social and cultural capital in relation to student retention.

Both human capital and social capital have, of course, been widely critiqued. At the heart of both critiques is a rejection of the idea that humans, or aspects of them, can or should be treated as a type of capital alongside wealth or physical resources.

Critics of the morality of human capital theory approach their critique from different angles. Steinberg (1985, p. 68) sees the notion as fundamentally unrealistic: 'On close examination, and despite all the trappings of scientific objectivity, "human capital" is a value-laden concept, one that treats the marketplace as though it were some kind of benevolent society, parceling out its rewards to the culturally deserving.' Marginson (1993, p. 54) appears to agree with that point, adding to it an ethical concern:

> Human capital theory assumes an unreal certainty about the connections between education, work and earnings. There are also deep ethical problems in the

conception of people as units of capital, controlled by economic forces external to them, rather than self-determining members of a democracy.

Baptiste (2001, pp. 197–8) makes the more general criticism, which can equally well be applied to all economic theories, that humans do not operate, at least wholly, as rational economic decision-makers: 'The theory … treats humans as lone wolves: radically isolated hedonists, creatures of habit (not intentions) who temper their avarice with economic rationality … educational programs that flow from such anthropology would be apolitical, adaptive and individualistic.'

Kivinen and Ahola (1999, p. 204) offer a more contemporary critique, noting that life is not a level playing field where all have the same opportunities:

> By contrasting reborn human capital ideology with what we have called the everyday reality of human risk capital facing graduates, we simply wish to draw attention to the widening gap between rhetoric and the real choices available. In the conditions of mass higher education, mass unemployment, a shrinking public sector and the new infocom industries … higher education certificates have become more and more a risk investment. If you succeed, the benefits are great … but on the whole, workers in the information society sail in three different boats. Alongside the buoyant vessel of the symbolic analysts, the second has a serious leak, and the third one is sinking fast.

While economists may calculate rates of return on investment in higher education, showing that, on average, it still makes long-term financial sense to study for a degree, the rates of return are not as good as they once were before mass participation, they vary a great deal depending upon the subject studied and institution attended, and they also vary between individuals; some are more fortunate or are better connected (i.e. have greater social capital) than others.

Tan (2014) offers a 'holistic' criticism of human capital theory, combining methodological, empirical, practical and moral elements. Despite the number and strength of these criticisms, however, he concludes that the theory 'seems to be here to stay because despite its shortcomings and imperfections, it would be fair to say that it is still a strong theory' (p. 436). In his judgement, there is no suitable alternative theory available at present to replace it.

Social capital theory has also been the subject of thorough critique. For a start, there are those who object to the phrase itself: '"social" and "capital" have contrasting features, capital being antisocial and exploitative and thus [the] phrase is misleading and manipulative' (Pawar 2006, p. 223). Similarly, Tlili and Obsiye (2014, p. 567) take objection to Coleman's particular version of social capital:

> Coleman's social capital is, paradoxically, not social enough, whether as structure, process or as a subjective and intersubjective enterprise. It figures as an unconditioned conditioner, insofar as it does not enter a network of relations with financial capital, human capital or any other variable related to structures of inequality and privilege.

Others take issue with the lack of an agreed definition, or the flexible way in which the term is used:

> Even if social capital has been a remarkably productive idea, it is not a good concept as most popular conceptualizations define social capital as several distinct phenomena or as phenomena that already have been conceptualized under other labels. (Bjørnskov and Sønderskov 2013, p. 1225)

> Social capital has aroused suspicion because of the huge range of social issues on which it has been deployed. (Schuller, Baron and Field 2000, p. 24)

Brunie (2009, p. 262) identifies three main ways in which the term is used:

> The relational approach focuses on how the relations an actor develops and maintains with other actors can allow him/her to access and mobilize valuable resources. The collective approach is often related to collective action, and emphasizes the quality of relationships within a group, both in cognitive and structural terms. The generalized approach views social capital as an individual attribute, and postulates generalized trust as a resource that binds society together and facilitates cooperation and civic endeavours.

Then there is the related question of how to measure social capital (Engbers, Thompson and Slaper 2016; Schuller, Baron and Field 2000; Vryonides 2007). This, in turn, inhibits empirical investigation: 'At present, we are still in the earliest stages of serious empirical investigation of social capital; while the available evidence suggests that the concept does indeed point to a coherent set of variables, we cannot yet be confident that this is the case, nor do we really have a clear sense as yet of its boundaries' (Field 2008, p. 158).

If the definition, measurement and investigation of social capital are issues, the question of how to encourage or create it is also moot:

> First, it does make sense to talk about constructive, goal-oriented outcomes as the product of social relations. Organizational involvement and intergenerational network closure, in particular, are connected with desirable outcomes for young people. Thus, there is some basis for the concept of social capital. Second ... this concept can be misleading because it suggests a quantity when the social production of desirable behavior is more accurately seen as a process. Third, the process is inherently problematic. We can only judge a *posteriori* whether a given arrangement contributes to the process. (Bankston and Zhou 2002, p. 314)

Then there are a series of more specific criticisms. Thus, Szreter (2002) argues that the theory downplays the role of the state, while Navarro (2002) – reviewing Putnam's theorization in the context of the United States – finds that it ignores the role of power and its distribution. Adkins (2005) offers a feminist critique.

Finally, Fine (2010, p. 126), who has devoted much of his career to critiquing the concept, offers the most widespread critique, including his findings that social capital

- is totally chaotic in definition, method and theory;
- is indiscriminately employed across applications and can be more or less anything, in principle if not in practice;
- is parasitic on, and crudely simplifying of, other social theory;
- misunderstands both social and capital;
- is complicit with mainstream economics, 'economics imperialism' and rational choice theory;
- neglects the economic, power, conflict, the state, gender, race, class, ethnicity, global, context, etc.;
- is self-help raised from individual to community level;
- fails to address criticism other than incorporating it as another factor;
- is a peculiar end-of-millennium product of the retreat from the dual extremes of postmodernism and neo-liberalism.

Despite the criticisms that have been made of both human capital and social capital, it would probably be fair to conclude that human capital remains a dominant influence in thinking about higher education and the economy, and that social capital is a strong and rising influence in thinking about the relations between higher education, the economy and society more generally.

There are continuing issues regarding the definition and application of both concepts, particularly social capital, yet they offer helpful and relatively straightforward ways for exploring higher education policy and practice, which clearly still have potential:

> One of the key merits of social capital is the way it *shifts the focus of analysis from the behaviour of individual agents to the pattern of relations between agents, social units and institutions*. ... Closely linked with this is the merit of social capital developing out of empirical research of diverse kinds to act as *a link between micro-, meso- and macro-levels of analysis*. ... An analogous argument applies about *multi-disciplinarity and inter-disciplinarity*. ... A further key merit of social capital as a concept is that it *reinserts issues of value into the heart of social scientific discourse*. ... This leads us to what we see as the key feature: *social capital's heuristic quality*. (Schuller, Baron and Field 2000, pp. 35–6, emphases in original)

Globalization and internationalization

Among the most discussed and researched aspects of higher education in the last two decades have been the linked issues of globalization and internationalization

(Kehm and Teichler 2007), which have been the subject of both several edited books (e.g. Ennew and Greenaway 2012; King, Marginson and Naidoo 2011; Maringe and Foskett 2010; Scott 1998a; Stromquist and Monkman 2000) and special issues of journals (e.g. Magyar and Robinson-Pant 2011; Maringe and Woodfield 2013; Sellar and Gale 2011; de Wit 2011). But what are globalization and internationalization, particularly as applied to higher education, and how do they differ? What impact are globalization and internationalization having on higher education provision and practice, what research issues are they raising and what critiques have been offered?

Three key points may be stressed immediately. First, the discussion in the higher education literature draws and builds on the broader discussion of globalization, in particular, in the social science literature (e.g. Beck 2000; Giddens 1999). Second, as we shall see, while distinctions may be drawn between the two terms, in practice they are often used interchangeably or in overlapping ways. Third, while they have attracted particular attention (in policy and research terms) in the last twenty years or so – following the massification of higher education spreading from North America to Europe, the Asia Pacific region and worldwide – these are not new phenomena. As Scott makes clear, internationalism at least has always been part of the university's mission:

> There are four topics relevant to the overall theme of internationalization and/or globalization. The first is the contrast between internationalism – a quality which the university has espoused from its earliest days – and globalization. The second topic is the very important changes that have taken place in HE [higher education], which are often summed up by the word massification. The third, linked to the first, is the radical shift from neo-colonial internationalization to post-colonial globalization. And the fourth and last topic is the even more radical configurations of time and space in which the university, as a key institution of the knowledge society of the future, is directly implicated. (1998b, pp. 122–3)

How, then, might we distinguish between globalization and internationalization? Teichler seeks to explain the difference in the following way:

> Internationalisation can best be defined as the totality of substantial changes in the context and inner life of higher education relative to an increasing frequency of border-crossing activities amidst a persistence of national systems, even though some signs of 'denationalisation' might be observed. … Globalisation initially seemed to be defined as the totality of substantial changes in the context and inner life of higher education related to growing interrelationships between different parts of the world whereby national borders are blurred or even seem to vanish. In recent years the term 'globalisation' is substituted for 'internationalisation' in the public debate on higher education, whereby a shift of meaning takes place … the term tends to be used for any supra-regional phenomenon related to higher education … and/or anything on a global scale related to higher education characterised by market and competition. (2004, pp. 22–3)

In his interpretation, then, while internationalization in higher education is about cross-border flows – of students, staff and knowledge – and international cooperation, globalization (which Teichler suggests has changed in meaning over time) represents a step change, with international trends and developments now impacting upon the national and local. Gacel-Ávila adds more flesh to this distinction, arguing that, while internationalization refers to mutually satisfactory relationships between nations, globalization encompasses forces outside of the control of individual nations:

> The phenomenon of globalisation does not tend to respect differences and border, thus … leading to homogenisation. In this sense, internationalisation can be understood as complementary or compensatory to globalizing tendencies, given that it allows for a resistance to the latter's denationalising and homogenising effects. (2005, p. 124)

Unusually – as it seems much more typical for academics to disagree, even, or perhaps especially, on the meanings of widely used terms – a third author, Dodds, makes much the same point, presenting internationalization as a relatively benign force in comparison to globalization:

> Some theorists have been happy to use the two concepts almost interchangeably. Others have described globalisation as a particularly 'intense' form of internationalisation. However, 'internationalisation' is generally seen as a less critical concept within academia than is 'globalisation'. (2008, p. 509)

Altbach and Knight, however, put it in another way, seeing internationalization as encompassing the responses that may be made to the forces of globalization:

> Globalization is the context of economic and academic trends that are part of the reality of the 21st century. Internationalization includes the policies and practices undertaken by academic systems and institutions – and even individuals – to cope with the global academic environment. (2007, p. 290)

Turning to the meanings of the two terms individually, Beerkens distinguishes four main interpretations of globalization, arguing that 'the main disagreement is between the notion of global as a geographical concept on one hand and as an authority-related, cultural, and institutional concept on the other' (2003, p. 133). Clearly, while also implying the former, the authors quoted above were emphasizing the latter interpretation.

Dodds (2008), based on a content analysis of the literature, also identifies a series of contested meanings of globalization: as flows of capital, people, information and culture (associated with King); as marketization (associated with Altbach); and as ideology. The consequences of globalization are seen as a concentration of linguistic and economic power, increased competition between higher education institutions, higher education institutions being seen as having a crucial role in maintaining or developing national competitive advantage, and changes in the nature of information and access to it. Dodds argues that, by contrast, the role of higher education institutions themselves in promoting globalization has been overlooked:

> Perhaps the only apparent point of consensus amongst contemporary researchers is the claim that globalisation affects HEIs [higher education institutions], rather than HEIs themselves being implicated in its promotion ... this position underplays the often important role of HEIs in encouraging cross-border flows and pressures, and global trends such as marketisation. (pp. 514–5)

This explanation suggests why globalization has been the subject of so much critique from academics, as will be discussed later.

As regards internationalization, a number of different distinctions or typologies have been presented. Haigh (2014, p. 6), for example, identified eight layers in the evolution of thinking about internationalization:

> (1) recruiting international students; (2) teaching international students; (3) growing the international enterprise university through the competitive recruitment of international staff and students; (4) compliance with standards set by international accreditation agencies; (5) 'internationalisation at home', which means internationalisation of the curriculum for local learners; (6) education for global citizenship; (7) connected e-learning; and (8) education for planetary, whole-Earth, consciousness.

These layers suggest a natural developmental process, moving from pragmatic concerns about increasing student recruitment towards an overarching concern for the welfare of the whole planet.

In a different vein, Engwall (2016) identifies four modes of internationalization – (a) import of ideas, (b) outsourcing (i.e. sending students abroad to study), (c) insourcing (attracting students from abroad to study) and (d) foreign direct investments (delivering higher education abroad) – with the first of these seen as the most important for higher education. The fourth of Engwall's modes is often termed cross-border or transnational higher education, and has amassed a substantial literature of its own (e.g. Bennell and Pearce 2003; Healey and Michael 2015; Kauppinen 2015; Naidoo 2009).

Bibliographic searches carried out using Scopus show the familiar story of a steady increase in the number of publications focusing on globalization and/or internationalization and higher education since the 1990s, with around 200 new publications each year now being produced with 'globalization' or 'internationalization', or both of these terms (there is a considerable overlap), in their titles, abstract or keywords.

The analysis of the Scopus results shows that the majority of authors in both listings are based in social science departments. Interestingly, authors based in the United Kingdom form the largest group for articles focusing on internationalization (the United Kingdom – 296 (e.g. Trahar and Hyland 2011; Walker 2014), the United States – 236 (e.g. Urban and Palmer 2014; Wamboye et al. 2015), Australia – 201 (e.g. Harman 2004; Levatino 2016), China – 123 (e.g. Jokila 2015; Liu and Metcalfe

2016), Germany – 76 (e.g. Bedenlier and Zavenski-Richter 2015; Berchem 1991)). The more usual order, with US-based authors well ahead, occurs for articles focusing on globalization (the United States – 600, the United Kingdom – 286, Australia – 221, China – 115, Canada – 96 (e.g. Larsen 2016; Pashby and Oliveira Andreotti 2016)). It may simply be that the two terms are more or less popular in different countries.

However, despite producing the largest number of authors on internationalization in higher education, and the second largest for globalization, none of the leading authors identified – Knight (14), Teichler (13) and Yemini (11) for internationalization, Marginson (20), Mok (15) and Teichler (10) again for globalization – have been primarily UK based.

Despite the dominance of the major Anglophone countries, plus China and Germany, in research and writing (in English) on globalization and internationalization in higher education, interest in this topic is widespread and, appropriately enough, global. Thus, for example, research has also focused on Colombia (Berry and Taylor 2014), Denmark (Fabricius, Mortensen and Haberland 2016), Finland (Ahola 2005), Japan (Umakoshi 1997), Latvia (Lulle and Buzinska 2017), Malaysia (Aziz and Abdullah 2014), Mexico (Berry and Taylor 2014), the Netherlands (Huang 2006), New Zealand (Jiang 2010), Norway (Gornitzka and Langfeldt 2008), Russia (Stukalova et al. 2015), South Africa (Dolby 2010), South Korea (Moon 2016), Sweden (Svensson and Wihlborg 2010), Thailand (Lavankura 2013) and Turkey (Akar 2010). Other authors have examined the position in particular world regions, such as Africa (Jowi 2009), Asia Pacific (Ng 2012), East Asia (Chao 2014) and Latin America (Gomes et al. 2012), or have researched a number of emerging market providers (Russell 2015).

It remains the case, however, that the impact of globalization and internationalization on higher education in the Western, developed world has been much more widely researched. This is not, of course, just because these countries contain the largest proportion of higher education researchers publishing in English, but also due to their dominance in the recruitment of international students (and staff):

> The core countries in the world system, the USA, the UK, Australia, France, Germany and Japan, receive most of the international students, whereas semi-periphery countries such as China, India and South Korea, and periphery countries, Malaysia and Vietnam, send most of the international students to other countries. (Barnett et al. 2016, p. 549)

A particular feature of this focus has been the interest in developments within the European Union, especially the effects of the Bologna process (e.g. Teichler 2009; Zmas 2015). Some, though, have researched the impact of the Bologna process outside of the European Union; for example, Ferrer (2010) has examined its effects on Latin American countries. Other Western international organizations or associations, such as the OECD have also attracted research attention for their work in encouraging globalization and internationalization (van der Wende 2007).

While the themes of globalization and internationalization encourage the adoption of a broad approach to research, practical considerations and researcher interests mean that a good deal of published research is more focused. This may be in terms, for example, of the disciplines studied (thus Bruner and Iannarelli (2011) examine management education in this context, while Larsen (2016) focuses on teacher education) or the mode of study (Hanna and Latchem (2002) consider the potential of open and distance learning).

By far the most common focus taken in research has been to examine, usually at a departmental, institutional or national level, the experience of international students (e.g. Castro et al. 2016; Knight 2012; Kritz 2016; Salisbury et al. 2009). Some of the research on the international student does, however, take a broader perspective, as, for example, Shields's research into student flows:

> Network analysis reveals that changes to international student flows are
> multifaceted and complex. However, there are clear trends in this complexity: even
> with the growth of new destinations for study, the network of international students
> has become more centralized, less densely connected, and less like a 'small world'. It
> shares strong structural similarities with the networks of world trade and the world
> polity, increasingly with the latter. (2013, p. 628)

Alongside the interest in the international student experience (see also the discussion in Chapter 5), a smaller but significant body of research has also built up on the academic staff experience of teaching international students, working with immigrant colleagues or working in other countries themselves (e.g. Bedenlier and Zawacki-Richter 2105; Gheorgiu and Stephens 2016; Teichler 2015). Part of this interest has focused on what has long been termed 'brain drain', the movement of qualified academics from developing to developed countries, or simply to countries with better academic job opportunities (Docquier and Rapoport 2012).

Interest in the student and staff experience of globalization and internationalization in higher education has led, naturally enough, to research into the impact upon the curriculum and teaching (e.g. Bovill, Jordan and Watters 2015; Korhonen and Weil 2015; Svensson and Wihlborg 2010). Particular foci here have been on taking a global perspective to teaching and learning, what this implies, and its impact, not just on international students, but on home students and teachers in the 'international classroom' as well. The idea of educating students to be global citizens has attracted considerable attention (e.g. Aktas et al. 2017; Pais and Costa 2017).

Another concern has been with the role of language, with English assuming the position of lingua franca in higher education, and universities in countries where English is not a mother tongue being encouraged or directed to offer more of their popular courses in the medium of English (Doiz, Lasagabaster and Sierra 2013; Duong and Chua 2016; Kedzierski 2016). While making provision more accessible to international students, the effects are not necessarily positive for home students or for 'successful internationalization':

> Ideally, the internationalization of university education should be about designing
> study programs that bring together, support and take nourishment from the
> knowledge, cultural practices, life experiences and linguistic resources of students

and staff from diverse backgrounds. … At present … language policies at Danish universities act as structural obstructions to this form of internationalization, because they institutionalize a non-integrated perspective on the local and the transnational. University language policies that make a sharp distinction between Danish (the local) and English (the non-local) actually nourish the paradoxes we have discussed … because they encourage a mindset that undermines a successful internationalization process. (Fabricius et al. 2016, n. p.)

In addition to examining the student and staff experience, and the impact upon the curriculum, higher education researchers interested in globalization and internationalization have also looked at their effect on research (Kwiek 2015a), governance and management (Enders 2004; King 2010), and on higher education institutions generally (Seeber et al. 2016). Thus, Maringe et al. note the different rationales for and responses to internationalization in different parts of the world:

In western universities, a commercial imperative appears to underpin the internationalisation processes and understanding. In Confucian and many Middle East nations, there is a deep-seated cultural imperative at the heart of the internationalisation agenda. In the poorer universities of the south, a curriculum-value driven process seems to characterise the internationalisation priorities of universities there. (2013, p. 9)

Based on a study of over 400 European higher education institutions, which would fit the first of Maringe et al.'s models, Seeber et al. identify competitive pressures underlying institutional and individual responses to internationalization:

The salience of a given rationale for a specific HEI [higher education institution] results from factors at multiple levels. Being embedded in a globally competitive arena for status spurs a conception of internationalization as instrumental to prestige. It appears that national contexts do not affect HEIs' rationales much, and that the amount of resources is less important than the resources competition for the selection of rationales. The immediate organizational context, both in terms of organizational goals and internal actors' interests, emerge as particularly relevant. (2016, p. 698)

There are clear links here to the research on ranking and league tables, discussed in Chapter 6.

Just as Haigh (2014), discussed earlier, identified a series of stages in the historical evolution of thinking about internationalization in higher education, so Knight, analogously, recognizes three generations of international universities:

The classic model or first generation is an internationalized university with a diversity of international partnerships, international students and staff, and multiple international and intercultural collaborative activities at home and abroad. This is the most common model. The second generation is called the satellite model, which includes universities with satellite offices around the world in the form of branch campuses, research centers, and management/contact offices. Internationally cofounded universities constitute the third and most recent generation of international universities. These are stand-alone institutions co-founded or co-developed by two or more partner institutions from different countries. (2015, p. 107)

Clearly, as Knight suggests, most universities have yet to get beyond the first generation, while many of those who have attempted to join the second generation have found that the transition did not go as smoothly as they had hoped.

As will be abundantly clear from the discussion so far, globalization and internationalization in higher education have been interpreted and addressed in a variety of ways. They have also raised many issues and been the subject of much critique. Some of these issues and critiques have been accepting of globalization and internationalization, but have argued that the responses to them have not been good enough. Thus, there have been reservations about the quality of provision, particularly in transnational or cross-border higher education (e.g. Arunasalam 2016), where assertions that provision was of equal standard to that made in the home institution have been severely questioned. Others have doubted the extent to which universities have achieved what they claim in their internationalization strategies (Ayoubi and Massoud 2007), or have queried the ethics of internationalization and its position on sustainability (Pashby and Oliveira Andreotti 2016).

Healey (2008) takes a different approach to the issue of sustainability, arguing that it is the policies and strategies that have led to increasing internationalization of higher education that are contradictory and unsustainable:

On the supply-side, the internationalisation of MESDC [main English-speaking destination countries] universities is a response to confused government policy, which has temporarily made the unregulated international student market more attractive than a highly regulated domestic market. ... To the extent that these policy frameworks are unsustainable in the longer term, the deregulation of domestic tuition fees and the freeing of universities from state control could well lead to a scenario in which many universities begin to retreat from internationalisation and return to their 'core activities' of research and teaching domestic students. On the demand side ... for mainstream students in developing countries, studying at a MESDC university has come to be regarded over the last 15 years as the only alternative for those who cannot secure a place at one of the leading universities in their home countries and who have the means to pay for a foreign education. As the higher education sectors in developing countries scale up and consumers become more sophisticated, it is likely that demand to study abroad, particularly at the lower status universities now so dependent on international students, will decline rather than continue to grow at recent rates. (pp. 122–3)

Perhaps even more concerningly, the recruitment of international students has been criticized as being inherently racist: 'The recruitment and reception of international students studying in the West are both structured by racialized logics, as both are embedded within the dominant global imaginary and its colonial myth of Western onto-epistemological supremacy … not only is resentment and interpersonal abuse toward international students framed by this imaginary, but also, ironically, efforts to welcome them as well' (Stein and de Andreotti 2016, p. 235; see also Lee, Jon and Byun 2017).

Fabricius et al. (2016) identify three paradoxes that arise from the dissonance between an unqualified acceptance of internationalization as a 'good thing' and its practical implications and impacts: internationalization and linguistic pluralism (which it tends to reduce), internationalization and intercultural understanding (with national groups of students often sticking together), and internationalization and competitiveness (where the evidence is either lacking or mixed).

A somewhat less trenchant critique of globalization and internationalization in higher education recognizes that the position in practice is rather more complex than is often implied. Thus, Marginson and Rhoades, in a much-cited article, stress the linkages and interrelationships between global, national and local levels or forces:

> We offer a Glonacal Agency Heuristic to frame comparative higher education research. 'Glonacal' incorporates three constituent terms – global, national, local. 'Agency' refers to organized agencies and to the agency of human action. … Our heuristic highlights the growing saliency of global agencies and relationships, including meta-national regions, in both the national and the local domains. At the same time, it emphasizes the continuing fecundity of local institutions and other agents at the national and global level. And it takes us beyond nation states, national markets, and national systems and institutions of higher education to consider organizational agencies and human agency at various levels. Such agencies and activities operate simultaneously in the three domains or planes of existence – global, national, local – amid multiple and reciprocal flows of activity. (2002, p. 305)

Focusing on just one of these levels, the local, Burnett and Huisman (2010) stress the importance of organizational culture in impacting on institutional responses.

However, the most thoroughgoing critique of globalization and internationalization in higher education – and one often delivered in a routine, condensed or shorthand form – is that is simply another expression of neo-liberalism (Harris 2008), or, at least, the way in which it is being interpreted and practised is: 'The current disillusionment about the co-opting of internationalization by neoliberal globalization stems from a kind of naïveté that internationalization itself already had a strong theoretical and practical basis for maintaining its own trajectory separate from economic globalization' (Beck 2012, p. 143).

These pressures are, perhaps, felt most keenly in developing nations:

> The globalisation of higher education is ultimately based on the market-driven fundamentals of globalisation. Thus it creates more challenges than opportunities, particularly for the non-western developing countries. The most prominent challenges include quality control, information management, its fitness for local societies, and costs and benefits. When all of these aspects accompany each other, it brings the dangers of total lack of … genuine educational values. (Yang 2003, p. 284)

What conclusions might we draw, then, about the significance of globalization and internationalization in, or to, higher education and higher education research? First, it is clear that the ideas, concepts or frameworks provided by globalization and internationalization have been, and are continuing to be, highly popular for thinking about and researching higher education. While it would probably not be true to say that this popularity was genuinely global, globalization and internationalization do draw attention to linkages between different parts of the world, and its developed and developing nations, in particular.

Second, globalization and internationalization, to a far greater extent than most frameworks applied to the study of higher education, draw attention to the division between what may be called pragmatic and idealistic conceptions of the purpose of higher education. At present the pragmatists – or neo-liberals as some would term them – are in the ascendant, with their concerns for recruiting as many international students as possible, and projecting the power and influence of specific higher education institutions or systems globally. The idealists, while being generally and genuinely critical, must largely confine themselves to improving the student experience and curriculum as best as they can.

Third, and finally, the point made by Dodds (2008), discussed earlier, deserves further emphasis. Higher education and higher education institutions have a major role to play in globalization and internationalization. They are at least as much drivers of these developments as responders to them, and the implications of this should not be overlooked.

Massification

An American researcher, Trow (1970, 1973), is widely credited for setting out the early thinking on mass higher education. Working in the United States, the first higher education system to allow and achieve mass participation, but with a keen comparative interest, particularly concerning the United Kingdom, he suggested the following definitions:

- 'elite' higher education systems enrolled less than 15 per cent of the age group;
- 'mass' higher education systems enrolled between 15 per cent and 50 per cent of the age group; and
- 'universal' higher education systems enrolled over 50 per cent of the age group.

While the break points may seem somewhat arbitrary, and others might prefer different labels for the groups, this model has been widely accepted and applied.

Trow (1973) explained the distinction between elite, mass and universal systems of higher education in the following fashion:

The old institutions cannot expand indefinitely; they are limited by their traditions, organizations, functions, and finance. In European countries, it is likely that an increased enrollment in higher education beyond about 15 percent of the age grade requires not merely the further expansion of the elite university systems, but the rapid development of mass higher education through the growth of popular nonelite institutions. Mass higher education differs from elite higher education not just quantitatively but qualitatively … if the transition is made successfully the system is then able to develop institutions that can grow without being transformed until they reach about 50 percent of the age grade. Beyond that, and thus far only in the United States, large sections of the population are sending nearly all their sons and daughters to some kind of higher education, and the system must again create new forms of higher education as it begins to move rapidly toward universal access. (pp. 6–7)

He recognized that, in a mass higher education system, the vast majority of students could not expect to attend Oxford, Harvard or an equivalent, but would be accommodated by less well-funded and lower-status institutions, including, in the United States, community colleges, and in the United Kingdom, further education colleges. In other words, while all students would be receiving an education at a higher level, they would be getting different sorts of higher education.

Returning to the theme twenty-six years later, Trow (1999) argued that, while his thesis had stood the test of time, the means by which it might be met were now more diverse, with the impact of information technology (through online learning) now very strong:

The elite-mass-universal access model I set forth in the early 1970s assumed that universal access to higher education would come through increased numbers of students in all countries enrolling or attending – much of it part time or at night – in non-elite institutions that might eventually and for some provide further links through credit transfer to degree-granting institutions. That has been happening, though still on a modest scale. Information technology now forces a revision of our conception of the conditions making for universal access: IT allows, and becomes the vehicle for, universal access to higher education of a different order of magnitude, with courses of every kind and description available over the Internet to people's homes and workplaces. (p. 327)

Writing in the same year, Altbach was able to argue that 'mass higher education has become the international norm at the end of the 20th century' (1999, p. 107). Of course, Trow and Altbach were not the only researchers writing about mass higher education. In the early years, names like McConnell (1973), Neave (1985) and Teichler (1998) were also prominent.

With the passage of time, some of the terms used and the foci of interest subtly changed. Thus, rather than talk simply about mass higher education, the rather ugly term 'massification' came into use to signify the process undergone to achieve mass higher education. And, instead of then anticipating a further expansion to universal higher education, the discussion turned instead to what happened 'post-massification' or in high-participation systems.

Bibliographic searches indicate that the term 'massification' has only recently been introduced, first appearing in the title of an article along with 'higher education' in 1998, and then again in 2007, with less than forty such articles having been published in total (according to Scopus). Articles focusing on mass higher education are rather more common, with between fifteen and thirty currently being published each year (according to Google Scholar).

Interest in mass higher education and massification has been widespread, with interest from developed and developing countries in all continents, including Australia (Pitman 2014), Chile (Leihy and Salazar 2016), China (Li 2012; Mok and Wu 2016; Zha 2011), Ethiopia (Tessema 2009) Germany (Powell and Solga 2011), Greece (Petmesidou 1998), Hong Kong (Lee 2016), Italy (Rossi 2010), Japan (Reiko 2001), Portugal (Dias 2015), Russia (Smolentseva 2016), Spain (Rosado and David 2006), Taiwan (Wang 2003), Turkey (Özoglu, Gür and Gümüs 2016), the United Kingdom (Scott 1995; Williams 1997) and Zambia (Kanyengo 2009). Other researchers have focused on world regions, most notably East Asia (Hayhoe 1995; Huang 2016; Mok 2016).

While much of the research literature has focused on describing and analysing the policies being applied in individual systems, there has also been an interest in particular topics. The most obvious of these has been the issues involved in teaching the large classes which mass higher education necessitates (e.g. Albertyn, Machika and Troskie-de Bruin 2016; Hornsby and Osman 2014), including how to provide useful feedback on assessment (Nicol 2010) and how the university library should respond (Kanyengo 2009).

The impact and effects of mass higher education have been extensively critiqued, as, of course, have virtually all higher education policies. These critiques have addressed a range of issues, including the impact on graduate employment, on the quality of provision, on widening participation and equity, on the institutions and sectors of higher education, and on students' perceptions of their experience.

The impact on graduate employment has undoubtedly taken most of the attention, with doubts expressed about whether the increasing number of graduates being produced by higher education could all gain graduate-level jobs, reaping the financial rewards for their investment in higher education. Thus, at one extreme, Ware (2015, p. 475) argues that a 'fraud' has been perpetrated, because 'a large minority of graduates earn no more than nongraduates or are in jobs for which they are "overeducated."'

There have, however, been many more measured analyses. Thus, in the UK context, using data on students who graduated in the 1980s and 1990s, Elias and Purcell (2004) concluded that

> while there may have been a decline from the high premium enjoyed by older graduates, for those who graduated in 1995 the average premium was holding up well, despite the expansion. Although we found differences between established graduate occupations and the newer areas of graduate employment, our evidence suggests that the development of new technical and managerial specialisms and occupational restructuring within organisations has been commensurate with the availability of an increased supply of highly qualified people. (p. 60)

In other words, while overall the graduate premium was not as great as it had been in the days of elite higher education, the UK economy was also upgrading and able to fruitfully absorb the rising number of graduates.

A longitudinal study of Finnish graduates came up with similarly nuanced findings, arguing that, while there were still financial returns to an investment in higher education, the financial risks were now greater:

> The changes in returns to university graduates over two decades seem to follow an intergenerational mechanism, where university education, so to speak, turns from one generation's human capital into the subsequent generation's human risk capital. Relative returns to both male and female graduates with an academic background are low at the early career stage for the age group born in 1966. Although their relative returns at the mature career stage are expected to be higher than those of the 1946 group, ever fewer will reach the average returns; even the human capital of offspring of academic families born in 1946 seems to be transforming into human risk capital of the respective group born in 1966. Graduates from non-academic families, however, can hardly avoid risks from one generation to the next. (Kivinen, Hedman and Kaipainen 2007, p. 245)

In Portugal, a study of the period from 2000 to 2010 concluded that fears of over-education and over-skilling were exaggerated, but that – as in Finland – there were also greater risks involved:

> Our findings suggest that, so far, there is little evidence of a generalised increase of combined overeducation and overskilling. New graduate jobs appear to show sufficient dynamism to keep these in check and at the moment overeducation coexists with significant pockets of underskilling. Our findings also suggest, however, that for a significant part of the young graduates' labour market in Portugal that dynamism may be limited, thus leading to greater heterogeneity in the job market. (Figueiredo et al. 2015, pp. 14–15)

In Taiwan, however, the picture appears less rosy, with evidence of both over-education and lower graduate salaries:

> The massification of higher education in Taiwan … promised bright prospects for students, parents, industries and higher education institutions. The massification had positive effects in terms of upgrading the industrial structure and maintaining regional competitiveness. At the individual level, the pressure of access to higher education substantially improved by providing extra places. Nevertheless, this process posed challenges for the career development of the younger generation. High-end job vacancies seem nowadays limited in Taiwan, which has led to declining wage levels, because of the overprovision of master's and doctoral courses. Rapid expansion makes this issue even worse because of the increasing incidence of overeducation or mismatch. (Chan and Lin 2015, p. 31)

Second to graduate employment, the impact of massification on the quality of provision has also been a concern. This was, of course, anticipated in Trow's analysis, as lower status and cheaper forms of provision had to be used to establish mass higher education. Thus, in the UK, Giannakis and Bullivant (2016) concluded that 'the rise in student numbers has been a contributing factor to the deterioration of quality in higher education', though they also noted that 'there may be however a range of other variables which may contribute to this' (p. 645).

In Australia, Pitman (2014) argued that, over the period from 2008 to 2014, the very understanding of higher education quality had changed in order to better accommodate the changes underway:

> The discursive relationship between mass higher education and higher education quality shifted from conceptualising quality as a function of economic productivity, through educational transformation and academic standards, to market competition and efficiency. Throughout, the student was more often positioned as a servant towards higher education quality, rather than its benefactor. (p. 348)

In Hong Kong, concerns have been more strongly expressed, with suggestions made that the move to mass higher education has been done 'on the cheap':

> Additional enrolments have been concentrated towards associate degrees. Whether these are suited as a terminal qualification to equip students for a knowledge-based economy appears to have been questioned by many graduates, who see it more as a stepping stone to an undergraduate degree. There is also limited evidence of employers seeing associate degree holders as ready for employment in managerial positions or in technologically-advanced industries. (Kember 2010, p. 177)

This links in with concerns about equity. Analysis suggests that, within some mass higher education systems, an elite higher education system remains more or less intact, with a hierarchy of institutions and courses from higher to lower status, and with students from less privileged backgrounds concentrated in the cheaper and lower-status parts of the system:

> The massification of higher education in Hong Kong has ... failed to enhance social mobility in the city ... the process of massification has been heavily shaped by the interests of the city's elites, who see higher education massification as a solution to such social and political problems as unemployment and regional integration, but remain reluctant to increase public spending on the sector. Consequently, the massification of higher education in Hong Kong has taken on a partial privatisation model in which expansion occurs almost exclusively in the private sector. As a result, publicly funded degree programmes have remained highly selective and are increasingly biased towards wealthy students. In the process, graduates from self-financed programmes are severely disadvantaged in terms of employability despite their investment. (Lee 2016, pp. 27–8)

Similar conclusions have been reached in Portugal, with Dias (2015, p. 118) noting: 'Despite the advances made in Portugal on access, and the system's expansion, equity of access and outcomes in higher education have not yet been achieved, whilst the democratisation process also remains unconvincing.'

The answer to this dilemma has been simply expressed, but clearly it would take a massive commitment to achieve:

> Massification and diversification cannot achieve equality of opportunities unless they are accompanied by the development of flexibility within systems to enable students to progress between different levels and sectors within national jurisdictions and between countries. Flexibility turns to be a most meaningful feature for ensuring greater access, and particularly greater equity in higher education. (Guri-Rosenblit, Sebkova and Teichler 2007, p. 386)

Mok (2016, p. 51) has noted that 'the intensification of "positional competition" among college graduates seems to reflect growing social inequality'. Rosado and David (2006, p. 361) have argued that the massification of higher education has led to 'massive universities rather [than] universities for the masses'. Part of the issue here has been where there are distinct sub-sectors within the system, as in Germany with its higher education and vocational educational systems (Powell and Solga 2011), and in the UK with higher education and further education (Smith and Bocock 1999), the latter of which now offers an increasing proportion of higher education provision.

Finally, there is the question of what the students themselves think of the developing mass higher education system in which they are enrolled. In many cases, of course, being the first in their family to attend higher education, they may have nothing to compare their experience with. In some systems, such as Chile, their politicization may have a notable impact (Fleet and Guzman-Concha 2016). In other systems, where student politicization is less of an issue, students' perceptions of massification are more likely to be related to questions of quality and cost.

Conclusions

Clearly, research into system policy within higher education is large in scope – typically national or international – and handles big issues, like globalization and massification. Yet, as we have seen, it is not without its faults and critiques. Here, I will draw attention to two particular areas of concern.

First, while the widespread attention paid to international and comparative studies in researching system policy is commendable, the relative ignorance of what happens at or below the level of the institution – in terms, for example, of policy implementation – is regrettable. This perspective is partly driven, of course, by the focus on using quantitative techniques and the nature of the data that is available for analysis.

Second, and this again is partly due to methodological focus, it seems a shame that those who research system policy are so far apart from those who research teaching and learning (where qualitative methods are widely in use). This is a symptom of higher education research being a growing and fracturing field, which, hopefully, books like this will do something both to chronicle and offer a remedy to.

Chapter 8
Research on Institutional Management

Introduction

Research into institutional management in higher education examines how universities and colleges are organized, managed, led and governed, the roles that higher education institutions take on, their funding arrangements and how these work in practice. Research into institutional management may be seen as occupying an intermediate position between research into system policy (see Chapter 7) and research into academic work (see Chapter 9), to both of which it is, of course, closely related.

Research into institutional management also has many similarities to research into system policy. It primarily employs documentary and multivariate analysis, at varying levels of sophistication; it emphasizes larger scales of analysis (typically individual institutions or, where institutional practices are being compared, at national level) than in other areas of higher education research; and remains dominated by men, including significant numbers of senior higher education managers (Tight 2003, 2012a).

Research trends

A bibliographic search using Scopus identified 847 published articles with the words 'higher', 'education' and 'management' in their titles, which might reasonably be assumed to focus on the topic of this chapter (though this will not be an exclusive listing). Unusually, more of them were authored by researchers based in the United Kingdom (143, or 17 per cent of the total) than in the United States (105, 12 per cent), suggesting that American researchers prefer different terminology. The sources for the articles were also very varied, with seventy-seven originating countries identified.

While the earliest article identified with 'higher', 'education' and 'management' in its title dates back to 1932, significant numbers were not being published until the 1990s, with 5 to 10 per year (indicative of when management – as opposed to administration – really started to assume importance in institutions and systems). Currently, between fifty and ninety such articles are being published each year.

Some higher education journals specialize, at least to some degree, in publishing articles on institutional management. They include *Tertiary Education and Management*, *Higher Education Management and Policy* (now discontinued) and the *Journal of Higher Education Policy and Management*, each of which also publishes many articles dealing with system policy, the focus of the previous chapter. Articles on higher education management also feature frequently in both generic higher education journals, such as *Higher Education*, and generic educational management journals, such as the *International Journal of Educational Management*.

As a topic, institutional management is characterized by both the development of new theory and the application of existing theories from other disciplines (often, of course, the disciplines from which the researchers themselves have come from or are still based in). Thus, institutional mission and diversity (which is considered in more detail later in this chapter), for example, have been the subject of some theorization; while theories on economies of scale, leadership and managerialism (the last of which is also considered in more detail later in this chapter), and, more generally, institutional theory, have been imported and applied from elsewhere.

Among the specific topics researched in institutional management, three currently stand out: funding and financial management (e.g. Essack, Naidoo and Barnes 2010; Fowles 2014; Gill and Gill 2000), governance (e.g. de Boer, Huisman and Meister-Scheytt 2010; Eckel 2000; Huisman 2009; Vilkinas and Peters 2014) and leadership (e.g. van den Bosch and Teelken 2000; Breakwell and Tytherleigh 2010; Odhiambo 2014).

Less popular topics for research include the role of middle management (e.g. Clegg and McAuley 2005; Santiago et al. 2006) and of gender (e.g. Goode and Bagilhole 1998; Luke 1997), and the growing importance attached to intellectual capital and knowledge management (e.g. Moss et al. 2007). Other topics researched vary widely, from alumni (e.g. Meer and Rosen 2010) to sexual harassment (e.g. Shultz, Scherman and Marshall 2000) to drinking policies (Colby, Raymond and Colby 2000).

Research designs and frameworks

The three research frameworks examined in more detail in this section – managerialism and collegiality, institutional mission and diversity, academic drift and institutional isomorphism – as well as being evidently popular topics for research into higher education institutional management, also illustrate interesting aspects of higher education research.

Thus, managerialism and collegiality are often presented as opposed approaches, with collegialism representing the 'traditional' way of running colleges and universities, and managerialism the 'modern', imposed strategy for coping with mass higher education. But are they as oppositional as many would make out?

Institutional diversity, like collegialism, is also regularly extolled as a desirable feature of higher education systems, while institutional mission expresses the need for contemporary institutions to label and market themselves (but perhaps not as diverse?). As with managerialism and collegiality, there are clearly tensions here.

Academic drift and institutional isomorphism – which encapsulate what is essentially the same idea – illustrate both the international divisions in higher education research and the extent to which it has produced 'original' theoretical frameworks and ideas. Academic drift was developed in the United Kingdom, seemingly from scratch, while institutional isomorphism, adopted from institutional theory, was applied in the United States, both to the same issue.

Managerialism and collegiality

A great deal has been written about managerialism – the belief that most significant decisions within contemporary organizations are made by managers with little involvement by other employees – over the last few decades. In the higher education sector, this discussion typically takes one of two forms: that this is a necessary development, given the size and complexity of contemporary universities; or that it is an unwelcome development and should be resisted. Critics often make favourable mention of an older idea, that of collegiality – the idea that decisions in universities and colleges can be made collectively by the academics affected, with the assistance and support of administrators – which is seen as the more traditional and desirable alternative.

Collegiality appears to have a lower profile in the higher education research literature than does managerialism, even though the idea of collegiality is of much longer standing. Thus, a search on Scopus found a total of just twenty-two articles with both 'managerialism' and 'higher education' in their titles, but only seven with both 'collegiality' and 'higher education'. However, while the first of the former was published only in the 1990s, the first of the latter dated to the 1970s, and there were many more earlier mentions of both 'collegiality' and 'higher education' in the text of articles.

While managerialism is a relatively recent entrant into the higher education literature, the discussion of collegiality goes back a long way; indeed, it might be said to be essentially historical in its importance. Writers on collegiality are likely to make reference to such seminal figures as Newman, in the English context, or Humboldt, in the German.

In the English system of higher education, the idea of collegiality is most closely associated with a collegial university organization, the classic, aspirational example of which is, of course, provided by Oxford and Cambridge (Tapper and Palfreyman 1998, 2000, 2002; Tapper and Salter 1992). Outside of Oxbridge, Tapper and Palfreyman (2000, p. 25) note the continuing importance of intellectual collegiality: 'Day-to-day working relationships as professionals interacting with colleagues to fulfil the purposes of teaching and research.'

The Oxbridge collegiate pattern of provision had an impact on the developing elite universities in America (Bess 1988; Duke 1996). In the UK, Durham also adopted this form of organization when it was established in the early nineteenth century, as did some of the newer English campus universities founded in the 1960s, such as Kent and Lancaster; though the extent to which they were really able to mimic Oxbridge was limited. Historically, the other English higher education institutions that made much of their collegiality were the teacher training colleges (Tight 2011; Wyatt 1977).

The historical associations of the term are now long gone, with the possible exception of Oxbridge, and most recent English authors acknowledge this. Thus, Dearlove (1997, p. 58) notes that 'collegial ideals are one thing but organisational reality has always been another', while Deem, Hillyard and Reed (2007, p. 85) argue that 'departmental and university collegiality, even amongst academics, was never as widespread as some of its proponents claim and rarely included women or blacks'.

Sahlin (2012) offers a more recent understanding of collegiality, emphasizing the importance of critical dialogue and peer review, and of 'a management structure with elected leaders' (p. 210). This begins to suggest an elision between collegiality and managerialism. Shattock goes further in explicitly linking collegiality with management: 'The main argument for a collegial style of management in universities is quite simply that it is the most effective method of achieving success in the core business' (2003, p. 88).

While Tapper and Palfreyman (2002) are correct in arguing that collegiality has featured little in academic analysis, there are a few examples. Thus, Hellawell and Hancock (2001) interviewed fourteen middle managers in one new UK university regarding their views on collegiality. They readily identified practical problems that got in the way of implementing collegial forms of management, which have had less and less traction as managerialism has advanced.

Over twenty years ago, Trow argued with respect to managerialism that 'the "ism" points to an ideology, to a faith or belief in the truth of a set of ideas which are independent of specific situations' (1994, p. 11), though another American author, Birnbaum (2000), preferred to simply dismiss managerialism as a fad. Writing about England, Trow went on to offer two – soft and hard – definitions of managerialism:

> The soft concept sees managerial effectiveness as an important element in the provision of higher education of quality at its lowest cost; it is focused around the idea of improving the 'efficiency' of existing institutions. The hard conception elevates institutional and system management to a dominant position in higher education; its advocates argue that higher education must be reshaped and reformed by the introduction of management systems which then become a continuing force ensuring the steady improvement in the provision of higher education. ... This 'hard' concept of managerialism is currently the dominant force. (1994, p. 11)

From the present-day perspective, the soft version sounds like common sense (and practice) to many, even where the hard version is the operational reality. Santiago and Carvalho (2004) offer a more recent account of the latter: 'It combines political, institutional and organizational assumptions with principles of rationality that apparently do not seem to be organized, but in which it is possible to detect some coherence around the notions of market, competition, individual choice, responsibility and efficiency' (pp. 427–8).

Shepherd (2017) offers an ideal type model of managerialism, drawn from the literature and based on six principles: 'Management is important and a good thing ... management is a discrete function ... management is rational and value neutral ... management is generic and universally applicable ... managers must have the right to manage ... private sector methods are superior' (pp. 5–7). This provides a clear template against which to evaluate practice.

Despite Santiago and Carvalho's evident concern that managerialism might be extending beyond the UK to other parts of Europe, in their studies (2004, 2012) of senior academic managers and policymakers in Portugal they found little evidence that managerialism had come to dominate in the higher education system. Within the UK, however, the commonly accepted view is that managerialism has dominated higher education, as well as other parts of the public sector, for at least three decades:

> New managerialism as a general set of ideological principles has permeated higher education ... many manager-academics have embraced these principles and the associated language. This seems to be especially so for those who are in senior positions or hold permanent managerial posts at any level. (Deem and Brehony 2005, p. 231)

The impact of managerialism, though, has varied by institutional type. Kok et al. (2008, 2010) surveyed academics in UK universities, concluding that 'it is the traditional university that is most affected. Their previous collegial approaches towards quality in research and teaching have been diluted by the increasing focus on cost-effectiveness, the need for greater student numbers, and moves towards more corporate-like orientations' (2010, pp. 109–10). By contrast, the newer universities – that is, the former polytechnics and colleges – had typically been run in a more managerial style throughout their recent history.

While the critique of managerialism in higher education has been particularly strong in the United Kingdom, it has also been evident in other countries around the world, including Australia (Anderson 2008), Austria (Pechar 2003), Canada (Hardy 1996), Finland (Salminen 2003), Hong Kong (Mok 1999), Ireland (O'Connor and White 2011), the Netherlands (Teelken 2012), New Zealand (Peters 2013), Portugal (Amaral, Magalhaes and Santiago 2003), South Africa (Adams 2006), Sweden (Sahlin 2012) and the United States (Roberts 2004).

These critiques are often fairly generic in nature. Thus, Beckmann and Cooper (2013) critique the rise of quality assurance, performance management and other aspects of what they term 'neoliberal managerialism'. They conclude that 'education's social purpose, for generating a critically aware, empathetic citizenry, freely engaged in democratic participation, has been eroded' (p. 20). A good number of the critiques take a gendered perspective (e.g. Bagilhole 2012; White, Carvalho and Riordan

2011). Others go beyond straightforward critique to argue that the adoption of business practices in higher education is partial, out of date or plain muddle-headed (e.g. Smyth 1989).

The critics are, however, by no means in agreement on how to counter managerialism in higher education. Some note the variety of resistance tactics in use (e.g. Anderson 2006), while others call for a new collegiality or a reassertion of its principles (e.g. Elton 1996; Harvey 1995). Some question the simplicity of the collegiality/managerialism dichotomy (Dearlove 1997, 2002). Burnes, Wend and Todnem (2014) similarly argue for a contemporary blending of collegiality and managerialism. Clegg and McAuley (2005) call, in the context of a study of middle managers in higher education, for a broader engagement with the management literature, noting that managers can be creative and innovative, while collegial systems may be discriminatory.

Looking at how a variety of universities and departments operate, McNay (1995) identifies four – rather than just two – university cultures, which he labels collegium, bureaucracy, corporation and enterprise. Here, collegium is clearly more or less equivalent to collegiality, while corporation is the closest to managerialism. Bureaucracy smacks of old-style managerial or governmental control, while enterprise suggests a direction we may be going in, with the student as our customer (see also the discussion in Chapter 6), and their potential employers and the government as key stakeholders.

Braun (1999) also identifies four governance models, explicitly building on earlier work by Clark and van Vught. Curiously, he does not credit McNay as a source though McNay contributes a chapter to his co-edited book (Braun and Merrien 1999), and is latterly referenced in connection with the UK position. Yet Braun's models – collegium, bureaucratic–oligarchic, market and new managerialism – are clearly analogous to those identified by McNay, though they make the collegiality/managerialism identification much more transparent.

While British academics in the 1980s and 1990s may have lacked the power or will to resist the managerial changes being imposed on them by the government and its agencies, later generations appear to have come to terms with these changes (of course, many of them will have known nothing else). Indeed, those with particular skills and mindsets appear to flourish. Thus, based on a survey of UK academics, Kolsaker (2008) concluded that

> despite worsening conditions, academics are much more positive and pragmatic than much of the literature suggests. Academics appear, on the whole, to accept managerialism not only as an external technology of control, but as a facilitator of enhanced performance, professionalism and status. (p. 522)

In an American contribution, Hatfield (2006) turns the collegiality/managerialism dichotomy on its head in showing how collegiality – in the sense of organizational citizenship – has become an element of performance to be assessed alongside teaching, research and service. In another American study, Apkarian et al. (2014) apply evidence from a national survey to assess whether key academic decisions are taken by managers or by academics and managers (dual control) in consort, and whether these patterns have changed over the period from 2000 to 2012. Using configurational analysis, they did not find a simple managerial/dual control dichotomy, but a complexity of patterns and changes over time. Four distinct institutional clusters were identified for both 2000 and 2012, with 'high campus participation' (i.e. more collegial) and 'low campus participation' (i.e. managerial) clusters both becoming stronger over the time period.

Institutional mission and diversity

Institutional diversity and institutional mission may be seen as integrally related. On the one hand, institutional diversity concerns the variety of higher education institutions – large and small, public or private, research-led or teaching-led, focused upon particular disciplines (e.g. art, business, education, medicine), forms of delivery (e.g. face-to-face, online) or types of students/clients (e.g. undergraduates, postgraduates, research students, companies) – that exist within a particular (national) system. On the other hand, institutional mission has to do with how the individual higher education institution thinks of itself and its roles, and how those roles are then articulated or marketed to its publics. Both diversity and mission, of course, are aspects of institutions that are by no means confined to higher education (Ostrom 2005).

The prevailing wisdom has long been that institutional diversity within higher education is a 'good thing', and that governments and policymakers should do all that they can to maintain and increase it. Thus, for example, in the American context, this was Birnbaum's expressed view over thirty years ago:

> Diversity is widely believed to be an essential characteristic of American higher education, one that in many ways differentiates postsecondary institutions in this country from those of other nations. Diversity has been identified as one of the basic reasons for higher education's high level of performance in this country and is an essential element in ensuring the system's responsiveness to societal needs. (1983, p. 1)

More recently, and in the same national context, Morphew expressed essentially the same opinion:

> Institutional diversity, or the existence of many different kinds of colleges and universities within a specific higher education system, has long been recognized as a positive and unique attribute of the U.S. higher education system. (Morphew 2009, p. 243)

The claim that this concern is unique to the United States, however, has to be challenged, as it is shared by other systems as well, for example, by many European nations, where different kinds of higher education institutions with different roles are, or have been, recognized. The perception of the United States as being different in this respect is partly due to the broad way in which its higher education sector is demarcated, which would correspond in other countries to the whole of post-secondary education. It is also a characteristic of those working within a particular system or nation to extol their virtues and/or 'uniqueness'. Institutional diversity – to varying degrees – is an international phenomenon; though we should also recognize the somewhat contrary desire of governments to ensure the underlying standard or quality of all higher education provision (see Chapter 6).

Institutional mission can be seen as a somewhat more recent concern, stemming largely from the massification of higher education and the growth in the numbers and size of higher education institutions. This, coupled with the tendency – some would say, necessity – to run universities and colleges like businesses (see the discussion of managerialism in the previous section), has led to individual institutions paying much more attention to what their purposes are, and what is distinctive about them, and then marketing this externally as their mission. Not surprisingly, given the much earlier massification of the American higher education system, institutional mission also became a concern there earlier and has remained important to this day.

Research and writing on institutional diversity and mission has been widespread and growing for decades, as evidenced by bibliographic searches on the Scopus database for articles with the words 'institutional', 'diversity', 'mission', 'higher' and 'education' in their title, abstract or keywords. These indicate that over sixty specialist articles are currently published on both institutional diversity and institutional mission each year.

An analysis of the data produced by Scopus indicates that 250 (45 per cent) of the articles identified dealing with institutional diversity were written by authors based in the United States, confirming the greater and longer-term interest in this topic there. Examples include articles by Morphew (2000a, 2009) and Wilton et al. (2015). Within the United States there have also been studies of institutional diversity as it relates to particular sub-sectors of higher education, such as Hispanic-serving institutions (e.g. Nunez, Crisp and Elizondo 2016) and Christian higher education (e.g. Nussbaum and Chang 2013).

Alongside the United States, other English-speaking nations – such as the United Kingdom (88, 16 per cent; e.g. Taylor 2003; Watts 1972), Australia (44, 8 per cent; e.g. Moodie 2005) and Canada (19, 3 per cent; e.g. Piche 2015) – also contributed significant, though smaller, numbers of articles. Authors based in Brazil, the Netherlands, Norway, Portugal (e.g. Teixeira et al. 2012), South Africa and Spain each contributed ten or more articles; but there are also examples from less expected sources, such as Slovakia (Caplanova 2003) and Thailand (Praphamontripong 2011). Other articles are more ambitious in territorial terms, examining the situation in a given continent, such as Europe (Huisman, Meek and Wood 2007) or Latin America (Balan 2012), while others take a transcontinental perspective, such as Pinheiro, Charles and Jones (2016), who compare the position in Australia, Canada and Norway.

The majority, 252 (53 per cent), of the articles identified dealing with institutional mission (there was, of course, some overlap with those examining diversity) were produced by authors based in the United States. Examples include the articles by Franklin (2012; focusing on the library's role), Morphew and Hartley (2006; focusing on mission statements), Pike, Kuh and Gonyea (2003; examining the relationship between institutional mission and student performance) and Woodrow (2006; focusing on Christian institutions). Much smaller numbers and proportions came from the other major English-speaking nations of the United Kingdom (48, 10 per cent; e.g. Filippakou and Tapper 2015; examining mission groups), Australia (15, 3 per cent; e.g. Chapman, Mangion and Buchanan 2015) and Canada (12, 3 per cent; e.g. Levin 1999).

As in the case of research and writing on institutional diversity, there were also interesting instances of publications from less obvious sources, such as Albania (Mora et al. 2015), China (Zhang 2007), Germany (Kosmutzky 2012), Jamaica (Ellis and Miller 2014), Norway (Sataoen 2016; focusing on third mission activities), Poland (Kwiek 2012) and the Ukraine (Hladchenko 2016). Similarly, a few authors examined developments in particular continents, such as Africa (Atuahene 2011) or Europe (Lepori and Kyvik 2010; focusing on universities of applied sciences), regions, such as Asia Pacific (Ng 2012; looking at internationalization), or took a truly global perspective (Puukka and Marmolejo 2008; examining universities' regional missions). Some studies have also focused on particular sectors within post-compulsory education, such as distance education (Lane 2012) and further education (Peeke 1994).

Not surprisingly, the findings from these studies could be somewhat contrasting. Thus, in an American study of institutional mission, Stich and Reeves (2016) concluded that

> beneath the generalized rhetoric of institutional mission statements lie powerful messages seemingly coded with varying forms of class-based academic capital. While students applying to lower-tier institutions are targeted through messages that stress values more aligned with a vocationally based education (irrespective of institutional type), students applying to upper-tier institutions are targeted through messages that communicate values more closely aligned with a particular educational narrative – that of a traditional liberal arts education. (p. 127)

Here the marketing role of the mission statement was clearly to the fore, with different strategies evident in institutions targeting different markets. Compare this, however, to the findings of Kosmutzky's study of German higher education institutions, which indicate that, where mission statements are 'forced on' institutions, they may not have the intended consequences:

> But expectations in the higher education policy discourse in the mid-1990s that mission statement development should guide universities to set priorities and profile them strategically (concentrating on strong subjects, sorting out weaker/ smaller subjects) have not been fulfilled. On the contrary, the detailed analysis of the contents of mission statements shows that, instead of articulating strategic profiles for the development of the organization, mission statements use their existing profiles for constructing advanced organizational images. (2012, p. 69)

Other German research has applied imprinting theory to university missions, recognizing the potential long-term impact of foundational views on the institution's purpose:

> Following recent trends and adapting to a service-oriented institutional logic regarding the contents of a mission statement seem to be hampered by the university's imprint. Moreover, our study shows that the persistence of imprints is influenced by the power and the reputation of a university ... our findings indicate that organizations are able to consciously decide whether they will retain or whether they will break with their imprints. With increasing power, the ability of an organization to persist with its imprint increases. ... In contrast to power, the effect of reputation shows a pull in the opposite direction. Universities with good reputations are more likely to frame their mission statements in line with the contemporary institutional logic, while this framing may play a less important role for universities with lower levels of reputation ... power enables organizations to enhance stability and to risk nonconformity to institutional requirements and trends while reputation is a burden that forces organizations to conform to the expectations of their environment. (Oertel and Soll 2017, p. 15)

Even in the United States, the concern with institutional mission is a relatively recent phenomenon, dating back, tellingly, about sixty years to the immediate post-war period in which higher education became a mass experience:

> In historical perspective, mission differentiation became prominent in the 1950s and 1960s, when state coordinating boards developed and enrollments expanded. Over the past four decades, statewide coordinators, planners and governing boards have considered various structural alternatives for achieving excellence and affordable access for diverse student populations. These alternatives included diversifying campus missions, facilitating transfer and articulation agreements, and providing mechanisms to demonstrate accountability. But even in states with master plans specifying a division of labor and responsibilities, colleges and universities at the same segmental level were able to develop an array of academic programs that were virtually identical from one campus to the next. (Bastedo and Gumport 2003, pp. 342–3)

When most people, rather than a small elite, go to university or college, it can no longer be expected that they will enjoy, or be able to afford, the same – or even a broadly similar – experience (see also the discussion on massification in Chapter 7). From the institution's perspective, there is the need to accommodate greater diversity, both in terms of student characteristics and what is provided for them under the banner of 'higher education'. When set against the demands for a quality higher education for all, this may then pose contradictory challenges:

> Colleges and universities in the US are caught in a bind. On the one hand they are social entities with clear public policy objectives of widening access, being affordable (even in a relatively high tuition and fee system compared to many

other nations), and being of high quality, particularly regarding undergraduate education. On the other hand, they exist in a highly market-driven environment in which public support has not kept pace with institutional needs and educational costs continue to rise. Thus, universities increasingly compete with one another for revenue, including student tuition and fees, private and public contract and research dollars, and income from auxiliary services. In effect, US colleges and universities are pursuing two different sets of priorities, but both are essential to their functioning. The first set of challenges asks institutions to be effective. However, the second set pushes institutions to pursue paths of prestige, which for most can run counter to their effectiveness objectives. (Eckel 2008, p. 176)

The link here with considerations of quality and ranking is clear (see Chapter 6). The discussion of academic drift and institutional isomorphism in the next section is also closely connected.

Like other popular frameworks for researching and thinking about institutional management, the notions of institutional diversity and mission have been widely debated and critiqued. As so often, a good part of this debate has been definitional; that is, what do we mean by institutional diversity and/or institutional mission, and how will we know them when we see them?

Huisman (1995) points out the biological roots of diversity studies, and makes an important distinction between the static concept of diversity (relating to variation at a particular time) and the more dynamic processes of differentiation and diversification. By contrast, with regard to institutional diversity, Birnbaum (1983, p. 37) notes that 'there is no commonly accepted definition that permits it to be used analytically'. He goes on to distinguish between internal diversity – that is the variation within a particular institution – and external diversity, the variation between institutions. With regard to the latter, several types of external diversity are identified: programmatic (the types of courses offered), procedural (how courses are offered), systemic (institutional type, size and control), constituential (student and staff characteristics), reputational, values and climate (or culture), and structural (how institutions are organized and governed). Clearly, measuring and comparing institutions in terms of so many variables is problematic, so most studies confine themselves to a limited number of variables.

Indeed, measurement is a concern in many studies of institutional diversity (e.g. Doucette, Richardson and Fenske 1985; Huisman, Meek and Wood 2007). Following an extensive review of the possible variables to use, and sensitivity testing with data from European systems and institutions, Huisman et al. (2015) conclude that

there is no textbook recipe for how to measure diversity, but the selection of dimensions, variables and analytical methods must be seen in the context of the specific goal of the study and its analytical framework. Good knowledge of the characteristics of measures and variables and their contextualization in the specific empirical setting considered are important issues in this respect. (pp. 377–8)

Two divergent approaches are those of Salini and Turri (2016), who, on the basis of a comparative study of England and Italy, advocate the use of revenue data to measure diversity; and Ferrari and Cowman (2004) who discuss the development of an inventory to accurately measure the perceptions of students at one American university regarding its mission and values.

In addition to the problems of definition and measurement, there are concerns with what the research on institutional diversity actually shows. Thus, in a review of existing diversity research, Van Vught (2008) notes that, even though there is a widespread acceptance that institutional diversity in higher education is a 'good thing', and many governments introduce policies designed to maintain and enhance it,

> environmental pressures (especially governmental regulation) as well as the dominance of academic norms and values are the crucial factors that influence the processes of differentiation and dedifferentiation in higher education systems. In all cases, the empirical observations point in the direction of dedifferentiation and decreasing levels of diversity. The overall impression is that, in empirical reality, the combination of strict and uniform governmental policies and the predominance of academic norms and values leads to homogenization. (pp. 164–5)

What van Vught terms homogenization is also commonly called academic drift (the subject of the next section) or, more broadly, institutional isomorphism. Fumasoli and Huisman (2013) describe the process by which institutions of higher education respond to changing government policy to maintain or adjust their profile within the system as 'institutional positioning'. They present:

> Institutional positioning as the linking pin between universities' actions and system level dynamics. The resource niche is a central concept of this framework and features the position, within the environment, in which universities locate themselves, by selecting the activities, and the relevant resources, according to which they can operate. (p. 163)

The close links between institutional diversity and institutional mission are very evident here, as the particular resource niche in which an individual institution endeavours to position itself clearly both reflects and helps determine its mission. There is also, though, a debate about the reality of the institutional mission. As already noted, there are pressures on institutions to claim excellence in as many areas of work as they reasonably can, thus giving an appearance of a lack of differentiation. Here the physical appearance of the institution – the 'campus space' – can be a much clearer guide to the true nature of the institution:

> While mission statements as artifacts give organizational structure and culture a verbally concrete form, mission itself acts in a rather tacit fashion. Teaching, research, and service compose the content of collegiate mission in general; but faculty members, administrators, and students likely carry out these activities without thinking of their basis in a mission statement. Because it stands out physically in daily institutional life, campus space makes mission, and thus structure and culture, even more tangible. Space behaves like statements of purpose to help define relations between an organization and its constituents. (Fugazzotto 2009, p. 290)

There are three sorts of conclusions that I would draw from this analysis of research on institutional diversity and institutional mission.

First, it is clear that, while the United States is the main origin for this research interest, and continues to dominate, there has been a growing interest internationally, particularly in Europe, and in comparing practice and progress in different countries or systems.

Second, in terms of institutional diversity, there is a clear tension between the desire to maintain and encourage diversity, on the one hand, and the wish to maintain and increase quality, with its concomitant trend towards homogenization.

Third, in terms of institutional mission, and related to the tensions regarding diversity, there are concerns about gaps between rhetoric and reality, and about the impact of marketization pressures on institutional performance.

Academic drift and institutional isomorphism

The theory of academic drift appears to have been first identified by Burgess and Pratt in the UK context, expressing the tendency of higher education institutions of lesser status to aspire to higher status. The first explicit mention of the term in print by these authors that I could find dates from 1972, where Burgess describes a process

> which my colleague John Pratt and I have called 'academic drift'. For over 100 years now it has been assumed that the achievement of status for an individual institution means moving out of the technical college tradition and into the academic one. (Burgess 1972, p. 13)

Two years later they expressed the idea more succinctly in relation to the development of the then polytechnic sector:

> We had every reason to suspect that the historical process of aspiration of colleges created specifically to be different from universities would overwhelm their best intentions, and they would increasingly aspire to university status and increasingly resemble university institutions. (Pratt and Burgess 1974, p. 172)

Academic drift has been a cornerstone of Burgess and Pratt's writing on UK higher education policy and institutional change throughout their careers (for a later example, see Pratt 1997, pp. 11–12), though, prior to 1972, it does not appear to have been explicitly labelled as academic drift (cf. Burgess and Pratt 1970, p. 5). As the quotations given from their work suggest, they have used 'academic drift' both retrospectively and prospectively. Academic drift may thus be viewed as a theory of institutional change.

Of course, neither Burgess nor Pratt was the first to link the words 'academic' and 'drift' together, and neither were they the first to use 'academic drift' to mean an aspiration towards a more academic status. Thus, it is used in this sense in a mid-1960s review of the development of technical education in Nigeria (Kilby 1964); and, forty years earlier, in an American article on the relation of the social worker to education, it is used in a slightly different sense (Hart 1923).

In addition to these previous uses of the term 'academic drift', there are also what we may call precursor theories. These demonstrate how similar ideas tend to crop up in academic life in different times and places. The clearest precursor in this case is the notion of institutional isomorphism, an institutional theory expressing the idea that organizations operating in the same sector tend towards increasing similarity of form and practice. DiMaggio and Powell (1983) suggest that there are three key mechanisms driving institutional isomorphism: coercive, mimetic and normative. The last of these consists largely of professionalization, a process in which higher education institutions are recognized as having a major role.

While clearly a theory that has a broader application than academic drift, the idea of, and mechanisms involved in, institutional isomorphism appear very similar to academic drift. Interestingly, there is no evidence in their writings that Burgess or Pratt knew of or used the theory of institutional isomorphism. There is, however, in the later writings of others, who use both terms almost interchangeably.

Institutional isomorphism has been widely applied, both explicitly and implicitly, in American higher education research, and well before academic drift came to be talked about in the United Kingdom, the United States and elsewhere (e.g. Riesman 1956). Schultz and Stickler (1965) write instead of the vertical or upward extension of higher education institutions and their programmes (see also Lachs 1965).

In America, a range of analogous terms are currently in usage alongside, or instead of, academic drift, including mission creep (e.g. Gonzales 2013) and mission drift (e.g. Jaquette 2013). Here there is a clear link to continuing debates regarding institutional missions and diversity in higher education on both sides of the Atlantic (see the previous section), as well as to more recent concerns with institutional rankings (see the section in Chapter 6).

Kivinen and Rinne (1996) identify a different precursor theory for academic drift, arguing that 'the concept of "academic drift" can ultimately be grounded in Emile Durkheim's (1964) theory of the social division of labor' (p. 97). This suggests that academic drift might be applied at levels other than that of the institution, not just to social groups but potentially to individuals as well.

Academic drift and institutional isomorphism have been applied to the study of higher education and its institutions in many countries, though chiefly in the Western developed world. These include, in addition to the United Kingdom (e.g. Neave 1978), other European nations (e.g. Belgium (Flanders): De Wit and Verhoeven 2003; Denmark: Christensen and Erno-Kjolhede 2011; Germany: Harwood 2005, 2010; Norway: Smeby 2006, Stensaker and Norgard 2001; Sweden: Kaiserfeld 2013; the Netherlands: Goedegebuure and Westerheijden 1991, Griffieon and de Jong 2013), groups of European countries as well as Europe in general (Gellert 1993; Maassen, Moen and Stensaker 2010; Neave 1979), Australia (e.g. Croucher and Woelert 2016; Franklin and McCaig 1979; Meek 1991), South Africa (e.g. Kraak 2009) and the United States (e.g. Baker, Orr and Young 2007; Morphew 2000b).

Some of these analyses have focused on particular disciplines, including, for example, agriculture (Harwood 2010), education (Baker, Orr and Young 2007), engineering (Christensen and Erno-Kjolhede 2011), information science (De Wit and Verhoeven 2003) and nursing (Laiho 2010), and the professions in general (Smeby 2006).

A bibliometric search using Google Scholar found a total of 2,631 publications that had used the term 'academic drift' since 1923. It has featured in publication titles far less commonly, however, with only 34 examples recorded, the first of which was in 1977 (Harman 1977). There has been a steady growth in the use of the term since the 1970s, when Burgess and Pratt started to popularize it. Thus, while Google Scholar records only four mentions of 'academic drift' in academic publications prior to 1970, in the 1970s there were 51; in the 1980s 151; in the 1990s, 324; in the 2000s, 909; and in the 2010s to date, 1,192.

Academic drift has, of course, been subject to development and critique. Early analyses were mainly concerned with either assessing whether the theoretical framework offered by academic drift applied in countries or systems other than the UK; or with critiquing its operation in the UK context.

Neave (1979), noting the prevalence of convergence theory (another analogue or precursor theory) in comparative education, set out to assess the applicability of academic drift elsewhere in Europe. After making an initial distinction between academic drift, institutional drift and policy drift (and, later, personnel drift and drift in curricular emphasis), he argued that academic drift might stem from faulty theory, policy implementation or manpower planning, or from a failure to distinguish between student and economic demand. He considered examples from France, Norway and the then Yugoslavia, finding plentiful evidence in each of policy drift, institutional drift, academic drift and drift in curricular emphasis. Two other early studies, in the Australian context, confirmed the applicability of the theory there, in this case in the colleges of advanced education (Franklin and McCaig 1979; Harman 1977), while Clark (1983) compared the American and British experiences.

Early critiques of the idea of academic drift tended to the view that this was simply a continuing historical trend, and that other institutions were always there to take on the lower-status roles which upwardly mobile institutions were shedding (e.g. Venables 1978). More recent discussions have accepted academic drift as both a theory and a reality, but have sought to understand why it takes place and whether (and how) it is possible to control it. Thus, Harwood (2005, 2010) has examined the development of agricultural colleges in Germany in the late nineteenth and early twentieth centuries, noting that, while some exhibited academic drift, others did not, depending on the attitudes and actions of the various stakeholders involved.

The debate on the impact of contemporary higher education policy notes the extent to which governments will go to either accommodate or try to prevent academic drift (De Wit and Verhoeven 2003). The informed view remains, however, that, notwithstanding the efforts of some governments in periodically creating new institutional sectors with defined responsibilities, in the medium to longer term academic drift is inevitable (Horta, Huisman and Heitor 2008).

Other researchers, like Neave, have sought to unpick the notion of academic drift. Kyvik (2007, p.333) distinguishes between 'six different, though related academisation processes which take place at student level (student drift), staff level (staff drift), programme level (programme drift), institutional level (institutional drift), sector level (sector drift), and governmental level (policy drift)'. There is a clear alignment between some of Kyvik's six levels and those proposed earlier by Neave. What Kyvik refers to as sector drift aligns closely with what most other authors mean when they use the term 'academic drift'.

Kaiserfeld (2013), in a study of eighteenth-century scientific academies, nineteenth-century institutions of higher vocational education and twentieth-century industrial research institutes, takes the discussion elsewhere. He links academic drift with what he terms epistemic drift, which he applied to 'denote a process by which ... scientists tend to place greater weight on the relevance of their research for politically, administratively, or commercially determined goals' (p. 172). Kaiserfeld uses the two processes of academic and epistemic drift to provide an explanation for the continued formation and development of hybrid organizations such as those he examined.

Conclusions

Institutional management is clearly a well-developed area for research into higher education, with close linkages both to business/management schools and to central university administrations. These established strengths do, however, suggest potential directions for future development.

Thus, in methodological terms, more interview-based and conceptual approaches may be used, as well as explicit observational techniques (as compared to the implicit, semi-autobiographical observational techniques that underlay much writing). More research at the level below the institution might also be encouraged, perhaps focusing on espoused management strategies and actual practice and experience. It would also be healthy to see more women and ethnic minority researchers becoming involved in this field, in which they remain significantly under-represented as practitioners.

Chapter 9
Research on Academic Work

Introduction

Higher education researchers, and academics in general, have long displayed a healthy interest in the nature of what they and their colleagues do: that is, academic work. While this may seem to some like obsessive navel gazing, it is an important area of research, as better understanding the different elements of academic work – teaching (see also Chapter 3), research (see also Chapter 10), management and administration (see also Chapter 8), consultancy, outreach activities and so on – can help to improve their delivery.

In one sense – as the cross-references to other chapters of this book in the previous paragraph suggest – all higher education research is research into academic work. In this chapter, therefore, the focus is a little narrower, concentrating on the overall experience of being an academic.

Research trends

A bibliographic search using Scopus identified 901 articles with the words 'academic' and 'work' in their titles, most of which were directly relevant and focused on the topic of this chapter. A minority of the articles identified discussed the academic work carried out by students, which, while relevant, is not the focus of this chapter.

Like most areas of higher education research, the search demonstrated that research and publication on academic work has multiplied in recent years. Thus, while less than ten articles a year were being published in the 1980s with the words 'academic' and 'work' in their titles, this had risen to over forty a year by the end of the 2000s, and around seventy to eighty a year currently.

As expected, over half of the articles identified were authored by researchers based in the main English-speaking countries, with 30 per cent coming from the United States (e.g. Beigi, Shirmohammedi and Kim 2016; Jensen 1982; Kleinhans et al. 2015), 12 per cent from the United Kingdom (e.g. Burgess 1996; Coate and Howson 2016; Locke 2012), 8 per cent from Australia (e.g. Currie and Eveline 2011; Harman 1990; Lafferty and Fleming 2000) and 4 per cent from Canada (e.g. Acker, Webber and Smyth 2016; Jones 2013; Martimianakis and Muzzin 2015).

Nevertheless, this means that nearly half (46 per cent) of the articles came from other countries. These included China (Lai and Li 2014), Finland (Ylijoki and Hendriksson 2015), Israel (Toren 1991), Korea (Lee and Jung 2017), Malaysia (Salehi, Rasdi and Ahmad 2015), New Zealand (Koopman-Boyden and Macdonald 2003), Norway (Nyhagen and Baschung 2013), Poland (Kwiek 2015b), Portugal (Santiago and Carvalho 2008), South Africa (Barkhuisen, Rothmann and van der Vijver 2016), Spain (Ramos, Palacin and Marquez 2015) and Sweden (Melin, Astvik and Bernhard-Oettel 2014).

Among the particular aspects of academic work being studied, the related issues of the work/family relationship and the position of women academics were popular. The former area of research focused on a range of related themes, including work/family conflict (Beigi, Shirmohammedi and Kim 2016), work–life balance (Cannizzo and Osbaldiston 2016), work–life choices (Isaac et al. 2014), well-being (Kinman and Jones 2008), coping strategies and health (Melin, Astvik and Bernhard-Oettel 2014), casualization (Courtney 2013, Jones 2013), insecurity (Knights and Clarke 2014) and burnout (Barkhuisen, Rothmann and van der Vijver 2016). More positively framed studies examined work/family enrichment (Salehi, Rasdi and Ahmad 2015) and the adoption of family-friendly policies in higher education (Feeney, Bernal and Bowman 2014).

The latter area includes a large number of studies which have examined the (changing) position of women in academe (e.g. Acker, Webber and Smyth 2016; Jensen 1982; Poole, Bornholt and Summers 1997; Toren 1991), as well as research that has targeted more specific questions, such as the role of women as senior academics (Coate and Howson 2016), their use of online technology (Menzies and Newson 2008), and whether men and women perform academic work differently (Ramos, Palacin and Marquez 2015). Other researchers have studied the particular circumstances of younger (e.g. Jones et al. 2012; Ylijoki and Hendriksson 2015), older (e.g. Davies and Jenkins 2013; Koopman-Boyden and Macdonald 2003) and expatriate academics (e.g. Austin et al. 2014; Smith 2009). The issue of part-time and temporary academic staff, seen as both a growing reliance and a problem as systems have massified, has also long been of research interest (e.g. Kimber 2003; Rajagopal and Farr 1989).

Taking a more managerial perspective, the issue of academic workload, how it is measured and how it has changed, has been a continuing focus for research (e.g. Bentley and Kyvik 2012; Burgess 1996; Harman 1990). More recently, this has included consideration of the impact of performance management or performativity more generally (e.g. Kenny 2017; Santiago and Carvalho 2008), and of competing work roles and how they are handled (Boyd and Smith 2016; Lai, Du and Li 2014). The increasing role of academic or educational development in preparing and supporting academics in their roles has also, naturally enough, become a topic for research (e.g. Amundsen and Wilson 2012; Boud and Brew 2013).

More generally, the question of how academic work has changed over time, and in particular systems, has been a concern (e.g. Beach 2013; Nyhagen and Baschung 2013). Here, data collected in the course of a succession of international/comparative studies, focusing primarily on Western, developed countries, has been particularly illuminating (Altbach 1996; Enders 2001). Most recently, studies of change in academic work have been re-focused as an examination of succeeding academic generations (e.g. Kleinhans et al. 2015; Kwiek 2015b).

Unsurprisingly, academic work has been the subject of edited and authored books; recent examples include Fitzgerald, White and Gunter (2012) and Leisyte and Wilkesmann (2016).

Research designs and frameworks

The three research frameworks to be considered in more detail here – academic tribes and territories, academic identities and communities of practice – each have their particular interest and adherents. Academic tribes and territories, associated in particular with Becher, can be seen as the English version of a more general framework, notably popular in the United States. The interest in academic identity, and how it is changing, is the specifically higher education version of a much more widespread interest – in psychology, sociology and other disciplines – in identity. Communities of practice, a framework developed on the borderlands between management and education, could be seen as another, more recent (but also more generic) version of tribes and territories.

Academic tribes and territories

Research and writing about tribes and territories in higher education is particularly associated with Becher, who published his key text on the topic, *Academic Tribes and Territories*, in 1989 (Becher 1989a). Becher had been working on the topic for several years when this book was published (Becher 1981, 1984, 1987), and continued to do so for more than a decade afterwards (e.g. Becher 1989b, 1990, 1994, 1999). A second edition of the book was published in 2001, with Trowler, who had been critical of some aspects of it, brought in as co-author (Becher and Trowler 2001).

Becher's research was driven by the underlying assumption that 'there are identifiable patterns to be found within the relationship between knowledge forms and their associated knowledge communities' (1989a, 150). In order to explore these patterns he undertook

> two long-term empirical investigations. ... The first, which occupied most of the period from 1980 to 1988, involved a study of research norms and practices in 12 contrasting disciplinary fields (biology, chemistry, economics, engineering, geography, history, law, mathematics, modern languages, pharmacy, physics and sociology). The second, which began in 1988 and was completed in 1993, focused specifically on the issue of graduate education in six of the same fields. Altogether,

> some 350 in-depth, semi-structured interviews with academics and research
> students provided the main data for the two studies. (Becher 1994, p. 151)

Data was collected in the United Kingdom and the United States (California), with a deliberate focus on high status departments.

Becher identified 'four basic sets of properties: hard/soft and pure/applied in the cognitive realm; convergent/divergent and urban/rural in the social' (1989a, p. 153). Hard disciplines (e.g. physics, pharmacy) are those with an agreed paradigm and where knowledge is cumulative; soft disciplines (e.g. history, sociology), by contrast, are more contested and less cumulative. Pure/applied concerns the degree to which research is directed towards understanding something that interests the researcher or towards solving practical problems. Chemistry and mathematics, for example, would be (primarily) classified as pure disciplines, engineering and law as applied.

The other two dichotomies identified by Becher may seem less obvious. Convergent/divergent, which other researchers have termed consensus (e.g. Braxton and Hargens 1996; Lodahl and Gordon 1972), has to do with how tightly knit the discipline is. Finally, while urban researchers are 'clustered around comparatively few salient topics', often working in collaboration, rural researchers are 'spread out thinly across a wide range of themes' (Becher 1989a, p. 79). This last dimension has been much less used than the others.

Becher's key text concluded that

> the overall picture is of academic institutions made up of basic organizational
> units whose constituent faculty members have relatively little mutuality of research
> interest … different categories of specialism (pure and applied, hard and soft, urban
> and rural) may well coexist within the confines of a single small department. …
> From this perspective, departments have indeed a notable resemblance to holding
> companies for their members, much as institutions can be portrayed as holding
> companies for their basic units. (1989a, pp. 163–4)

Becher traces his interest in this topic as a response to being irritated with the simplistic arguments put forward by Snow (1959, 1964) in his analysis of the 'two cultures' (i.e. science and art) in academic life. Becher also quotes Bailey (1977), who had previously used tribes and territories as a metaphor for academic life. Becher's categorization of the disciplines builds upon earlier work, most notably by Pantin (1968), Kuhn (1962), Biglan (1973a,b) and Kolb (1984). Other precursors included Hagstrom (1965), Storer (1967, 1972) and Whitley (1984/2000), all of whom Becher refers to and discusses.

Biglan appears to have been the major influence, however, and his work continues to be so to this day, sometimes linked with that of Kolb as the Biglan/Kolb model. Interestingly, this model has evolved in parallel to Becher's, but is more popular on the American side (Biglan and Kolb were both American) than the European side of the Atlantic: another example of the tendency of researchers, at least those focusing on higher education, to operate within national 'silos' (Shahjahan and Kezar 2013; Tight 2014b).

Biglan (1973a,b) used multidimensional scaling to compare the judgements of academics at one university and one small college in the United States about the similarities, or differences, between different disciplinary areas. He concluded that there were three key characteristics that differentiated between disciplines: (i) the existence of a paradigm; (ii) a concern with application; and (iii) a concern with life systems. While Becher kept the hard/soft and pure/applied dimensions (i.e. the cognitive realm, as he termed it), he discarded the life/non-life dichotomy and added the convergent/divergent and urban/rural dimensions (his social realm) instead.

Biglan's findings have been tested and verified by a series of American scholars, including Cresswell and Bean (1981a,b), Malaney (1986) and Stoecker (1993), with the last of these arguing that the expanded classification put forward by Becher also merited further consideration. Interestingly, in an extensive overview of research in this area, Braxton and Hargens (1996, p. 6) argued that Biglan had been fortunate in gaining attention for his work while Storer (1967, 1972) earlier had not. Biglan's classification has, however, stood up to the test of time (Simpson 2015).

Braxton and Hargens were measured in their assessment of Becher's contribution, noting that his framework was 'obviously at an early stage of development' (1996, p. 8). They concluded:

> Most of the disciplinary differences revealed by our survey are related to variations in levels of scholarly consensus. … Faculty in high-consensus fields are more oriented to research. … Academic departments in high-consensus fields tend to be more effective organizations … high-consensus fields tend to be more universalistic. (p. 36)

As this line of research continued in America (e.g. Fuchs 1992), others were also studying the effects of disciplinarity in higher education in the UK (Evans 1988, 1993).

Becher (1996, 1999) later extended his analysis to include a range of the professions (medicine, pharmacy, law, accountancy, architecture and structural engineering) and their relationships with higher education. The second edition of *Academic Tribes and Territories* (Becher and Trowler 2001) also updated and expanded the first, including some new material and data to take the emphasis away from elite universities and the research role, and to recognize the specific concerns and issues faced by women and ethnic minority academics.

The idea of tribes and territories has been widely applied within higher education research. A search through Google Scholar found a total of around 6,200 academic publications that used the exact phrase 'academic tribes and territories'. Of these, a much smaller number, just twelve (mostly Becher's and Trowler's books, and reviews thereof), used the term in their titles. Interest in, and publishing on, tribes and territories in higher education has expanded decade by decade, and particularly most recently, such that 90 per cent of the articles mentioning academic tribes and territories have been published since 2000.

Becher's model of academic tribes and territories has been applied in a variety of contexts within higher education. It is, for example, referenced and acknowledged in research focusing on academic cultures, sub-cultures and identities (Silver

2003; Välimaa 1998; Ylijoki 2000), academic development (Bath and Smith 2004; Blackmore 2007), doctoral education (Parry 2007), higher education research (Tight 2008), interdisciplinarity (Bird 2001), internationalization (Clifford 2009), knowledge validation (Donald 1995), leadership and management (Kekäle 1999), quality (Kekäle 2002), research (Brew 2008), teacher education (Menter 2011) and teaching and learning (Lindblom-Ylanne et al. 2006; Neumann 2001; Smeby 1996).

The notion of tribes and territories has also been utilized by researchers working in particular fields or disciplines (i.e. tribes), including geography (Johnston 1996), health (Pirrie 1999), management (Tranfield 2002), psychology (Donald 1995), sociology (Ylijoki 2000), tourism studies (Tribe 2010) and women's studies (Stanley 1997).

Becher's framework has been most commonly applied by researchers who were based, like he was, in the UK (e.g. Menter 2011; Silver 2003). His work has spread internationally as well, however, with the idea of tribes and territories applied by researchers in a variety of countries, including Australia (Brew 2008; Krause 2014; Neumann 2001), Canada (Donald 1995), Italy (Boffo and Moscati 1998), Finland (Lindblom-Ylanne et al. 2006; Välimaa 1998) and Norway (Smeby 1996). Higher education researchers based in the United States, and researching disciplinarity and/ or academic work (e.g. Brint et al. 2005; Cashin and Downey 1995), are much more likely to refer to Biglan, Kolb and other American researchers, and to overlook Becher.

Interestingly, some of the research referred to links tribes and territories with other theoretical frameworks. For example, Hyland (2012) links discipline with identity (academic or student; see the next section), referencing his own work when he refers to academic culture, and Becher when he refers to academic tribe. Tribes and territories have also been linked to the idea of threshold concepts (discussed in Chapter 4), which suggests that, within any discipline, there are particular concepts which students find difficult to understand, and which represent thresholds that they need to overcome if they are to progress (Carmichael 2012). A third example is communities of practice, which offers another framework for thinking about how academics work together (Parker 2002, Tight 2008), and is discussed later in this chapter.

Becher's latter-day co-author, Trowler, returned to the topic of tribes and territories recently (2009) in a critical vein: 'The problem with this kind of categorization is that while it seems to make sense when disciplines are viewed through the wrong end of a telescope, from a great distance, the distinctions begin to fall apart in the analytical band when one looks at disciplines close up' (p. 183). Trowler suggests a more flexible analysis informed by ideas of structure, agency and context. Trowler subsequently co-edited a review of the state of thinking on the topic (Trowler et al. 2012), concluding that 'the metaphor of tribes and territories has probably outlived its usefulness' (p. 257).

Earlier criticisms of Becher's work noted its focus on the research function in elite institutions, and on what might be termed the traditional disciplines. His later research went some way towards answering these criticisms, and other researchers have also filled in gaps by applying the idea of tribes and territories to a broader range of disciplines (e.g. Pirrie 1999; Tranfield 2002; Tribe 2010). Similarly, it would be quite possible to extend the analysis to characterize different kinds (sub-tribes) of sub-disciplines, as well as interdisciplinary developments.

A more fundamental objection to the tribes and territories framework is that it promotes the idealization and simplification of disciplines (Välimaa 1998), a criticism which Trowler (2009) seems to share. Trowler is also not alone in arguing that the tribes and territories framework can no longer bear the weight that is being put upon it (see, for example, Brew 2008). Bearing these critiques in mind, we might conclude that the tribes and territories framework has both strengths and limitations; and that, while some higher education researchers have rejected it, others continue to use it. We might then ask whether there were alternative and/or better frameworks available for thinking about academics, disciplines and their relationships, and about the policies that impact upon them.

There are quite a few alternative theoretical frameworks that might be applied, including two – communities of practice and academic identity – that have already been mentioned and which are discussed in more detail in the succeeding sections of this chapter. Communities of practice offers a way of thinking about the groups or networks which help guide, regulate and make meaning of our lives, in work and outside. Theories of identity have been developed over many decades in both psychology and sociology, and have been fairly widely applied to the study of both students' and academics' identities.

Modes of knowledge offer a third alternative framework, one particularly associated with the work of Gibbons and his collaborators (Gibbons et al. 1994; Nowotny et al. 2001), who have argued that what they call Mode 1 knowledge – conventional university research and scholarship of the kind originally studied by Becher – is being increasingly superseded by Mode 2 knowledge. The latter is typically transdisciplinary, and is likely to be created (and used) outside rather than inside universities, though perhaps in collaboration with academics. While the strength of the argument is debatable, Mode 2 type knowledge creation and organization has been increasingly studied (e.g. Adler et al. 2000; Kogan 2005).

Academic identities

Research and writing on academic identity – as on most other topics in higher education research – has grown substantially over the last few decades. Thus, while only one or two articles with the term 'academic identity' in their titles, indicating their focus on this topic, were published each year during the 1990s – according to a search using Scopus – the current figure is around fifty to sixty per year. While a few of these consider academic identity at other levels of education – for example, among secondary school students preparing for university and college – the great majority are concerned with higher education. Interest in academic identity has grown to the extent that a biennial international conference on the topic has been in successful operation for several years (Grant et al. 2014).

Research into academic identity focuses on both higher education students and academic staff, and also extends to others involved in the academy. While much of the interest in students' academic identity is focused on undergraduates (e.g. Attenborough 2011; Jensen and Jetten 2016), students at other levels have also been studied, including those taking doctorates (Alexander, Harris-Huemmert and McAlpine 2014). For academic staff there has been a particular focus on new or younger academics (e.g. Archer 2008; McAlpine, Amundsen and Turner 2014; Smith 2017; van Winkel et al. 2017), and on how their academic identities have been affected by changes in higher education policy and practice. The academic identity of older, established academics has also been of interest, however (Calvert, Lewis and Spindler 2011; Henkel 2000; Weiland 1995), particularly those designated as academic managers (Barry, Berg and Chandler 2006), who face the challenge of balancing their roles as academics and as managers.

In addition to the continuing interest in the academic identities of students and academics, more recently there has been a small but growing body of research examining the academic identities of others who work in the academy, notably academic administrators – that is those who keep higher education institutions running (e.g. Collinson 2006; Whitchurch and Gordon 2010) – and academic developers – that is those who train academics (e.g. Leibowitz, Ndebele and Winberg 2014). An interesting difference here is that, while those who research academic administrators are predominantly academics, those researching academic developers are overwhelmingly themselves academic developers, concerned with understanding and promoting the nature and significance of their own roles.

Within the general literature on academic identity, particular emphasis has been placed by some researchers on investigating the effects of gender (e.g. Stroude et al. 2015; Tsouroufli 2016; Walker 1998), ethnicity (e.g. Miller-Cotto and Byrnes 2016; Oyserman and Lewis 2017; White and Lowenthal 2011) and, most recently, sexuality (Maritz and Prinsloo 2015; Rothmann 2016).

Another strong focus for research has been on the role of the discipline in forming and supporting students' and academics' academic identity. For example, researchers have examined the topic in the context of the disciplines of communication (Gronbeck 2005), design (Jawitz 2009), engineering education (Winberg 2008), English (Chan 2016), experimental psychology (Ash 1980), health professions (Boyd and Smith 2016), nurse education (Findlow 2012), occupational therapy (Fortune et al. 2016), science (Henkel 2004) and teacher education (White et al. 2014). A clear interest here has been on disciplines that are relatively new to the academy, such that their academic identity would have to be consciously developed.

A related focus for research has been on students' or academics' professional identity (e.g. Jensen and Jetten 2016), particularly in disciplines (e.g. education, engineering, nursing) with a strong link to a specific profession. Other researchers have examined academics' organizational identity – that is their identity with their employer rather than their discipline – particularly in the context, all too common these days, of organizational (Mills et al. 2005) or curriculum restructuring (Moore 2003).

The key role of academic writing in developing academic identity has been another specialist interest for researchers on this topic, particularly for those with a background in linguistics (e.g. Cheung et al. 2016; Hyland 2002; Lea and Stierer 2009; Tang and John 1999). There are close links here to research on academic literacies (discussed in Chapter 4). A related literature examines the impact of digital technologies on academic identity (e.g. Hanson 2009; Kirkup 2010 (who studied academics who blog), McNaughton and Billot 2016 (who examined the use of videoconferencing)).

While much of the literature on academic identity examined here, naturally enough, comes from the main English-speaking countries, there are examples of its application in research based elsewhere, including, for example, China (Huang, Pang and Yu 2016), Finland (Ylijoki and Ursin 2013), Indonesia (Gaus and Hall 2013), Macau (Hao 2016), the Netherlands (van Winkel et al. 2017) and Sweden (Barry, Berg and Chandler 2006).

There has also been interest in the development and application of particular methodologies for researching academic identity. Thus, Learmonth and Humphreys (2011) explore the use of autoethnography to study their experience of academic conferences (see also Ai 2017), while McLean (2012) employs discursive psychology rather than the more usual sociological approaches, and Pick, Symons and Teo (2015) consider the examination of narrative fiction as a means of exploring aspects of academic identity that are more difficult to access.

Pifer and Baker (2016) usefully summarize the driving forces underlying much of the research into academic identity:

A personal approach to understanding the salience of identity for individuals is critical to the development of satisfied and successful faculty members and, ultimately, the state of the profession. Full consideration of experiences in the professoriate must go beyond the formal roles of teaching, research, and service to explore the equally important influence of discipline and career stage, interpersonal relationships, familial responsibilities and community roles, and individual characteristics and identities. Members of today's academy seek meaningful professional careers that validate and integrate their identities at all stages of their work. (p. 203)

Most of the literature on academic identity is not so much critical of academic identity as using it to help mount a critique on something else. A rare example of the former is a brief piece by Neary and Winn (2016), who simply dismiss academic identity research as inadequate: 'The concept of "academic identity" is not adequate to the critical task for which it is utilised as it fails to deal with the real nature of work in capitalist society' (p. 409). They then outline an alternative Marxist approach.

Without a doubt, the most common critique currently mounted in academic identity research concerns the impact of managerialism and/or neo-liberalism on academic work (e.g. Beck and Young 2005; Degn 2016; Henkel 2000; Watson 2011; Winter 2009; see also the discussion of managerialism in Chapter 8). This literature typically argues that practices have changed dramatically during the last few decades, and that the 'traditional' (or, for the more cynical, mythical) academic identity – of an individual who researched, taught or learnt what they choose, without limitation and under little pressure – is under threat.

For example, here is Archer (2008) arguing that the identities available to many academics are now limited and under continual re-negotiation:

> The contemporary neoliberal context, with its emphasis on performativity, mitigates against the achievement of secure or stable academic identities … the 'authentic' and 'successful' academic is a desired yet refused identity for many younger academics, and is especially amplified through matrices of 'race'/ethnicity, social class, gender and age. Hence younger academics from minority ethnic and working-class backgrounds, and those who are contract researchers, find it particularly difficult to inhabit identities of success/authenticity with any sense of permanence or legitimacy. That is, they must negotiate on a daily basis not only their attempts at 'becoming' but also the threat of 'unbecoming'. (p. 401)

A similar analysis is provided by Barry, Berg and Chandler (2006), based on a comparative study of England and Sweden: 'Academics in Sweden and England have been (re)negotiating the relations of organization and identity in the face of pressures to make them more managerial … academics have been engaged in *academic shape shifting*, to manage expectations as they draw on their experience, within a field of opportunities and constraints, seen here as compromises, in order to (re)position themselves and cope with recent change' (p. 290, emphasis in original).

Another key issue commonly identified in the academic identity literature concerns the growing complexity of academic life, something that is fairly evident from the range of topics focused on in that literature:

> The issue of academic identity is complex and … cannot, in any simple sense, be read off from descriptions of mainly teaching, research, or management roles. Academic identities were being actively shaped and developed in response to the changes in university structures and external environments; hybridity in relationship to discipline and place was common. Yet respondents in all roles were able to maintain highly distinctive, strongly framed academic projects of the self. The newer emerging identities, or hybrids, were mostly not shaped by a reference to nostalgia for an elitist past, but were based on different epistemological assumptions derived from other professional and practice based loyalties. (Clegg 2008, p. 34)

Indeed, the impact of managerialism and/or neo-liberalism is seen as one of the main reasons driving both change and increasing complexity:

> Our results speak for multiplicity and diversification of the ways in which academic identity is understood and enacted. Although academic identity has never formed a unified and monolithic entity but has been differentiated foremost by disciplinary communities and also by institutional settings, it seems that this differentiation has multiplied due to the managerial and structural transformations in the university environment. Furthermore, the identity constructions embedded in the nine

narratives presented in this study include polarized notions of academic roles, duties, commitments and status. Being a rebel, loser, overloaded worker, or a member of the precariat is totally different from being a winner, mobile careerist, or change agent, and has different implications. The respective identities of a devoted parent and a bystander fall between these opposites, stirring further the overall picture of what being an academic may mean. (Ylijoki and Ursin 2013, p. 1147)

In these circumstances, we can, of course, no longer talk of an academic identity as if it is relatively uniform and shared (as if it ever was); we must instead recognize an increasing diversity of academic identities, driven in part by the academic roles we are given or sign up for, and in part by how we choose or are able to interpret them.

Communities of practice

The origins of the use of the term 'communities of practice' may be traced to a research group in California in the 1980s (Kimble 2006). Who actually came up with the term is, however, unclear, though Lave and/or Wenger are usually credited. Wenger (1998) suggests that Lave first came up with the term sometime before they wrote their 1991 book together; though he also reports that she credits him with it. Prior to coming up with the term, the researchers involved had been engaged, separately and collectively, in a range of related projects. Lave showed a particular interest in the everyday use of mathematics (Lave 1988; Lave, Murtaugh and de la Rocha 1984; Rogoff and Lave 1984), while others in the group were more concerned with organizational learning (e.g. Brown, Collins and Duguid 1989; Brown and Duguid 1991).

As with many such initiatives, a key stimulus to the development of communities of practice was a reaction against previous thinking, in this case the notion that skills and knowledge could be learnt in a classroom and then seamlessly transferred to a real-life (work or non-work) setting. Instead, learning was seen as situated within the particular circumstances in which the learner found themselves, and would vary depending upon those circumstances. In other words, the researchers were seeking to emphasize the social (or sociocultural) rather than the psychological aspects of learning.

Of course, both the terms 'community' and 'practice' have long been in use, but Lave and Wenger do appear to be the first to have linked them together as 'communities of practice'. Early writers on communities of practice drew particular attention to the 'community' element, referencing Williams (1976/1988), who describes community as a 'warmly persuasive word' that 'never seems to be used unfavourably' (p. 76). One consequence of this is that the 'practice' element has had to be re-emphasized periodically (e.g. Brown and Duguid 2001).

In their key early text, *Situated Learning: Legitimate Peripheral Participation*, Lave and Wenger (1991) note that their original intention had been 'to rescue the idea of *apprenticeship*' (p. 29). They use data from studies of Mayan midwives, Vai and Gola tailors (eventually written up in Lave 2011; see also Scribner and Cole 1981), US navy quartermasters, supermarket butchers and non-drinking alcoholics as 'examples of apprenticeship from different cultural and historical traditions' (Lave and Wenger 1991, p. 62). But, rather than focus on apprenticeship as such, they discuss learning as both a situated and social practice:

> In our view, learning is not merely situated in practice – as if it were some independently reifiable process that just happened to be located somewhere; learning is an integral part of generative social practice in the lived-in world. (p. 35)

The groups whose behaviours they analysed they termed communities of practice, within which 'newcomers' could learn from 'old-timers' through a process they termed legitimate peripheral participation: 'Viewing learning as legitimate peripheral participation means that learning is not merely a condition for membership, but is itself an evolving form of membership' (p. 53). Legitimate peripheral participation 'provides a way to speak about the relations between newcomers and old-timers, and about activities, identities, artifacts, and communities of knowledge and practice' (p. 29). They defined a community of practice as 'a set of relations among persons, activity, and world, over time and in relation with other tangential and overlapping communities of practice' (p. 98).

At any one time, of course, every individual would likely be involved in a number of communities of practice – at work or in their social lives – though some would probably be much more significant than others. Individuals' experiences within communities of practice might not be positive, and issues of power were crucial: 'Control and selection, as well as the need for access, are inherent in communities of practice' (p. 103).

Following the publication of their key text, other authors produced studies of different communities of practice. For example, Orr's (1996) study of photocopier technicians is stated in the book's foreword as putting 'the flesh of everyday life on Lave and Wenger's idea of a community of practice' (p. xiii), though Orr doesn't himself reference Lave or Wenger in the book.

In a second key text, Wenger (1998) uses claims processing as another example of a community of practice. In this text, Wenger also adds further detail to the theory. Stressing practice as well as community, he identifies 'three dimensions of the relation by which practice is the source of coherence of a community … mutual engagement … a joint enterprise … a shared repertoire' (pp. 72–3). In a later article, linking communities of practice with boundaries and identities, he argues:

> Communities of practice are the basic building blocks of a social learning system because they are the social 'containers' of the competences that make up such a system. By participating in these communities, we define with each other what constitutes competence in a given context. (Wenger 2000, p. 229)

Working with two other collaborators (Wenger, McDermott and Snyder 2002), Wenger then produced a guidebook to the cultivation of communities of practice, arguing that they were an essential key to success in a global knowledge economy. Lave continued to focus on the practice of learning (Lave 1993), and went on to study other communities, including the British involved in the port wine trade in Porto (Lave 2001). This divergence in interest is reflected in the contributions Lave and Wenger made separately to a recent edited collection on learning theory (Lave 2009; Wenger 2009).

By the mid-2000s, when the theory of communities of practice had been developed, discussed and applied for a decade and a half, it was time for some appraisal of what had been achieved. Unsurprisingly, Cox noted that

> usage of the term is very diverse. Sometimes it is a conceptual lens through which to examine the situated social construction of meaning. At other times it is used to refer to a virtual community or informal group sponsored by an organization to facilitate knowledge sharing or learning. (2005, p. 527)

Not surprisingly, in the organizational literature, the latter had become the dominant usage. Others also noted this shift in usage and practice (e.g. Lea 2005). Kimble (2006) went further in identifying three periods in the development of the theory, arguing that communities of practice had 'undergone a transition from being a heuristic device to a theory and from a theory to an application' (p. 230). Kimble also noted that the popularity and diversity of use of communities of practice was leading to increasing critique.

Communities of practice has been described as 'one of the most articulated and developed concepts within broad social theories of learning' (Barton and Tusting 2005b, p. 1). As continuing evidence of this, a search on Google Scholar indicates that over 220,000 academic articles mention the term, with around 3,600 using it in their titles. This usage has increased rapidly, decade by decade, since Lave and Wenger first introduced the idea to the academic world.

Lang and Canning (2010) carried out a citation analysis of Lave and Wenger's (1991) book over the period between 1991 and 2001, with a particular focus on educational research in the United Kingdom, and, to a lesser extent, in the United States. They found that

> in the 10 years following the publication of the book, until the end of 2001, the journal citation data provided by the Web of Knowledge citation index lists 856 citations to this text. Of these citations, 371 appeared in education journals. ... Within education, the majority of citations to *Situated Learning* come from US-based writers. Writers in the UK ... were slower to cite this text after its appearance, but their citation rate increased markedly from 1998 onward. (Lang and Canning 2010, p. 296)

The extensive literature that now exists on communities of practice includes a number of books devoted to the topic (e.g. Barton and Tusting 2005a; Hughes, Jewson and Unwin 2007; Kimble, Hildreth and Bourdon 2008a, b; Kopaczyk and Jucker 2013), as well as numerous articles in academic journals. Of course, not all of these are concerned with higher education, but many are, at least to some extent.

Of those articles and books that do concern themselves with communities of practice as applied to higher education, one telling point is the range of disciplinary contexts they deal with. For example, in addition to the more common contexts of education and business/management, there are publications focusing on communities of practice in relation to accounting (Stephenson 2017), architecture (Morton 2012), English (Kopaczyk and Jucker 2013), information science (Cox 2005), linguistics (Holmes and Meyerhoff 1999), music (Hewitt 2009; Virkkula 2016), psychology (Linehan and McCarthy 2001), the STEM disciplines (science, technology, engineering and mathematics; Kezar, Gehrke and Bernstein-Sierra 2017) and tourism (Albrecht 2012).

Articles focusing on communities of practice from within the broad business/management discipline are probably the most common (e.g. Easterby-Smith et al. 1998; Ng and Pemberton 2013; Warhurst 2008), but articles based within and focused on education are also numerous (e.g. Edwards 2005; Hammersley 2005; Hodkinson and Hodkinson 2003). In the interface between the business/management and education disciplines, there have been numbers of studies applying communities of practice to, for example, apprenticeship (its original focus; Fuller and Unwin 2003), workplace learning (Fuller et al. 2005), organizational learning (Contu and Willmott 2003) and organizational change (Hendry 1996).

As well as the sheer volume and disciplinary distribution of writing about communities of practice, its geographical spread is also notable. In addition to the obvious English-speaking nations of Australia (e.g. Nagy and Burch 2009; Pharo et al. 2014), Canada (e.g. Hodges 1998; Morita 2004), Ireland (Donnelly 2008), New Zealand (e.g. Albrecht 2012; Janson and Howard 2004) and the United Kingdom (e.g. Cousin and Deepwell 2005; Elwood and Klenowski 2002), there are examples of English language outputs on higher education from authors based in China (Zhan and Wan 2016), Finland (Annala and Makinen 2016), Germany (Johnson 2001), Japan (Umino and Benson 2016), Malaysia (Ng and Pemberton 2013), the Netherlands (Cremers and Valkenburg 2008) and South Africa (Hodgkinson-William, Slay and Sieborger 2008). Clearly then, if not completely global, thinking and writing about communities of practice has certainly been widespread.

The range of topics which communities of practice theory has been used to research is also impressive. Within higher education, this includes themes such as academic development (Donnelly 2008; Malcolm and Zukas 2000), academic writing (Kent et al. 2017), access provision (James, Busher and Suttill 2016), assessment (Elwood and Klenowski 2002; Grainger et al. 2017; Price 2005), corporate universities (Nagy and Burch 2009), curriculum reform (Annal and Makinen 2016), group work (Fearon, McLaughlin and Eng 2012), guest lectures (Albrecht 2012), learning technology (Dempster et al. 2004), microblogging (Lewis and Rush 2013), online seminars (Putz and Arnold 2001), practice-based learning (Hodge, Wright and Mozeley 2014), research students (Janson and Howard 2004), second language learning (Morita 2004), studying abroad (Umino and Benson 2016), teacher education (Hodges 1998), teaching (Klein and Connell 2008) and theory (Tummons 2012).

One particular area in which communities of practice theory has taken on a life of its own is in the study of online communities (e.g. Huysman, Wenger and Wulf 2003; Johnson 2001; Palloff and Pratt 2007; Renninger and Shumar 2002). Of note here is the parallel use of analogous frameworks. Thus, Hildreth and Kimble (2004) propose the use of a networks of practices model, while Garrison, Anderson and Archer (2000, 2010) develop a community of inquiry framework. We may also note the use of further, similarly named, frameworks in studies of group and societal learning, including, for example, both community of learners (Brown 1994) and learning communities (Lenning et al. 2013). Rogoff (2003, p. 284), a previous co-author of Lave's, uses a similar concept of 'guided practice' instead of legitimate peripheral participation.

Communities of practice has also been linked to, or compared with, a range of other theories, including, for example, activity theory (Edwards 2005; Engeström 2009; discussed in Chapter 4), actor–network theory (Fox 2000), ecological learning systems (Hall 2017), habitus (Mutch 2003), learning architectures (Tummons 2014) and tribes and territories (Tight 2008; discussed earlier in this chapter).

As already indicated, communities of practice theory has been the subject of a variety of critiques over the two decades since it was first articulated. These critiques have extended beyond the concerns with diversity and shift in usage (Handley et al. 2006; Hughes 2007; Lea 2005), the lack of attention paid to power relations (Contu and Wilmott 2003; Fuller et al. 2005), and the relative attention given to community as opposed to practice, though these concerns remain. Thus, Easterby-Smith et al. (1998) have argued that the theory can only be applied to particular kinds of community, while Edwards (2005) suggests that it has little to say about the learning of new things as opposed to established practices. Fuller et al. (2005) consider that it underplays the roles of teaching and learner identity (discussed in the previous subsection).

Given these varied and persistent critiques, perhaps the most concerning criticism is that communities of practice theory has not been developed further; Lang and Canning (2010) found little in the way of cumulative research. It might be argued that communities of practice are too easy to apply, providing a ready-made and swiftly intelligible theoretical framework for thinking about any group of individuals with shared interests. Does labelling such groups as communities of practice advance our analysis sufficiently far forward?

Conclusions

Academic work is, then, both a lively and a contested area of higher education research. Academics display a continuing interest in researching and understanding their own practice, and the three theoretical frameworks considered in detail in this chapter – academic tribes and territories, academic identities, communities of practice – have clear linkages and overlaps. They also have the benefit of not just focusing on academics themselves, but of allowing the study of the role of students alongside that of academics, as well as the other members of (non-academic) staff who contribute to the academic enterprise. These two latter areas are relatively under-researched when compared to studies focusing solely on academics, so should be priorities for further research.

Chapter 10
Research on Knowledge and Research

Introduction

The subject of this chapter – rather like the previous chapter – may sound rather introspective. Researching research, and the knowledge which it is expected to lead to, does sound a bit circular. Yet research is one of the key roles of higher education (along with teaching, which was examined in Chapter 3) and knowledge is probably the simplest and most fundamental way of explaining what higher education is about. So it is critically important to better understand how we go about creating, organizing and disseminating knowledge, in order that we might improve both our practices and our understanding.

Research trends

Research into research and knowledge in higher education is fairly extensive. Thus, a search using Scopus identified 1,285 articles with the words 'research', 'higher' and 'education' in their titles, and a further 523 with the words 'knowledge', 'higher' and 'education'. Currently, over 100 such articles are being published each year focusing on research in higher education, and over 50 on knowledge in higher education.

Publication of such research in the English language is heavily influenced, of course, by researchers based in the main English language speaking countries of Australia (e.g. Gaze and Stevens 2011; St George 2006), Canada (e.g. Jones and Oleksiyenko 2011; Metcalfe and Fenwick 2009), the United Kingdom (e.g. Aitkin 1991; Brennan 2012; Olssen and Peters 2005) and the United States (e.g. Dundar and Lewis 1998; Kellams 1975; Perna 2016). However, these researchers together only account for a minority of the total publications: 42 per cent of those focused on research in higher education, and 38 per cent of those focused on knowledge in higher education.

Researchers from other countries contribute the majority of published articles on these topics, including authors based in Brazil (Guzman and Trivelato 2011), China (Chen and Hu 2012; Zhang, Bao and Sun 2016), the Czech Republic (Kohoutek 2013), Finland (Valimaa and Hoffman 2008), Germany (Kosmutzky and Krucken

2014; Orr 2004), Hong Kong (Jung and Horta 2013), Indonesia (Waworuntu and Holsinger 1989), Italy (Abramo, Cicero and D'Angelo 2012), Korea (Shin, Lee and Kim 2013), the Netherlands (De Weert 1999), Norway (Bleiklie 2005; Kyvik and Skodvin 2003), the Philippines (Quimbo and Sulabo 2014), Romania (Bucur, Kifor and Marginean 2016), South Africa (Abrahams and Fitzgerald 2015; Buckley 2012), Spain (Pastor, Serrano and Zaera 2015), Sweden (Jacob and Hellstrom 2014) and Switzerland (Lepori 2008). Clearly, interest in these topics in northern Europe and East Asia is strong.

Within these broad topics of knowledge and research, researchers were studying and writing about a diverse range of subjects. Taking knowledge in higher education first, two popular foci for policy-related research were the linked notions of the knowledge economy (e.g. Abrahams and Fitzgerald 2015; Olssen and Peters 2005; Sum and Jessop 2013) and the knowledge society (e.g. Bleiklie 2005; De Weert 1999; Valimaa and Hoffman 2008). While research on the former is firmly linked to the vocational purpose and impact of higher education, research on the latter may take a broader approach, considering the role of higher education in developing useful citizens as well as workers.

Other researchers have focused on the more immediately practical issues of how the knowledge produced by higher education institutions is, or should be, managed (e.g. Guzman and Trivelato 2011; Moss, Kubacki, Hersh and Gunn 2007), and/or on how it can be shared and transferred (e.g. Buckley 2012; Harris, Li and Moffat 2013; Kitagawa and Lightowler 2013).

More fundamentally, some researchers have been interested in the nature of knowledge and how this is changing. In this area, the research on modes of knowledge (Gibbons et al. 1994; Nowotny et al. 2001) – arguing that Mode 1 knowledge, that is conventional university research and scholarship, is being superseded by Mode 2 knowledge, which is typically transdisciplinary, and likely to be created (and used) outside rather than inside higher education, though perhaps in collaboration with academics – has been particularly influential (this is also discussed in the section on academic tribes and territories in Chapter 9). In a related way, applying actor–network theory, Fenwick and Edwards (2014) have drawn attention to the construction and development of networks of knowledge.

Turning to research on research in higher education, two key areas for study have been research policy (e.g. Aitkin 1991; Jacob and Hellstrom 2014; Metcalfe and Fenwick 2009; see also Chapter 7), particularly research funding and strategies (e.g. Litwin 2009; Silander and Haake 2016), and research productivity (its measurement and variation) (e.g. Dundar and Lewis 1998; Pastor, Serrano and Zaera 2015; Waworuntu and Holsinger 1989). Of interest here has been how research productivity can or should be measured, and how it varies between different kinds of institution. A particular focus has been on the links between research, innovation and economic productivity (e.g. Cai 2017).

Closely related to this last point, some researchers have focused on the role of research in 'newer' institutions (e.g. Kyvik and Skodvin 2003; Lepori 2008; Lepori and Kyvik 2010); that is, universities and colleges without an existing research 'tradition', but where changing policy has meant that they have had to rapidly develop one. Other topics studied include research collaboration (e.g. Shin, Lee and Kim 2013), and the impact of research assessment and evaluation schemes (e.g. Bucur, Kifor and Marginean 2016; Orr 2004). Research into research as an academic role, alongside teaching and management, was considered in Chapter 9.

Finally, and critically so for a book of this nature, we must recognize the growing body of research into higher education research, to which, of course, this book is a contribution. The instinct for higher education researchers to assess the overall output of their field goes back at least four decades (Kellams 1975). Some of these assessments have focused on a particular country or region, such as the United States (Kezar 2000; Perna 2016), Europe (Kehm 2015) or East Asia (Chen and Hu 2012; Horta, Jung and Yonezawa 2015; Jung and Horta 2013; Kim and Yung 2017). Others have taken a comparative approach (Blair 2015), examined particular kinds of higher education research (Kohoutek 2013; Kosmutzky and Krucken 2014; Kuzhabekova, Hendel and Chapman 2015) or the application of specific methodologies (Andreotti et al. 2016).

Research designs and frameworks

The three research frameworks considered in detail in this section – the research/teaching nexus, interdisciplinarity, and professional and vocational disciplines – each relate to strongly held positions in higher education policy and practice, and hence have become major areas for research.

Thus, the research/teaching nexus encapsulates the idea that the two major functions of higher education – research and teaching – are, in some way or ways, indelibly and symbiotically linked to each other.

Those who favour interdisciplinarity argue that working within a single discipline – or, more usually, sub-discipline – misses the broader picture, and that most real-world problems require collaboration between researchers from a variety of disciplines to solve.

The professional and vocational disciplines currently occupy a very strong position within the higher education curriculum, reflecting the view that the main purpose of higher education is to prepare students for their future work roles.

Yet, as we shall see, each of these positions have been challenged, and are a matter for debate, and thus represent very important and live areas for research.

The research/teaching nexus

The research/teaching nexus or the teaching/research nexus – the two terms are used interchangeably, with the order perhaps reflecting the prominence attached to the two roles by the writers concerned – has been the subject of increasing discussion in the higher education research literature over the last two decades. The earliest identification of this relationship as a nexus that I have been able to find is over forty years old (Jauch and Gentry 1976, p. 163), but discussion of the linkages between research and teaching dates back well before then (e.g. in 1969, Martin and Berry referred to the teaching/research dilemma; see also Schmitt 1965). It was a significant issue during the nineteenth century, as modern universities came into being, and has been a regular subject for debate since then.

By using the term 'research/teaching nexus', authors are implying that the linkage between research and teaching – as the two major functions of higher education – is close, essential and undeniable. For them, a university is not worthy of the title unless it engages in both teaching and research (Flood Page 1972). Similarly, the academics that the universities employ are not proper academics if they do not research as well as teach; and students may also be expected to engage in research at some level as part of their learning experience. These views are all matters of debate, however, and they clearly do not reflect actual practice in all higher education institutions or departments.

Concerns about the research/teaching nexus appear to stem from at least three main, and inter-related, originating debates: the ongoing debate about the nature of higher education and the university, which has been in progress ever since universities were first established; the post-war, large-scale, quantitative and mainly American studies which found little or no relationship between research and teaching; and, in reaction to these, attempts to develop closer linkages between research and teaching, which found a particular expression in the scholarship of teaching and learning movement (discussed further in Chapter 3; see also Neumann 1996).

Academics have always been keenly interested in the nature or idea of the university and higher education. They are also prone to justifying their opinions and practices in this regard by reference to some hallowed authority or 'tradition', often within a particular national template. Thus, English academics might quote or reference Newman (1852/1976), while those working in German systems would use Humboldt (1809/1970; see also Clark 1993; Gellert, Leitner and Schramm 1990), and American authors might refer to Kerr (1963/2001).

One of the most interesting aspects of these authors is the different positions they took on the relation between research and teaching. Thus, Newman saw the university, or at least its component colleges, as, in essence, a finishing school for young gentlemen. Research was not the business of the university, but was to be carried out in separate specialist institutions. Humboldt, by contrast, saw the unity of research and teaching as at the core of the university, with all teaching carried out through research.

While Newman has been widely used to support the Oxbridge collegiate tradition, and Humboldt is seen as one of the originators of the research-led university, Kerr can be viewed as an early advocate of the modern mass higher education system, within which research and teaching could coexist in varying relations alongside other university roles, such as community service and industrial consultancy.

One natural response to these continuing debates about the roles of research and teaching is to try and measure their association. This has been a particularly popular approach in the United States in the post-war period, using available institutional (e.g. Colbeck 1998; Friedrich and Michalak 1983; Harry and Goldner 1972) or national (e.g. Fox 1992) data sets. Typically, these studies have looked for statistical associations between variables representative of research (such as numbers of publications and research grants) and teaching (such as evaluations of quality); and typically they have found either no association or a small positive correlation. Other variables which intervene in the supposedly positive research/teaching relationship are then sometimes sought, but with little success.

More recently, researchers in other systems, such as the United Kingdom (e.g. Coate, Barnett and Williams 2001; Jenkins 2004; Zaman 2004) and Australia (e.g. Brew 1999) have started to look for evidence of the research/teaching nexus. Tellingly – and probably partly in response to the US studies, and partly because of a relative lack of useable quantitative data sets – these studies have tended to be qualitative.

The plethora of quantitative studies of the research/teaching relationship in the United States have lent themselves to the production of meta-analyses; that is, analyses where the data examined in a series of related studies are pooled and re-examined as a much larger data set. In an early study of this kind, Feldman (1987) re-examined twenty-nine American quantitative studies of research/teaching relations. He concluded that 'research productivity is positively but very weakly correlated with overall teaching effectiveness' (p. 240). He then explored possible mediating variables and factors – instructors' rank and age, their other characteristics, time and effort, context (career stage, discipline, type of institution).

Probably the most quoted meta-analysis, however, is a more recent one by Hattie and Marsh (1996). They re-examined the studies identified by Feldman, together with another twenty-nine, meaning that a total of fifty-eight studies were included in their meta-analysis. They came to the same conclusion as Feldman, leading them to suggest: 'Perhaps the most profitable research direction is to inquire why the belief of complementarity exists' (p. 533; see also Marsh and Hattie 2002). In a smaller meta-analysis (thirty studies), Braxton (1996) came to a similar conclusion, arguing that research and teaching could be viewed as either complementary (but not directly connected) or unrelated.

By contrast, Coate, Barnett and Williams (2001), in a multidisciplinary, interview-based study within English universities, found evidence for six possible relationships between teaching and research: integration, research as a positive influence on teaching, teaching as a positive influence on research, separate activities with little impact on each other, research as a negative influence on teaching and teaching as a negative influence on research.

The idea of the research/teaching nexus has been widely applied in the last three decades in higher education policy and research, though authors – particularly those based in the United States – do not always use the term. Thus, we may note published articles in the English language by authors based in, for example, Australia (e.g. Ramsden and Moses 1992; de Rome, Boud and Genn 1985; Stappenbelt 2013), Canada (e.g. Shore, Pinker and Bates 1990), Denmark (e.g. Jensen 1988), Finland (e.g. Annala and Makinen 2011), Korea (e.g. Shin 2011), the Netherlands (e.g. Hu et al. 2015; Visser-Wijnveen et al. 2010), New Zealand (e.g. Harland 2016; Robertson and Bond 2001), Norway (e.g.

Kyvik and Smeby 1994), Portugal (e.g. Farcas, Bernardes and Matos 2016; Lopes et al. 2013), Spain (e.g. Geraldo et al. 2010), Sweden (e.g. Geschwind and Brostrom 2015), the United Kingdom (e.g. Brown and McCartney 1998; Buckley 2011; Douglas 2013) and the United States (e.g. Faia 1976; Noser, Manakyan and Tanner 1996; Serow 2000). There have also been some comparative studies undertaken and reported (e.g. Gellert, Leitner and Schramm 1990; Gottlieb and Keith 1997).

Though much of the interest in the research/teaching nexus in higher education has been generic in nature, the concept has also been applied within a wide range of specific disciplines. These include, for example, accounting (Duff and Marriott 2016), the built environment (Durning and Jenkins 2005), dentistry (Kieser and Herbison 2001), engineering (Stappenbelt 2013), geography (Le Heron, Baker and McEwen 2006), history (McLean and Barker 2004), hospitality management (Ball and Mohamed 2010), information systems/management (Grant and Wakerlin 2009), nurse and teacher education (Lopes et al. 2013), politics and international relations (Lightfoot and Piotukh 2014) and sport history (Johnes 2004).

Much of the discussion of the research/teaching nexus has focused on its significance for higher education. Clark (1994, 1997), for example, argues in favour of a strong research/teaching/study nexus, noting the forces of research drift and teaching drift (see also the discussion of academic drift and institutional isomorphism in Chapter 8) which act to weaken this nexus, and identifying contrary enabling forces, most notably, in America, the graduate school.

More detailed analyses, while still tending to assert the unquestionable importance of the research/teaching nexus, focus in on particular aspects:

- advice on how the research/teaching nexus may be developed or strengthened (e.g. Baldwin 2005; Brew 2006; Douglas 2013; Kreber 2006);
- examining staff and student attitudes towards the research/teaching nexus (e.g. Buckley 2011; Healey et al. 2010; Kyvik and Smeby 1994);
- discussing how the research/teaching nexus works, or is articulated (e.g. Barnett 1992; Elton 1986; Horta et al. 2012; Kogan 2004); and
- suggesting how the research/teaching nexus might best be researched (e.g. Trigwell and Prosser 2009).

Naturally enough, as an idea that has been debated within higher education over a long period of time, the research/teaching nexus has come in for a good deal of criticism. Some of this critique has centred on the varied ways in which the term, and its component parts, are used and understood (e.g. Jenkins 2004; Neumann 1992; Simons and Elen 2007; Trowler and Wareham 2008). Thus, Hughes (2005) organized his critique in terms of five 'myths'

> of the mutually beneficial relationship between research and teaching … of a generalizable and static relationship … that scholarship is separate from research and teaching … of superiority of the lecturer as researcher … of disinterested research into the relationship between research and teaching. (p. 16)

Other authors have based their assessment on contemporary, and changing, policy and practice. Thus, Henkel (2004) notes that the idea of the research/teaching nexus would have been unnecessary if research and teaching had not become somewhat disassociated. Similarly, Scott (2005) draws attention to the contradiction between practice, where research and teaching may effectively overlap, and policy, where funding regimes are treating the two roles as separate and distinct. Locke (2012) goes so far as to suggest that it implies a need for a reconfiguration of the academic profession.

It is important to stress, therefore, that this experience is not universal. Thus, Taylor (2007) comparing institutional management practices regarding research and teaching in England and Sweden, found that the more sympathetic and less interventionist approach taken in the latter had not pressurized the research/teaching nexus. Leisyte et al. (2009), in another comparative study – of higher education governance in England and the Netherlands – bring in a temporal component, arguing that the nexus is not stable.

Interdisciplinarity

Conventionally, higher education institutions have been organized internally in terms of disciplines, or groups of related disciplines, where each discipline has its own defined subject area and way of looking at the world. Academics are trained within particular disciplines, and they typically specialize in one area of that discipline for research purposes. Disciplines and sub-disciplines have their own networks, journals and conferences, and each tend to see themselves as critical for or central to the academy, while having little to do with other disciplines (Abbott 2001; Collins 1998). A discipline may be defined as

> a branch of knowledge, instruction, learning, teaching, or education. …
> So, 'discipline' is a body of knowledge or skills that can be taught and learned.
> (Alvargonzalez 2011, p. 387)

That, at least, is the conventional view. Against it may be set the alternative view – which has recurred, in varying ways, throughout history – that seeks to work across disciplinary boundaries, in both teaching and research. This alternative view sees disciplines as limiting academic thinking, and being blind to the complex nature of real-world problems (Klein 2004). In its modern guise, this alternative view is most commonly termed 'interdisciplinarity'.

Interdisciplinarity has been lauded, by its advocates, as the answer to all that is wrong within the academy. Nissani (1997), for example, makes a tenfold case for interdisciplinarity – it enables creative breakthroughs, brings in an outsider's perspective, allows cross-disciplinary oversights, reveals disciplinary cracks, is ideal for addressing complex or practical problems, argues for a unity of knowledge, permits flexibility in research, counters the law of diminishing returns stemming from single discipline approaches, and supports social change and academic freedom.

Tarrant and Thiele (2017) go even further in arguing, in the context of environmental science and sustainability research, that 'whether universities can successfully address the pressing challenges of the twenty-first century will depend on their developing increased capacity for interdisciplinary scholarship and teaching' (p. 360).

Choi and Pak (2006, p. 355) define interdisciplinarity as 'a synthesis of two or more disciplines, establishing a new level of discourse and integration of knowledge'. For others, however, the term is much more contested and open to interpretation:

> Interdisciplinarity is among the most talked about but most misunderstood topics in education on all levels today. Seen as the savior of research and teaching … or the seeds of destruction, interdisciplinarity's proponents and critics talk past each other. Seldom do they seek common terms; typically, they mean very different approaches when they refer to interdisciplinarity. They erroneously dichotomize disciplines and interdisciplines, confuse specialization and synthesis, and misconstrue 'integration'. They also date the historical turn to interdisciplinarity too late. (Graff 2016, p. 775)

Similarly, in an analysis of interviews with academics and administrators at a UK university, Cuevas-Garcia (2017) identifies twelve different 'interpretative repertoires', some of them contradictory, used to think and argue about interdisciplinarity.

In addition to interdisciplinarity, a range of related terms with overlapping meanings are in use, including condisciplinarity, cross-disciplinarity, metadisciplinarity, multidisciplinarity, pluridisciplinarity, postdisciplinarity and transdisciplinarity (Hoffmann, Schmidt and Nersessian 2013; Jantsch 1970). Of these, multidisciplinarity and transdisciplinarity are in most common use alongside interdisciplinarity. Two slightly different, but confirmatory, sets of distinctions between this triumvirate are made by Choi and Pak, and Alvargonzalez:

> *Multidisciplinarity* draws on knowledge from different disciplines but stays with the boundaries of those fields. *Interdisciplinarity* analyses, synthesizes and harmonizes links between disciplines into a coordinated and coherent whole. *Transdisciplinarity* integrates the natural, social and health sciences in a humanities context, and in so doing transcends each of their traditional boundaries. (Choi and Pak 2006, p. 359, emphases in original)

> multidisciplinarity refers to an activity associated with many, multiple, or more than one existing discipline … interdisciplinarity refers to an activity that exists among existing disciplines or in a reciprocal relationship between them … transdisciplinarity is that which concerns transcending the disciplines, going across and through the different disciplines, and beyond each individual discipline. (Alvargonzalez 2011, p. 388)

The three terms could be seen, therefore, as suggesting different levels of radicality along the same spectrum, with multidisciplinarity the least challenging to a conventional disciplinary perspective, and transdisciplinarity the most. Interdisciplinarity, perhaps, offers the best of both worlds, in engaging a range of disciplines in a common cause while leaving them essentially intact. The term does, however, cover a range of approaches; thus, Huutoniemi et al. 2010 offer a typology, which takes into account the scope and goals of the project, and whether the focus is empirical, methodological or theoretical.

Bibliographic searches, using Scopus and Google Scholar, for articles published with the words 'interdisciplinarity', 'disciplinarity' or 'multidisciplinarity' in their titles, show that 'interdisciplinarity' is clearly the more popular term, and that the numbers of articles focusing on it have been steadily increasing, from a handful a year in the 1990s to over 150 per year in the 2010s (according to Google Scholar).

These publications include an increasing number of overviews of the field in book form (e.g. Barry and Born 2013; Callard and Fitzgerald 2015; Davies, Devlin and Tight 2010; Frodeman, Klein, Mitcham and Holbrook 2010; Lattuca 2001). Perhaps unsurprisingly, the practice of interdisciplinarity has also been the subject of many bibliographic or bibliometric studies (e.g. Braun and Schubert 2003; Hellsten and Leydesdorff 2016; Morillo, Bordons and Gomez 2001; Mugabushaka, Kyriakou and Papazoglou 2016; Schummer 2004), typically focusing upon either the incidence of interdisciplinarity in particular areas or how to measure it.

Many articles have provided case studies of experience with interdisciplinary approaches in particular subject areas or disciplines; for example, business (Ryan and Neumann 2013), climatic change (Hellsten and Leydesdorff 2016), cultural studies (McCulloch 2014), education (Jay; Rose and Milligan 2017), English (Moran and Drakakis 2010), environmental management (O'Brien, Marzano and White 2013), environmental science (MacMynowski 2007), ethnography/computer science (Goulden et al. 2017), fisheries research (Haapasaari, Kulmala and Kuikka 2012), geography (Lau and Pasquini 2004), nanoscience/technology (Schummer 2004), neuroscience/social science (Fitgerald and Callard 2015), sustainability science (Bursztyn and Drummond 2014) and urban planning (Shandas and Brown 2016).

Here, while English and geography would be recognized by most as established disciplines, topics like climatic change or fisheries research would not, and might, therefore, be seen as ripe for interdisciplinary exploration. Some of the other examples given – such as ethnography/computer science and neuroscience/social science – clearly signal collaborations between disciplines or methodologies.

Some authors have focused on the impact of interdisciplinarity on the curriculum (Knight et al. 2013; Olson and Brosnan 2017), on learning (Lattuca, Voight and Fath 2004), or on the university as a whole (Franks et al. 2007; Koski 2011); while others have analysed the experience of students (Bradbeer 1999; Gardner et al. 2014; Strengers 2014) and academics engaged in interdisciplinary study or research (Blackmore and Kandiko 2011; Garforth and Kerr 2011; Martimianakis and Muzzin 2015). Sanz-Menendez, Bordons and Zulueta (2001, p. 47) have described this experience:

Interdisciplinarity emerges as a double-edged process: of jumping into a new area with people of different disciplines, in coherence with the traditional disciplinary research teams; and of specialization in a field traditionally dominated by a single group of disciplinary backgrounds, in which researchers from different areas join the teams. Thus specialization–fragmentation–hybridization all come together.

More practical publications have attempted to set out how to practice interdisciplinarity. Thus, Choi and Pak (2007, pp. E229–30) identify twelve 'promoters' of interdisciplinary teamwork success – including good selection of team members, personal commitment of team members, incentives, institutional support and changes in the workplace, a common goal and shared vision, and clarity and rotation of roles – and twelve barriers – including poor selection of the disciplines and team members, poor process of team functioning, language problems, insufficient time, insufficient funding, institutional constraints and unequal power among disciplines. These might be said, however, to be almost wholly generic in nature, as well as being fairly obvious.

Many and diverse issues and criticisms have been raised regarding interdisciplinarity, demonstrating a considerable range of opinions. Those in favour of increasing interdisciplinarity have argued that this is hampered by the continuing strength of the disciplines, their domain specificity (MacLeod 2016), and their control of reward structures (Reybold and Halx 2012): 'If institutions with traditional discipline-based structures want to provide students with interdisciplinary opportunities, teachers need to be adequately supported in terms of workload, career rewards and pedagogy' (Pharo and Bridle 2012, p. 65).

From the student perspective, engaging in interdisciplinary study imposes additional demands, particularly if those responsible for teaching lack the necessary sympathy or training:

> Barriers to interdisciplinarity arise because of differences in disciplinary epistemologies, discourses and traditions of teaching and learning. Students also bring to bear very different learning approaches and styles. Some of these learning styles are much more adaptive to particular disciplinary knowledge structures than others. Students face a number of bewildering challenges as they first try to adapt to their chosen area of specialisation, then to move between it and other disciplines and finally to be able to work equally effectively in them all. (Bradbeer 1999, p. 394)

Some would refer to these problems as being about the different academic literacies (see Chapter 4) practised in different disciplines.

Others have argued that the demands of government and other higher education stakeholders to engage in interdisciplinarity to a greater extent are hampered by the existing organizational structures of higher education:

> In the Australian context, the paradox of interdisciplinarity primarily concerns the proliferation of a programmatic discourse of interdisciplinarity in government reports and government policy and strategy documents, often tied to notions of innovation and applicability, parallel to the persistence or even reinforcement of modes of governance and associated mechanisms that almost exclusively rely on rigid discipline-based classification systems to evaluate and fund research ... there is a significant mismatch between the discourse of interdisciplinarity and associated conceptions of knowledge on the one hand, and current, relatively inflexible governmental research funding and evaluation practices on the other. (Woelert and Millar 2013, p. 755)

To overcome this may require, along with other changes in governance and organization, a different, but broader, quality assurance strategy:

> Interdisciplinarity provides a counterpoint to the disciplinary mode of academic quality control, as it can be set directly against disciplinary autonomy. As an evaluative concept, interdisciplinarity implies a higher level academic accountability, which renders disciplinary communities more broadly responsive for their epistemic goals and procedures. (Huutoniemi 2016, p. 180)

In contrast, there are those, not necessarily opposed to the underlying aims of interdisciplinarity, who argue that it may be unnecessary, since the existing disciplines, as well as being strong and entrenched, have also shown themselves to be highly adaptable:

> In thinking about the relations between disciplinarity and interdisciplinarity ... it would be a mistake to contrast the homogeneity and closure of disciplines with the heterogeneity and openness of interdisciplinarity. On the one hand, interdisciplinary research can involve hypostatization and closure, limiting as well as transforming the possibility for new forms, methods and sites of research. On the other hand, disciplines themselves are often remarkably heterogeneous or internally divided. (Barry, Born and Weszkalnys 2008, p. 26)

There is a sense here, as in the following contribution, that the difference between interdisciplinarity and disciplinarity may not be so great as some would argue; it is more to do with how they are practised:

> We do not believe that the case has been fully made, theoretically or empirically, for the general superiority of interdisciplinary over disciplinary knowledge. The established disciplines are not as static or as isolated as advocates of interdisciplinarity sometimes suggest. Although there are certainly successful examples of interdisciplinarity, established academic disciplines remain dynamic centers of knowledge production that are open to external developments even while insisting on internal standards. (Jacobs and Frickel 2009, p. 60)

For some, the rise of interdisciplinarity is actually seen as posing a threat to disciplines, as in the case of applied social studies and sociology:

> While sociology 'exports' concepts, methodologies and personnel it lacks the internal disciplinary integrity of other 'exporter' disciplines, such as economics, political science and anthropology. The consequence is an increasingly blurred distinction between sociology as a discipline and the interdisciplinary area of applied social studies with a potential loss of disciplinary identity. (Holmwood 2010, p. 639)

This does, though, come across as being overly defensive and somewhat insecure.

Finally, there are those who maintain that interdisciplinarity is either exaggerated, undesirable or is being done in the wrong way. Thus, Schummer (2004, p. 425) argues that, even in the commonly identified interdisciplinary field of nanoscience/ technology, much of what is going on is not interdisciplinary: 'Current nanoscale research reveals no particular patterns and degrees of interdisciplinarity and … its apparent multidisciplinarity consists of different largely mono-disciplinary fields which are rather unrelated to each other and which hardly share more than the prefix nano.'

Barrett (2012, p. 109) claims that an over-emphasis on interdisciplinary approaches to teaching and research may have negative impacts upon the academy: 'The implications of a widespread shift towards "hyperinterdisciplinary" and entirely problem-focused curricula and programmes of study, such as "short-termism" and "hyper-specialisation" in terms of the work and identities of university teachers, researchers and students, do not seem overly positive.'

Price (2014, p. 52) argues that what he terms 'condisciplinarity' or 'mainstream interdisciplinarity' is inadequate for generating a full understanding of the complexity of reality, and that what is needed instead is a critical realist approach:

> Critical realist interdisciplinarity is preferable because it acknowledges inter alia the empirical, actual and real layers of reality, which allows it to develop depth-explanations of phenomena. In practice, this means that critical realist interdisciplinarity can potentially provide explanations that, compared to condisciplinarity, are broader (include more of the human and non-human context) and deeper (include for example individuals' conscious and unconscious psychological motivations).

This sounds, however, more of a claim for the superiority of a critical realist approach, than an argument for interdisciplinarity.

We might conclude, therefore, that the jury remains out on interdisciplinarity. Is it the solution to higher education's problems, making its teaching and research much more relevant, accessible and useful? Or is it a threat to the well-established patterns of academic organization, which have proven their worth over the decades and centuries? As ever, we note that more research is needed.

Professional and vocational disciplines

The debate about the relationship between higher education and the professions and/ or vocations is – like the related debate about the purpose of the university – as old as higher education itself. In one sense, higher education was always concerned with the development of (at least some of) its students for a future profession, that of academic work (the focus of Chapter 9) itself. But, much more broadly, the link between it and other professions – classically divinity, then law and medicine, and most recently teaching, nursing and a multitude of others – has been strong.

There are, of course, many who argue that the (only or chief) role of higher education, so far as teaching is concerned, is the preparation of students for their future employment. Governments, employers' organizations and other stakeholders have, regularly and repeatedly, driven this point home, and have argued that universities and colleges need to do yet more to make their graduates more employable. There are others, though, including sometimes governments and employers, who recognize that the teaching/learning process in higher education has other purposes as well, not least the development of well-rounded, broadly educated and thoughtful individuals, who can contribute to society as well as the economy throughout their lifetimes. The tension between these vocational and liberal purposes of higher education is of longstanding.

The relationship between higher education and professional/vocational preparation has become even closer in recent decades, as more and more professions – most notably teaching and the various branches of health care – have determined that their entrants need to be graduates, and have moved their preparation from specialist colleges into higher education institutions. As well as contributing to the expansion of higher education, this has meant that most universities now have a very vocational look, with the majority of their departments and courses now preparing their students for specific professions (Brint et al. 2005).

Not surprisingly, these developments and debates have underpinned a considerable amount of research and writing. Bibliographic searches using Scopus show that the number of articles with the words 'professional' and 'higher education' in their title, and thus focusing on this topic, has increased significantly in recent years. Whereas there were only a handful of such articles published each year during the 1990s, the current figure is around fifty per year. A similar trend may be seen with articles focusing on vocational higher education (there is, of course, some overlap), though the overall numbers are lower.

There are specialist sub-literatures focusing on every profession you can think of, including, for example, accounting (Merwe, McChlery and Visser 2014), business (Schellekens, Paas and Merrienboer 2003), hospitality (Gross and Manoharan 2016), nurse education (Bergström 2010), pharmacy (Paor 2016), policing (Nikolou-Walker and Meaklim 2007), political science (Nyström 2009), psychology (Nyström 2009), social work (Baartman and Ruijs 2011; Bommel, Kwakman and Boshuizen 2012) and teacher education (Baeten, Struyven and Dochy 2013; Burn 2006; Higginbotham 1969). Note that this list includes both obvious professions, such as accounting and teaching, and disciplines, such as political science and psychology, which are not so closely linked to a single profession, or indeed any profession at all.

Research has examined many varied aspects of the relationship between higher education and the professions, including the curriculum and how it is taught (Leonard, Fitzgerald and Riordan 2016; Lizzio and Wilson 2004; Merwe, McChlery and Visser 2014), and how the students involved are then assessed (Baartman, Gulikers and Dijkstra 2013; Bergström 2010). Of course, many professional bodies have a direct engagement with these issues, setting out comprehensive requirements for what students need to do to achieve professional status, and monitoring what higher education institutions do to ensure that they do so.

More specialist topics for research are the role of internships, placements or work-based learning in professional higher education (e.g. Wan et al. 2013), how entrepreneurialism can best be encouraged among the student body (Bjornali and Støren 2012), and how students' future professional identities can be developed

(Trede, Macklin and Bridges 2012). Of course, the undergraduate degree is no longer seen as the only engagement with higher education, so there is also interest and research into continuing professional development or education (Burrow et al. 2016; Cho and Rathbun 2013).

Lurking near the heart of any critical discussion of professional and/or vocational disciplines in higher education is the longstanding debate already referred to about the – complementary or opposed, depending upon your point of view – vocational and liberal roles of higher education. This may not only be reflected in the stances taken by particular researchers, but may also be reified in national policy.

Thus, there are countries or systems – such as Australia, Finland, Germany, the Netherlands, Sweden, Taiwan and, to an extent, the UK – where vocational and 'academic' higher education are, or have been, organized in different sectors, though with some inevitable cross-over (e.g. Huang and Lee 2012; Husband and Jeffrey 2016; Kuijpers and Meijers 2012; Lindell and Stenstrom 2005; Moodie and Wheelahan 2009; Parry 2015; Poortman et al. 2014; Webb et al. 2017; Wolter and Kerst 2015).

In such systems, much of the debate over the professional/vocational function of higher education resolves around either the status accorded to the vocational sector (which is typically seen as being of lower status), and/or the linkages between the vocational and academic sectors. For example, in the Australian context, Bandias, Fuller and Pfitzner (2011) argue that

> various efforts to strengthen the connections between higher education and vocational education have been made in Australia over the last 25 years with limited success. This has been due, in large part, to structural rigidities, differences in curriculum and differences in pedagogy and assessment. While these issues remain complex, reform is vital if a fully effective tertiary system is to be achieved. This will require significant changes affecting funding, regulation and system governance in both sectors. Traditionally, higher education has concentrated on longer study programmes with a focus on adaptable skills for professional occupations. Vocational education, on the other hand has focused on more immediate vocational outcomes in trades and para-professional occupations. However, the vocational focus of higher education has increased in recent years and vocational education has responded to the demands of industry for higher level skills by refocusing on middle level and advanced training. (pp. 590–1)

An alternative approach is to not focus on the vocational sector or on particular programmes with a designated vocational outcome, but to view all higher education as leading to professional employment (e.g. Bjornali and Støren 2012; Gallifa 2009; Nyström 2009; Schomburg 2007). This is not to disregard its liberal role, but to acknowledge that an underlying purpose of higher education is to prepare its students for higher status careers. The issue, then, becomes how well they do this: what proportion of graduates enter such careers, and how well do they, and their employers, think that their higher education has prepared them?

Research of this kind, taking a comparative perspective, has shown that there are significant differences between different professions/disciplines. Nilsson (2010), for example, reports on a Swedish study that compared medicine and engineering:

> In the case of medicine, the educational and professional competence bases overlap significantly, and the professional education programme is viewed as a direct vocational preparation. However, the physicians argue that the transition to the workplace is associated with a need to reprioritise knowledge. The engineers consider the educational and professional competence bases to be only loosely coupled. Rather than focusing on the substance of the educational programme, the engineers consider the educational programme to constitute a broad foundation facilitating further learning and professional development in the workplace. (p. 255)

In a broader study of Greek higher technological education, Kostoglou, Vassilakoupoulos and Koilias (2013) found that

> there are significant differences among the graduates of different specialties regarding their major employment characteristics, such as professional status, type of employment and moreover the relevance between present work and bachelor studies and the satisfaction from employment and wages. 'ICT' [information and communication technologies] and 'ENG' [engineering] graduates appear to be in a better position in the labor market regarding the above employment variables. On the other hand 'Agriculture', 'Management and Economics' and 'Graphics and Arts' graduates suffer higher unemployment rates than all other specialties. The specialties related to health services being dominated by women present the highest relevance between work and studies and high employment rates; however their wages and the satisfaction from them are significantly lower than all the others. (pp. 534–5)

In other words, the linkage between higher education and profession or employment works better in some areas than others, and also has a gendered component. How stable these relationships are over time is, of course, another issue, and one which research and policy have the ability to effect.

For example, research into the quality of professional/vocational provision has a clear focus on how higher education targeted at working life should be organized and presented. Thus, Kuijpers and Meijers (2012) argue that

> a learning environment that stimulates real-life work experiences, that gives the students opportunities to influence their own course of study by offering them the opportunity to make choices, and also fosters a dialogue about these experiences and choices, contributes to the use of career competencies. There is clearly a positive relationship between a powerful career-related learning environment and career reflection (characterized by reflective behaviour), work exploration (characterized by exploring behaviour), career action (characterized by proactive behaviour) and networking (characterized by interactive behaviour). (p. 462)

Such an approach, while clearly beneficial, does not, of course, guarantee that all of its graduates will transition seamlessly into successful professional careers (see also the discussion of the transition to work in Chapter 5).

Conclusions

Arguably, then, while research into knowledge and research in higher education may seem to be highly introspective, it focuses on some of the most critical issues affecting universities and colleges, and their various stakeholders. These have profound implications for their organization and practices, not just of research but in teaching as well. Perhaps, therefore, rather more effort should be expended on researching these topics – relatively speaking – than on the seemingly more imperative and immediate issues of teaching and learning, course design and so forth.

Chapter 11
Conclusions

This book has provided a synthesis and overview of higher education research internationally. It has done this by analysing the trends in higher education research in eight themes or areas of interest: teaching and learning (Chapter 3), course design (Chapter 4), the student experience (Chapter 5), quality (Chapter 6), system policy (Chapter 7), institutional management (Chapter 8), academic work (Chapter 9), and knowledge and research (Chapter 10). For each theme three research designs or frameworks, or pairs of designs or frameworks, were explored in detail, with their origins and meaning, application and usage, and development and critique carefully examined.

The primary methods used in undertaking this mapping and synthesis have been meta-analysis and systematic review, aiming to identify and analyse all research-based publications (principally journal articles, but also books and book chapters) produced on the themes, research designs and frameworks identified. The main limitation on the analysis was its restriction to English language publications. Considerable use was made of search engines and databases – notably Scopus and Google Scholar – to help identify relevant publications.

While I would not claim to have successfully identified and read every publication of relevance – how could I? – I have made extensive efforts to do so, as the unusually long references list that follows this chapter testifies. Bear in mind also that the references list does not include the totality of the publications examined, but merely a selection, chosen to include both key works and indicative examples of particular kinds of research.

In this chapter, the aim is twofold. First, to draw some general lessons from the research that has been analysed. This will involve looking across themes and frameworks, rather than attempting to summarize them any further, to identify commonalities in the processes of research, and in the development and application of theory and methodology.

Second, to use this synthesis as a kind of palimpsest to try and identify what is missing: what hasn't been researched, which methods or theories haven't been applied, and where, therefore, higher education researchers might usefully address their energies in the future. This may, of course, be an even more useful exercise than synthesizing what has already been achieved.

What have we learnt?

The diligent reader, who has either been through the entire book or read several chapters, will have noted a number of similarities or commonalities in the points being made, and the conclusions being drawn, in successive chapters and sections. Here I shall draw attention to and discuss seven of these:

1   The tendency for newly articulated theories or frameworks to have pre-existing or precursor analogues.

2   The tendency for what is essentially the same theory or framework to be given different titles by different researchers.

3   The opposing tendency, for the same theory or framework to be interpreted and applied in very different ways by different researchers.

4   The tendency for perspectives on particular topics to change over time, and for theories and frameworks themselves to change and develop.

5   The finding that, while some theories or frameworks have been developed within higher education research, many more have been developed outside of it in a variety of disciplines, and then imported and applied within higher education research.

6   The tendency for many higher education researchers to confine themselves to, and operate within, national and methodological silos.

7   The presence of an underlying neo-liberal critique informing many of the topics researched and approaches employed within higher education research.

It is my strong suspicion – though at present I only have limited evidence for this – that many of these points also apply to research into other fields, as well as to research into higher education.

Pre-existing or precursor theories or frameworks

It is common to find that newly articulated theories or frameworks have predecessors: pre-existing or precursor theories or frameworks covering much the same topic or issue, and often with the same or a similar name.

This is not to say that the advocates of the newly articulated theory or framework have knowingly appropriated an existing theory or framework, while claiming no knowledge of the precursor. Rather, it is to recognize that, in increasingly well-researched fields with longstanding issues, it is not surprising if researchers come up independently with similar ideas at different times. We should also recognize that nowadays, with the development of the internet and the increasing volume of data available on it, it has become much easier to search for this sort of information.

One obvious example of this phenomenon is phenomenography (see Chapter 3), a research design developed in Sweden in the late 1960s and onwards by Marton and his colleagues. The term had been previously used to mean much the same thing by both Sonnemann (1954) in psychopathology and Needleman (1963) in psychoanalysis, in both cases to distinguish it from phenomenology; something which Marton, in particular, long denied had any connection with phenomenography.

Another example of this tendency is academic drift (see Chapter 8), which in the UK is particularly associated with the work of Burgess and Pratt from the 1970s onwards. Yet, bibliographic searches show the term being used in much the same way as early as in the 1920s. Meanwhile, in the United States, an institutional theory termed institutional isomorphism was being employed in higher education research in much the same way as academic drift was in the United Kingdom, Europe and Australia. American higher education researchers were also using a range of synonyms for the phenomenon, including vertical or upward extension, mission creep and mission drift.

Analogous or differently titled theories or frameworks

A second common tendency is for what are essentially the same theories or frameworks to be given different titles by different authors. In a way this is a contemporaneous version of the previous tendency, reflecting the ease with which researchers working in different places, and not in contact with each other, may come up with parallel ideas. In other cases, it has to do with changing fashions, with authors wanting to put a new spin on an existing idea or take it in a different direction.

The example of academic drift and institutional isomorphism has already been mentioned. Another example suggestive of changing fashions is that of student retention (see Chapter 5), a phrasing which has now largely replaced the harsher and more negative terms of student withdrawal or dropout, which were formerly in widespread usage. A third example is the scholarship of teaching and learning, formerly the scholarship of teaching (see Chapter 3), which, while widely recognized and used, may also be known by the more prosaic term 'pedagogical research'.

The tendency for different researchers to use different titles for the same theoretical framework is not, however, totally endemic. Indeed, the opposite phenomenon may occur, where the same term is agreed and used by widely separated groups of researchers (though geographical separation is, of course, far less important now than it used to be). Perhaps the best example of this in higher education research is learning approaches (see Chapter 3), a framework that was developed more or less simultaneously – though using varied methodologies – by researchers in Sweden, Australia and the UK.

Theories or frameworks being used in very different ways

A related tendency – indeed, one that may be thought of as virtually universal – is where theories or frameworks, with an agreed label or title, are used or applied in very different ways. This may be thought of as a natural developmental trend, as a new idea is disseminated and picked up by other researchers over time, and then applied by them, perhaps with only partial knowledge of the original theoretical framework in question, to their own concerns and in their own context. It would be amazing, of course, were it otherwise; and this is, after all, a key way in which theories and frameworks develop.

A good example of this is communities of practice theory (see Chapter 9), originally developed in the United States in the late 1980s or early 1990s by Lave and Wenger. After their initial development of the theory, the two progenitors went their different ways, and their subsequent writings reflect their different interests which had been combined in the framework. Thus, Lave was more interested in exploring everyday learning practices, and her research was taken up in higher education by those interested in empowering and enabling students and academics through group activities. Wenger, on the other hand, was more interested in the use of communities of practice as a management tool, which, in higher education – as in business – appealed to those in management positions charged with improving the quality of provision.

Changing perspectives and trends

Another linked tendency is where the meaning of a particular research framework changes over time as the underlying topic on which it is focused also changes. In other words, researchers are using the same label to refer to their studies of the same topic, but what that label and topic now encompasses has changed, so that it would not necessarily be recognizable to former researchers in the same field.

An example of this is research into the student experience (see Chapter 5), where what was once considered as the student experience – that is in most cases their classroom learning experience – has now been broadened to include all aspects of student life while they are students. Indeed, the research interest may extend to consider their lives before and after they were students as well.

A similar, and related, example concerns the changing popularity of student retention and student engagement as research frameworks (see Chapter 5). These two frameworks are addressing essentially the same issue – how to retain or engage students in higher education – but the latter carries a more positive message (what can be done to help students enjoy and commit to their higher education), while the former, with its emphasis on how to stop students withdrawing from higher education, seems negative by comparison. It seems hopeful, therefore, that the latter has now overtaken the former in terms of its popularity as a research framework.

We should also recognize here, of course, that all theoretical frameworks develop over time – at least, those that are seen as having value do. Activity systems theory (see Chapter 4) is a good example. Thus, authors typically recognize at least three generations in the development of activity system theory from its origins in Soviet psychology. Contemporary activity systems theory is witnessing further developments, as in the identification and use of contradictions, the notion of expansive learning and the methodology of the change laboratory.

Developed inside or outside higher education research

The analyses presented in this book have also confirmed, as suggested in Chapter 2, that, while some of the theories and frameworks considered have been wholly or largely developed within higher education research, many others have been developed in external disciplines, and then imported into and applied to researching higher education. This has occurred because many of those involved in researching higher education come from or remain based in other disciplines/departments, and bring their own theories and frameworks with them.

Examples of the theories or frameworks developed within higher education research include phenomenography, and teaching and learning approaches (see Chapter 3), threshold concepts (Chapter 4), the research/teaching nexus and interdisciplinarity (both of which are considered in Chapter 10). Interestingly, there is a clear distinction between these theories or frameworks, with the first three being identifiable as theories (indeed, as has been argued, phenomenography may also be considered as a research design), while the last two are essentially frameworks for undertaking research.

Examples of the theories or frameworks developed outside of higher education research, but then imported into and applied to it, include academic literacies and activity systems (both considered in Chapter 4, the former imported from linguistics and the latter from psychology), quality assurance/management (Chapter 6, imported from business/management), institutional diversity and managerialism (both considered in Chapter 8, the former imported from biology, the latter from business/management), academic tribes and territories (Chapter 9, which has its origins in anthropology) and academic identity (also Chapter 9, with origins in both psychology and sociology).

The distinction between being developed inside or outside higher education research (or, more generally, educational research) is not, however, always so clear cut. Thus, the theories of human and social capital (discussed in Chapter 7) and communities of practice (Chapter 9) may each be considered to have developed, to some extent, on the borders between disciplines (economics in the case of human capital, sociology for social capital, and business/management for communities of practice) and the field of higher education research (or educational research more generally), as their application is wholly, largely or significantly directed towards educational issues.

National and methodological silos

Another common finding is the strong tendency for researchers to work in 'silos' – that is, narrowly restricted specialisms – and to have contact, either directly or through their citations (Tight 2006, 2008), with only a limited number of other researchers with similar interests. This is not unusual for researchers in general, of course, as it makes a lot of sense to focus one's interests, and then to develop and maintain contacts chiefly with those who have similar interests.

However, researching in silos often goes further than simply a focus on a specialism, and in at least two different ways, both of which may be seen in higher education research.

First, many higher education researchers also operate in a methodological silo; that is, they have a commitment to, and/or are comfortable with, a particular set of methodologies or methods, and carry out all or the great majority of their research using them. The most obvious example of this is the way in which many researchers – throughout the social sciences as well as within higher education research – commit themselves to either qualitative or quantitative methods, with relatively few being comfortable to use either, both or a mixed methods approach.

Methodological 'silo-ing' may, however, be more extreme or specialized than this. Thus, there are researchers who find so much value in a particular method – be it phenomenography, factor analysis or focus group interviewing – that they devote a large part of their career to its application. On the positive side, doing so enables them to perfect their expertise; but the ability to appreciate and engage with a range of methods is also a strength. For example, researchers interested in teaching and learning approaches (see Chapter 3) have managed to learn from both qualitative (phenomenography) and quantitative (surveys and multivariate analyses) approaches, while typically remaining committed to one or the other.

Second, there are national research silos as well. US-based researchers seem particularly prone to this (Shahjahan and Kezar 2013; Tight 2007, 2014b), typically only referencing publications produced by other US-based researchers and published in US-based journals. Most US-based journals focused on higher education only or chiefly publish articles from US-based authors. This is also reflected in the tendency, already noted, for US-based researchers to refer to what are essentially the same theories or frameworks by different names to those used in other parts of the world.

This is, of course, understandable, as the United States has a large and complex higher education system. It also has a relatively long tradition of researching higher education, as its system was the first to undergo massification (discussed in Chapter 7); and a particular preference for quantitative forms of research, as massification led to the development and use of large databases. Yet, this tendency is also regrettable, as comparative analyses can help to advance understanding.

The United States is not the only country, however, where higher education researchers tend to work in a national silo. In English language publications, the same tendency can be detected, though to a lesser degree, among UK-based researchers. Outside the anglophone world, those publishing in English as their second language are, by contrast, effectively forced to engage with research from other, English-speaking countries. This is also inevitably the case for those working in smaller countries, where there will not be a sufficient volume of research publications to engage with unless the researchers look beyond their own system.

Interestingly, the national 'silo-ing' of higher education researchers does not apply to every topic researched, but, for a topic to be researched on a truly international basis, it has to start in the United States and then spread elsewhere. The clearest example of this is the scholarship of teaching and learning (discussed in Chapter 3), a movement which originated in the United States but was then enthusiastically picked up elsewhere.

An underlying neo-liberal critique

Finally, we may note the frequency with which a neo-liberal critique is advanced in research and writing on higher education. This is not universal; some researchers simply carry out and write up their research, without feeling the need to engage much in critique, let alone of neo-liberalism. Others focus on other critiques, which tend to be more specific to the topic being researched.

The prevalence of neo-liberal critique also depends to a considerable degree on the nature of the topic being researched, being much more common when the research is policy related, representing something of a dissonance between the researcher's perspective and the policy being researched. Thus, criticism of neo-liberal policy is particularly strong in research into quality, system policy, institutional management, and knowledge and research (the subjects of Chapters 6, 7, 8 and 10); somewhat apparent in studies of the student experience and academic work (Chapters 5 and 9); and barely present in research into teaching and learning and course design (Chapters 3 and 4).

The particular topics which are most likely to attract a neo-liberal critique include the transition to work (discussed in Chapter 5), quality assurance/management, the student as consumer or customer, ranking and league tables (all discussed in Chapter 6), human and social capital, globalization and internationalization, massification (all discussed in Chapter 7), managerialism, institutional mission and diversity (discussed in Chapter 8), the research/teaching nexus, and professional and vocational disciplines (discussed in Chapter 10). This is where the 'traditional' liberalism of the academy is most likely to come into conflict with the contemporary neo-liberalism of higher education policy (and policy more generally).

What remains to be researched?

It is a commonplace of research writing, not just in higher education research but generally, that one of the first conclusions of any piece of research is that 'more research is needed'. The authors then set out just what kinds of further research they believe is necessary. In part, of course, this is a self-serving conclusion, since the authors/researchers have a direct interest in further employment, but it does also reflect the reality that research, in answering (at least partially) some questions, almost always identifies further questions that need answering.

Before going on to try and identify here what remains to be researched, it is useful to reflect, however, upon how much we already know. Meta-analyses, systematic reviews and syntheses, such as those presented in this book, clearly identify the vast amount of research-based literature on higher education being published each year. Thus, an analysis of the output of English language academic journals focusing exclusively on higher education research in 2016 (Tight 2018) suggested that, for the 86 journals identified, over 40,000 pages (or about 16,000,000 words) were published. Bearing in mind that this is only part, though a major part, of the total output, and that the amount published is growing rapidly year by year, the cumulative total of research on higher education is massive.

The first thing which anyone who is thinking of undertaking further research into higher education should do, therefore, is to identify what has already been done on their topic. It is highly likely that there will be a great deal of relevance; perhaps focusing on other countries, other types of institutions, other levels of education (see Hattie 2009) or other disciplinary areas, but still relevant. In light of this existing research, the researcher then needs to determine what it is that their own proposed research is going to add – which may just be exploring a particular issue in their own context – and perhaps modify their plans accordingly.

Of course, a great deal, the majority, of higher education research is small-scale, examining a particular issue in one class, department or institution. As well as being interesting to the researchers involved, and relevant for their department and/or institution, their findings – if published and disseminated – will add to the accumulating body of knowledge on that issue. While there may be a degree of wheel reinvention going on, the research should still be of some value.

However, beyond simply adding another small mite to the existing body of knowledge on a particular topic or issue, are there other aspects of higher education that remain to be researched? Based on the research carried out for this book, I would firmly suggest that there are many. Some of them require relatively large-scale research and thinking, while others could be fairly small-scale; some are chiefly empirical, while others focus more on theory or methodology; so there are opportunities here for all kinds of researchers.

Starting with larger-scale research, there is a clear need – especially outside of the United States, where such research is already common – to engage more in large-scale, comparative and longitudinal studies. More sets of 'big data' – both quantitative and qualitative – are becoming available in more countries, and they require detailed study to uncover what they have to say about different aspects of higher education. We need to overcome the reservations that many have about working with quantitative data, and improve our training programmes in this area.

Comparative studies, comparing practices and experiences between departments, disciplines, institutions and, particularly, countries, are of special value, because they allow the analysis of alternative populations and strategies. Longitudinal studies are also of critical importance because – unlike the much more typical, short-term cross-sectional studies – they enable us to track developments over time. These also include historical studies, making use of the available data for past years.

Of course, such larger-scale studies immediately raise questions of resourcing, but, with higher education now a much larger-scale activity, and governments and other stakeholders keen to keep a watching eye on what is going on, these should be resolvable. Large-scale research also offers greater scope for informing and persuading policymakers as to the options and possibilities.

At the smaller scale, there are so many possibilities for further research, that could be fruitfully carried out by individuals or small teams, that I will limit myself to mentioning a few of particular interest to myself (but see also Tight 2012a):

- There is plentiful scope for more detailed studies of the broader student experience, probably making use of students as researchers. These should focus less on the 'typical' student – full-time, campus-based, young and undergraduate – and more on the huge numbers of other kinds of students (mature, part-time, distant, postgraduate, etc.).

- There is also a need for more detailed studies of the academic-staff experience, including, in particular, the burgeoning number of part-time and sessional academic staff. More attention should also be given to the growing variety of non-academic staff (management and administration, support staff, etc.) who contribute to the higher education experience.

- More emphasis needs to be given in research to the non-vocational aims and outcomes of higher education – community and social involvement, lifelong learning, etc. – alongside the vocational ones that otherwise tend to dominate (as in studies of the transition to work; see Chapter 5).

- It would also be useful and revealing to see more research on failed initiatives. If you read many of what I would term 'small-scale evaluative case studies', which research the impact of an initiative at course, department or institutional level, you will probably have noticed that they are almost invariably positive; that is they worked, to a greater or lesser extent. Logic, anecdotal evidence and personal experience all suggest, however, that this is not a representative sample; many, perhaps most, initiatives fail. It would be just as interesting, and perhaps more helpful, to hear of these, though I can readily understand why some researchers – and particularly their funders or employers – would not wish to publicize them.

Turning now to theory and methodology, we may start by arguing for the application and development of a wider range of methodologies and theories, and for research into topics at different levels (i.e. from the individual through to international studies).

In theoretical terms, it seems apparent that some frameworks may have come to the end of their useful life, and are ripe for replacement or improvement. For example, in the study of learning approaches (see Chapter 3), is there much more to be gained, theoretically or practically, from the dichotomous recognition of deep and surface learning approaches, when practices are clearly rather more complex than that? One might also question what the threshold concepts framework has added to studies of course design (see Chapter 4), or whether the ritual denouncements of managerialism (see Chapter 8), and of neo-liberal approaches in general, are overly defensive and simplistic.

In methodological terms, it would be good to see greater use made of autobiographical, biographical and life history approaches in qualitative studies. In quantitative studies, on the other hand, as well as a greater engagement in general and with the varied forms of multivariate analysis, more use could be made of simpler techniques. The reporting of averages, ranges and other distributional statistics, and of cross-tabulations between variables, for example, has much to offer and should be immediately accessible to most. Much greater use could also be made of mixed methodological approaches.

Higher education research is a rich and rapidly developing field. It has much to offer the researcher, whether new to research and/or to the field, or older and well-practised. There are many useful lifetimes of further research to be done here.

References

A work of this nature produces many references. To keep this list within reasonable bounds, journals that are referenced on several occasions or more have been abbreviated, as follows:

AE – Accounting Education
AEHE – Assessment and Evaluation in Higher Education
AER – Australian Educational Researcher
AHHE – Arts and Humanities in Higher Education
AJE – Australian Journal of Education
ALHE – Active Learning in Higher Education
ALT-J – Research in Learning Technology
AMJ – Academy of Management Journal
AMR – Academy of Management Review
APER – Asia Pacific Educational Review
APJE – Asia Pacific Journal of Education

BJEP – British Journal of Psychology
BJES – British Journal of Educational Studies
BJET – British Journal of Educational Technology
BJS – British Journal of Sociology
BJSE – British Journal of Sociology of Education

CCJRP – Community College Journal of Research and Practice
CE – Comparative Education
CER – Comparative Education Review
CHE – Christian Higher Education
CIM – Clinical and Investigative Medicine
ComE – Communication Education

DSCPE – Discourse: Studies in the Cultural Politics of Education

EAR – Educational Action Research
EC – Education as Change
EcER – Economics of Education Review
EdR – Educational Research

EE – Education Economics
EER – Environmental Education Research
EERJ – European Educational Research Journal
EJDE – European Journal of Dental Education
EJE – European Journal of Education
EJEE – European Journal of Engineering Education
EJHE – European Journal of Higher Education
EJPE – European Journal of Political Education
EnE – Engineering Education
EP – Educational Psychology
EPR – Educational Psychology Review
EPT – Educational Philosophy and Theory
ERE – Educational Research and Evaluation
ERR – Educational Research Review
ES – Educational Studies
ESP – English for Special Purposes
ET – Education + Training
EurR – European Review

GE – Gender and Education

HE – Higher Education
HEE – Higher Education in Europe
HEM – Higher Education Management
HEMP – Higher Education Management and Policy
HEP – Higher Education Policy
HEQ – Higher Education Quarterly
HER – Higher Education Review
HERD – Higher Education Research and Development

IETI – Innovations in Education and Teaching International
IHE – Innovative Higher Education
IJAD – International Journal for Academic Development
IJED – International Journal of Educational Development
IJEM – International Journal of Education Management
IJER – International Journal of Educational Research
IJFYHE – International Journal of the First Year in Higher Education
IJIE – International Journal of Inclusive Education
IJMCE – International Journal of Mentoring and Coaching in Education
IJRME – International Journal of Research and Method in Education
IJSE – International Journal of Science Education
IJSRM – International Journal of Social Research Methods
IPHER – International Perspectives on Higher Education Research
IRE – International Review of Education

IREE – International Review of Economics Education
IRRODL – International Review of Research in Open and Distance Learning
IS – Instructional Science

JAP – Journal of Applied Psychology
JCD – Journal of Counselling and Development
JCPA – Journal of Comparative Policy Analysis
JCR – Journal of Critical Realism
JCSD – Journal of College Student Development
JCSR – Journal of College Student Retention
JEAH – Journal of Educational Administration and History
JEAP – Journal of English for Academic Purposes
JEB – Journal of Education for Business
JEMS – Journal of Ethnic and Migration Studies
JEP – Journal of Education Policy
JER – Journal of Educational Research
JET – Journal of Education and Teaching
JEW – Journal of Education and Work
JFHE – Journal of Further and Higher Education
JGHE – Journal of Geography in Higher Education
JHBSE – Journal of Human Behavior in the Social Environment
JHE – Journal of Higher Education
JHEPM – Journal of Higher Education Policy and Management
JHHE – Journal of Hispanic Higher Education
JHLSTE – Journal of Hospitality, Leisure, Sport and Tourism Education
JKE – Journal of the Knowledge Economy
JME – Journal of Management Education
JMHE – Journal of Marketing in Higher Education
JMS – Journal of Management Studies
JNE – Journal of Negro Education
JPE – Journal of Political Economy
JPSE – Journal of Political Science Education
JS – Journal of Sociology
JSIE – Journal of Studies in International Education
JTIB – Journal of Teaching in International Business
JVB – Journal of Vocational Behavior
JVET – Journal of Vocational Education and Training

LI – Learning and Instruction
LID – Learning and Individual Differences
LRE – London Review of Education

MCA – Mind, Culture and Activity
MS – The Manchester School

NDTL – New Directions in Teaching and Learning

OL – Open Learning
ORE – Oxford Review of Education
OS – Organizational Science

PFE – Policy Futures in Education
PS – Political Science and Politics

QAE – Quality Assurance in Education
QHE – Quality in Higher Education
QQ – Quality and Quantity
QSE – Qualitative Studies in Education

RCIE – Research in Comparative and International Education
RE – Research Evaluation
REE – Race Ethnicity and Education
RER – Review of Educational Research
ResHE – Research in Higher Education
RevHE – Review of Higher Education
RP – Research Policy
RPE – Research Papers in Education

SAJHE – South African Journal of Higher Education
SCE – Studies in Continuing Education
SE – Science Education
SEE – Studies in Educational Evaluation
SF – Social Factors
SHE – Studies in Higher Education
SIR – Social Indicators Research
SJER – Scandinavian Journal of Educational Research
SocE – Sociology of Education
SPP – Science and Public Policy
SSJ – Social Science Journal
SWE – Social Work Education

TEM – Tertiary Education and Management
THE – Teaching in Higher Education
TIHE – The Internet and Higher Education
TLI – Teaching and Learning Inquiry
TP – Theory and Psychology
TPE – Technology, Pedagogy and Education
TQM – Total Quality Management
TQMBE – Total Quality Management and Business Excellence

TS – Teaching Sociology
TT – Teachers and Teaching

VL – Vocations and Learning

Abbott, A. (2001) *Chaos of Disciplines*. Chicago, IL, University of Chicago Press.
Abdullah, F. (2006) Measuring Service Quality in Higher Education. *Marketing Intelligence and Planning*, 24, 1, 31–47.
Abrahams, L., and Fitzgerald, P. (2015) Would 'Good' Values Yield Good 'Value'? *JKE*, 6, 125–37.
Abramo, G., Cicero, T., and D'Angelo, C. (2012) Revisiting Size Effects in Higher Education Research Productivity. *HE*, 63, 6, 701–17.
Acker, S., Webber, M., and Smyth, E. (2016) Continuity or Change? *NASPA Journal about Women in Higher Education*, 9, 1, 1–20.
Ackerman, R., and Schibrowsky, J. (2007) A Business Marketing Strategy applied to Student Retention. *JCSR*, 9, 3, 307–36.
Adams, C., Buetow, S., Edlin, R., Zdravkovic, N., and Heyligers, J. (2016) A Collaborative Approach to Integrating Information and Academic Literacy into the Curricula of Research Methods Courses. *Journal of Academic Librarianship*, 42, 222–31.
Adams, F. (2006) Managerialism and Higher Education Governance. *SAJHE*, 20, 1, 5–16.
Adams, J., Cochrane, M., and Dunne, L. (eds) (2012a) *Applying Theory to Educational Research*. Chichester, Wiley-Blackwell.
Adams, J., Cochrane, M., and Dunne, L. (2012b) Introduction. pp. 1–10 in J. Adams, M. Cochrane and L. Dunne (eds) *Applying Theory to Educational Research*. Chichester, Wiley-Blackwell.
Addison. N. (2014) Doubting Learning Outcomes in Higher Education Contexts. *International Journal of Art and Design Education*, 33, 3, 313–25.
Adkins, L. (2005) Social Capital. *Feminist Theory*, 6, 2, 195–211.
Adler, N., Hellstrom, T., Jacob, M., and Norrgren, F. (2000) A Model for the Institutionalisation of University-Industry Partnerships. In M. Jacob and T. Hellstrom (eds) *The Future of Knowledge Production in the Academy*. Buckingham, Open University Press.
Adler, P., and Kwon, S.-W. (2002) Social Capital. *AMR*, 27, 1, 17–40.
Adler-Kassner, L., Majewski, J., and Koshnick, D. (2012) The Value of Troublesome Knowledge. *Composition Forum*, 26, 17pp.
Adsit, J. (2017) The Writer and Meta-Knowledge about Writing. *New Writing*, DOI:10.1080/14790726.2017.1299764.
Aguillo, I., Bar-Ilan, J., Levene, M., and Ortega, J. (2010) Comparing University Rankings. *Scientometrics*, 85, 243–56.
Ahier, J. (2000) Financing Higher Education by Loans and Fees. *JEP*, 15, 6, 683–70.
Ahola, S. (2005) Global and Local Priorities in Higher Education Policies. *TEM*, 11, 1, 37–53.
Ai, B. (2017) Constructing an Academic Identity in Australia. *HERD*, DOI:10.1080/07294360.2017.1303459.
Ainley, P. (2008) The Varieties of Student Experience. *SHE*, 33, 5, 615–24.
Aitkin, D. (1991) How Research Came to Dominate Higher Education and What Ought to be Done About It. *ORE*, 17, 3, 235–47.
Akar, H. (2010) Globalization and its Challenges for Developing Countries. *APER*, 11, 447–57.
Akerlind, G. (2005a) Academic Growth and Development. *HE*, 50, 1, 1–32.
Akerlind, G. (2005b) Variation and Commonality in Phenomenographic Research Methods. *HERD*, 24, 4, 321–34.

Akerlind, G., McKenzie, J., and Lupton, M. (2014) The Potential of Combining Phenomenography, Variation Theory and Threshold Concepts to Inform Curriculum Design in Higher Education. *IPHER*, 10, 227–47.

Aktas, F., Pitts, T., Richards, J., and Silova, I. (2017) Institutionalizing Global Citizenship. *JSIE*, 21, 1, 65–80.

Ala-Vähälä, T. (2016) Reception of the Quality Assurance Commitments of the Bologna Process in Finnish Higher Education Institutions. *QHE*, 22, 2, 103–16.

Albers, C. (2008) Improving Pedagogy through Action Learning and Scholarship of Teaching and Learning. *TS*, 36, 1, 79–86.

Albertyn, R., Machika, P., and Troskie-de Bruin, C. (2016) Towards Responsible Massification. *Africa Education Review*, 13, 3–4, 49–64.

Albrecht, J. (2012) Authentic Learning and Communities of Practice in Tourism Higher Education. *Journal of Teaching in Travel and Tourism*, 12, 3, 260–76.

Alexander, P., Harris-Huemmert, S., and McAlpine, L. (2014) Tools for Reflection on the Academic Identities of Doctoral Students. *IJAD*, 19, 3, 162–73.

Alhazmi, A., and Nyland, B. (2013) The Saudi Arabian International Student Experience. *Compare*, 43, 3, 346–65.

Almeida, P., Teixiera-Dias, J., Martinho, M., and Balasooriya, C. (2011) The Interplay between Students' Perceptions of Context and Approaches to Learning. *RPE*, 26, 2, 149–69.

Alperin, J. (2013) Brazil's Exception to the World-class University Movement. *QHE*, 19, 2, 158–72.

Alsop, G., and Tompsett, C. (2006) Making Sense of 'Pure' Phenomenography in Information and Communication Technology in Education. *ALT-J*, 14, 3, 241–59.

Altbach, P. (ed.) (1996) *The International Academic Profession*. Princeton, NJ: Carnegie Foundation for the Advancement of Learning.

Altbach, P. (1999) The Logic of Mass Higher Education. *TEM*, 5, 2, 107–24.

Altbach, P., and Knight, J. (2007) The Internationalization of Higher Education. *JSIE*, 11, 3–4, 290–305.

Alvargonzalez, D. (2011) Multidisciplinarity, Interdisciplinarity, Transdisciplinarity and the Sciences. *International Studies in the Philosophy of Science*, 25, 4, 387–403.

Alves, M., and Korhonen, V. (2016) Transitions and Trajectories from Higher Education to Work and Back. *EERJ*, 15, 6, 676–95.

Amaral, A., Magalhaes, A., and Santiago, R. (2003) The Rise of Academic Managerialism in Portugal. pp. 131–53 in A. Amaral, L. Meek and I. Larsen (eds) *The Higher Education Managerial Revolution?* Dordrecht, Kluwer.

Amaral, A., and Teixeira, P. (2000) The Rise and Fall of the Private Sector in Portuguese Higher Education. *HEP*, 13, 3, 245–66.

Aminbeidokhti, A., Jamshidi, L., and Hoseini, A. (2016) The Effect of the Total Quality Management on Organizational Innovation in Higher Education mediated by Organizational Learning. *SHE*, 41, 7, 1153–68.

Amos, T., and Fischer, S. (1998) Understanding and Responding to Student Learning Difficulties within the Higher Education Context. *SAJHE*, 12, 2, 17–23.

Amsler, S., and Bolsmann, C. (2012) University Ranking as Social Exclusion. *BJSE*, 33, 2, 283–301.

Amundsen, C., and Wilson, M. (2012) Are We Asking the Right Questions? *RER*, 82, 1, 90–126.

Anderberg, E., Svensson, L., Alvegard, C., and Johansson, T. (2008) The Epistemological Role of Language Use in Learning. *ERR*, 3, 14–29.

Anderson, G. (2006) Carving out Time and Space in the Managerial University. *Journal of Organizational Change Management*, 19, 5, 578–92.

Anderson, G. (2008) Mapping Academic Resistance in the Managerial University. *Organization*, 15, 2, 251–70.

Anderson, V., McGrath, T., and Butcher, A. (2014) Asian-born New Zealand-educated Graduates' Transition to Work. *APJE*, 34, 1, 65–79.

Andreotti, V., Stein, S., Pashby, K., and Nicolson, M. (2016) Social Cartographies as Performative Devices in Research on Higher Education. *HERD*, 35, 1, 84–91.

Andriani, L., and Christoforou, A. (2016) Social Capital. *Journal of Economic Issues*, 50, 1, 4–22.

Angulo-Ruiz, L., and Pergelova, A. (2013) The Student Retention Puzzle Revisited. *Journal of Nonprofit and Public Sector Marketing*, 25, 334–53.

Annala, J., and Makinen, M. (2011) The Research-Teaching Nexus in Higher Education Curriculum Design. *Transnational Curriculum Inquiry*, 8, 1, 3–21.

Annala, J., and Makinen, M. (2016) Communities of Practice in Higher Education. *SHE*, DOI:10.1080/03075079.2015.1125877.

Ansah, F. (2015) A Strategic Quality Assurance Framework in an African Higher Education Context. *QHE*, 21, 2, 132–50.

Apkarian, J., Mulligan, K., Rotondi, M., and Brint, S. (2014) Who Governs? *TEM*, 20, 2, 151–64.

Archer, A. (2008a) The Place is Suffering. *ESP*, 27, 255–66.

Archer, L. (2008b) Younger Academics' Constructions of 'Authenticity', 'Success' and Professional Identity. *SHE*, 33, 4, 385–403.

Aronson, P., Callahan, T., and Davis, T. (2015) The Transition from College to Work during the Great Recession. *Journal of Youth Studies*, 18, 9, 1097–18.

Arunasalam, N. (2016) Impact of UK and Australian Transnational Higher Education in Malaysia. *JSIE*, 20, 3, 242–59.

Ash, M. (1980) Experimental Psychology in Germany before 1914. *Psychological Research*, 42, 75–86.

Asif, M., Awan, M., Khan, M., and Ahmad, N. (2013) A Model for Total Quality Management in Higher Education. *QQ*, 47, 1883–904.

Asikainen, H., and Gijbels, D. (2017) Do Students Develop Towards More Deep Approaches to Learning during Studies? *EPR*, 29, 205–34.

Ashwin, P. (ed.) (2005) *Changing Higher Education*. London, Routledge.

Ashwin, P. (2009) *Analysing Teaching-Learning Interactions in Higher Education*. London, Continuum.

Ashwin, P., Abbas, A., and McLean, M. (2014) How Do Students' Accounts of Sociology Change over the Course of their Undergraduate Degrees? *HE*, 67, 2, 219–34.

Ashworth, P., and Greasley, K. (2009) The Phenomenology of 'Approach to Studying'. *SHE*, 34, 5, 561–76.

Ashworth, P., and Lucas, U. (2000) Achieving Empathy and Engagement. *SHE*, 25, 3, 295–308.

Asif, M., Awan, M., Khan, M., and Ahmad, N. (2013) A Model for Total Quality Management in Higher Education. *QQ*, 47, 1883–904.

Astin, A. (1975) *Preventing Students from Dropping Out*. San Francisco, CA, Jossey-Bass.

Attenborough, F. (2011) 'I don't f***ing care!' *Discourse and Communication*, 5, 2, 99–121.

Atuahene, F. (2011) Re-thinking the Missing Mission of Higher Education. *Journal of Asian and African Studies*, 46, 4, 321–41.

Austerlitz, N. (2007) The Internal Point of View. *Art, Design and Communication in Higher Education*, 5, 3, 165–77.

Austin, A., Chapman, D., Farah, S., Wilson, E., and Ridge, N. (2014) Expatriate Academic Staff in the United Arab Emirates. *HE*, 68, 4, 541–57.

Axel, E. (1997) One Developmental Line in European Activity Theories. pp. 128–46 in M. Cole, Y. Engeström and O. Vasquez (eds) *Mind, Culture and Activity*. Cambridge, Cambridge University Press.

Ayoubi, R., and Massoud, H. (2007) The Strategy of Internationalization in Universities. *IJEM*, 21, 4, 329–49.

Aziz, M., and Abdullah, D. (2014) Finding the Next 'Wave' in Internationalization of Higher Education. *APER*, 15, 493–502.

Baartman, L., and Ruijs, L. (2011) Comparing Students' Perceived and Actual Competence in Higher Professional Education. *AEHE*, 36, 4, 385–98.

Baartman, L., Gulikers, J., and Dijkstra, A. (2013) Factors Influencing Assessment Quality in Higher Vocational Education. *AEHE*, 38, 8, 978–97.

Baeten, M., Kyndt, E., Struyven, K., and Dochy, F. (2010) Using Student-centred Learning Environments to Stimulate Deep Approaches to Learning. *ERR*, 5, 243–60.

Baeten, M., Struyven, K., and Dochy, F. (2013) Student-centred Teaching Methods. *SEE*, 39, 1, 14–22.

Bagilhole, B. (2012) A Cross-national Analysis of Gender Equality and the Shift from Collegiality to Managerialism in Higher Education Policy. *Acta Pedagogica Vilnensia*, 28, 23–36.

Bailey, F. (1977) *Morality and Expediency*. Oxford, Basil Blackwell.

Bailey, J. (2000) Students as Clients in a Professional/Client Relationship. *JME*, 24, 3, 353–65.

Baillie, C., Bowden, J., and Meyer, J. (2013) Threshold Capabilities. *HE*, 65, 2, 227–46.

Baker, B., Orr, M., and Young, M. (2007) Academic Drift, Institutional Production and Professional Distribution of Graduate Degrees in Educational Leadership. *Educational Administration Quarterly*, 43, 3, 279–318.

Balan, J. (2012) Research Universities in Latin America. *Social Research*, 79, 3, 741–70.

Baldwin, G. (2005) *The Teaching-Research Nexus*. Melbourne, University of Melbourne, Centre for the Study of Higher Education.

Ball, R., and Wilkinson, R. (1994) The Use and Abuse of Performance Indicators in UK Higher Education. *HE*, 27, 4, 417–27.

Ball, S. (1995) Intellectuals or Technicians? *BJES*, 43, 3, 255–71.

Ball, S., and Mohamed, M. (2010) Insights on How Students Perceive the Research-Teaching Nexus. *JHLSTE*, 9, 2, 89–101.

Bamwesiga, P., Fejes, A., and Dahlgren, L.-O. (2014) A Phenomenographic Study of Students' Conceptions of Quality in Learning in Higher Education in Rwanda. *SCE*, 35, 3, 337–50.

Bandias, S., Fuller, D., and Pfitzner, D. (2011) Vocational and Higher Education in Australia. *JHEPM*, 33, 6, 583–94.

Bankston, C., and Zhou, M. (2002) Social Capital as Process. *Sociological Inquiry*, 72, 2, 285–317.

Baptiste, I. (2001) Educating Lone Wolves. *Adult Education Quarterly*, 51, 3, 184–201.

Barkhuizen, N., Rothmann, S., and Vijver, F. van de (2016) Burnout and Work Engagement of Academics in Higher Education Institutions. *Stress Health*, 30, 322–32.

Barnabè, F., and Riccaboni, A. (2007) Which Role for Performance Measurement Systems in Higher Education? *SEE*, 33, 302–19.

Barnard, A., Croft, W., Irons, R., Cuffe, N., Bandara, W., and Rowntree, P. (2011) Peer Partnership to enhance Scholarship of Teaching. *HERD*, 30, 4, 435–48.

Barnard, A., McCosker, H., and Gerber, R. (1999) Phenomenography. *Qualitative Health Research*, 9, 2, 212–26.

Barnard, E. (1960) Crisis in Higher Education. *The Massachusetts Review*, 1, 4, 701–16.

Barnett, G., Lee, M., Jiang, K., and Park, H. (2016) The Flow of International Students from a Macro Perspective. *Compare*, 46, 4, 533–59.

Barnett, R. (1987) The Maintenance of Quality in the Public Sector of UK Higher Education. *HE*, 16, 3, 279–301.

Barnett, R. (1992) Linking Teaching and Research. *JHE*, 63, 6, 619–36.

Baron, P., and Corbin, L. (2012) Student Engagement. *HERD*, 31, 6, 759–72.

Barradell, S. (2013) The Identification of Threshold Concepts. *HE*, 65, 2, 265–76.

Barrett, B. (2012) Is Interdisciplinarity Old News? *BJSE*, 33, 1, 97–114.

Barrett, M., Harmin, M., Maracle, B., Patterson, M., Thomson, C., Flowers, M., and Bors, K. (2017) Shifting Relations with the More-than-Human. *EER*, 23, 1, 131–43.

Barry, A., and Born, G. (eds) (2013) *Interdisciplinarity*. London, Routledge.

Barry, A., Born, G., and Weszkalnys, G. (2008) Logics of Interdisciplinarity. *Economy and Society*, 37, 1, 20–49.

Barry, J., Berg, E., and Chandler, J. (2006) Academic Shape Shifting. *Organization*, 13, 2, 275–98.

Barton, D. (1994) *Literacy*. Oxford, Blackwell.

Barton, D., and Tusting, K. (eds) (2005a) *Beyond Communities of Practice*. Cambridge, Cambridge University Press.

Barton, D., and Tusting, K. (2005b) Introduction. pp. 1–13 in D. Barton and K. Tusting (eds) *Beyond Communities of Practice*. Cambridge, Cambridge University Press.

Bartsch, R. (2013a) Designing SoTL Studies. *NDTL*, 136, 17–33.

Bartsch, R. (2013b) Designing SoTL Studies. *NDTL*, 136, 35–48.

Bastalich, W., Behrend, M., and Bloomfield, R. (2014) Is Non-subject Based Research Training a 'Waste of Time', Good Only for the Development of Professional Skills? *THE*, 19, 4, 373–84.

Bastedo, M., and Gumport, P. (2003) Access to What? *HE*, 46, 3, 341–59.

Bath, D., and Smith, C. (2004) Academic Developers. *IJAD*, 9, 1, 9–27.

Beach, D. (2013) Changing Higher Education. *JEP*, 28, 4, 517–33.

Bean, J. (1980) Dropouts and Turnover. *ResHE*, 12, 2, 155–87.

Bean, J., and Metzner, B. (1985) A Conceptual Model of Nontraditional Undergraduate Student Attrition. *RER*, 55, 4, 485–540.

Beaty, L. (2006) Foreword. pp. xi–xii in Meyer, J., and Land, R. (eds) *Overcoming Barriers to Student Understanding*. London, Routledge.

Bebbington, A., Guggenheim, S., Olson, E., and Woolcock, M. (2004) Exploring Social Capital Debates at the World Bank. *Journal of Development Studies*, 40, 5, 33–64.

Becher, T. (1981) Towards a Definition of Disciplinary Cultures. *SHE*, 6, 2, 109–22.

Becher, T. (1984) The Cultural View. pp. 165–98 in B. Clark (ed.) *Perspectives on Higher Education*. Berkeley, CA, University of California Press.

Becher, T. (1987) The Disciplinary Shaping of the Profession. pp. 271–303 in B. Clark (ed.) *The Academic Profession*. Berkeley, CA, University of California Press.

Becher, T. (1989a) *Academic Tribes and Territories*. Milton Keynes, Open University Press.

Becher, T. (1989b) Historians on History. *SHE*, 14, 3, 263–78.

Becher, T. (1990) Physicists on Physics. *SHE*, 15, 1, 3–20.

Becher, T. (1994) The Significance of Disciplinary Differences. *SHE*, 19, 2, 151–61.

Becher, T. (1996) The Learning Professions. *SHE*, 21, 1, 43–55.

Becher, T. (1999) *Professional Practices*. New Brunswick, NJ, Transaction.

Becher, T., and Trowler, P. (2001) *Academic Tribes and Territories*. Buckingham, Open University Press, second edition.

Beck, J., and Young, M. (2005) The Assault on the Professions and the Restructuring of Academic and Professional Identities. *BJSE*, 26, 2, 183–97.

Beck, K. (2012) Globalization/s. *Canadian Journal of Education*, 35, 3, 133–48.

Beck, U. (2000) *What is Globalization?* Malden, MA, Polity.

Becker, G. (1962) Investment in Human Capital. *Journal of Political Economy*, 70, 5, Part 2, 9–49.

Becker, G. (1964) *Human Capital*. New York: National Bureau of Economic Research/ Columbia University Press.

Beckmann, A., and Cooper, C. (2013) Neoliberal Globalization, Managerialism and Higher Education in England. *Educational Policy Analysis and Strategic Research*, 8, 1, 5–24.

Beckwith, J. (1991) Approaches to Learning, Their Context and Relationship to Assessment Performance. *HE*, 22, 1, 17–30.

Bedenlier, S., and Zawacki-Richter, O. (2015) Internationalization of Higher Education and the Impacts on Academic Faculty Members. *RCIE*, 10, 2, 185–201.

Beerkens, E. (2003) Globalisation and Higher Education Research. *JSIE*, 7, 2, 128–48.

Beigi, M., Shirmohammadi, M., and Kim, S. (2016) Living the Academic Life. *Work*, 53, 459–68.

Bennell, P., and Pearce, T. (2003) The Internationalisation of Higher Education. *IJED*, 23, 215–32.

Bennett, C., and Dewar, J. (2012) An Overview of the Scholarship of Teaching and Learning in Mathematics. *PRIMUS*, 22, 6, 458–73.

Bennett, R., Hobson, J., Jones, A., Martin-Lynch, P., Scutt, C., Strehlow, K., and Veitch, S. (2016) Being Chimaera. *HERD*, 35, 2, 217–28.

Benson, R., and Brack, C. (2009) Developing the Scholarship of Teaching. *THE*, 14, 1, 71–80.

Bentley, P., and Kyvik, S. (2012) Academic Work from a Comparative Perspective. *HE*, 63, 4, 529–47.

Benzie, H., Pryce, A., and Smith, K. (2017) The Wicked Problem of Embedding Academic Literacies. *HERD*, 36, 2, 227–40.

Berchem, T. (1991) The Internationalisation of Higher Education. *HE*, 21, 3, 297–304.

Berg, D., Gunn, A., Hill, M., and Haigh, M. (2016) Research in the Work of New Zealand Teacher-Educators. *HERD*, 35, 6, 1125–38.

Bergman, L. (2016) Supporting Academic Literacies. *THE*, 21, 5, 516–31.

Bergström, P. (2010) Process-based Assessment for Professional Learning in Higher Education. *IRRODL*, 11, 2, 33–48.

Bernhard, A. (2012) Quality Assurance in an International Higher Education Area. *TEM*, 18, 2, 153–69.

Berry, C. (1999) University League Tables. *HER*, 31, 2, 3–10.

Berry, C., and Taylor, J. (2014) Internationalisation in Higher Education in Latin America. *HE*, 67, 5, 585–601.

Bess, J. (1988) *Collegiality and Bureaucracy in the Modern University*. New York, Teachers College Press.

Bevitt, S. (2015) Assessment Innovation and Student Experience. *AEHE*, 40, 1, 103–19.

Biesta, G., Allan, J., and Edwards, R. (2011) The Theory Question in Research Capacity Building in Education. *BJES*, 59, 3, 225–39.

Biggeri, L., Bini, M., and Grilli, L. (2001) The Transition from University to Work. *Journal of the Royal Statistical Society A*, 164, 2, 293–305.

Biggs, J. (1976) Dimensions of Study Behaviour. *BJEP*, 46, 1, 68–80.

Biggs, J. (1979) Individual Differences in Study Processes and the Quality of Learning Outcomes. *HE*, 8, 4, 381–94.

Biggs, J. (1993) What do Inventories of Students' Learning Processes really Measure? *BJEP*, 63, 1, 3–19.

Biggs, J. (1999) What the Student does. *HERD*, 18, 1, 57–75.

Biggs, J., and Collis, K. (1982) *Evaluating the Quality of Learning*. New York, Academic Press.

Biglan, A. (1973a) The Characteristics of Subject Matter in Different Academic Disciplines. *JAP*, 57, 3, 195–203.

Biglan, A. (1973b) Relationships between Subject Matter Characteristics and the Structure and Output of University Departments. *JAP*, 57, 3, 204–13.

Billing, D. (1998) Quality Management and Organisational Structure in Higher Education. *JHEPM*, 20, 2, 139–59.

Billing, D. (2004) International Comparisons and Trends in External Quality Assurance of Higher Education. *HE*, 47, 1, 113–37.

Billing, D., and Thomas, H. (2000) The International Transferability of Quality Assessment Systems for Higher Education. *QHE*, 6, 1, 31–40.

Bird, E. (2001) Disciplining the Interdisciplinary. *BJSE*, 22, 4, 463–78.

Birnbaum, R. (1983) *Maintaining Diversity in Higher Education*. San Francisco, CA, Jossey-Bass.

Birnbaum, R. (2000) *Management Fads in Higher Education*. San Francisco, CA, Jossey-Bass.

Bjornali, E., and Støren, L. (2012) Examining Competence Factors that encourage Innovative Behaviour by European Higher Education Graduate Professionals. *Journal of Small Business and Enterprise Development*, 19, 3, 402–23.

Bjørnskov, C., and Sønderskov, K. (2013) Is Social Capital a Good Concept? *SIR*, 114, 1225–42.

Black, M., and Rechter, S. (2013) A Critical Reflection on the Use of an Embedded Academic Literacy Program for Teaching Sociology. *JS*, 49, 4, 456–70.

Blackmore, P. (2007) Developing Tribes and Territories. *Educational Developments*, 8, 2, 1–4, 10–11, 14.

Blackmore, P., and Kandiko, C. (2011) Interdisciplinarity within an Academic Career. *RPE*, 16, 1, 123–34.

Blackmur, D. (2008) A Critical Analysis of the INQAAHE Guidelines of Good Practice for Higher Education Quality Assurance Agencies. *HE*, 56, 6, 723–34.

Blair, A. (2015) Similar or Different? A comparative analysis of higher education research in political science and international relations between the United States of America and the United Kingdom. *JPSE*, 11, 2, 174–89.

Blair, E. (2014) Academic Development through the Contextualization of the Scholarship of Teaching and Learning. *IJAD*, 19, 4, 330–40.

Bleiklie, I. (2005) Organizing Higher Education in a Knowledge Society. *HE*, 49, 1, 31–59.

Bligh, B., and Flood, M. (2017) Activity Theory in Empirical Higher Education Research. *TEAM*, 23, 2, 125–52.

Blunden, A. (2007) Modernity, the Individual and the Foundations of Cultural-Historical Activity Theory. *MCA*, 14, 4, 253–65.

Boer, H. de, Huisman, J., and Meister-Scheytt, C. (2010) Supervision in 'Modern' University Governance. *SHE*, 35, 3, 317–33.

Boeve, A., Meijer, R., Bosker, R., Vugteveen, J., Hoekstra, R., and Albers, C. (2016) Implementing the Flipped Classroom. *HE*, DOI 10.1007/s10734-016-0104-y.

Boffo, S., and Moscati, R. (1998) Evaluation in the Italian Higher Education System. *EJE*, 33, 3, 349–60.

Bogue, G., and Johnson, B. (2010) Performance Incentives and Public College Accountability in the United States. *HEMP*, 22, 2, 9–30.

Bommel, M. van, Kwakman, K., and Boshuizen, H. (2012) Experiences of Social Work Students with learning Theoretical Knowledge in Constructivist Higher Vocational Education. *JVET*, 64, 4, 529–42.

Boon, S., Johnston, B., and Webber, S. (2007) A Phenomenographic Study of English Faculty's Conceptions of Information Literacy. *Journal of Documentation*, 63, 2, 204–28.

Booth, A. (2004) Rethinking the Scholarly. *AHHE*, 3, 3, 247–66.

Booth, S. (1997) On Phenomenography, Learning and Teaching. *HERD*, 16, 2, 135–58.

Bornmann, L., Mittag, S., and Daniel, H-D. (2006) Quality Assurance in Higher Education. *HE*, 52, 3, 687–709.

Bosch, H. van den, and Teelken, C. (2000) Organisation and Leadership in Higher Education. *HEP*, 13, 4, 379–97.

Boshier, R. (2009) Why is the Scholarship of Teaching and Learning such a Hard Sell? *HERD*, 28, 1, 1–15.

Boshier, R., and Huang, Y. (2008) In the House of Scholarship of Teaching and Learning (SoTL), Teaching Lives Upstairs and Learning in the Basement. *THE*, 13, 6, 645–56.

Bouckenooghe, D., Cools, E., De Clerq, D., Vanderheyden, K., and Fatima, T. (2016) Exploring the Impact of Cognitive Style Profiles on Different Learning Approaches. LID (pre-publication).

Boud, D., and Brew, A. (2013) Reconceptualising Academic Work as Professional Practice. *IJAD*, 18, 3, 208–21.

Bougnol, M.-L., and Dula, J. (2015) Technical Pitfalls in University Rankings. *HE*, 69, 5, 859–66.

Bourdieu, P. (1986) The Forms of Capital. pp. 241–58 in J. Richardson (ed.) *Handbook of Theory and Research for the Sociology of Education*. New York, Greenwood Press.

Boustedt, J., Eckerdal, A., McCartney, R., Mostrom, J., Ratcliffe, M., Sanders, K., and Zander, C. (2007) Threshold Concepts in Computer Science. *ACM SIGSE Bulletin*, 39, 1, 504–8.

Bovill, C., Jordan, L., and Watters, N. (2015) Transnational Approaches to Teaching and Learning in Higher Education. *THE*, 20, 1, 12–23.

Bowden, J. (2005) Reflections on the Phenomenographic Team Research Process. pp. 11–31 in J. Bowden and P. Green (eds) *Doing Developmental Phenomenography*. Melbourne, RMIT University Press.

Bowden, J., and Marton, F. (1998) *The University of Learning*. London, Kogan Page.

Bowles, T., and Brindle, K. (2017) Identifying Facilitating Factors and Barriers to improving Student Retention Rates in Tertiary Teaching Courses. *HERD*, DOI:10.1080/07294360.2016.1264927.

Bowman, N., and Bastedo, M. (2009) Getting on the Front Page. *ResHE*, 50, 5, 415–36.

Boyd, P., and Smith, C. (2016) The Contemporary Academic. *SHE*, 41, 4, 678–95.

Boyer, E. (1990) *Scholarship Reconsidered*. Princeton, NJ: Carnegie Foundation for the Advancement of Teaching.

Boyer Commission on Educating Undergraduates in the Research University (1998) *Reinventing Undergraduate Education*.

Bradbeer, I., Healey, M., and Kneale, P. (2004) Undergraduate Geographers' Understanding of Geography, Learning and Teaching. *JGHE*, 28, 1, 17–34.

Bradbeer, J. (1999) Barriers to Interdisciplinarity. *JGHE*, 23, 3, 381–96.

Brady, N., and Bates, A. (2016) The Standards Paradox. *EERJ*, 15, 2, 155–74.

Braine, G. (2002) Academic Literacy and the Nonnative Speaker Graduate Student. *JEAP*, 1, 59–68.

Brandenburg, R., and Wilson, J. (eds) (2013) *Pedagogies for the Future*. Rotterdam, Sense.

Braun, D. (1999) Changing Governance Models in Higher Education. *Swiss Political Science Review*, 5, 3, 1–24.

Braun, D., and Merrien, F.-X. (eds) (1999) *Towards a New Model of Governance for Universities?* London, Jessica Kingsley.

Braun, T., and Schubert, A. (2003) A Quantitative View on the Coming of Age of Interdisciplinarity in the Sciences, 1980-99. *Scientometrics*, 58, 1, 183–9.

Braxton, J. (1996) Contrasting Perspectives on the Relationship between Teaching and Research. *New Directions for Institutional Research*, 90, 5–14.

Braxton, J., and Hargens, L. (1996) Variation among Academic Disciplines. In J. Smart (ed), *Higher Education*. New York, Agathon Press, Volume 11, 1–46.

Braxton, J., Milem, J., and Sullivan, A. (2000) The Influence of Active Learning on the College Student Departure Process. *JHE*, 71, 5, 569–90.

Breakwell, G., and Tytherleigh, M. (2010) University Leaders and University Performance in the United Kingdom. *HE*, 60, 5, 491–506.

Brekke, I. (2007) Ethnic Background and the Transition from Education to Work among University Graduates. *JEMS*, 33, 8, 1299–321.

Brennan, J. (2012) Is There a Future for Higher Education Institutions in the Knowledge Society? *EurR*, 20, 2, 195–202.

Brew, A. (1999) Research and Teaching. *SHE*, 24, 3, 291–301.

Brew, A. (2001) Conceptions of Research. *SHE*, 26, 3, 271–85.

Brew, A. (2006) *Research and Teaching*. Basingstoke, Palgrave Macmillan.

Brew, A. (2008) Disciplinary and Interdisciplinary Affiliations of Experienced Researchers. *HE*, 56, 4, 423–48.

Brew, A., and Ginns, P. (2008) The Relationship between Engagement in the Scholarship of Teaching and Learning and Students' Course Experiences. *AEHE*, 33, 5, 535–45.

Brint, S., Riddle, M., Turk-Bicakci, L. and Levy, C. (2005) From the Liberal to the Practical Arts in American Colleges and Universities. *JHE*, 76, 2, 151–80.

Broecke, S. (2015) University Rankings. *EE*, 23, 2, 137–61.

Brown, A. (1994) The Advancement of Learning. *EdR*, 23, 8, 4–12.

Brown, J. S., Collins, A., and Duguid, P. (1989) Situated Cognition and the Culture of Learning. *EdR*, 18, 1, 32–42.

Brown, J. S., and Duguid, P. (1991) Organizational Learning and Communities-of-Practice. *OS*, 2, 1, 40–57.

Brown, J. S., and Duguid, P. (2001) Knowledge and Organization. *OS*, 12, 2, 198–213.

Brown, K., Shephard, K., Warren, D., Hesson, G., and Fleming, J. (2016) Using Phenomenography to Build an Understanding of how University People conceptualise their Community-engaged Activities. *HERD*, 35, 4, 643–57.

Brown, L., and Jones, I. (2013) Encounters with Racism and the International Student Experience. *SHE*, 38, 7, 1004–19.

Brown, R. (2013) Mutuality meets the Market. *HEQ*, 67, 4, 420–37.

Brown, R., and McCartney, S. (1998) The Link between Research and Teaching. *IETI*, 35, 2, 117–29.

Brownlee, J., Walker, S., Lennox, S., Exley, B., and Pearce, S. (2009) The First Year University Experience. *HE*, 58, 5, 599–618.

Bruce, C. (1994) Research Students' Early Experiences of the Dissertation Literature Review. *SHE*, 19, 2, 217–29.

Bruce, C., Pham, B., and Stoodley, I. (2004) Constituting the Significance and Value of Research. *SHE*, 29, 2, 219–38.

Bruner, R., and Iannarelli, J. (2011) Globalization of Management Education. *Journal of Teaching in International Business*, 22, 232–42.

Brunie, A. (2009) Meaningful Distinctions within a Concept. *Social Science Research*, 38, 251–65.

Buckley, C. (2011) Student and Staff Perceptions of the Research-Teaching Nexus. *IETI*, 48, 3, 313–22.

Buckley, S. (2012) Higher Education and Knowledge Sharing. *IETI*, 49, 3, 333–44.

Bucur, A., Kifor, C., and Marginean, S. (2016) Evaluation of the Quality and Quantity of Research Results in Higher Education. *QQ*, DOI 10.1007/s11135-016-0452-9.

Budd, R. (2016) Undergraduate Orientations towards Higher Education in Germany and England. *HE*, DOI 10.1007/s10734-015-9977-4.

Buhl, H. (2007) Well-being and the Child-Parent Relationship at the Transition from University to Work Life. *Journal of Adolescent Research*, 22, 5, 550–71.

Bunce, L., Baird, A., and Jones, S. (2016) The Student-as-Consumer Approach in Higher Education and its Effects on Academic Performance. *SHE*, DOI:10.1080/03075079.2015.1127908.

Burgar, P. (1994) Enforcing Academic Rules in Higher Education. *ResHE*, 35, 1, 43–55.

Burgess, T. (1972) Introduction. pp. 7–19 in T. Burgess (ed.), *The Shape of Higher Education*. London, Cornmarket Press.

Burgess, T. (1996) Planning the Academic's Workload. *HE*, 32, 1, 63–75.

Burgess, T., and Pratt, J. (1970) *Policy and Practice*. London, Allen Lane The Penguin Press.

Burn, K. (2006) Promoting Critical Conversations. *JET*, 32, 3, 243–58.

Burnes, B., Wend, P., and Todnem, R. (2014) The Changing Face of English Universities. *SHE*, 39, 6, 905–26.

Burnett, S.-A., and Huisman, J. (2010) Universities' Responses to Globalisation. *JSIE*, 14, 2, 117–42.

Burquel, N., and van Vught, F. (2010) Benchmarking in European Higher Education. *TEM*, 16, 3, 243–55.

Burrow, S., Mairs, H., Pusey, H., Bradshaw, T., and Keady, J. (2016) Continuing Professional Education. *International Journal of Nursing Studies*, 63, 139–45.

Burrows, R. (2012) Living with the h-Index? *Sociological Review*, 60, 2, 355–72.

Bursztyn, M., and Drummond, J. (2014) Sustainability Science and the University. *EER*, 20, 3, 313–32.

Buultjens, M., and Robinson, P. (2011) Enhancing Aspects of the Higher Education Student Experience. *JHEPM*, 33, 4, 337–46.

Byun, K., Jon, K.-E., and Kim, D. (2013) Quest for Building World-class Universities in South Korea. *HE*, 65, 5, 645–59.

Cabrera, A., Nora, A., and Castenada, M. (1993) College Persistence. *JHE*, 64, 2, 123–39.

Cai, Y. (2017) From an Analytical Framework for understanding the Innovation Process in Higher Education to an Emerging Research Field of Innovations in Higher Education. *RevHE*, 40, 4, 585–616.

Callard, F., and Fitzgerald, D. (2015) *Rethinking Interdisciplinarity across the Social Sciences and Neurosciences*. Basingstoke, Palgrave Macmillan.

Callender, C. (2014) Student Numbers and Funding. *HEQ*, 68, 2, 164–86.

Calvert, M., Lewis, T., and Spindler, J. (2011) Negotiating Professional Identities in Higher Education. *Research in Education*, 86, 25–38.

Cameron, J., Roxburgh, M., Taylor, J., and Lauder, W. (2011) An Integrative Literature Review of Student Retention in Programmes of Nursing and Midwifery Education. *Journal of Clinical Nursing*, 20, 1372–82.

Campbell, J., Smith, D., Boulton-Lewis, G., Brownlee, J., Burnett, P., Carrington, S., and Purdie, N. (2001) Students' Perceptions of Teaching and Learning. *TT*, 7, 2, 173–87.

Campbell, T., and Campbell, D. (1997) Faculty/Student Mentor Program. *ResHE*, 38, 6, 727–42.

Cannizzo, F., and Osbaldiston, N. (2016) Academic Work/Life Balance. *JS*, 52, 4, 890–906.

Caplanova, A. (2003) Does the Institutional Type Matter? *TEM*, 9, 4, 317–40.

Caraca, J., Conceicao, P., and Heitor, M. (2000) Towards a Public Policy for the Research University in Portugal. *HEP*, 13, 2, 181–201.

Carini, R., Kuh, G., and Klein, S. (2006) Student Engagement and Student Learning. *ResHE*, 47, 1, 1–32.

Carmichael, P. (2012) Tribes, Territories and Threshold Concepts. *EPT*, 44, S1, 31–42.

Carr, W. (2006) Education without Theory. *BJES*, 54, 2, 136–59.

Carroll, M., Razvi, S., Goodliffe, T., and Al-Habsi, F. (2009) Progress in Developing a National Quality Management System for Higher Education in Oman. *QHE*, 15, 1, 17–27.

Case, J. (2008) Alienation and Engagement. *HE*, 55, 3, 321–32.

Case, J. (2015) Emergent Interactions. *THE*, 20, 6, 625–35.

Case, J., and Marshall, D. (2009) Approaches to Learning. pp. 9–21 in M. Tight, K.-H. Mok, J. Huisman and C. Morphew (eds) *The Routledge International Handbook of Higher Education*. New York, Routledge.

Case, J., and Gunstone, R. (2003) Going Deeper than Deep and Surface Approaches. *THE*, 8, 1, 55–69.

Cashin, W., and Downey, R. (1995) Disciplinary Differences in What is Taught and in Students' Perceptions of What they Learn and of How they are Taught. *NDTL* 64, 81–92.

Cassidy, S. (2004) Learning Styles. *EP*, 24, 4, 419–44.

Castle, E. (2002) Social Capital. *Rural Sociology*, 67, 3, 331–49.

Castro, P., Woodin, J., Lundgren, U., and Byram, M. (2016) Student Mobility and Internationalisation in Higher Education. *Language and Intercultural Communication*, 16, 3, 418–36.

Chalcraft, D., Hilton, T., and Hughes, T. (2015) Customer, Collaborator or Co-creator? *JMHE*, 25, 1, 1–4.

Chamorro-Premuzic, T., and Furnham, A. (2009) Mainly Openness. *LID*, 19, 524–9.

Chan, E. (2016) 'Being an English Major, being a Humanities Student'. *SHE*, 41, 9, 1656–73.

Chan, S.-J., and Lin, L.-W. (2015) Massification of Higher Education in Taiwan. *HEP*, 28, 1, 17–33.

Chao, R. (2014) Pathways to an East Asian Higher Education Area. *HE*, 68, 4, 559–75.

Chapman, A., Mangion, A., and Buchanan, R. (2015) Institutional Statements of Commitment and Widening Participation Policy in Australia. *PFE*, 13, 8, 995–1009.

Charmaz, K. (2006) *Constructing Grounded Theory*. London, Sage.

Chen, C.-L., and Liang, T.-L. (2011) The Design and Implementation of a Blended Knowledge Management Course in Higher Education. *Procedia Engineering*, 15, 4152–56.

Chen, H., Lattuca, L., and Hamilton, E. (2008) Conceptualizing Engagement. *Journal of Engineering Education*, 339–53.

Chen, S.-Y., and Hu, L.-F. (2012) Higher Education Research as a Field in China. *HERD*, 31, 5, 655–66.

Cheng, D. (2001) Assessing Student Collegiate Experience. *AEHE*, 26, 6, 525–38.

Cheung, K., Elander, J., Stupple, E., and Flay, M. (2016) Academics' Understanding of the Authorial Academic Writer. *SHE*, DOI:10.1080/03075079.2016.1264382.

Chevalier, A., and Jia, X. (2016) Subject-specific League Tables and Students' Application Decisions. *MS*, 84, 5, 600–20.

Cho, M.-H., and Rathbun, G. (2013) Implementing Teacher-centred Online Teacher Professional Development (oTPD) Programme in Higher Education. *IETI*, 50, 2, 144–56.

Choi, B., and Pak, A. (2006) Multidisciplinarity, Interdisciplinarity and Transdisciplinarity in Health Research, Services, Education and Policy. *CIM*, 29, 6, 351–64.

Choi, B., and Pak, A. (2007) Multidisciplinarity, Interdisciplinarity and Transdisciplinarity in Health Research, Services, Education and Policy. *CIM*, 30, 6, E224–32.

Choi, B., and Rhee, B. (2014) The Influences of Student Engagement, Institutional Mission and Cooperative Learning Climate on the Generic Competency Development of Korean Undergraduate Students. *HE*, 67, 1, 1–18.

Christensen, S., and Erno-Kjolhede, E. (2011) Academic Drift in Danish Professional Engineering Education. *EJEE*, 36, 3, 285–99.

Christenson, S., Reschly, A., and Wylie, C. (eds) (2012) *Handbook of Research on Student Engagement*. New York, Springer.

Christie, F. (2017) The Reporting of University League Table Employability Rankings. *JEW*, 30, 4, 403–18.

Christie, H., Tett, L., Cree, V., and McCune, V. (2016) 'It All Just Clicked'. *SHE*, 41, 3, 478–90.

Clark, B. (1983) *The Higher Education System*. Berkeley, CA, University of California Press.

Clark, B. (1993) The Research Foundations of Post-Graduate Education. *HEQ*, 47, 4, 301–15.

Clark, B. (1994) The Research-Teaching-Study Nexus in Modern Systems of Higher Education. *HEP*, 7, 1, 11–17.

Clark, B. (1997) The Modern Integration of Research Activities with Teaching and Learning. *JHE*, 68, 3, 241–55.

Clarke, M. (2002) Some Guidelines for Academic Quality Rankings. *HEE*, 27, 4, 443–59.

Clarke, R. (1986) Students' Approaches to Learning in an Innovative Medical School. *BJEP*, 56, 3, 309–21.

Clegg, S. (2008) Academic Identities under Threat? *BERJ*, 34, 3, 329–45.

Clegg, S., and McAuley, J. (2005) Conceptualising Middle Management in Higher Education. *JHEPM*, 27, 1, 19–34.

Clewes, D. (2003) A Student-centred Conceptual Model of Service Quality in Higher Education. *QHE*, 9, 1, 69–85.

Cliff, A. (2015) The National Benchmark Test in Academic Literacy. *Language Matters*, 46, 1, 3–21.

Clifford, V. (2009) Engaging the Disciplines in Internationalising the Curriculum. *IJAD*, 14, 2, 133–43.

Clift, J., and Imrie, B. (1980) The Design of Evaluation for Learning. *HE*, 9, 1, 61–80.

Clouder, L. (2005) Caring as a 'Threshold Concept'. *THE*, 10, 4, 505–17.

Coate, K., Barnett, R., and Williams, G. (2001) Relationships between Teaching and Research in Higher Education in England. *HEQ*, 55, 2, 158–74.

Coate, K., and Howson, C. (2016) Indicators of Esteem. *BJSE*, 37, 4, 567–85.

Coates, H. (2005) The Value of Student Engagement for Higher Education Quality Assurance. *QHE*, 11, 1, 25–6.

Coates, H. (2010) Development of the Australasian Survey of Student Engagement (AUSSE). *HE*, 60, 1, 1–17.

Coates, H., and Krause, K.-L. (2005) Investigating Ten Years of Equity Policy in Australian Higher Education. *JHEPM*, 27, 1, 35–46.

Coertjens, L., Donche, V., De Maeyer, S., van Daal, T., and Van Petegem, P. (2017) The Growth Trend in Learning Strategies during the Transition from Secondary to Higher Education in Flanders. *HE*, DOI 10.1007/s10734-016-0093-x.

Coffey, M., and Gibbs, G. (2001) The Evaluation of the Student Evaluation of Educational Quality Questionnaire (SEEQ) in UK Higher Education. *AEHE*, 26, 1, 89–93.

Coffin, C., and Donohue, J. (2012) Academic Literacies and Systemic Functional Linguistics. *JEAP*, 11, 64–75.

Cohen, L., Manion, L., and Morrison, K. (2007). *Research Methods in Education*. London, Routledge, sixth edition.

Colbeck, C. (1998) Merging in a Seamless Blend. *JHE*, 69, 6, 647–71.

Colby, J., Raymond, G., and Colby, S. (2000) Evaluation of a College Policy Mandating Treatment for Students with Substantiated Drinking Problems. *JCSD*, 41, 4, 395–404.

Cole, M., and Engeström, Y. (1993) A Cultural-Historical Approach to Distributed Cognition. pp. 1–46 in G. Salomon (ed.) *Distributed Cognitions*. Cambridge, Cambridge University Press.

Coleman, J. (1988) Social Capital in the Creation of Human Capital. *American Journal of Sociology*, 94, Supplement, S95–S120.

Collier-Reed, B., and Ingerman, A. (2013) Phenomenography. *IPHER*, 9, 243–60.

Collier-Reed, B., Ingerman, A., and Berglund, A. (2009) Reflections on Trustworthiness in Phenomenographic Research. *EC*, 13, 2, 339–55.

Collins, C., and Rhoads, R. (2010) The World Bank, Support for Universities and Asymmetrical Power Relations in International Development. *HE*, 59, 2, 181–205.

Collins, R. (1998) *The Sociology of Philosophies*. Cambridge, MA: Belknap Press.

Collinson, J. (2006) Just 'Non-Academics'? Research Administrators and Contested Occupational Identity. *Work, Employment and Society*, 20, 2, 267–88.

Contu, A., and Willmott, H. (2003) Re-embedding Situatedness. *Organization Science*, 14, 3, 283–96.

Cooper, H. (2010) *Research Synthesis and Meta-Analysis*. Los Angeles, CA, Sage, fourth edition.

Cope, C. (2004) Ensuring Validity and Reliability in Phenomenographic Research Using the Analytical Framework of a Structure of Awareness. *Qualitative Research Journal*, 4, 2, 5–18.

Cope, C., and Staehr, L. (2005) Improving Students' Learning Approaches through Intervention in an Information Systems Learning Environment. *SHE*, 30, 2, 181–97.

Coradini, O. (2010) The Divergences between Bourdieu's and Coleman's Notions of Social Capital and their Epistemological Limits. *Social Science Information*, 49, 4, 563–83.

Coria, M., Deluca, M., and Martinez, M. (2010) Curricular Changes in Accredited Undergraduate Programmes in Argentina. *QHE*, 16, 3, 247–55.

Cottrell, S., and Jones, E. (2003) Researching the Scholarship of Teaching and Learning. *IHE*, 27, 3, 169–81.

Courtney, K. (2013) Adapting Higher Education through Changes in Academic Work. *HEQ*, 67, 1, 40–55.

Cousin, G., and Deepwell, F. (2005) Designs for Network Learning. *SHE*, 30, 1, 57–66.

Cox, A. (2005) What are Communities of Practice? *Journal of Information Science*, 31, 6, 527–40.

Cox, B., Thompson, K., Anderson, A., Mintz, A., Locks, T., Morgan, L., Edelstein, J., and Wolz, A. (2017) College Experience for Students with Autism Spectrum Disorder. *JCSD*, 58, 1, 71–87.

Craig, J. (2014) What Have We Been Writing About? *JPSE*, 10, 1, 23–36.

Cranton, P. (2011) A Transformative Perspective on the Scholarship of Teaching and Learning. *HERD*, 30, 1, 75–86.

Crawford, K., Gordon, S., Nicholas, J., and Prosser, M. (1994) Conceptions of Mathematics and How it is Learned. *LI*, 4, 331–45.

Crawford, K., Gordon, S., Nicholas, J., and Prosser, M. (1998) University Mathematics' Students Conceptions of Mathematics. *SHE*, 23, 1, 87–94.

Creagh, T. (2015) The History, Content and Evolution of *The International Journal of the First Year in Higher Education*. *IJFYHE*, 6, 1, 1–10.

Cremers, P., and Valkenburg, R. (2008) Teaching and Learning about Communities of Practice in Higher Education. pp. 333–54 in C. Kimble, P. Hildreth and I. Bourdon (eds) *Communities of Practice, volume 1*. Charlotte, NC, Information Age.

Creswell, J., and Bean, J. (1981a) Research Output, Socialization and the Biglan Model. *ResHE*, 15, 1, 69–91.

Creswell, J., and Bean, J. (1981b) The Biglan Studies of Differences Among Academic Areas. *RevHE*, 4, 3, 1–16.

Crosling, G., Thomas, L., and Heagney, M. (2008) *Improving Student Retention in Higher Education*. London, Routledge.

Croucher, G., and Woelert, P. (2016) Institutional Isomorphism and the Creation of the Unified National System of Higher Education in Australia. *HE*, 71, 439–53.

Cruickshank, M. (2003) Total Quality Management in the Higher Education Sector. *TQMBE*, 14, 10, 1159–67.

Csizmadia, T., Enders, J., and Westerheijden, D. (2008) Quality Management in Hungarian Higher Education. *HE*, 56, 4, 439–55.

Cuevas-Garcia, C. (2017) Understanding Interdisciplinarity in its Argumentative Context. *Interdisciplinary Science Reviews*, DOI:10.1080/03080188.2016.1264133.

Currie, J., and Eveline, J. (2011) E-technology and Work/Life Balance for Academics with Young Children. *HE*, 62, 4, 533–50.

Curtis, S., and Klapper, R. (2005) Financial Support Systems. *International Journal of Social Economics*, 32, 1/2, 121–32.

Cutajar, M. (2017) The Student Experience of Learning using Networked Technologies. *TPE*, DOI:10.1080/1475939X.2017.1327451.

Cuthbert, R. (1988) Quality and Management in Higher Education. *SHE*, 13, 1, 59–68.

Cuthbert, R. (2010) Students as Customers? *HER*, 42, 3, 3–25.

Dahlgren, L. (1989) Fragments of an Economic Habitus. *EJPE*, 4, 4, 547–58.

Dahlgren, L., Handal, G., Szkudlarek, T., and Bayer, M. (2007) Students as Journeymen between Cultures of Higher Education and Work. *HEE*, 32, 4, 305–16.

Dahlgren, L., and Marton, F. (1976) *Investigations into the learning and teaching of basic concepts in economics*. Report No. 54, Institute of Education, University of Göteborg.

Dahlgren, L., and Marton, F. (1978) Students' Conceptions of Subject Matter. *SHE*, 3, 1, 25–35.

Dahlin, B. (2007) Enriching the Theoretical Horizons of Phenomenography, Variation Theory and Learning Studies. *SJER*, 51, 4, 327–46.

Dall'Alba, G., Walsh, E., Bowden, J., Martin, E., Marton, F., Masters, G., Ramsden, P., and Stephanou, A. (1989) Assessing Understanding. *Research in Science Education*, 19, 57–66.

Damian, R., Grifoll, J., and Rigbers, A. (2015) On the Role of Impact Evaluation of Quality Assurance from the Strategic Perspective of Quality Assurance Agencies in the European Higher Education Area. *QHE*, 21, 3, 251–69.

Damme, D. van (2001) Quality Issues in the Internationalization of Higher Education. *HE*, 41, 4, 415–41.

Daniel, R., and Daniel, L. (2013) Enhancing the Transition from Study to Work. *AHHE*, 12, 2–3, 138–53.

Daniels, H. (2004) Cultural Historical Activity Theory and Professional Learning. *International Journal of Disability, Development and Education*, 51, 2, 185–200.

Danskin, E. (1979) Quality and Quantity in Higher Education in Thailand and Philippines. *CE*, 15, 3, 313–22.

Davies, E., and Jenkins, A. (2013) The Work-to-Retirement Transition of Academic Staff. *Employee Relations*, 35, 3, 322–38.

Davies, M., Devlin, M., and Tight, M. (eds) (2010) *Interdisciplinary Higher Education*. Bingley, Emerald.

Davies, P., Qiu, T., and Davies, N. (2014) Cultural and Human Capital, Information and Higher Education Choices. *JEP*, 29, 6, 804–25.

Davies, P., and Mangan, J. (2007) Threshold Concepts and the Integration of Understanding in Economics. *SHE*, 32, 6, 711–26.

Daza, L. (2016) The Role of Social Capital in Students' Perceptions of Progress in Higher Education. *ERE*, 22, 1–2, 65–85.

De Freitas, S., Morgan, J., and Gibson, D. (2015) Will MOOCs transform Learning and Teaching in Higher Education? *BJET*, 46, 3, 455–71.

De La Harpe, B., Radloff, A., and Wyber, J. (2000) Quality and Generic (Professional) Skills. *QHE*, 6, 3, 231–43.

Dearlove, J. (1997) The Academic Labour Process. *HER*, 30, 1, 56–75.

Dearlove, J. (2002) A Continuing Role for Academics. *HEQ*, 56, 3, 257–75.

Deem, R., and Brehony, K. (2005) Management as Ideology. *ORE*, 31, 2, 217–35.

Deem, R., Hillyard, S., and Reed, M. (2007) *Knowledge, Higher Education and the New Managerialism*. Oxford, Oxford University Press.

Deem, R., Mok, K.-H., and Lucas, U. (2008) Transforming Higher Education in whose Image? *HEP*, 21, 83–97.

Degn, L. (2016) Academic Sensemaking and Behavioural Responses. *SHE*, DOI:10.1080/03075079.2016.1168796.

Delaney, A. (2008) Why Faculty-Student Interaction Matters in the First Year Experience. *TEM*, 14, 3, 227–41.

Delaney, J., and Doyle, W. (2014) State Spending on Higher Education Capital Outlays. *ResHE*, 55, 5, 433–66.

Delucchi, M., and Korgen, K. (2002) 'We're the Customer – We Pay the Tuition'. *TS*, 30, 1, 100–7.

Dempster, J., Beetham, H., Jackson, P., and Richardson, S. (2004) Creating Virtual Communities of Practice for Learning Technology in Higher Education. *ALT-J*, 11, 3, 103–17.

D'Eon, M., and Harris, C. (2000) If Students are not Customers, What are They? *Academic Medicine*, 75, 1173–7.

DeShields, O., Kara, A., and Kaynak, E. (2005) Determinants of Business Students' Satisfaction and Retention in Higher Education. *IJEM*, 19, 2–3, 128–39.

Dey, E., and Astin, A. (1993) Statistical Alternatives for Studying College Student Retention. *ResHE*, 34, 5, 569–81.

Dhalin, B., and Regmi, M. (1997) Conceptions of Learning among Nepalese Students. *HE*, 33, 4, 471–93.

Dias, D. (2015) Has Massification of Higher Education led to more Equity? *IJIE*, 19, 2, 103–20.

Dietrich, J., Jokisaari, M., and Nurmi, J.-E. (2012) Work-related Goal Appraisals and Stress during the Transition from Education to Work. *JVB*, 80, 82–92.

Dill, D. (2000) Designing Academic Audit. *QHE*, 6, 3, 187–207.

Dill, D., and Soo, M. (2005) Academic Quality, League Tables and Public Policy. *HE*, 49, 4, 495–533.

DiMaggio, P., and Powell, W. (1983) The Iron Cage Revisited. *ASR*, 48, 2, 147–60.

Ding, X. (2016) Exploring the Experiences of International Students in China. *JSIE*, 20, 4, 319–38.

DiSarro, D. (2014) Let's CHAT! *New Writing*, 11, 3, 438–51.

Diseth, A. (2007) Students' Evaluation of Teaching, Approaches to Learning and Academic Achievement. *SJER*, 51, 2, 185–204.

Dobbins, M., and Knill, C. (2009) Higher Education Policies in Central and Eastern Europe. *Governance*, 22, 3, 397–430.

Docquier, F., and Rapoport, H. (2012) Globalization, Brain Drain and Development. *Journal of Economic Literature*, 50, 3, 681–730.

Dodds, A. (2008) How does Globalisation Interact with Higher Education? *CE*, 44, 4, 505–17.

Doiz, A., Lasagabaster, D., and Sierra, J. (2013) Globalisation, Internationalisation, Multilingualism and Linguistic Strains in Higher Education. *SHE*, 38, 9, 1407–21.

Dolby, N. (2010) Internationalizing Higher Education. *Teachers College Record*, 112, 7, 1758–91.

Donald, J. (1995) Disciplinary Differences in Knowledge Validation. *NDTL*, 64, 7–17.

Donnelly, R. (2008) Virtual Problem-based Learning Communities of Practice for Teachers and Academic Developers. pp. 67–88 in C. Kimble, P. Hildreth and I. Bourdon (eds) *Communities of Practice, volume 2*. Charlotte, NC, Information Age.

Doucette, D., Richardson, R., and Fenske, R. (1985) Defining Institutional Mission. *JHE*, 56, 2, 189–205.

Douglas, A. (2013) Advice from the Professors in a University Social Sciences Department on the Teaching-Research Nexus. *THE*, 18, 4, 377–88.

Douglass, J. (2010) Creating a Culture of Aspiration. *Procedia: Social and Behavioral Sciences*, 2, 6981–95.

Duff, A., and Marriott, N. (2016) The Teaching-Research Gestalt. *SHE*, DOI:10.1080/03075079.2016.1152465.

Duke, A. (1996) *Importing Oxbridge*. New Haven, CT, Yale University Press.

Duke, Z., and Mudge, P. (2016) 'Dissolving Boundaries'. *Journal of Adult Theological Education*, 13, 2, 147–62.

Dundar, H., and Lewis, D. (1998) Determinants of Research Productivity in Higher Education. *ResHE*, 39, 6, 607–31.

Duong, V., and Chua, C. (2016) English as a Symbol of Internationalization in Higher Education. *HERD*, 35, 4, 669–83.

Durning, B., and Jenkins, A. (2005) Teaching/Research Relations in Departments. *SHE*, 30, 4, 407–26.

Eagle, L., and Brennan, R. (2007) Are Students Customers? *QAE*, 15, 1, 44–60.

Easterby-Smith, M., Snell, R., and Gherardi, S. (1998) Organizational Learning. *Management Learning*, 29, 3, 259–72.

Ebenezer, J., and Erickson, G. (1996) Chemistry Students' Conceptions of Solubility. *SE*, 80, 2, 181–201.

Eckel, P. (2000) The Role of Shared Governance in Institutional Hard Decisions. *RevHE*, 24, 1, 15–39.

Eckel, P. (2008) Mission Diversity and the Tension between Prestige and Effectiveness. *HEP*, 21, 175–92.

Edwards, A. (2005) Let's Get Beyond Community and Practice. *Curriculum Journal*, 16, 1, 49–65.

Elias, P., and Purcell, K. (2004) Is Mass Higher Education Working? *National Institute Economic Review*, 190, 60–74.

Elken, M., Hovdhaugen, E., and Stensaker, B. (2016) Global Rankings in the Nordic Region. *HE*, DOI 10.1007/s10734-015-9975-6.

Ellis, J., and Miller, P. (2014) Providing Higher Education in Post-modern Times. *RCIE*, 9, 1, 83–91.

Ellis, R., Ginns, P., and Piggott, L. (2009) E-learning in Higher Education. *HERD*, 28, 3, 303–18.

Elton, L. (1986) Research and Teaching. *HE*, 15, 3–4, 299–304.

Elton, L. (1996) Task Differentiation in Universities. *TEM*, 2, 2, 138–45.

Elwood, L., and Klenowski, V. (2002) Creating Communities of Shared Practice. *AEHE*, 27, 3, 243–56.

Enders, J. (ed.) (2001) *Academic Staff in Europe*. Westport, CT; Greenwood.

Enders, J. (2004) Higher Education, Internationalisation and the Nation-state. *HE*, 47, 3, 361–82.

Enders, J., and Westerheijden, D. (2014) The Dutch Way of New Public Management. *PS*, 33, 3, 167–76.

Engbers, T., Thompson, M., and Slaper, T. (2016) Theory and Measurement in Social Capital Research. *SIR*, DOI 10.1007/s11205-016-1299-0.

Engeström, Y. (2001) Expansive Learning at Work. *JEW*, 14, 1, 133–56.

Engeström, Y. (2009) Expansive Learning. pp. 53–73 in K. Illeris (ed.) *Contemporary Theories of Learning*. London, Routledge.

Engeström, Y. (2015) *Learning by Expanding*. New York, Cambridge University Press, second edition (first edition published in 1987).

Engeström, Y., and Sannino, A. (2010) Studies of Expansive Learning. *ERR*, 5, 1, 1–24.

Engwall, L. (2016) The Internationalisation of Higher Education. *EurR*, 24, 2, 221–31.

Ennew, C., and Greenaway, D. (eds) (2012) *The Globalization of Higher Education*. Basingstoke, Palgrave Macmillan.

Entwistle, N. (1984) Contrasting Perspectives on Learning. pp. 1–18 in F. Marton, D. Hounsell and N. Entwistle (eds) *The Experience of Learning*. Edinburgh, Scottish Academic Press.

Entwistle, N. (1988) Motivational Factors in Students' Approaches to Learning. pp. 21–51 in R. Schmeck (ed.) *Learning Strategies and Learning Styles*. Dordrecht, Springer.

Entwistle, N., Hanley, M., and Hounsell, D. (1979) Identifying Distinctive Approaches to Studying. *HE*, 8, 4, 365–80.

Entwistle, N., and Marton, F. (1984) Changing Conceptions of Learning and Research. pp. 211–36 in F. Marton, D. Hounsell and N. Entwistle (eds) *The Experience of Learning*. Edinburgh, Scottish Academic Press.

Entwistle, N., and McCune, V. (2004) The Conceptual Bases of Study Strategy Inventories. *EPR*, 16, 4, 325–45.

Entwistle, N., and Tait, H. (1990) Approaches to Learning, Evaluations of Teaching, and Preferences for Contrasting Academic Environments. *HE*, 19, 2, 169–94.

Erkkila, T. (2014) Global University Rankings, Transnational Policy Discourse and Higher Education in Europe. *EJE*, 49, 1, 91–101.

Ertl, H., Hayward, G., Wright, S., Edwards, A., Lunt, I., Mills, D., and Yu, K. (2008) *The Student Learning Experience in Higher Education*. York, Higher Education Academy.

Essack, S., Naidoo, I., and Barnes, G. (2010) Government Funding as Leverage for Quality Teaching and Learning. *HEMP*, 22, 3, 93–105.

Evans, C. (1988) *Language People*. Milton Keynes, Open University Press.

Evans, C. (1993) *English People*. Buckingham, Open University Press.

Evans, S. (2016) Making the Transition to Higher Education in Hong Kong. *JFHE*, DOI:10.1 080/0309877X.2016.1224327.

Everaert, P., Opdecam, E., and Maussen, S. (2017) The Relationship between Motivation, Learning Approaches, Academic Performance and Time Spent. *AE*, 26, 1, 78–107.

Fabricius, A., Mortensen, J., and Haberland, H. (2016) The Lure of Internationalisation. *HE*, DOI 10.1007/s10734-015-9978-3.

Faia, M. (1976) Teaching and Research. *ResHE*, 4, 235–46.

Fanghanel, J. (2013) Going Public with Pedagogical Inquiries. *Teaching and Learning Inquiry*, 1, 1, 59–70.

Farcas, D., Bernardes, S., and Matos, M. (2016) The Research-Teaching Nexus from the Portuguese Academics' Perspective. *HE*, DOI 10.1007/s10734-016-0046-4.

Fearon, C., McLaughlin, H., and Eng, T. (2012) Using Student Group Work in Higher Education to Emulate Professional Communities of Practice. *ET*, 54, 2/3, 114–25.

Federkeil, G. (2002) Some Aspects of Ranking Methodology. *HEE*, 27, 4, 389–97.

Feeney, M., Bernal, M., and Bowman, L. (2014) Enabling Work? *SPP*, 41, 750–64.

Feldman, K. (1987) Research Productivity and Scholarly Accomplishment of College Teachers as related to their Instructional Effectiveness. *ResHE*, 26, 3, 227–98.

Felix, A. (2009) The Adult Heritage Spanish Speaker in the Foreign Language Classroom. *International Journal of Qualitative Studies in Education*, 22, 2, 145–62.

Fenwick, T., and Edwards, R. (2014) Networks of Knowledge, Matters of Learning and Criticality in Higher Education. *HE*, 67, 1, 35–50.

Ferenz, O. (2005) EFL Writers' Social Networks. *JEAP*, 4, 339–51.

Ferrari, J., and Cowman, S. (2004) Toward a Reliable and Valid Measure of Institutional Mission and Values Perception. *Journal of Beliefs and Values*, 25, 1, 43–54.

Field, J. (2008) *Social Capital*. London, Routledge, second edition.

Figueiredo, H., Biscaia, R., Rocha, V., and Teixeira, P. (2015) Should We Start Worrying? *SHE*, DOI:10.1080/03075079.2015.1101754.

Filippakou, O. (2011) The Idea of Quality in Higher Education. *DSCPE*, 32, 1, 15–28.

Filippakou, O., and Tapper, T. (2008) Quality Assurance and Quality Enhancement in Higher Education. *HEQ*, 62, 1–2, 84–100.

Filippakou, O., and Tapper, T. (2015) Mission Groups and the New Politics of British Higher Education. *HEQ*, 69, 2, 121–37.

Findlow, S. (2012) Higher Education Change and Professional-Academic Identity in Newly 'Academic' Disciplines. *HE*, 63, 1, 117–33.

Fine, B. (2001) *Social Capital versus Social Theory.* London, Routledge.

Fine, B. (2010) *Theories of Social Capital.* London, Pluto Press.

Finnegan, F., and Merrill, B. (2017) 'We're as Good as Anybody Else'. *BJSE*, 38, 3, 307–24.

Finnie, R. (2004) The School-to-Work Transition of Canadian Post-secondary Graduates. *JHEPM*, 26, 1, 35–58.

Fire, N., and Casstevens, W. (2013) The Use of Cultural Historical Activity Theory (CHAT) within a Constructivist Learning Environment to develop Core Competencies in Social Work. *Journal of Teaching in Social Work*, 33, 1, 41–58.

Fitzgerald, D., and Callard, F. (2015) Social Science and Neuroscience beyond Interdisciplinarity. *Theory, Culture and Society*, 32, 1, 3–32.

Fitzgerald, T., White, J., and Gunter, H. (2012) *Hard Labour?* Bingley, Emerald.

Fleet, N., and Guzman-Concha, C. (2016) Mass Higher Education and the 2011 Student Movement in Chile. *Bulletin of Latin American Research*, DOI:10.1111/blar.12471.

Flood Page, C. (1972) Teaching and Research. *Universities Quarterly*, 27, 1, 102–18.

Foot, K. (2014) Cultural-Historical Activity Theory. *JHBSE*, 24, 329–47.

Ford, N. (1981) Recent Approaches to the Study and Teaching of 'Effective' Learning in Higher Education. *RER*, 51, 3, 345–77.

Forsman, J., Linder, C., Moll, R., Fraser, D., and Andersson, S. (2014) A New Approach to Modelling Student Retention through an application of Complexity Thinking. *SHE*, 39, 1, 68–86.

Fortune, T., Ennals, P., Bhopti, A., Neilson, C., Darzins, S., and Bruce, C. (2016) Bridging Identity 'Chasms'. *THE*, 21, 3, 313–25.

Fouche, I., van Dyk, T., and Butler, G. (2017) An 'Enlightening Course that Empowers First Years'? *JEAP*, 27, 14– 30.

Fourie, M., and Alt, H. (2000) Challenges to Sustaining and Enhancing Quality of Teaching and Learning in South African Universities. *QHE*, 6, 2, 115–24.

Fowles, J. (2014) Funding and Focus. *ResHE*, 55, 3, 272–87.

Fowles, J., Frederickson, G., and Koppell, J. (2016) University Rankings. *Public Administration Review*, 76, 5, 790–803.

Fox, M. (1992) Research, Teaching and Publication Productivity. *SocE*, 65, 4, 293–305.

Fox, S. (2000) Communities of Practice, Foucault and Actor-Network Theory. *JMS*, 37, 6, 853–67.

Francis, H. (1993) Advancing Phenomenography. *Nordisk Pedagogik*, 13, 2, 68–75.

Franklin, B. (2012) Surviving to Thriving. *Journal of Library Administration*, 52, 1, 94–107.

Franklin, P., and McCaig, R. (1979) Academic Drift in Tertiary Education. *Journal of Educational Administration*, 17, 2, 259–62.

Franks, D., Dale, P., Hindmarsh, R., Fellows, C., Buckridge, M., and Cybinski, P. (2007) Interdisciplinary Foundations. *SHE*, 32, 2, 167–85.

Fransson, A. (1977) On Qualitative Differences in Learning IV. *BJEP*, 47, 3, 244–57.

Frederiks, M., Westerheijden, D., and Weusthof, P. (1994) Effects of Quality Assessment in Dutch Higher Education. *EJE*, 29, 2, 181–99.

Freeman, B. (2014) Benchmarking Australian and New Zealand University Meta-policy in an increasingly regulated Tertiary Environment. *JHEPM*, 36, 1, 74–87.

Freire, P. (1972) *Pedagogy of the Oppressed*. Translated by M. Ramer. Harmondsworth, Penguin.

Freire, P. (1974) *Education for Critical Consciousness*. London, Sheed and Ward.

Friedrich, R., and Michalak, S. (1983) Why Doesn't Research Improve Teaching? *JHE*, 54, 2, 145–63.

Frodeman, R., Klein, J., Mitcham, C., and Holbrook, B. (eds) (2010) *The Oxford Handbook of Interdisciplinarity*. Oxford, Oxford University Press.

Frost, P., and Fukami, C. (1997) Teaching Effectiveness in the Organizational Sciences. *AMJ*, 40, 6, 1271–81.

Fryer, L. (2017) (Latent) Transitions to Learning at University. *HE*, DOI 10.1007/s10734-016-0094-9.

Fuchs, S. (1992) *The Professional Quest for Truth*. Albany, NY, State University of New York Press.

Fugazzotto, S. (2009) Mission Statements, Physical Space and Strategy in Higher Education. *IHE*, 34, 285–98.

Fuller, A., Hodkinson, H., Hodkinson, P., and Unwin, L. (2005) Learning as Peripheral Participation in Communities of Practice. *BERJ*, 31, 1, 49–68.

Fuller, A., and Unwin, L. (2003) Learning as Apprentices in the Contemporary UK Workplace. *JEW*, 16, 4, 407–26.

Fumasoli, T., and Huisman, J. (2013) Strategic Agency and System Diversity. *Minerva*, 51, 155–69.

Gacel-Ávila, G. (2005) The Internationalisation of Higher Education. *JSIE*, 9, 2, 121–36.

Gallagher, P. (2015) Graduate Transition into Work. *JEW*, 28, 5, 461–80.

Gallifa, J. (2009) Professional Integration in Higher Education. *JHEPM*, 31, 3, 229–37.

Gardner, S., and Gopaul, B. (2012) The Part-time Doctoral Student Experience. *International Journal of Doctoral Studies*, 7, 63–78.

Gardner, S., Jansujwicz, J., Hutchins, K., Cline, B., and Levesque, V. (2014) Socialization to Interdisciplinarity. *HE*, 67, 3, 255–71.

Garforth, L., and Kerr, A. (2011) Interdisciplinarity and the Social Sciences. *BJS*, 62, 4, 657–76.

Garrison, R., Anderson, T., and Archer, W. (2000) Critical Inquiry in a Text-based Environment. *TIHE*, 2, 2–3, 87–105.

Gartell, M. (2012) The College-to-Work Transition during the 1990s. *Applied Economics*, 44, 11, 1449–69.

Gasiewski, J., Eagan, K., Garcia, G., Hurtado, S., and Chang, M. (2012) From Gatekeeping to Engagement. *HE*, 53, 2, 229–61.

Gates, T., Heffernan, K., and Sudore, R. (2015) Social Work Students as Market Consumers. *SWE*, 34, 7, 881–94.

Gatfield, T., Barker, M., and Graham, P. (1999) Measuring Student Quality Variables and the Implications for Management Practices in Higher Education Institutions. *JHEPM*, 21, 2, 239–52.

Gaus, N., and Hall, D. (2013) Neoliberal Governance in Indonesian Universities. *International Journal of Sociology and Social Policy*, 35, 9–10, 666–82.

Gaze, B., and Stevens, C. (2011) Running Risks of Gender Inequity. *JEP*, 26, 5, 621–39.

Geertsema, J. (2016) Academic Development, SoTL and Educational Research. *IJAD*, 21, 2, 122–34.

Gellert, C. (1993) Academic Drift and Blurring of Boundaries in Systems of Higher Education. *HEE*, 18, 2, 78–84.

Gellert, C., Leitner, E., and Schramm, J. (eds) (1990) *Research and Teaching at Universities*. Frankfurt am Main, Peter Lang.

George, D. (2007) Market Overreach. *Journal of Socio-economics*, 36, 965–97.

Geraldo, J., Trevitt, C., Carter, S., and Fazey, J. (2010) Rethinking the Research-Teaching Nexus in Undergraduate Education. *EERJ*, 9, 1, 81–91.

Geschwind, L., and Brostrom, A. (2015) Managing the Teaching-Research Nexus. *HERD*, 34, 1, 60–73.

Gewirtz, S., Dickson, M., Power, S., Halpin, D., and Whitty, G. (2005) The Deployment of Social Capital Theory in Educational Policy and Provision. *BERJ*, 31, 6, 651–73.

Gheorgiu, E., and Stephens, C. (2016) Working with 'The Others'. *SSJ*, 53, 521–33.

Giannakis, M., and Bullivant, N. (2016) The Massification of Higher Education in the UK. *JFHE*, 40, 5, 630–48.

Gibbons, M., Limoges, C., Nowotny, H., Schwartzman, S., Scott, P., and Trow, M. (1994) *The New Production of Knowledge*. London, Sage.

Gibbons, S., Neumayer, E., and Perkins, R. (2015) Student Satisfaction, League Tables and University Applications. *EER*, 48, 148–64.

Gibbs, G., Morgan, A., and Taylor E. (1982) A Review of the Research of Ference Marton and the Goteborg Group. *HE*, 11, 2, 123–45.

Gibson, A.-M., Shaw, J., Hewitt, A., Easton, C., Robertson, S., and Gibson, N. (2016) A Longitudinal Examination of Students' Health Behaviours during their First Year at University. *JFHE*, DOI:10.1080/0309877X.2016.1188902.

Giddens, A. (1999) *Runaway World*. London, Profile.

Gift, S., and Bell-Hutchinson, C. (2007) Quality Assurance and the Imperatives for Improved Student Experiences in Higher Education. *QHE*, 13, 2, 145–57.

Gilardi, S., and Guglielmetti, C. (2011) University Life of Non-traditional Students. *JHE*, 82, 1, 33–53.

Gill, T., and Gill, S. (2000) Financial Management of Universities in Developing Countries. *HEP*, 13, 2, 125–30.

Ginns, P. Prosser, M., and Barrie, S. (2007) Students' Perceptions of Teaching Quality in Higher Education. *SHE*, 32, 5, 603–15.

Giret, J.-F. (2011) Does Vocational Training Help Transition to Work? *EJE*, 46, 2, 244–56.

Glassick, C., Huber, M., and Maeroff, G. (1997) *Scholarship Assessed*. San Francisco, CA: Jossey-Bass.

Goedegebuure, L., Kaiser, F., Maassen, P., Meek, L., van Vught, F., and de Weert, E. (eds) (1993) *Higher Education Policy*. Oxford, Pergamon.

Goedegebuure, L., and Westerheijden, D. (1991) Changing Balances in Dutch Higher Education. *HE*, 21, 4, 495–520.

Goglio, V. (2016) One Size Fits All? *JHEPM*, 38, 2, 212–26.

Goldingay, S., Hitch, D., Carrington, A., Nipperess, S., and Rosario, V. (2016) Transforming Roles to Support Student Development of Academic Literacies. *RP*, 17, 3, 334–46.

Gomes, A., Robertson, S., and Dale, R. (2012) The Social Condition of Higher Education. *Globalisation, Societies and Education*, 10, 2, 221–45.

Gonzalez, C. (2012) The Relationship between Approaches to Teaching, Approaches to e-Teaching and Perceptions of the Teaching Situation in Relation to e-Learning among Higher Education Teachers. *IS*, 40, 975–98.

Gonzalez, L. (2013) Faculty Sensemaking and Mission Creep. *RevHE*, 36, 2, 179–209.

Goode, J., and Bagilhole, B. (1998) Gendering the Management of Change in Higher Education. *Gender, Work and Organization*, 5, 3, 148–64.

Goodfellow, R. (2005) Academic Literacies and e-Learning. *IJER*, 43, 481–94.

Goos, M., Gannaway, D., and Hughes, C. (2011) Assessment as an Equity Issue in Higher Education. *AER*, 38, 95–107.

Gordon, C., and Debus, R. (2002) Developing Deep Learning Approaches and Personal Teacher Efficacy within a Preservice Teacher Education Context. *BJEP*, 72, 483–511.

Gornitzka, A., and Langfeldt, L. (eds) (2008) *Borderless Knowledge*. Dordrecht, Springer.

Gottlieb, E., and Keith, B. (1997) The Academic Research-Teaching Nexus in Eight Advanced-Industrialized Countries. *HE*, 34, 3, 397–420.

Goulden, M., Greiffenhagen, C., Crowcroft, J., McAuley, D., Mortier, R., Radenkovic, N., and Sathiaseelen, A. (2017) Wild Interdisciplinarity. *IJSRM*, 20, 2, 137–50.

Gounko, T., and Smale, W. (2007) Russian Higher Education Reforms. *European Education*, 39, 2, 60–82.

Gourlay, L. (2009) Threshold Practices. *LRE*, 7, 2, 181–92.

Gourlay, L. (2015) 'Student Engagement' and the Tyranny of Participation. *THE*, 20, 4, 402–11.

Graff, H. (2016) The 'Problem' of Interdisciplinarity in Theory, Practice and History. *Social Science History*, 40, 775–803.

Grainger, P., Christie, M., Thomas, G., Dole, S., Heck, D., Marshman, M., and Carey, M. (2017) Improving the Quality of Assessment by using a Community of Practice to explore the Optimal Construction of Assessment Rubrics. *RP*, 18, 3, 410–22.

Grant, B., Burford, J., Bosanquet, A., and Loads, D. (2014) Of Zombies, Monsters and Song. *THE*, 19, 3, 315–21.

Grant, D., Mergen, E., and Widrick, S. (2002) Quality Management in US Higher Education. *TQM*, 13, 2, 207–15.

Grant, K., and Wakerlin, S. (2009) Reconceptualising the Concept of a Nexus? *THE*, 14, 2, 133–46.

Greaves, K. (2015) Is Scholarship of Teaching and Learning in Practical Legal Training a Professional Responsibility? *The Law Teacher*, 49, 1, 22–38.

Green, D., Loertscher, J., Minderhout, V., and Lewis, J. (2017) For Want of a Better Word. *HERD*, DOI:10.1080/07294360.2017.1325848.

Greenbank, P. (2008) Widening Participation in Higher Education. *RPCE*, 11, 2, 199–215.

Greene, T., Marti, N., and McClenney, K. (2008) The Effort-Outcome Gap. *JHE*, 79, 5, 513–39.

Griffioen, D., and de Jong, U. (2013) Academic Drift in Dutch Non-university Higher Education Evaluated. *HEP*, 26, 2, 173–91.

Grise-Owens, E., Owens, L., and Miller, J. (2016) Conceptualizing the Scholarship of Teaching and Learning for Social Work Education. *Journal of Social Work Education*, 52, 1, 6-17.

Groccia, J., Alsudairi, M., and Boskis, W. (eds) (2012) *Handbook of College and University Teaching*. Thousand Oaks, CA, Sage.

Gronbeck, B. (2005) Is Communication a Humanities Discipline? *AHHE*, 4, 3, 229–46.

Grosemans, I., Coertjens, L., and Kyndt, E. (2017) Exploring Learning and Fit in the Transition from Higher Education to the Labour Market. *ERR*, 20, 67–84.

Gross, M., and Manoharan, A. (2016) The Balance of Liberal and Vocational Values in Hospitality Higher Education. *Journal of Hospitality and Tourism Education*, 28, 1, 44–57.

Guiffrida, D., and Douthit, K. (2010) The Black Student Experience at Predominantly White Colleges. *Journal of Counseling and Development*, 88, 3, 311–18.

Guilbault, M. (2016) Students as Customers in Higher Education. *JMHE*, 26, 2, 132–42.

Guile, D. (2009) Conceptualizing the Transition from Education to Work as Vocational Practice. *BERJ*, 35, 5, 761–79.

Gunn, R., and Hill, S. (2008) The Impact of League Tables on University Application Rates. *HEQ*, 62, 3, 273–96.

Guri-Rosenblit, S., Sebkova, H., and Teichler, U. (2007) Massification and Diversity of Higher Education Systems. *HEP*, 20, 373–89.

Gurung, R., Ansberg, P., Alexander, P., Lawrence, N., and Johnson, D. (2008) The State of the Scholarship of Teaching and Learning in Psychology. *Teaching of Psychology*, 35, 4, 249–61.

Guzman, G., and Trivelato, L. (2011) Packaging and Unpackaging Knowledge in Mass Higher Education. *HE*, 62, 4, 451–65.

Guzman-Simon, F., Garcia-Jimenez, E., and Lopez-Cobo, I. (2017) Undergraduate Students' Perspectives on Digital Competence and Academic Literacy in a Spanish University. *Computers in Human Behavior*, 74, 196–204.

Gvaramadze, I. (2008) From Quality Assurance to Quality Enhancement in the European Higher Education Area. *EJE*, 43, 4, 443–55.

Haan, H. de (2014) Where is the Gap between Internationalization Strategic Planning and its Implementation? *TEM*, 20, 2, 135–50.

Haapasaari, P., Kulmala, S., and Kuikka, S. (2012) Growing into Interdisciplinarity. *Ecology and Society*, 17, 1, 6, 12pp.

Hagel, P., Carr, R., and Devlin, M. (2012) Conceptualising and Measuring Student Engagement through the Australasian Survey of Student Engagement (AUSSE). *AEHE*, 37, 4, 475–86.

Haggis, T. (2003) Constructing Images of Ourselves? *BERJ*, 29, 1, 89–104.

Haggis, T. (2009) What have we been Thinking of? *SHE*, 34, 4, 377–90.

Hagstrom, W. (1965) *The Scientific Community*. New York, Basic Books.

Haigh, M. (2014) From Internationalisation to Education for Global Citizenship. *HEQ*, 68, 1, 6–27.

Haigh, N., Gossman, P., and Jiao, X. (2011) Undertaking an Institutional 'Stock-take' of SoTL. *HERD*, 30, 1, 9–23.

Hailikari, T., Kordts-Freudinger, R., and Postareff, L. (2016) Feel the Progress. *International Journal of Higher Education*, 5, 3, 79–90.

Halbesleben, J., Becker, J., and Buckley, M. (2003) Considering the Labor Contributions of Students. *JEB*, 78, 255–7.

Halbesleben, J., and Wheeler, A. (2009) Student Identification with Business Education Models. *JME*, 33, 2, 166–95.

Hall, V. (2017) Exploring Teacher-Student Interactions. *JFHE*, 41, 2, 120–32.

Hallett, F. (2013) Study Support and the Development of Academic Literacy in Higher Education. *THE*, 18, 5, 518–30.

Hallett, F. (2014) The Dilemma of Methodological Idolatry in Higher Education. *IPHER*, 10, 203–25.

Hallinger, P., and Lu, J. (2013) Learner Centred Higher Education in East Asia. *IJEM*, 27, 6, 594–612.

Halpern, D. (2005) *Social Capital*. Cambridge, Polity Press

Hamann, K., Pollock, P., and Wilson, B. (2009) Who SoTls where? *PS*, 42, 4, 729–35.

Hammel, J., Magasi, S., Mirza, M., Fischer, H., Preissner, K., Peterson, E., and Suarez-Balcazar, Y. (2015) A Scholarship of Practice Revisited. *Occupational Therapy in Health Care*, 29, 4, 352–69.

Hammer, S., and Green W. (2011) Critical Thinking in a First Year Management Unit. *HERD*, 30, 3, 303–15.

Hammersley, M. (2005) What Can the Literature on Communities of Practice tell us about Educational Research? *IJRME*, 28, 1, 5–21.

Handley, K., Sturdy, A., Fincham, R., and Clark, T. (2006) Within and Beyond Communities of Practice. *JMS*, 43, 3, 641–53.

Hanifan, L. (1916) The Rural School Community Center. *Annals of the American Academy of Political and Social Science*, 67, 130–8.

Hanna, D., and Latchem, C. (2002) Beyond National Borders. *JSIE*, 6, 2, 115–33.

Hanna, J. (1930) Student Retention in Junior Colleges. *JER*, 22, 1, 1–8.

Hanson, J. (2009) Displaced but not Replaced. *THE*, 14, 5, 553–64.

Hao, Z. (2016) In Search of a Professional Identity. *HE*, 72, 1, 101–13.

Hardy, C. (1996) *The Politics of Collegiality*. Montreal/Kingston, McGill-Queen's University Press.

Harland, T. (2016) Teaching to enhance Research. *HERD*, 35, 3, 461–72.

Harland, T., Hussain, R., and Bakar, A. (2014) The Scholarship of Teaching and Learning. *THE*, 19, 1, 38–48.

Harman, G. (1977) Academic Staff and Academic Drift in Australian Colleges of Advanced Education. *HE*, 6, 3, 313–35.

Harman, G. (2001) The Politics of Quality Assurance. *AJE*, 45, 2, 168–82.

Harman, G. (2004) New Directions in Internationalizing Higher Education. *HEP*, 17, 101–20.

Harman, G., and Wood, F. (1990) Academics and their Work under Dawkins. *AER*, 17, 2, 53–74.

Harper, G., and Kember, D. (1986) Approaches to Study of Distance Education Students. *BJET*, 17, 3, 212–22.

Harris, D. (2017) Threshold Concepts in Teaching Leisure Studies. *Leisure Studies*, 36, 2, 282–92.

Harris, R., Li, Q., and Moffat, J. (2013) The Impact of Higher Education Institution-Firm Knowledge Links on Establishment-level Productivity in British Regions. *MS*, 81, 2, 143–62.

Harris, S. (2008) Internationalising the University. *EPT*, 40, 2, 346–57.

Harry, J., and Goldner, N. (1972) The Null Relationship between Teaching and Research. *SocE*, 45, 1, 47–60.

Hart, J. (1923) The Relation of the Social Worker to Education. *SF*, 1, 5, 572–5.

Hartley, P., Woods, A., and Pill, M. (eds) (2005) *Enhancing Teaching in Higher Education*. London, Routledge.

Harvey, L. (1995) The New Collegialism. *TEM*, 1, 2, 153–60.

Harvey, L., and Williams, J. (2010a) Fifteen Years of *Quality in Higher Education*. *QHE*, 16, 1, 3–36.

Harvey, L., and Williams, J. (2010b) Fifteen Years of *Quality in Higher Education* (Part Two). *QHE*, 16, 2, 81–113.

Harwood, J. (2005) *Technology's Dilemma*. Bern, Peter Lang.

Harwood, J. (2010) Understanding Academic Drift. *Minerva*, 48, 413–27.

Haselgrove, S. (ed) (1994) *The Student Experience*. Buckingham, Open University Press.

Hatch, T. (2009) The Scholarship of Teaching and Web-based Representations of Teaching in the United States. *EAR*, 17, 1, 63–78.

Hatfield, R. (2006) Collegiality in Higher Education. *Journal of Organizational Culture, Communication and Conflict*, 10, 1, 11–19.

Hattie, J. (2009) *Visible Learning*. Abingdon, Routledge.

Hattie, J., and Marsh, H. (1996) The Relationship between Teaching and Research. *RER*, 66, 4, 507–42.

Haug, G. (2003) Quality Assurance/Accreditation in the Emerging European Higher Education Area. *EJE*, 38, 3, 229–40.

Hayhoe, R. (1995) An Asian Multiversity? *CER*, 39, 3, 299–321.

Hazelkorn, E. (2008) Learning to Live with League Tables and Ranking. *HEP*, 21, 193–215.

Healey, M. (2000) Developing the Scholarship of Teaching in Higher Education. *HERD*, 19, 2, 169–89.

Healey, M. (2003) Promoting Lifelong Professional Development in Geography Education. *Professional Geographer*, 55, 1, 1–17.

Healey, M., Jordan, F., Pell, B., and Short, C. (2010) The Research-Teaching Nexus. *IETI*, 47, 2, 235–46.

Healey, N. (2008) Is Higher Education *really* Internationalising? *HE*, 55, 333–55.

Healey, N., and Michael, L. (2015) Towards a New Framework for Analysing Transnational Education. *HEP*, 28, 369–91.

Hedgcock, J., and Lee, H. (2017) An Exploratory Study of Academic Literacy Socialization. *JEAP*, 26, 17–28.

Heikkila, A., and Lonka, K. (2006) Studying in Higher Education. *SHE*, 31, 1, 99–117.

Hellawell, D., and Hancock, N. (2001) A Case Study of the Changing Role of the Academic Middle Manager in Higher Education. *RPE*, 16, 2, 183–97.

Hellsten, I., and Leydesdorff, L. (2016) The Construction of Interdisciplinarity. *Journal of the Association for Information Science and Technology*, 67, 9, 2181–93.

Hendel, D., and Lewis, D. (2005) Quality Assurance of Higher Education in Transition Countries. *TEM*, 11, 3, 239–58.

Hendel, D., and Stolz, I. (2008) A Comparative Analysis of Higher Education Ranking Systems in Europe. *TEM*, 14, 3, 173–89.

Henderson, B., and Buchanan, H. (2007) The Scholarship of Teaching and Learning. *ResHE*, 48, 5, 523–43.

Hendry, C. (1996) Understanding and Creating Whole Organizational Change through Learning Theory. *Human Relations*, 49, 5, 621–41.

Henkel, M. (2000) *Academic Identities and Policy Change in Higher Education*. London, Jessica Kingsley.

Henkel, M. (2004) Teaching and Research. *HEMP*, 16, 2, 19–30.

Herbert, S., and Pierce, R. (2013) Gesture as Data for a Phenomenographic Analysis of Mathematical Conceptions. *IJER*, 60, 1, 1–10.

Hernandez, J. (2002) A Qualitative Exploration of the First-year Experience of Latino College Students. *NASPA Journal*, 40, 1, 69–84.

Herrmann, K. (2013) The Impact of Cooperative Learning on Student Engagement. *ALHE*, 14, 3, 175–87.

Herrmann, K., Bager-Elsborg, A., and McCune, V. (2016) Investigating the Relationships between Approaches to Learning, Learning Identities and Academic Achievement in Higher Education. *HE*: DOI 10.1007/s10734-016-9999-6.

Herrmann, K., Bager-Elsborg, A., and Parpala, A. (2016) Measuring Perceptions of the Learning Environment and Approaches to Learning. *SJER*, DOI:10.1080/00313831.2016.1172497.

Higginbotham, P. (1969) The Concepts of Professional and Academic Studies in relation to Courses in Institutions of Higher Education (particularly Colleges of Education). *BJES*, 17, 1, 54–65.

Hildreth, P., and Kimble, C. (eds) (2004) *Knowledge Networks*. Hershey, PA, Idea Group.

Hirst, E., Henderson, R., Allan, M., Bode, J., and Kocatepe, M. (2004) Repositioning Academic Literacy. *Australian Journal of Language and Literacy*, 27, 1, 66–80.

Hladchenko, M. (2016) The Organizational Identity of Ukrainian Universities as claimed through their Mission Statements. *TEM*, 22, 4, 376–89.

Hodge, P., Wright, S., and Mozeley, F. (2014) More-than-Human Theorising. *IPHER*, 10, 83–102.

Hodges, D. (1998) Participation as Dis-Identification with/in a Community of Practice. *MCA*, 5, 4, 272–90.

Hodgkinson-Williams, C., Slay, H., and Sieborger, I. (2008) Developing Communities of Practice within and outside Higher Education Institutions. *BJET*, 39, 3, 433–42.

Hodkinson, P., and Hodkinson, H. (2003) Individuals, Communities of Practice and the Policy Context. *SCE*, 25, 1, 3–21.

Hodson, P., and Thomas, H. (2003) Quality Assurance in Higher Education. *HE*, 45, 3, 375–87.

Hoecht, A. (2006) Quality Assurance in UK Higher Education. *HE*, 51, 4, 541–63.

Hofer, A., Townsend, R., and Brunetti, K. (2012) Troublesome Concepts and Information Literacy. *Portal: libraries and the academy*, 12, 4, 387–405.

Hoffmann, M., Schmidt, J., and Nersessian, N. (2013) Philosophy *of* and *as* Interdisciplinarity. *Synthese*, 190, 1857–64.

Hogg, R., and Hogg, M. (1995) Continuous Quality Improvement in Higher Education. *International Statistical Review*, 63, 1, 35–48.

Holden, R., and Hamblett, J. (2007) The Transition from Higher Education into Work. *ET*, 49, 7, 516–85.

Holloway, M., Alpay, E., and Bull, A. (2010) A Quantitative Approach to Identifying Threshold Concepts in Engineering Education. *EnE*, 11pp.

Holmegaard, H., Madsen, L., and Ulriksson, L. (2016) Where is the Engineering I Applied For? *European Journal of Engineering Education*, 41, 2, 154–71.

Holmes, J., and Meyerhoff, M. (1999) The Community of Practice. *Language in Society*, 28, 2, 173–83.

Holmwood, J. (2010) Sociology's Misfortune. *BJS*, 61, 4, 639–58.

Holt, D., Palmer, S., Munro, J., Solomonides, I., Gosper, M., Hicks, M., Sankey, M., Allan, G., and Hollenbeck, R. (2013) Leading the Quality Management of Online Learning Environments in Australian Higher Education. *Australasian Journal of Educational Technology*, 29, 3, 387–402.

Holt, R. (2008) Using Activity Theory to Understand Entrepreneurial Opportunity. *MCA*, 15, 1, 52–70.

Holzman, L. (2006) What Kind of a Theory is Activity Theory? *TP*, 16, 1, 5–11.

Hornsby, D., and Osman, R. (2014) Massification in Higher Education. *HE*, 67, 6, 711–19.

Horsburgh, M. (1999) Quality Monitoring in Higher Education. *QHE*, 5, 1, 9–25.

Horspool, A., and Lange, C. (2012) Applying the Scholarship of Teaching and Learning. *AEHE*, 37, 1, 73–88.

Horstschraer, J. (2012) University Rankings in Action? *EcER*, 31, 1162–76.

Horta, H. (2010) The Role of the State in the Internationalization of Universities in Catching-up Countries. *HEP*, 23, 1, 63–81.

Horta, H., Dautel, V., and Veloso, F. (2012) An Output Perspective on the Teaching-Research Nexus. *SHE*, 37, 2, 171–87.

Horta, H., Huisman, J., and Heitor, M. (2008) Does Competitive Research Funding Encourage Diversity in Higher Education? *SPP*, 35, 3, 146–58.

Horta, H., Jung, J., and Yonezawa, A. (2015) Higher Education Research in East Asia. *HEP*, 28, 411–17.

Hosier, A. (2017) Creating Learning Outcomes from Threshold Concepts for Information Literacy Instruction. *College and Undergraduate Libraries*, 24, 1, 1–13.

Hou, A. (2012) Impact of Excellence Programs on Taiwan Higher Education in terms of Quality Assurance and Academic Excellence, Examining the Conflicting Role of Taiwan's Accrediting Agencies. *APER*, 13, 77–88.

Hou, A., Morse, R., and Chiang, C.-L. (2012) An Analysis of Mobility in Global Rankings. *HERD*, 31, 6, 841–57.

Hou, Y.-C., Morse, R., Ince, M., Chen, H.-J., Chiang, C.-L., and Chan, Y. (2015) Is the Asian Quality Assurance System going Glonacal? *SHE*, 40, 1, 83–105.

Houston, D., and Paewai, S. (2013) Knowledge, Power and Meanings Shaping Quality Assurance in Higher Education. *QHE*, 19, 3, 261–82.

Hovdhaugen, E., Frolich, N., and Aamodt, P. (2013) Informing Institutional Management. *EJE*, 48, 1, 165–77.

Howie, P., and Bagnall, R. (2013) A Critique of the Deep and Surface Approaches to Learning Model. *THE*, 18, 4, 389–400.

Hrn iar, M., and Madzík, P. (2017) A 3D View of Issues of Quality in Higher Education. *TQMBE*, 28, 5–6, 633–62.

Hu, H., and McCormick, A. (2012) An Engagement-based Student Typology and its Relationship to College Outcomes. *ResHE*, 53, 738–54.

Hsieh, T.-L. (2014) Motivation matters? *HE*, 68, 3, 417–33.

Hu, Y., van der Rijst, R., van Veen, K., and Verloop, N. (2015) The Role of Research in Teaching. *HEP*, 28, 535–54.

Huang, F. (2006) Internationalization of Curricula in Higher Education Institutions in comparative perspective. *HE*, 51, 4, 521–39.

Huang, F. (2016) The Impact of Mass and Universal Higher Education on Curriculum and Instruction. *HE*, DOI 10.1007/s10734-016-0061-5.

Huang, H.-I., and Lee, C.-F. (2012) Strategic Management for Competitive Advantage. *JHEPM*, 34, 6, 611–28.

Huang, J., van den Brink, H., and Groot, W. (2009) A Meta-analysis of the Effect of Education on Social Capital. *EcER*, 28, 454–64.

Huang, M.-H. (2012) Opening the Black Box of QS World University Rankings. *RE*, 21, 71–8.

Huang, X.-H. (2014) The Move to Quality Assurance in Chinese Higher Education. *LRE*, 12, 3, 286–99.

Huang, Y., Pang, S.-K., and Yu, S. (2016) Academic Identities and University Faculty Responses to New Managerialist Reforms. *SHE*, DOI:10.1080/03075079.2016.1157860.

Hubball, H., and Burt, H. (2006) The Scholarship of Teaching and Learning. *IHE*, 30, 5, 327–44.

Hubbell, L. (2015) Students Aren't Consumers. *Academic Questions*, 28, 82–9.

Huber, M., and Morreale, S. (eds) (2002) *Disciplinary Styles in the Scholarship of Teaching and Learning*. Washington, DC: American Association for Higher Education and the Carnegie Foundation for the Advancement of Teaching.

Hughes, J. (2007) Lost in Translation. pp. 30–40 in J. Hughes, N. Jewson and L. Unwin (eds) *Communities of Practice*. London, Routledge.

Hughes, J., Jewson, N., and Unwin, L. (eds) (2007) *Communities of Practice*. London, Routledge.

Hughes, M. (2005) The Mythology of Research and Teaching Relationships in Universities. pp. 14–26 in R. Barnett (ed.) *Reshaping the University*. Maidenhead, Open University Press.

Huisman, J. (1995) *Differentiation, Diversity and Dependency in Higher Education*. Utrecht, Uitgeverij Lemma BV.

Huisman, J. (ed) (2009) *International Perspectives on the Governance of Higher Education*. New York, Routledge.

Huisman, J., Meek, L., and Wood, F. (2007) Institutional Diversity in Higher Education. *HEQ*, 61, 4, 563–77.

Huisman, J., Lepori, B., Seeber, M., Frolich, N., and Scordato, L. (2015) Measuring Institutional Diversity across Higher Education Systems. *RE*, 24, 369–79

Humboldt, W von. (1970) On the Spirit and the Organisational Framework of Intellectual Institutions in Berlin. *Minerva*, 8, 242–50 (original written 1809/1810).

Hunter, J., and Schmidt, F. (2004) *Methods of Meta-Analysis*. Thousand Oaks, CA: Sage, second edition.

Husband, G., and Jeffrey, M. (2016) Advanced and Higher Vocational Education in Scotland. *RPE*, 21, 1–2, 66–72.

Hutchings, P., and Huber, M. (2008) Placing Theory in the Scholarship of Teaching and Learning. *AHHE*, 7, 3, 229–44.

Hutchings, P., Huber, M., and Ciccone, A. (2011) *The Scholarship of Teaching and Learning Reconsidered*. San Francisco, CA, Jossey-Bass.

Hutchings, P., and Shulman, L. (1999) The Scholarship of Teaching. *Change*, 31, 5, 10–15.

Huutoniemi, K. (2016) Interdisciplinarity as Academic Accountability. *Social Epistemology*, 30, 2, 163–85.

Huutoniemi, K., Klein, J., Bruun, H., and Hukkinen, J. (2010) Analyzing Interdisciplinarity. *RP*, 39, 79–88.

Huysman, M., Wenger, E., and Wulf, V. (eds) (2003) *Communities and Technologies*. Dordrecht, Kluwer.

Hyland, K. (2002) Authority and Invisibility. *Journal of Pragmatics*, 34, 1091–112.

Hyland, K. (2012) *Disciplinary Identities*. Cambridge, Cambridge University Press.

Iammarino, S. and Marinelli, E. (2015) Education-Job (Mis)Match and Interregional Migration. *Regional Studies*, 49, 5, 866–82.

Ingerman, A., and Booth, S. (2003) Expounding on Physics. *IJSE*, 25, 12, 1489–508.

Isaac, C., Byars-Winston, A., McSorley, R., Schultz, A., Kaatz, A., and Carnes, M. (2014) *Advances in Health Sciences Education*, 19, 29–41.

Ishikawa, M. (2009) University Rankings, Global Models and Emerging Hegemony. *JSIE*, 13, 2, 159–73.

Islam, R., and Shafiq, S. (2016) Surface and Deep Approaches to Learning in Higher Education. *Bangladesh Journal of Educational Research*, 2, 1, 45–56.

Ivanic, R. (1998) *Writing and Identity*. Amsterdam, John Benjamins.

Jacob, M., and Hellstrom, T. (2014) Opportunity from Crisis. *SHE*, 39, 8, 1321–31.

Jacobs, C. (2005) On Being an Insider on the Outside. *THE*, 10, 4, 475–87.

Jacobs, J., and Frickel, S. (2009) Interdisciplinarity. *Annual Review of Sociology*, 35, 43–65.

Jain, R., Sinha, G., and Sahney, S. (2011) Conceptualizing Service Quality in Higher Education. *Asian Journal on Quality*, 12, 3, 296–314.

Jamelske, E. (2009) Measuring the Impact of a University First-year Experience Program on Student GPA and Retention. *HE*, 57, 3, 373–91.

James, N., Busher, H., and Suttill, B. (2016) 'We All Know Why We're Here'. *JFHE*, 40, 6, 765–79.

James, R., Krause, K.-L., and Jennings, C. (2010) *The First Year Experience in Australian Universities*. Melbourne, University of Melbourne Centre for the Study of Higher Education.

Janson, A., and Howard, L. (2004) The Odyssey of PhD Students Becoming a Community of Practice. *Business Communication Quarterly*, 67, 2, 168–81.

Jantsch, E. (1970) Inter- and Transdisciplinary University. *Policy Sciences*, 1, 4, 403–28.

Jaquette, O. (2013) Why do Colleges become Universities? *ResHE*, DOI 10.1007/s11162-013-9283-x, 30pp.

Jarvis, D. (2014) Regulating Higher Education. *Policy and Society*, 33, 155–66.

Jauch, L., and Gentry, J. (1976) Perceptions of Faculty Evaluation in the Soft Sciences. *ResHE*, 5, 1259–170.

Jawitz, J. (2009) Academic Identities and Communities of Practice in a Professional Discipline. *THE*, 14, 3, 241–51.

Jay, T., Rose, J., and Milligan L. (2017) Adoption, Adaption and Integration. *IJRME*, 40, 3, 223–30.

Jenkins, A. (2004) *A Guide to the Research Evidence on Teaching-Research Relations*. York, Higher Education Academy.

Jensen, D., and Jetten, J. (2016) The Importance of Developing Students' Academic and Professional Identities in Higher Education. *JCSD*, 57, 8, 1027–42.

Jensen, J.-J. (1988) Research and Teaching in the Universities of Denmark. *HE*, 17, 1, 17–26.

Jensen, K. (1982) Women's Work and Academic Culture. *HE*, 11, 1, 67–83.

Jeremic, V., Bulajic, M., Martic, M., and Radojicic, Z. (2011) A Fresh Approach to Evaluating the Academic Ranking of World Universities. *Scientometrics*, 87, 587–96.

Jiang, X. (2010) A Probe into the Internationalisation of Higher Education in the New Zealand Context. *EPT*, 42, 8, 881–97.

Jobbins, D. (2002) *The Times/The Times Higher Education Supplement* League Tables in Britain. *HEE*, 27, 4, 383–8.

Joensman, K., and Greek, M. (2017) Lecturers' Text Competencies and Guidance towards Academic Literacy. *EAR*, 25, 3, 354–69.

Johnes, M. (2004) The Teaching-Research Nexus in a Sports History Module. *JHLSTE*, 3, 1, 47–52.

Johnson, C. (2001) A Survey of Current Research on Online Communities of Practice. *IHE*, 4, 45–60.

Johnson, D., Wasserman, T., Yildirim, N., and Yonia, B. (2014) Examining the Effects of Stress and Campus Climate on the Persistence of Students of Color and White Students. *ResHE*, 55, 1, 75–100.

Johnston, C. (2001) Student Perceptions of Learning in First Year in an Economics and Commerce Faculty. *HERD*, 20, 2, 169–84.

Johnston, R. (1996) Academic Tribes, Disciplinary Containers and the Realpolitik of Opening Up the Social Sciences. *Environment and Planning A*, 28, 1943–7.

Jokila, S. (2015) The Internationalization of Higher Education with Chinese Characteristics. *APJE*, 35, 1, 125–39.

Jones, A., and Bennett, R. (2016) Reaching beyond an Online/Offline Divide. *TPE*, DOI:10.1 080/1475939X.2016.1201527.

Jones, C., and Asensio, M. (2001) Experiences of Assessment. *Journal of Computer Assisted Learning*, 17, 314–21.

Jones, D. (2015) Opening Up the Pandora's Box of Sustainability League Tables of Universities. *SHE*, DOI:10.1080/03075079.2015.1052737.

Jones, G. (2013) The Horizontal and Vertical Fragmentation of Academic Work and the Challenge for Academic Governance and Leadership. *APER*, 14, 75–83.

Jones, G., and Oleksiyenko, A. (2011) The Internationalization of Canadian University Research. *HE*, 61, 1, 41–57.

Jones, G., Weinrib, J., Metcalfe, A., Fisher, D., Rubenson, K., and Snee, I. (2012) Academic Work in Canada. *HEQ*, 66, 2, 189–206.

Jones, L., Castellanos, J., and Cole, D. (2002) Examining the Ethnic Minority Student Experience at Predominantly White Institutions. *JHHE*, 1, 1, 19–39.

Joo, K. (2014) A Cultural-Historical Activity Theory Investigation of Contradictions in Open and Distance Higher Education among alienated Adult Learners in Korea National Open University. *IRRODL*, 15, 1, 41–61.

Joseph, M., and Joseph, P. (1997) Employers' Perceptions of Service Quality in Higher Education. *JMHE*, 8, 2, 1–13.

Jowi, J. (2009) Internationalization of Higher Education in Africa. *HEP*, 22, 263–81.

Jung, J., and Horta, H. (2013) Higher Education Research in Asia. *HEQ*, 67, 4, 398–419.

Jungert, T. (2013) Social Identities among Engineering Students and through their transition to work. *SHE*, 38, 1, 39–52.

Jury, M., Smeding, A., Stephens, N., Nelson, J., Aeleni, C., and Darnon, C. (2017) The Experience of Low-SES Students in Higher Education. *Journal of Social Issues*, 73, 1, 23–41.

Justice, C., Rice, J., Warry, W., Inglis, S., Miller, S., and Sammon, S. (2007) Inquiry in Higher Education. *IHE*, 31, 201–14.

Kahn, P. (2014) Theorising Student Engagement in Higher Education. *BERJ*, 40, 6, 1005–18.

Kahn, P., Goodhew, P., Murphy, M., and Walsh, L. (2013) The Scholarship of Teaching and Learning as Collaborative Working. *HERD*, 32, 6, 901–14.

Kahu, E. (2013) Framing Student Engagement in Higher Education. *SHE*, 38, 5, 758–73.

Kaiserfeld, T. (2013) Why New Hybrid Organizations are Formed. *Minerva*, 51, 171–94.

Kali, Y., Levin-Peled, R., and Dori, Y. (2009) The Role of Design Principles in Designing Courses that promote Collaborative Learning in Higher Education. *Computers in Human Behavior*, 25, 1067–78.

Kane, S., Chalcraft, D., and Volpe, G. (2014) Notions of Belonging. *IJME*, 12, 193–201.

Kanji, G., Malek, A., and Tambi, B. (1999) Total Quality Management in UK Higher Education Institutions. *TQM*, 10, 1, 129–53.

Kanji, G., Tambi, A., and Wallace, W. (1999) A Comparative Study of Quality Practices in Higher Education Institutions in the US and Malaysia. *TQM*, 10, 3, 357–71.

Kanuka, H. (2011) Keeping the Scholarship in the Scholarship of Teaching and Learning. *International Journal for the Scholarship of Teaching and Learning*, 5, 1, article 3.

Kanyengo, C. (2009) A Library Response to the Massification of Higher Education. *HEP*, 22, 373–87.

Kauppinen, I. (2015) Towards a Theory of Transnational Academic Capitalism. *BJSE*, 36, 2, 336–53.

Kaye, T., Bickel, R., and Birtwistle, T. (2006) Criticising the Image of the Student as Consumer. *Education and the Law*, 18, 2–3, 85–129.

Kearney, S. (2013) Improving Engagement. *AEHE*, 38, 7, 875–91.

Kedzierski, M. (2016) English as a Medium of Instruction in East Asia's Higher Education Sector. *CE*, 52, 3, 375–91.

Kehm, B. (2014) Global University Rankings. *EJE*, 49, 1, 102–12.

Kehm, B. (2015) Higher Education as a Field of Study and Research in Europe. *EJE*, 50, 1, 60–74.

Kehm, B., Michelsen, S., and Vabo, A. (2010) Towards the Two-cycle Degree Structure. *HEP*, 23, 2, 227–45.

Kehm, B., and Teichler, U. (2007) Research on Internationalisation in Higher Education. *JSIE*, 11, 3–4, 260–73.

Kekäle, J. (1999) 'Preferred' Patterns of Academic Leadership in Different Disciplinary (Sub)Cultures. *HE*, 37, 3, 217–38.

Kekäle, J. (2002) Conceptions of Quality in Four Different Disciplines. *TEM*, 8, 1, 65–80.

Kellams, S. (1975) Research Studies on Higher Education. *ResHE*, 3, 139–54.

Kember, D. (1997) A Reconceptualisation of the Research into University Academics' Conceptions of Teaching. *LI*, 7, 3, 255–75.

Kember, D. (2000) Misconceptions about the Learning Approaches, Motivation and Study Practices of Asian Students. *HE*, 40, 1, 99–121.

Kember, D. (2001) Beliefs about Knowledge and the Process of Teaching and Learning as a Factor in Adjusting to Study in Higher Education. *SHE*, 26, 2, 205–21.

Kember, D. (2010) Opening Up the Road to Nowhere. *HE*, 59, 2, 167–79.

Kember, D., Biggs, J., and Leung, D. (2004) Examining the Multidimensionality of Approaches to Learning through the Development of a Revised Version of the Learning Process Questionnaire. *BJEP*, 74, 261–80.

Kember, D., and Gow, L. (1990) Cultural Specificity of Approaches to Study. *BJEP*, 60, 3, 356–63.

Kember, D., and Kwan, K.-P. (2000) Lecturers' Approaches to Teaching and their Relationship to Conceptions of Good Teaching. *IS*, 28, 469–90.

Kenny, J. (2017) Re-empowering Academics in a Corporate Culture. *HE*, DOI 10.1007/s10734-017-0143-z.

Kent, A., Berry, D., Budds, K., Skipper, Y., and Williams, H. (2017) Promoting Writing amongst Peers. *HERD*, DOI:10.1080/07294360.2017.1300141.

Kerby, M. (2015) Toward a New Predictive Model of Retention in Higher Education. *JCSR*, 17, 2, 138–61.

Kerr, C. (2001) *The Uses of the University*. Cambridge, MA, Harvard University Press, 5th edition. First published in 1963.

Kettley, N. (2010) *Theory Building in Educational Research*. London, Continuum.

Kezar, A. (2000) Higher Education Research at the Millenium. *RevHE*, 23, 4, 443–68.

Kezar, A., Gehrke, S., and Bernstein-Sierra, S. (2017) Designing for Success in STEM Communities of Practice. *RevHE*, 40, 2, 217–44.

Kezar, A., and Kinzie, J. (2006) Examining the Ways Institutions Create Student Engagement. *JCSD*, 47, 2, 149–72.

Kieser, J., and Herbison, P. (2001) Student Learning and the Teaching-Research Nexus in Oral Biology. *EJDE*, 5, 60–2.

Kift, S. (2009) *Articulating a Transition Pedagogy to Scaffold and the Enhance the First Year Student Learning Experience in Australian Higher Education*. Strawberry Hills, NSW; Australian Teaching and Learning Council.

Kift, S. (2015) A Decade of Transition Pedagogy. *HERDSA Review of Higher Education*, 2, 51–86.

Kilby, T. (1964) Technical Education in Nigeria. *Bulletin of the Oxford University Institute of Economic and Statistics*, 26, 2, 181–94.

Kiley, M., and Wisker, G. (2009) Threshold Concepts in Research Education and Evidence of Threshold Crossing. *HERD*, 28, 4, 431–41.

Kilinc, A., and Aydin, A. (2013) Turkish Student Science Teachers' Conceptions of Sustainable Development. *IJSE*, 35, 5, 731–52.

Killen, P., and Gallagher, E. (2013) Sketching the Contours of the Scholarship of Teaching and Learning in Theology and Religion. *Teaching Theology and Religion*, 16, 2, 107–24.

Kilpatrick, S., Johns, S., Barnes, R., Fischer, S., McLennan, D., and Magnusson, K. (2016) Exploring the Retention and Success of Students with Disability in Australian Higher Education. *IJIE*, DOI:10.1080/13603116.2016.1251980.

Kim, M. (2012) Cultural-Historical Activity Theory Perspectives on constructing ICT-mediated Metaphors of Teaching and Learning. *European Journal of Teacher Education*, 35, 4, 435–48.

Kim, Y., Horta, H., and Jung, J. (2017) Higher Education Research in Hong Kong, Japan, China and Malaysia. *SHE*, 42, 1, 149–68.

Kimber, M. (2003) The Tenured 'Core' and the Tenuous 'Periphery'. *JHEPM*, 25, 1, 41–50.

Kimble, C. (2006) Communities of Practice. In E. Tomadaki and P. Scott (eds) *Innovative Approaches for Learning and Knowledge Sharing*. EC-TEL Workshop Proceedings, pp. 218–34.

Kimble, C., Hildreth, P., and Bourdon, I (eds) (2008a) *Communities of Practice, volume 1*. Charlotte, NC, Information Age.

Kimble, C., Hildreth, P., and Bourdon, I. (eds) (2008b) *Communities of Practice, volume 2*. Charlotte, NC, Information Age.

Kinchin, I., Cabot, L., Kobus, M., and Woolford, (2011) Threshold Concepts in Dental Education. *EJDE*, 15, 210–15.

King, R. (2010) Policy Internationalization, National Variety and Governance. *HE*, 60, 6, 583–94.

King, R., Marginson, S., and Naidoo, R. (eds) (2011) *Handbook on Globalization and Higher Education*. Cheltenham, Edward Elgar.

Kinman, G., and Jones, F. (2008) A Life beyond Work? *JHBSE*, 17, 1–2, 41–60.

Kinnunen, P., and Simon, B. (2012) Phenomenography and Grounded Theory as Research Methods in Computing Education Research Field. *Computer Science Education*, 22, 2, 199–218.

Kirkgoz, Y. (2013) Students' Approaches to Learning in an English-medium Higher Education. *Journal of Language Teaching and Learning*, 2, 30–9.

Kirkup, G. (2010) Academic Blogging. *LRE*, 8, 1, 75–84.

Kitagawa, F., and Lightowler, C. (2013) Knowledge Exchange. *RE*, 22, 1–14.

Kivinen, O., and Ahola, S. (1999) Higher Education as Human Risk Capital. *HE*, 38, 2, 191–208.

Kivinen, O., Hedman, J., and Kaipainen, P. (2007) From Elite University to Mass Higher Education. *Acta Sociologica*, 50, 3, 231–47.

Kivinen, O., and Rinne, R. (1996) The Problem of Diversification in Higher Education. pp. 95–116 in L. Meek, L. Goedegeburre, O. Kivinen and R. Rinne (eds), *The Mockers and Mocked*. Oxford, Pergamon.

Kleijnen, J., Dolmans, D., Willems, J., and Hout, H. van (2011) Does Internal Quality Management Contribute to More Control or to Improvement of Higher Education? *QAE*, 19, 2, 141–55.

Klein, J. (2004) Interdisciplinarity and Complexity. *E:CO*, 6, 1–2, 2–10.

Klein, J., and Connell, N. (2008) The Identification and Cultivation of Appropriate Communities of Practice in Higher Education. pp. 65–81 in C. Kimble, P. Hildreth and I. Bourdon (eds) *Communities of Practice, volume 1*. Charlotte, NC, Information Age.

Klein, L., and Schwartzman, S. (1993) Higher Education Policies in Brazil. *HE*, 25, 1, 21–34.

Kleinhans, K., Chakradhar, K., Muller, S., and Waddill, P. (2015) Multigenerational Perceptions of the Academic Work Environment in Higher Education in the United States. *HE*, 70, 1, 89–103.

Knight, D., Lattuca, L., Kimball, E., and Reason, R. (2013) Understanding Interdisciplinarity. *IHE*, 38, 143–58.

Knight, J. (2012) Student Mobility and Internationalization. *RCIE*, 7, 1, 20–33.

Knight, J. (2015) International Universities. *JSIE*, 19, 2, 107–21.

Knights, D., and Clarke, C. (2014) It's a Bittersweet Symphony, This Life. *OSt*, 35, 3, 335–57.

Knoke, D., and Isaac, L. (1976) Quality of Higher Education and Sociopolitical Attitudes. *SF*, 54, 3, 524–9.

Kobrak, P. (1992) Black Student Retention in Predominantly White Regional Universities. *JNE*, 61, 4, 509–30.

Koenen, A.-K., Dochy, F., and Berghmans, I. (2015) A Phenomenographic Analysis of the Implementation of Competence-based Education in Higher Education. *Teaching and Teacher Education*, 50, 1, 1–12.

Koenig-Lewis, N., Asaad, Y., Palmer, A., and Petersone, E. (2015) The Effects of Passage of Time on Alumni Recall of 'Student Experience'. *HEQ*, DOI:10.1111/hequ.12063

Kogan, M. (2004) Teaching and Research. *HEMP*, 16, 2, 9–18.

Kogan, M. (2005) Modes of Knowledge and Patterns of Power. *HE*, 49, 1, 9–30.

Kohoutek, J. (2013) Three Decades of Implementation Research in Higher Education. *HEQ*, 67, 1, 56–79.

Kok, S.-K., Douglas, A., and McClelland, B. (2008) Shifting Higher Education Management. *International Journal of Learning*, 15, 4, 227–39.

Kok, S.-K., Douglas, A., McClelland, B., and Bryde, D. (2010) The Move Towards Managerialism. *TEM*, 16, 2, 99–113.

Kolb, D. (1984) Learning Styles and Disciplinary Differences. pp. 232–55 in A. Chickering (ed.) *The Modern American College*. San Francisco, CA, Jossey-Bass.

Koljatic, M., and Kuh, G. (2001) A Longitudinal Assessment of College Student Engagement in Good Practices in Undergraduate Education. *HE*, 42, 3, 351–71.

Kolsaker, A. (2008) Academic Professionalism in the Managerialist Era. *SHE*, 33, 5, 513–25.

Koopman-Boyden, P., and Macdonald, L. (2003) Ageing, Work Performance and Managing Ageing Academics. *JHE*, 25, 1, 29–40.

Kopaczyk, J., and Jucker, A. (eds) (2013) *Communities of Practice in the History of English*. Amsterdam, John Benjamins.

Korhonen, V., and Weil, M. (2015) The Internationalisation of Higher Education. *Journal of Research in International Education*, 14, 3, 198–212.

Koris, R., Ortenblad, A., Kerem, K., and Ojala, T. (2015) Student-Customer Orientation at a Higher Education Institution. *JMHE*, 25, 1, 29–44.

Korosteleva, E. (2010) Threshold Concepts through *Enactive* Learning. *International Studies Perspectives*, 11, 37–50.

Koski, L. (2011) Interdisciplinarity in the Context of University Politics. *EERJ*, 10, 1, 148–52.

Kosmutzky, A. (2012) Between Mission and Market Position. *TEM*, 18, 1, 57–77.

Kosmutzky, A., and Krucken, G. (2014) Growth or Steady State? *HE*, 67, 4, 457–72.

Kostoglou, V., Vassilakoupoulos, M., and Koilias, C. (2013) Higher Technological Education Specialties and Graduates' Vocational Status and Prospects. *ET*, 56, 6, 520–37.

Koutsantoni, D. (2006) Rhetorical Strategies in Engineering Research Articles and Research Theses. *JEAP*, 5, 19–36.

Kraak, A. (2009) South African Technikons and Policy Contestation over Academic Drift. pp. 961–75 in R. Maclean and D. Wilson (eds), *International Handbook of Education for the Changing World of Work*. Dordrecht, Springer.

Krause, K.-L. (2012) Addressing the Wicked Problem of Quality in Higher Education. *HERD*, 31, 3, 285–97.

Krause, K.-L. (2014) Challenging Perspectives on Learning and Teaching in the Disciplines. *SHE*, 39, 1, 2–19.

Krause, K.-L. and Coates, H. (2008) Students' Engagement in First-year University. *AEHE*, 33, 5, 493–505.

Kreber, C. (2005) Reflection on Teaching and the Scholarship of Teaching. *HE*, 50, 2, 323–59.

Kreber, C. (ed) (2006) *Exploring Research-based Teaching*. San Francisco, CA, Jossey-Bass.

Kreber, C. (2013) Empowering the Scholarship of Teaching. *SHE*, 38, 6, 857–69.

Kreber, C. (2015) Reviving the Ancient Virtues in the Scholarship of Teaching, with a slight critical twist. *HERD*, 34, 3, 568–80.

Kreber, C., and Cranton, P. (2000) Exploring the Scholarship of Teaching. *JHE*, 71, 4, 476–95.

Kritz, M. (2016) Why do Countries differ in their Rates of Outbound Student Mobility? *JSIE*, 20, 2, 99–117.

Kuh, G. (2003) What We're Learning about Student Engagement from NSSE. *Change*, 35, 2, 24–32.

Kuh, G., Cruce, T., Shoup, R., Kinzie, J., and Gonyea, R. (2008) Unmasking the Effects of Student Engagement on First-year College Grades and Persistence. *JHE*, 79, 5, 540–63.

Kuhn, T. (1962) *The Structure of Scientific Revolutions*. Chicago, IL, University of Chicago Press.

Kuijpers, M., and Meijers, F. (2012) Learning for Now or Later? *SHE*, 37, 4, 449–67.

Kuzhabekhova, A., Hendel, D., and Chapman, D. (2015) Mapping Global Research on International Higher Education. *ResHE*, 56, 861–82.

Kwiek, M. (2012) Changing Higher Education Policies. *SPP*, 39, 641–54.

Kwiek, M. (2015a) The Internationalization of Research in Europe. *JSIE*, 19, 4, 341–59.

Kwiek, M. (2015b) Academic Generations and Academic Work. *SHE*, 40, 8, 1354–76.

Kwon, S.-W., and Adler, P. (2014) Social Capital. *AMR*, 39, 4, 412–22.

Kyndt, E., Dochy, F., Struyven, K., Cascallar, E. (2011) The Perception of Workload and Task Complexity and its Influence on Students' Approaches to Learning. *European Journal of Psychology in Education*, 26, 393–415.

Kyvik (2007) Academic Drift. pp. 333–8 in Centre for Higher Education Policy Studies (ed.) *Towards a Cartography of Higher Education Policy Change*. Enschede, CHEPS.

Kyvik, S., and Skodvin, O.-J. (2003) Research in the Non-university Higher Education Sector. *HE*, 45, 2, 203–22.

Kyvik, S., and Smeby, J.-C. (1994) Teaching and Research. *HE*, 28, 2, 227–39.

La Lopa, J. (2013) The Scholarship of Teaching. *Journal of Culinary Science and Technology*, 11, 2, 183–202.

Lachs, J. (1965) Graduate Programs in the Undergraduate College. *JHE*, 36, 6, 121–30.

Ladegaard, H. (2017) The Disquieting Tension of 'The Other'. *Journal of Multilingual and Multicultural Development*, 38, 3, 268–82.

Lafferty, G., and Fleming, J. (2000) The Restructuring of Academic Work in Australia. *BJSE*, 21, 2, 257–67.

Lai, M., Du, P., and Li, L. (2014) Struggling to Handle Teaching and Research. *THE*, 19, 8, 966–79.

Lai, M., Lam, K., and Lim, C. (2016) Design Principles for the Blend in Blended Learning. *THE*, 21, 6, 716–29.

Laiho, A. (2010) Academicisation of Nursing Education in the Nordic Countries. *HE*, 60, 6, 641–56.

Lamarra, N. (2009) Higher Education Quality Assurance Processes in Latin America. *PFE*, 7, 5, 486–97

Lamb, P., Sandberg, J., and Liesch, P. (2011) Small Firm Internationalization Unveiled Through Phenomenography. *Journal of International Business Studies*, 42, 672–93.

Land, R. (2011) There Could Be Trouble Ahead. *IJAD*, 16, 2, 175–8.

Land, R. (2012) Crossing Tribal Boundaries. pp. 175–85 in P. Trowler, M. Saunders and V. Bamber (eds) *Tribes and Territories in the 21st Century*. London, Routledge.

Land, R., Cousin, G., Meyer, J., and Davies, P. (2005) Threshold Concepts and Troublesome Knowledge (3). In C. Rust (ed) *Improving Student Learning*. Oxford, Oxford Centre for Staff and Learning Development.

Land, R., Meyer, J., and Flanagan, M. (eds) (2016) *Threshold Concepts in Practice*. Rotterdam, Sense.

Land, R., Meyer, J., and Smith, J. (eds) (2008) *Threshold Concepts within the Disciplines*. Rotterdam, Sense.

Lane, A. (2012) A Review of the Role of National Policy and Institutional Mission in European Distance Teaching Universities with respect to Widening Participation in Higher Education Study through Open Educational Resources. *Distance Education*, 33, 2, 135–50.

Lang, I., and Canning, R. (2010) The Use of Citations in Educational Research. *JFHE*, 34, 2, 291–301.

Langemeyer, I., and Roth, W.-M. (2006) Is Cultural-Historical Activity Theory Threatened to Fall Short of its own Principles and Possibilities as a Dialectical Social Science? *Outlines*, 2, 20–42.

Lanning, S., McGregor, M., Crain, G., Van Ness, C., Keselyak, N., and Killip, J. (2014) The Status of the Scholarship of Teaching and Learning in Dental Education. *Journal of Dental Education*, 78, 10, 1353–63.

Larrechea, E., and Castro, A. (2009) New Demands and Policies on Higher Education in the Mercosur. *PFE*, 7, 5, 473–85.

Larsen, M. (2016) Globalisation and Internationalisation of Teacher Education. *Teaching Education*, 27, 4, 396–409.

Lattuca, L. (2001) *Creating Interdisciplinarity*. Nashville, TN, Vanderbilt University Press.

Lattuca, L., Voight, L., and Fath, K. (2004) Does Interdisciplinarity promote Learning? *RevHE*, 28, 1, 23–48.

Lau, L., and Pasquini, M. (2004) Meeting Grounds. *Interdisciplinary Science Reviews*, 29, 1, 49–64.

Lautenbach, G. (2014) A Theoretically Driven Teaching and Research Framework. *ES*, 40, 4, 361–76.

Lavankura, P. (2013) Internationalizing Higher Education in Thailand. *JSIE*, 17, 5, 663–76.

Lave, J. (1988) *Cognition in Practice*. Cambridge, Cambridge University Press.

Lave, J. (2001) Getting to be British. pp. 281–324 in D. Holland and J. Lave (eds) *History in Person*. Santa Fe, NM, School of American Research Press.

Lave, J. (2009) The Practice of Learning. pp. 200–8 in K. Illeris (ed.) *Contemporary Theories of Learning*. London, Routledge.

Lave, J. (2011) *Apprenticeship in Critical Ethnographic Practice*. Chicago, IL: University of Chicago Press.

Lave, J., Murtaugh, M., and de la Rocha, O. (1984) The Dialectic of Arithmetic in Grocery Shopping. pp. 67–94 in B. Rogoff and J. Lave (eds) *Everyday Cognition*. Cambridge, MA: Harvard University Press.

Lave, J., and Wenger, E. (1991) *Situated Learning*. Cambridge, Cambridge University Press.

Law, A., and Mooney, G. (2006) The Maladies of Social Capital I. *Critique*, 34, 2, 127–43.

Law, D., and Meyer, J. (2010) Adaptation and Validation of the Inventory of Learning Styles for Quality Assurance in a Hong Kong Post-secondary Education Context. *QHE*, 16, 3, 269–83.

Le Heron, R., Baker, R., and McEwen, L. (2006) Co-learning. *JGHE*, 30, 1, 77–87.

Lea, M. (2004) Academic Literacies. *SHE*, 29, 6, 739–56.

Lea, M. (2005) 'Communities of Practice' in Higher Education. pp. 180–97 in D. Barton and K. Tusting (eds) *Beyond Communities of Practice*. Cambridge, Cambridge University Press.

Lea, M., and Stierer, B. (2009) Lecturers' Everyday Writing as Professional Practice in the University as Workplace. *SHE*, 34, 4, 417–28.

Lea, M., and Street, B. (1998) Student Writing in Higher Education. *SHE*, 23, 2, 157–72.

Lea, M., and Street, B. (2006) The 'Academic Literacies' Model. *TP*, 45, 4, 368–77.

Leach, L. (2016) Exploring Discipline Differences in Student Engagement in One Institution. *HERD*, 35, 4, 772–86.

Learmonth, M., and Humphreys, M. (2011) Autoethnography and Academic Identity. *Organization*, 19, 1, 99–117.

Lechner, C., Tomasik, M., and Silbereisen, R. (2016) Preparing for Uncertain Careers. *JVB*, 95–6, 90–101.

Lecusay, R., Rossen, L., and Cole, M. (2008) Cultural-Historical Activity Theory and the Zone of Proximal Development in the Study of Idioculture Design and Implementation. *Cognitive Systems Research*, 9, 92–103.

Lee, J., Jon, J.-E., and Byun, K. (2017) Neo-Racism and Neo-Nationalism within East Asia. *JSIE*, 21, 2, 136–55.

Lee, S.-J., and Jung, J. (2017) Work Experiences and Knowledge Transfer among Korean Academics. *SHE*, DOI:10.1080/03075079.2017.1301416.

Lee, S.-Y. (2016) Massification without Equalisation. *JEW*, 29, 1, 13–31.

Lee, Y.-J. (2011) More than just Story-telling. *Journal of Curriculum Studies*, 43, 3, 403–24.

Leiber, T., Stensaker, B., and Harvey, L. (2015) Impact Evaluation of Quality Assurance in Higher Education. *QHE*, 21, 3, 288–311.

Leibowitz, B., and Bozalek, V. (2016) The Scholarship of Teaching and Learning from a Social Justice Perspective. *THE*, 21, 2, 109–22.

Leibowitz, B., Ndebele, C., and Winberg, C. (2014) 'It's an amazing learning curve to be part of the project'. *SHE*, 39, 7, 1256–69.

Leihy, P., and Salazar, J. (2016) The Moral Dimension in Chilean Higher Education's Expansion. *HE*, DOI 10.1007/s10734-016-0034-8.

Leisyte, L., Enders, J., and de Boer, H. (2009) The Balance between Teaching and Research in Dutch and English Universities in the Context of University Governance Reforms. *HE*, 58, 5, 619–35.

Leisyte, L., and Wilkesmann, U. (eds) (2016) *Organizing Academic Work in Higher Education*. London, Routledge.

Lenning, O., Hill, D., Saunders, K., Solan, A., and Stokes, A. (2013) *Powerful Learning Communities*. Sterling, VA, Stylus.

Leonard, S., Fitzgerald, R., and Riordan, G. (2016) Using Developmental Evaluation as a Design Thinking Tool for Curriculum Innovation in Professional Higher Education. *HERD*, 35, 2, 309–21.

Leonardo, Z., and Manning, L. (2017) White Historical Activity Theory. *REE*, 20, 1, 15–29.

Lepori, B. (2008) Research in Non-university Higher Education Institutions. *HE*, 56, 1, 45–58.

Lepori, B., and Kyvik, S. (2010) The Research Mission of Universities of Applied Sciences and the Future Configuration of Higher Education Systems in Europe. *HEP*, 23, 3, 295–316.

Leuze, K. (2011) How Structure Signals Status. *JEW*, 24, 5, 449–75.

Levatino, A. (2016) Transnational Higher Education and International Student Mobility. *HE*, DOI 10.1007/s10734-016-9985-z.

Levin, J. (1999) Missions and Structures. *HE*, 37, 4, 377–99.

Lewis, B., and Rush, D. (2013) Experience of Developing Twitter-based Communities of Practice in Higher Education. *Research in Learning Technology*, 21, http://dx.doi.org/10.3402/rlt.v21i0.18598.

Li, J. (2012) The Student Experience in China's Revolutionary Move to Mass Higher Education. *HEP*, 25, 453–75.

Li, M., Shankar, S., and Tang, K. (2011) Why Does the USA dominate University League Tables? *SHE*, 36, 8, 923–37.

Li, Y., and Kaye, M. (1998) A Case Study for Comparing Two Service Quality Measurement Approaches in the Context of Teaching in Higher Education. *QHE*, 4, 2, 103–13.

Lightfoot, S., and Piotukh, V. (2014) The Research-Teaching Nexus in Politics and International Relations in the UK. *Politics*, doi:10.1111/1467-9256.12045.

Lilley, W., and Hardman, J. (2017) 'You Focus, I'm Talking'. *Africa Education Review*, DOI:10.1080/18146627.2016.1224592.

Lillis, T., and Scott, M. (2007) Defining Academic Literacies Research. *Journal of Applied Linguistics*, 4, 1, 5–32.

Lim, D. (1999) Quality Assurance in Higher Education in Developing Countries. *AEHE*, 24, 4, 379–90.

Lim F. (2010) Do Too Many Rights Make a Wrong? *QHE*, 16, 3, 211–22.

Lin, N. (2001) *Social Capital*. Cambridge, Cambridge University Press.

Lindblom-Ylanne, S., Trigwell, K., Nevgi, A., and Ashwin, P. (2006) How Approaches to Teaching are Affected by Discipline and Teaching Context. *SHE*, 31, 3, 285–98.

Lindell, M., and Stenstrom, M.-L. (2005) Between Policy and Practice. *Journal of Workplace Learning*, 17, 3, 194–211.

Linder, C., and Marshall, D. (2003) Reflection and Phenomenography. *LI*, 13, 271–84.

Linehan, C., and McCarthy, J. (2001) Reviewing the 'Community of Practice' Metaphor. *MCA*, 8, 2, 129–47.

Ling, F., Ng, P., and Leung, M.-Y. (2011) Predicting the Academic Performance of Construction Engineering Students by Teaching and Learning Approaches. *Journal of Professional Issues in Engineering Education and Practice*, 137, 4, 277–84.

Liow, S., Betts, M., and Lit, J. (1993) Course Design in Higher Education. *SHE*, 18, 1, 65–79.

Lipsey, M., and Wilson, D. (2001) *Practical Meta-Analysis*. Thousand Oaks, CA: Sage.

Littell, J., Corcoran, J., and Pillai, V. (2008) *Systematic Reviews and Meta-Analysis*. Oxford, Oxford University Press.

Litwin, J. (2009) The Efficacy of Strategy in the Competition for Research Funding in Higher Education. *TEM*, 15, 1, 63–77.

Liu, H., and Metcalfe, A. (2016) Internationalizing Chinese Higher Education. *HE*, 71, 3, 399–413.

Liu, N., and Cheng, Y. (2005) The Academic Ranking of World Universities. *HEE*, 30, 2, 127–36.

Lizzio, A., and Wilson, K. (2004) Action Learning in Higher Education. *SHE*, 29, 4, 469–88.

Lo, W. (2017) The Recalibration of Neoliberalisation. *HE*, 73, 759–73.

Locke, W. (2012) The Dislocation of Teaching and Research and the Reconfiguring of Academic Work. *LRE*, 10, 3, 261–74.

Lodahl, J., and Gordon, G. (1972) The Structure of Scientific Fields and the Functioning of University Graduate Departments. *American Sociological Review*, 37, 1, 57–72.

Lofstrom, E., and Nevgi, A. (2007) From Strategic Planning to Meaningful Learning. *BJET*, 38, 2, 312–24.

Lofthouse, R., and Leat, D. (2013) An Activity Theory Perspective on Peer Coaching. *IJMCE*, 2, 1, 8–20.

Lomas, L. (2007) Are Students Customers? *QHE*, 13, 1, 31–44.

Long, C. (2009) From Whole Number to Real Number. *Pythagoras*, 70, 32–42.

Lonka, K., and Lindblom-Ylanne, S. (1996) Epistemologies, Conceptions of Learning and Study Practices in Medicine and Psychology. *HE*, 31, 1, 5–24.

Lopes, A., Boyd, P., Andrew, N., and Pereira, F. (2013) The Research-Teaching Nexus in Nurse and Teacher Education. *HE*, DOI 10.1007/s10734-013-9700-2.

Louie, B., Drevdahl, D., Purdy, J., and Stackman, R. (2003) Advancing the Scholarship of Teaching through Collaborative Self-Study. *JHE*, 74, 2, 150–71.

Loughland, T., Reid, A., and Petocz, P. (2002) Young People's Conceptions of Environment. *EER*, 8, 2, 187–97.

Lovaglio, P., Vacca, G., and Verzillo, S. (2016) Human Capital Estimation in Higher Education. *Advances in Data Analysis and Classification*, 10, 465–89.

Luca, M., and Smith, J. (2013) Salience in Quality Disclosure. *Journal of Economics and Management Strategy*, 22, 1, 58–77.

Lucas, U. (2011) Towards a 'Scholarship of Teaching and Learning'. *AE*, 20, 3, 239–43.

Lucas, U., and Mladenovic, R. (2007) The Potential of Threshold Concepts. *LRE*, 5, 3, 237–48.

Luckett, K. (2007) The Introduction of External Quality Assurance in South African Higher Education. *QHE*, 13, 2, 97–116.

Luitjen-Lub, A., Van der Wende, M., and Huisman, J. (2005) On Cooperation and Competition. *JSIE*, 9, 2, 147–63.

Luke, C. (1997) Women in Higher Education Management in Thailand. *Asian Journal of Women's Studies*, 3, 4, 98–123.

Lulle, A., and Buzinska, L. (2017) Between a 'Student Abroad' and 'Being from Latvia'. *JEMS*, 43, 8, 1362–78.

Lundquist, R. (1997) Quality Systems and ISO 9000 in Higher Education. *AEHE*, 22, 2, 159–72.

Luxon, T., and Peelo, M. (2009) Internationalisation. *IETI*, 46, 1, 51–60.

Lybeck, L., Marton, F., Stromdahl, H., and Tullberg, A. (1988) The Phenomenography of the 'Mole Concept' in Chemistry. pp. 81–108 in P. Ramsden (ed.) *Improving Learning*. London, Kogan Page.

Maassen, P. (1987) Quality Control in Dutch Higher Education. *EJE*, 22, 2, 161–70.

Maassen, P. (1997) Quality in European Higher Education. *EJE*, 32, 2, 111–27.

Maassen, P., Moen, E., and Stensaker, B. (2010) Reforming Higher Education in the Netherlands and Norway. *PS*, 32, 5, 479–95.

Maassen, P., and Stensaker, B. (2005) The Black Box Revisited. pp. 213–26 in I. Bleiklie and M. Henkel (eds) *Governing Knowledge*. Dordrecht, Springer.

MacDougall, M. (2010) Threshold Concepts in Statistics and Online Discussion as a Basis for Curriculum Innovation in Undergraduate Medicine. *MSOR Connections*, 10, 3, 21–4, 41.

MacLeod, M. (2016) What makes Interdisciplinarity Difficult? *Synthese*, DOI 10.1007/s11229-016-1236-4.

Macmillan, M. (2014) Student Connections with Academic Texts. *THE*, 19, 8, 943–54.

MacMynowski, D. (2007) Pausing at the Brink of Interdisciplinarity. *Ecology and Society*, 12, 1, 20, 14pp.

Maffei, A., Daghini, L., Archenti, A., and Lohse, N. (2016) CONALI Ontology. *Procedia CIRP*, 50, 765–72.

Magyar, A., and Robinson-Pant, A. (2011) Special Issue on University Internationalisation. *TT*, 17, 6, 663–76.

Mak, A., and Kennedy, M. (2012) Internationalising the Student Experience. *IHE*, 37, 323–34.

Malaney, G. (1986) Differentiation in Graduate Education. *ResHE*, 25, 1, 82–96.

Malcolm, J., and Zukas, M. (2000) Becoming an Educator. pp. 51–64 in I. McNay (ed.) *Higher Education and its Communities*. Buckingham, Open University Press.

Malcolm, J., and Zukas, M. (2001) Bridging Pedagogic Gaps. *THE*, 6, 1, 33–42.

Manatos, M., Sarrico, C., and Rosa, M. (2017) The Integration of Quality Management in Higher Education Institutions. *TQMBE*, 28, 1–2, 159–75.

Mann, S. (2001) Alternative Perspectives on the Student Experience. *SHE*, 26, 1, 7–19.

Mantai, L. (2017) Feeling Like a Researcher. *SHE*, 42, 4, 636–50.

Marginson, S. (1993) *Education and Public Policy in Australia*. Melbourne, Cambridge University Press.

Marginson, S., and Rhoades, G. (2002) Beyond National States, Markets and Systems of Higher Education. *HE*, 43, 3, 281–309.

Marginson, S., and van der Wende, M. (2007) To Rank or to be Ranked. *JSIE*, 11, 3–4, 306–29.

Maringe, F., and Foskett, N. (eds) (2010) *Globalization and Internationalization in Higher Education*. London, Continuum.

Maringe, F., Foskett, N., and Woodfield, S. (2013) Emerging Internationalisation Models in an Uneven Global Terrain. *Compare*, 43, 1, 9–36.

Maringe, F., and Woodfield, S. (2013) Contemporary Issues on the Internationalisation of Higher Education. *Compare*, 43, 1, 1–8.

Marinkovich, J., Velasquez, M., Cordova, A., and Cid, C. (2016) Academic Literacy and Genres in University Learning Communities. *Ilha do Desterro*, 69, 3, 95–113.

Marquis, E., Healey, M., and Vine, M. (2016) Fostering Collaborative Teaching and Learning Scholarship through an International Writing Group Initiative. *HERD*, 35, 3, 531–44.

Marschall, M. (2004) Citizen Participation and the Neighborhood Context. *Political Research Quarterly*, 57, 2, 231–44.

Marsh, H., and Hattie, J. (2002) The Relation between Research Productivity and Teaching Effectiveness. *JHE*, 73, 5, 603–41.

Marshall, L., and Meachem, L. (2007) Direct or Directed. *Learning, Media and Technology*, 32, 1, 41–52.

Martensson, K., Roxa, T., and Olsson, T. (2011) Developing a Quality Culture through the Scholarship of Teaching and Learning. *HERD*, 30, 1, 51–62.

Martimianakis, M., and Muzzin, L. (2015) Discourses of Interdisciplinarity and the Shifting Topography of Academic Work. *SHE*, 40, 8, 1454–70.

Martin, T., and Berry, K. (1969) The Teaching-Research Dilemma. *JHE*, 40, 9, 691–703.

Martinez, M., and Nilson, M. (2006) Assessing the Connection between Higher Education Policy and Performance. *Educational Policy*, 20, 2, 299–322.

Martiz, J., and Prinsloo, P. (2015) 'Queering' and Querying Academic Identities in Postgraduate Education. *HERD*, 34, 4, 695–708.

Marton, F. (1981) Phenomenography. *IS*, 10, 177–200.

Marton, F. (1986) Phenomenography. *Journal of Thought*, 21, 3, 28–49.

Marton, F. (1988) Phenomenography. pp. 176–205 in D. Fetterman (ed.) *Qualitative Approaches to Evaluation in Education*. New York, Praeger.

Marton, F. (1992) Phenomenography and 'The Art of Teaching All Things to All Men'. *QSE*, 5, 3, 253–67.

Marton, F. (2000) The Structure of Awareness. pp. 102–16 in J. Bowden and E. Walsh (eds) *Phenomenography*. Melbourne, RMIT University Press.

Marton, F., and Booth, S. (1997) *Learning and Awareness*. Mahwah, NJ: Lawrence Erlbaum.

Marton, F., Dall'Alba, G., and Beaty, E. (1993) Conceptions of Learning. *IJER*, 19, 277–99.

Marton, F., Hounsell, D., and Entwistle, N. (eds) (2005) *The Experience of Learning*. Edinburgh, University of Edinburgh, third (internet) edition.

Marton, F., and Pong, W. (2005) On the Unit of Description in Phenomenography. *HERD*, 24, 4, 335–48.

Marton, F., and Saljo, R. (1976a) On Qualitative Differences in Learning I. *BJEP*, 46, 1, 4–11.

Marton, F., and Saljo, R. (1976b) On Qualitative Differences in Learning II. *BJEP*, 46, 2, 115–27.

Marton, F., and Saljo, R. (1984) Approaches to Learning. pp. 36–55 in F. Marton, D. Hounsell and N. Entwistle (eds) *The Experience of Learning*. Edinburgh, Scottish Academic Press.

Marton, F., and Trigwell, K. (2000) Variatio Est Mater Studiorum. *HERD*, 19, 3, 381–95.

Mathison, K. (2015) Effects of the Performance Management Context on Australian Academics' Engagement with the Scholarship of Teaching and Learning. *AER*, 42, 97–116.

Matthews, N., Simon, J., and Kelly, E. (2016) 'Diagnosing' Academic Literacy Needs in Higher Education. *Pedagogy, Culture and Society*, 24, 3, 445–57.

Mavor, S., and Trayner, B. (2001) Aligning Genre and Practice with Learning in Higher Education. *ESP*, 20, 345–66.

May, T. (2001) *Social Research*. Buckingham, Open University Press, third edition.

McAlpine, L., Amundsen, C., and Turner, G. (2014) Identity-trajectory. *BERJ*, 40, 6, 952–69.

McConnell, T. (1973) Beyond the Universities. *HE*, 2, 2, 160–71.

McCroskey, L., Richmond, V., and McCroskey, J. (2002) The Scholarship of Teaching and Learning. *ComE*, 51, 4, 383–91.

McCulloch, A. (2009) The Student as Co-producer. *SHE*, 34, 2, 171–83.

McCulloch, G. (2014) Interdisciplinarity in Action. *JEAH*, 46, 2, 160–73.

McGrath, L., and Kaufhold, K. (2016) English for Specific Purposes and Academic Literacies. *THE*, 21, 8, 933–47.

McInnis, C. (1997) Defining and Assessing the Student Experience in the Quality Management Process. *TEM*, 3, 1, 63–71.

McInnis, C. (2001) Researching the First Year Experience. *HERD*, 20, 2, 105–14.

McKinney, K. (ed) (2013) *The Scholarship of Teaching and Learning in and across the Disciplines*. Bloomington, IN, Indiana University Press.

McLaughlin, J., and Durrant, P. (2016) Student Learning Approaches in the UAE. *HERD*, DOI:10.1080/07294360.2016.1176998.

McLean, A., Bond, C., and Nicholson, H. (2015) An Anatomy of Feedback. *SHE*, 40, 5, 921–32.

McLean, M. (2001) Can we relate Conceptions of Learning to Student Academic Achievement? *THE*, 6, 3, 399–413.

McLean, M., and Barker, H. (2004) Students Making Progress and the 'Research-Teaching Nexus' Debate. *THE*, 9, 4, 407–19.

McLean, N. (2012) Researching Academic Identity. *IJAD*, 17, 2, 97–108.

McLellan, C. (2008) Speaking of Internationalization. *JSIE*, 12, 2, 131–47.

McLendon, M., Hearn, J., and Deaton, R. (2006) Called to Account. *Educational Evaluation and Policy Analysis*, 28, 1, 1–24.

McMillan, J., and Cheney, G. (1996) The Student as Consumer. *ComE*, 45, 1, 1–15.

McMurtry, A. (2006) Linking Complexity with Cultural Historical Activity Theory. *IJRME*, 29, 2, 209–19.

McNally, B., Chipperfield, J., Dorsett, P., Del Fabbro, L., Frommolt, V., Goetz, S., Lewohl, J., Molineux, M., Pearson, A., Reddan, G., Roiko, A., and Rung, A. (2017) Flipped Classroom Experiences. *HE*, 73, 281–98.

McNaughton, S., and Billot, J. (2016) Negotiating Academic Teacher Identity Shifts during Higher Education Contextual Change. *THE*, 21, 6, 644–58.

McNay, I. (1995) From the Collegial Academy to Corporate Enterprise. pp. 105–15 in
T. Schuller (ed.), *The Changing University?* Buckingham, Open University Press.

Meade, P., and Woodhouse, D. (2000) Evaluating the Effectiveness of the New Zealand
Academic Audit Unit. *QHE*, 6, 1, 19–29.

Meek, L. (1991) The Transformation of Australian Higher Education from Binary to Unitary
System. *HE*, 21, 4, 461–94.

Meer, J., and Rosen, S. (2010) Family Bonding with Universities. *ResHE*, 51, 641–58.

Meister, L. (2017) Threshold Concepts and Ways of Thinking and Practising. *The Interpreter
and Translator Trainer*, 11, 1, 20–37.

Melin, M., Astvik, W., and Bernhard-Oettel, C. (2014) New Work Demands in Higher
Education. *QHE*, 20, 3, 290–308.

Melles, G., and Lockhart, J. (2012) Writing Purposefully in Art and Design. *AHHE*, 11, 4,
346–62.

Menahem, G. (2008) The Transformation of Higher Education in Israel since the 1990s.
Governance, 21, 4, 499–526.

Mendoza, P., Suarez, J., and Bustamente, E. (2016) Sense of Community in Student
Retention at a Tertiary Technical Institution in Bogota. *Community College Review*, 44, 4,
286–314.

Menter, I. (2011) Four 'Academic Sub-tribes', but one Territory? *JET*, 37, 3, 293–308.

Menzies, H., and Newson, J. (2008) Time, Stress and Intellectual Engagement in Academic
Work. *Gender, Work and Organization*, 15, 5, 504–22.

Meredith, M. (2004) Why do Universities compete in the Ratings Game? *ResHE*, 45, 5,
443–61.

Merwe, N. van der, McChlery, S., and Visser, S. (2014) Balancing Academic and
Professional Pedagogies. *THE*, 19, 3, 276–88.

Metcalfe, A., and Fenwick, T. (2009) Knowledge for Whose Society? *HE*, 57, 209–25.

Meyer, D., and Kadolph, S. (2005) The Scholarship of Teaching and Learning in Textiles and
Apparel. *Clothing and Textiles Research Journal*, 23, 4, 209–15.

Meyer, J., and Land, R. (2003) *Threshold Concepts and Troublesome Knowledge.* Enhancing
Teaching-Learning Environments in Undergraduate Courses, Occasional Report 4, 14
pp. Edinburgh, School of Education, University of Edinburgh.

Meyer, J., and Land, R. (2005) Threshold Concepts and Troublesome Knowledge (2). *HE*, 49,
3, 373–88.

Meyer, J., and Land, R. (eds) (2006a) *Overcoming Barriers to Student Understanding.*
London, Routledge.

Meyer, J., and Land, R. (2006b) Threshold Concepts and Troublesome Knowledge. pp. 3–18
in J. Meyer and R. Land (eds) *Overcoming Barriers to Student Understanding.* London,
Routledge.

Meyer, J., and Land, R. (2006c) Threshold Concepts and Troublesome Knowledge. pp. 19–32
in J. Meyer and R. Land (eds) *Overcoming Barriers to Student Understanding.* London,
Routledge.

Meyer, J., Land, R., and Baillie, C. (eds) (2010) *Threshold Concepts and Transformational
Learning.* Rotterdam, Sense.

Meyer, J., and Shanahan, P. (2002) On Variations in Conceptions of 'Price' in Economics.
HE, 43, 2, 203–25.

Meyer, J., Ward, S., and Latreille, P. (2009) Threshold Concepts and Metalearning Capacity.
IREE, 8, 1, 132–54.

Miettinen, R. (2006) Epistemology of Transformative Material Activity. *Journal for the
Theory of Social Behaviour*, 36, 4, 389–408.

Miller, J., Martineau, L., and Clark, R. (2000) Technology Infusion and Higher Education.
IHE, 24, 3, 227–40.

Miller-Cotto, D., and Byrnes, J. (2016) Ethnic/Racial Identity and Academic Achievement. *Developmental Review*, 41, 51–70.

Millot, B. (2015) International Rankings. *International Journal of Educational Development*, 40, 156–65.

Mills, E. (1955) Broadening Student Experience in Mental Hygiene and Abnormal Psychology. *American Psychologist*, 10, 2, 74–8.

Mills, M., Bettis, P., Miller, J., and Nolan, R. (2005) Experiences of Academic Unit Reorganization. *RevHE*, 28, 4, 597–619.

Mironenko, I. (2014) Concerning Interpretations of Activity Theory. *Integrative Psychological Behavior*, 47, 376–93.

Mitchell, L., and Mitchell, E. (2015) Using SoTL as a Lens to Reflect and Explore for Innovation in Education and Librarianship. *Technical Services Quarterly*, 32, 1, 46–58.

Modell, S. (2005) Students as Consumers? *Accounting, Auditing and Accountability Journal*, 18, 4, 537–63.

Moed, H. (2017) A Critical Comparative Analysis of Five World University Rankings. *Scientometrics*, 110, 967–90.

Moerkerke, G. (2015) Modern Customers and Open Universities. *OL*, 30, 3, 235–51.

Mohrman, K., Ma, W., and Baker, D. (2008) The Research University in Transition. *HEP*, 21, 1, 5–27.

Mok, K.-H. (1999) The Cost of Managerialism. *JHEPM*, 21, 1, 117–27.

Mok, K.-H. (2000) Impact of Globalization. *CER*, 44, 2, 148–74.

Mok, K.-H. (2005) The Quest for World-class University. *QAE*, 13, 4, 277–304.

Mok, K.-H. (2016) Massification of Higher Education, Graduate Employment and Social Mobility in the Greater China Region. *BJSE*, 37, 1, 51–71.

Mok, K.-H., and Wu, A. (2016) Higher Education, Changing Labour Market and Social Mobility in the Era of Massification in China. *JEW*, 29, 1, 77–97.

Molesworth, M., Scullion, R., and Nixon, E. (eds.) (2011) *The Marketisation of Higher Education and the Student as Consumer*. London, Routledge.

Monks, J., and Ehrenberg, R. (1999) U.S. News and World Report's College Rankings. *Change*, 31, 6, 42–51.

Montgomery, C. (2010) *Understanding the International Student Experience*. Basingstoke, Palgrave Macmillan.

Montgomery, C., and McDowell, L. (2009) Social Networks and the International Student Experience. *JISE*, 13, 4, 455–66.

Montoro, C. (2016) Learn or Earn? *Learning, Culture and Social Interaction*, http://dx.doi.org/10.1016/j.lcsi.2016.05.001.

Moodie, G. (1988) The Debates about Higher Education Quality in Britain and the USA. *SHE*, 13, 1, 5–13.

Moodie, G. (2005) How Different are Higher Education Institutions in the UK, US and Australia? *HEQ*, 69, 1, 3–36.

Moodie, G., and Wheelahan, L. (2009) The Significance of Australian Vocational Education Institutions in opening Access to Higher Education. *HEQ*, 63, 4, 356–70.

Moon, R. (2016) Internationalisation without Cultural Diversity? *CE*, 52, 1, 91–108.

Moore, R. (2003) Curriculum Restructuring in South African Higher Education. *SHE*, 28, 3, 303–19.

Mora, J.-G., Ferreira, C., Vidal, J., and Vieira, M.-J. (2015) Higher Education in Albania. *TEM*, 21, 1, 29–40.

Morales, M. (2017) Cultural Historical Activity Theory. *Asia-Pacific Education Researcher*, 26, 1–2, 85–96.

Moran, J., and Drakakis, J. (2010) *Interdisciplinarity*. London, Routledge, second edition.

Morgan, A., Taylor, E., and Gibbs, G. (1982) Variations in Students' Approaches to Studying. *BJET*, 13, 2, 107–13.

Morgan, D., Kearney, R., and Regens, J. (1976) Assessing Quality among Graduate Institutions of Higher Education in the United States. *Social Science Quarterly*, 57, 3, 670–9.

Morgan, H. (2012) The Social Model of Disability as a Threshold Concept. *SWE*, 31, 2, 215–26.

Morillo, F., Bordons, M., and Gomez, I. (2001) An Approach to Interdisciplinarity through Bibliometric Indicators. *Scientometrics*, 51, 1, 203–22.

Morita, N. (2004) Negotiating Participation and Identity in Second Language Academic Communities. *TESOL Quarterly*, 38, 4, 573–603.

Morley, L. (2001) Producing New Workers. *QHE*, 7, 2, 131–8.

Morphew, C. (2000a) The Realities of Strategic Planning. *RevHE*, 23, 3, 257–80.

Morphew, C. (2000b) Institutional Diversity, Program Acquisition and Faculty Members. *HEP*, 13, 1, 55–77.

Morphew, C. (2009) Conceptualizing Change in the Institutional Diversity of US Colleges and Universities. *JHE*, 80, 3, 243–69.

Morphew, C., and Hartley, M. (2006) Mission Statements. *JHE*, 77, 3, 456–71.

Morrison, A. (2017) The Responsibilized Consumer. *Cultural Studies Critical Methodologies*, 17, 3, 197–204.

Morselli, D., Costa, M. and Margiotta, U. (2014) Entrepreneurship Education based upon the Change Laboratory. *IJME*, 12, 333–48.

Morton, J. (2012) Communities of Practice in Higher Education. *Linguistics and Education*, 23, 100–11.

Moss, G., Kubacki, K., Hersh, M., and Gunn, R. (2007) Knowledge Management in Higher Education. *EJE*, 42, 3, 377–94.

Motova, G., and Pykkö, R. (2012) Russian Higher Education and European Standards of Quality Assurance. *EJE*, 47, 1, 25–36.

Mugabushaka, A.-M., Kyriakou, A., and Papazoglou, T. (2016) Bibliometric Indicators of Interdisciplinarity. *Scientometrics*, 107, 593–607.

Mugler, F., and Landbeck, R. (1997) Learning in the South Pacific and Phenomenography across Cultures. *HERD*, 16, 2, 227–39.

Murray, N., and Nallaya, S. (2016) Embedding Academic Literacies in University Programme Curricula. *SHE*, 41, 7, 1296–312.

Murray, R. (ed) (2008) *The Scholarship of Teaching and Learning in Higher Education*. Maidenhead, Open University Press.

Mutch, A. (2003) Communities of Practice and Habitus. *Organization Studies*, 24, 3, 383–401.

Nagy, J., and Burch, T. (2009) Communities of Practice in Academe (CoP-iA). *ORE*, 35, 2, 227–47.

Naidoo, V. (2009) Transnational Higher Education. *JSIE*, 13, 3, 310–30.

Nalbone, D., Kovach, R., Fish, J., McCoy, K., Jones, K., and Wright, H. (2016) Social Networking Sites as a Tool for Student Transitions. *JCSR*, 17, 4, 489–512.

Navarro, V. (2002) A Critique of Social Capital. *International Journal of Health Services*, 32, 3, 423–32.

Neary, M., and Winn, J. (2016) Against Academic Identity. *HERD*, 35, 2, 409–12.

Neave, G. (1978) Polytechnics. *SHE*, 3, 1, 105–11.

Neave, G. (1979) Academic Drift. *SHE*, 4, 2, 143–59.

Neave, G. (1985) Elite and Mass Higher Education in Britain. *CER*, 29, 3, 347–61.

Neave, G. (1988) On the Cultivation of Quality, Efficiency and Enterprise. *EJE*, 23, 1/2, 7–23.

Neave, G. (1994) The Politics of Quality. *EJE*, 29, 2, 115–34.

Needleman, J. (1963) A Critical Introduction to Ludwig Binswanger's Existential Psychoanalysis. In L. Binswanger, *Being-in-the-World*. Translated by J. Needleman. New York, Basic Books.

Nelson, K., Clarke, J., Kift, S., and Creagh, T. (2011) *Trends in Policies, Programs and Practices in the Australasian First Year Experience Literature 2000–10*. Brisbane, Queensland University of Technology.

Neumann, R. (1992) Perceptions of the Teaching-Research Nexus. *HE*, 23, 159–71.

Neumann, R. (1996) Researching the Teaching-Research Nexus. *AJE*, 40, 1, 5–18.

Neumann, R. (2001) Disciplinary Differences and University Teaching. *SHE*, 26, 2, 135–46.

Nevill, A., and Rhodes, C. (2004) Academic and Social Integration in Higher Education. *JFHE*, 28, 2, 179–93.

Newman, J. (1976) *The Idea of a University Defined and Illustrated*. Oxford, Clarendon Press, edited by I. Ker. Originally published in 1852.

Newman, M., Trenchs-Parera, M., and Pujol, M. (2003) Core Academic Literacy Principles versus Culture-specific Practices. *ESP*, 22, 45–71.

Ng, L., and Pemberton, J. (2013) Research-based Communities of Practice in UK Higher Education. *SHE*, 38, 10, 1522–39.

Ng, S. (2012) Rethinking the Mission of Internationalization of Higher Education in the Asia-Pacific Region. *Compare*, 42, 3, 439–59.

Nicholls, G. (2005) New Lecturers' Constructions of Learning, Teaching and Research in Higher Education. *SHE*, 30, 5, 611–25.

Nicol, D. (2010) From Monologue to Dialogue. *AEHE*, 35, 5, 501–17.

Nicola-Richmond, K., Pepin, G., and Larkin, H. (2016) Transformation from Student to Occupational Therapist. *Australian Occupational Therapy Journal*, 63, 95–104.

Nicola-Richmond, K., Pepin, G., Larkin, H., and Taylor, C. (2018) Threshold Concepts in Higher Education. *HERD*, 37, 1, 101–14.

Nikolou-Walker, E., and Meaklim, T. (2007) Vocational Training in Higher Education. *RPE*, 12, 3, 357–76.

Nilsson, K.-A., and Wahlen, S. (2000) Institutional Response to the Swedish Model of Quality Assurance. *QHE*, 6, 1, 7–18.

Nilsson, P. (2013) Developing a Scholarship of Teaching in Engineering. *RP*, 14, 2, 196–208.

Nilsson, S. (2010) On the Meaning of Higher Education in Professional Practice. *JEW*, 23, 3, 255–74.

Nissani, M. (1997) Ten Cheers for Interdisciplinarity. *SSJ*, 34, 2, 201–16.

Nkrumah-Young, K., Huisman, J., and Powell, P. (2008) The Impact of Funding Policies on Higher Education in Jamaica. *CE*, 44, 2, 215–27.

Noaman, A., Ragab, A., Madbouly, A., Khedra, A., and Fayoumi, A. (2017) Higher Education Quality Assessment Model. *SHE*, 42, 1, 23–46.

Noelke, C., Gebel, M., and Kogan, I. (2012) Uniform Inequalities. *European Sociological Review*, 28, 6, 704–16.

Norton, L., Richardson, J., Hartley, J., Newstead, S., and Mayes, J. (2005) Teachers' Beliefs and Intentions concerning Teaching in Higher Education. *HE*, 50, 4, 537–71.

Noser, T., Manakyan, H., and Tanner, J. (1996) Research Productivity and Perceived Teaching Effectiveness. *ResHE*, 37, 3, 299–321.

Nowotny, H., Scott, P., and Gibbons, M. (2001) *Re-thinking Science*. Cambridge, Polity Press.

Nunez, A.-M., Crisp, G., and Elizondo, D. (2016) Mapping Hispanic-serving Institutions. *JHE*, 87, 1, 55–83.

Nunez, I. (2013) Transcending the Dualisms of Activity Theory. *JCR*, 12, 2, 141–65.

Nunez, I. (2014) *Critical Realist Activity Theory*. London, Routledge.

Nussbaum, K., and Chang, H. (2013) The Quest for Diversity in Christian Higher Education. *CHE*, 12, 1–2, 5–19.

Nussbaumer, D. (2012) An Overview of Cultural Historical Activity Theory (CHAT) Use in Classroom Research 2000 to 2009. *ER*, 64, 1, 37–55.

Nyberg, A., and Wright, P. (2015) 50 Years of Human Capital Research. *Academy of Management Perspectives*, 29, 3, 287–95.

Nyhagen, G., and Baschung, L. (2013) New Organisational Structures and the Transformation of Academic Work. *HE*, 66, 4, 409–23.

Nyström, S. (2009) The Dynamics of Professional Identity Formation. *VL*, 2, 1, 1–18.

O'Brien, L., Marzano, M., and White, R. (2013) 'Participatory Interdisciplinarity'. *SPP*, 40, 51–61.

O'Brien, M., Varga-Atkins, T., Umoquit, M., and Tso, P. (2012) Cultural-Historical Activity Theory and 'the Visual' in Research. *IJRME*, 35, 3, 251–68.

O'Connor, P., and White, K. (2011) Similarities and Differences in Collegiality/Managerialism in Irish and Australian Universities. *GE*, 23, 7, 903–19.

Odhiambo, G. (2011) Higher Education Quality in Kenya. *QHE*, 17, 3, 299–315.

Odhiambo, G. (2014a) The Challenges and Future of Public Higher Education Leadership in Kenya. *JHEPM*, 36, 2, 183–95.

Odhiambo, G. (2014b) Quality Assurance for Public Higher Education. *HERD*, 33, 5, 978–91.

Oermann, M. (2014) Defining and Assessing the Scholarship of Teaching in Nursing. *Journal of Professional Nursing*, 30, 5, 370–5.

Oertel, S., and Soll, M. (2017) Universities between Traditional Forces and Modern Demands. *HE*, 73, 1–18.

Ohrstedt, M., and Lindfors, P. (2016) Students' Adoption of Course-specific Approaches to Learning in Two Parallel Courses. *EJPE*, 31, 209–23.

Ojo, E., and Booth, S. (2009) Internationalisation of Higher Education in a South African University. *EC*, 13, 2, 309–23.

Okay-Somerville, B., and Scholarios, D. (2015) Position, Possession or Process? *SHE*, DOI:10.1080/03075079.2015.1091813.

Olson, R., and Brosnan, C. (2017) Examining Interprofessional Education through the Lens of Interdisciplinarity. *Minerva*, DOI 10.1007/s11024-017-9316-2.

Olssen, M., and Peters, M. (2005) Neoliberalism, Higher Education and the Knowledge Economy. *JEP*, 20, 3, 313–45.

O'Mahony, K., and Garavan, T. (2012) Implementing a Quality Management Framework in a Higher Education Organisation. *QAE*, 20, 2, 184–200.

O'Neil, M., and Jackson, L. (1983) Nominal Group Technique. *SHE*, 8, 2, 129–38.

Opheim, V. (2007) Equal Opportunities? *JEW*, 20, 3, 255–82.

Ordorika, I., and Lloyd, M. (2015) International Rankings and the Contest for University Hegemony. *JEP*, 30, 3, 385–405.

Orr, D. (2004) Research Assessment as an Instrument for Steering Higher Education. *JHEPM*, 26, 3, 345–62.

Orr, J. (1996) *Talking About Machines*. Ithaca, NY: ILR Press.

Oseguera, L., Locks, A., and Vega, I. (2009) Increasing Latina/o Students' Baccalaureate Attainment. *JHHE*, 8, 1, 23–53.

O'Shea, S. (2015) Arriving, Surviving and Succeeding. *JCSD*, 56, 5, 499–517.

Ostrom, E. (2005) *Understanding Institutional Diversity*. Princeton, NJ, Princeton University Press.

O'Sullivan, S. (2011) Applying the Scholarship of Teaching and Learning in an Irish Context. *TS*, 39, 3, 303–19.

Owlia, M., and Aspinwall, E. (1996) Quality in Higher Education. *TQM*, 7, 2, 161–71.

Oyserman, D., and Lewis, N. (2017) Seeing the Destination AND the Path. *Social Issues and Policy Review*, 11, 1, 159–94.

Özoglu, M., Gür, B. and Gümüs, S. (2016) Rapid Expansion of Higher Education in Turkey *HEP*, 29, 1, 21–39.

Pace, R. (1984) *Measuring the Quality of College Student Experiences*. Los Angeles, CA: Higher Education Research Institute, University of California, Los Angeles.

Paino, M., Blankenship, C., Grauerholz, L., and Chin, J. (2012) The Scholarship of Teaching and Learning in Teaching Sociology. *TS*, 40, 2, 93–106.

Pais, A., and Costa, M. (2017) An Ideology Critique of Global Citizenship Education. *Critical Studies in Education*, DOI:10.1080/17508487.2017.1318772.

Palloff, R., and Pratt, K. (2007) *Building Online Learning Communities*. San Francisco, CA: Jossey-Bass, second edition.

Pang, M., and Marton, F. (2003) Beyond 'Lesson Study'. *IS*, 31, 175–94.

Pantin, C. (1968) *The Relations Between the Sciences*. Cambridge, Cambridge University Press.

Paor, C. de (2016) The Contribution of Professional Accreditation to Quality Assurance in Higher Education. *QHE*, 22, 3, 228–41.

Papadimitriou, A. (2011) Reforms, Leadership and Quality Management in Greek Higher Education. *TEM*, 17, 4, 355–72.

Parker, J. (2002) A New Disciplinarity. *THE*, 7, 4, 373–86.

Parry, G. (2015) English Higher Education and its Vocational Zones. *RCIE*, 10, 4, 493–509.

Parry, S. (2007) *Disciplines and Doctorates*. Dordrecht, Springer.

Pascarella, E., and Terenzini, P. (1980) Predicting Freshmen Persistence and Voluntary Dropout from a Theoretical Model. *JHE*, 51, 1, 60–75.

Pascarella, E., and Terenzini, P. (1991) *How College Affects Students*. San Francisco, CA: Jossey-Bass.

Pascarella, E., and Terenzini, P. (2005) *How College Affects Students Volume 2*. San Francisco, CA: Jossey-Bass.

Pashby, K., and Oliveira Andreotti, V. de (2016) Ethical Internationalisation in Higher Education. *EER*, 22, 6, 771–87.

Pask, G. (1976) Styles and Strategies of Learning. *BJEP*, 46, 2, 128–48.

Pastor, J., Serrano, L., and Zaera, I. (2015) The Research Output of European Higher Education Institutions. *Scientometrics*, 102, 1867–93.

Patrick, W., and Stanley, E. (1998) Teaching and Research Quality Indicators and the Shaping of Higher Education. *ResHE*, 39, 1, 19–41.

Pawar, M. (2006) 'Social' Capital? *SSJ*, 43, 211–26.

Paxton, M. (2012) Student Voice as a Methodological Issue in Academic Literacies Research. *HERD*, 31, 3, 381–91.

Paxton, M., and Frith, V. (2014) Implications of Academic Literacies Research for Knowledge Making and Curriculum Design. *HE*, 67, 2, 171–82.

Pearson, J. (2017) Processfolio. *Critical Inquiry in Language Studies*, DOI:10.1080/15427587.2017.1279544.

Pearson, M. (2012) Building Bridges. *JHEPM*, 34, 2, 187–99.

Pechar, H. (2003) In Search of a New Profession. pp. 109–29 in A. Amaral, L. Meek and I. Larsen (eds) *The Higher Education Managerial Revolution?* Dordrecht, Kluwer.

Pedrosa-de-Jesus, M., and Silva Lopes, B. da (2011) The Relationship between Teaching and Learning Conceptions, Preferred Teaching Approaches and Questioning Practices. *RPE*, 26, 2, 223–43.

Peeke, G. (1994) *Mission and Change*. Buckingham, Open University Press.

Peeters, M., Beltyukova, A., and Martin, B. (2013) Educational Testing and Validity of Conclusions in the Scholarship of Teaching and Learning. *American Journal of Pharmaceutical Education*, 77, 9, article 186.

Pelkonen, A., Teräväinen, T. and Waltari, S.-T. (2008) Assessing Policy Coordination Capacity. *SPP*, 35, 4, 241–52.

Pelliccione, L. and Raison, G. (2009) Promoting the Scholarship of Teaching through Reflective e-Portfolios in Teacher Education. *JET*, 35, 3, 271–81.

Penn-Edwards, S., and Donnison, S. (2011) Engaging with Higher Education Academic Support. *EJE*, 46, 4, 566–80.

Pennington, G., and O'Neil, M. (1994) Enhancing the Quality of Teaching and Learning in Higher Education. *QAE*, 2, 3, 13–18.

Perkins, D. (1999) The Many Faces of Constructivism. *Educational Leadership*, 57, 3, 6–11.

Perna, L. (2016) Throwing down the Gauntlet. *RevHE*, 39, 3, 319–38.

Peters, M. (2013) Managerialism and the Neoliberal University. *Contemporary Readings in Law and Social Justice*, 5, 1, 11–26.

Peterson, G., and Stakenas, R. (1981) Performance-based Education. *JHE*, 52, 4, 352–68.

Peterson, S., Kovel-Jarboe, P., and Schwartz, S. (1997) Quality Improvement in Higher Education. *QHE*, 3, 2, 131–41.

Petmesidou, M. (1998) Mass Higher Education and the Social Sciences in Greece. *International Sociology*, 13, 3, 359–84.

Pharo, E., and Bridle, K. (2012) Does Interdisciplinarity Exist behind the Façade of Traditional Disciplines? *JGHE*, 36, 1, 65–80.

Pharo, E., Davison, A., McGregor, H., Warr, K., and Brown, P. (2014) Using Communities of Practice to Enhance Interdisciplinary Teaching. *HERD*, 33, 2, 341–54.

Pherali, T. (2011) *Phenomenography as a Research Strategy*. Saarbrucken, Lambert Academic Publishing.

Piche, P. (2015) Institutional Diversity and funding Universities in Ontario. *JHEPM*, 37, 1, 52–68.

Picione, R., and Freda, M. (2016) Possible Use in Psychology of Threshold Concept in Order to Study Sensemaking Processes. *Culture and Psychology*, 22, 3, 362–75.

Pick, D., Symons, C., and Teo, S. (2015) Chronotypes and Timespace Contexts. *SHE*, DOI:10.1080/03075079.2015.1085008.

Pifer, M., and Baker, V. (2016) Professional, Personal and Relational. *Identity*, 16, 3, 190–205.

Pike, G., and Kuh, G. (2005) A Typology of Student Engagement for American Colleges and Universities. *ResHE*, 46, 2, 185–209.

Pike, G., Kuh, G., and Gonyea, R. (2003) The Relationship between Institutional Mission and Students' Involvement and Educational Outcomes. *ResHE*, 44, 2, 241–61.

Pike, G., Smart, J., and Ethington, C. (2012) The Mediating Effects of Student Engagement on the Relationships between Academic Disciplines and Learning Outcomes. *ResHE*, 53, 550–75.

Pinheiro, R., Charles, D., and Jones, G. (2016) Equity, Institutional Diversity and Regional Development. *HE*, 72, 3, 307–22.

Pirrie, A. (1999) Rocky Mountains and Tired Indians. *BERJ*, 25, 1, 113–26.

Pitkethly, A., and Prosser, M. (2001) The First Year Experience Project. *HERD*, 20, 2, 185–98.

Pitman, T. (2014) Reinterpreting Higher Education Quality in Response to Policies of Mass Education. *QHE*, 20, 3, 348–63.

Pitman, T. (2016) The Evolution of the Student as a Customer in Australian Higher Education. *AER*, 43, 345–59.

Pittaway, S. (2012) Staff and Student Engagement. *Australian Journal of Teacher Education*, 37, 4, 3, 10pp.

Pompili, G. (2010) Quality in Search of Meanings. *QHE*, 16, 3, 235–45.

Poole, M., Bornholt, L., and Summers, F. (1997) An International Study of the Gendered Nature of Academic Work. *HE*, 34, 3, 373–96.

Poortman, C., Reenalda, M., Nijhof, W., and Nieuwenhuis, L. (2014) Workplace Learning in Dual Higher Professional Education. *VL*, 7, 167–90.

Popadiuk, N., and Arthur, N. (2014) Key Relationships for International Student University-to-Work Transitions. *JCD*, 41, 2, 122–40.

Portes, A. (2000) The Two Meanings of Social Capital. *Sociological Forum*, 15, 1, 1–12.

Powell, J., and Solga, H. (2011) Why are Higher Education Participation Rates in Germany so Low? *JEW*, 24, 1–2, 49–68.

Pozzoli, D. (2009) The Transition to Work for Italian University Graduates. *Labour*, 23, 1, 131–69.

Praphamontripong, P. (2011) Government Policies and Institutional Diversity of Private Higher Education. *JCPA*, 13, 4, 411–24.

Pratasavitskaya, A., and Stensaker, B. (2010) Quality Management in Higher Education. *QHE*, 16, 1, 37–50.

Pratt, J. (1997) *The Polytechnic Experiment 1965–92*. Buckingham, Open University Press.

Pratt, J., and Burgess, T. (1974) *Polytechnics*. London, Pitman.

Price, D., and Tovar, E. (2014) Student Engagement and Institutional Graduation Rates. *CCJRP*, 38, 9, 766–82.

Price, L. (2014) Critical Realist versus Mainstream Interdisciplinarity. *JCR*, 13, 1, 52–76.

Price, L., and Kirkwood, A. (2014) Using Technology for Teaching and Learning in Higher Education. *HERD*, 33, 3, 549–64.

Price, M. (2005) Assessment Standards. *AEHE*, 30, 3, 215–30.

Pring, R. (2005) *Philosophy of Educational Research*. London, Continuum, second edition.

Prosser, M. (1993) Phenomenography and the Principles and Practices of Learning. *HERD*, 12, 1, 21–31.

Prosser, M., Martin, E., Trigwell, K., Ramsden, P., and Middleton, H. (2008) University Academics' Experience of Research and its Relationship to their Experience of Teaching. *IS*, 36, 3–16.

Prosser, M., and Trigwell, K. (1997) Using Phenomenography in the Design of Programs for Teachers in Higher Education. *HERD*, 16, 1, 41–54.

Prosser, M., and Trigwell, K. (1999) *Understanding Learning and Teaching*. Buckingham, Open University Press.

Prosser, M., and Trigwell, K. (2006) Confirmatory Factor Analysis of the Approaches to Teaching Inventory. *BJEP*, 76, 405–19.

Proulx, R. (2007) Higher Education Ranking and League Tables. *HEE*, 32, 1, 71–82.

Punch, K. (1998) *Introduction to Social Research*. London, Sage.

Pusser, B., and Marginson, S. (2013) University Rankings in Critical Perspective. *JHE*, 84, 4, 544–68.

Putnam, R. (2000) *Bowling Alone*. New York: Simon & Schuster.

Putz, P., and Arnold, P. (2001) Communities of Practice. *Education, Communication and Information*, 1, 2, 181–95.

Puukka, J., and Marmolejo, F. (2008) Higher Education Institutions and Regional Mission. *HEP*, 21, 217–44.

Pyvis, D. (2011) The Need for Context-sensitive Measures of Educational Quality in Transnational Higher Education. *THE*, 16, 6, 733–44.

Quimbo, M., and Sulabo, E. (2014) Research Productivity and its Policy Implications in Higher Education Institutions. *SHE*, 39, 10, 1955–71.

Quinlan, K., Male, S., Baillie, C., Stamboulis, A., Fill, J., and Jaffer, Z. (2013) Methodological Challenges in Researching Threshold Concepts. *HE*. 17pp. DOI 10.1007/s10734-013-9623-y.

Quinn, A., Lemay, G., Larden, P., and Johnson, D. (2009) Service Quality in Higher Education. *TQMBE*, 20, 2, 139-52.

Rajagopal, I., and Farr, W. (1989) The Political Economy of Part-time Academic Work in Canada. *HE*, 18, 3, 267–85.

Rambiritch, A. (2015) Accountability Issues in Testing Academic Literacy. *Perspectives in Education*, 33, 1, 26–41.

Ramirez, G. (2014) Trading Quality Across Borders. *TEM*, 20, 2, 121–34.

Ramos, A., Palacin, F., and Marquez, M. (2015) Do Men and Women Perform Academic Work Differently? *TEM*, 21, 4, 263–76.

Ramsden, P. (1985) Student Learning Research. *HERD*, 4, 1, 51–69.

Ramsden, P. (1987) Improving Teaching and Learning in Higher Education. *SHE*, 12, 3, 275–86.

Ramsden, P. (1991) A Performance Indicator of Teaching Quality in Higher Education. *SHE*, 16, 2, 129–50.

Ramsden, P. (1992) *Learning to Teach in Higher Education*. London, Routledge.

Ramsden, P. (1993) Theories of Learning and Teaching and the Practice of Excellence in Higher Education. *HERD*, 12, 1, 87–97.

Ramsden, P., and Entwistle, N. (1981) Effects of Academic Departments on Students' Approaches to Studying. *BJEP*, 51, 3, 368–83.

Ramsden, P., and Moses, I. (1992) Associations between Research and Teaching in Australian Higher Education. *HE*, 23, 3, 273–95.

Reason, R. (2009) Student Variables that predict Retention. *NASPA Journal*, 46, 3, 482–501.

Reid, A. (2001) Variations in the Ways that Instrumental and Vocal Students Experience Learning Music. *Music Education Research*, 3, 1, 26–40.

Reid, A., and Petocz (2002) Students' Conceptions of Statistics. *Journal of Statistics Education*, 10, 2 – www.amstat.org/publications/jse/v10n2/reid.html.

Reiko, Y. (2001) University Reform in the Post-massification Era in Japan. *HEP*, 14, 277–91.

Renninger, K., and Shumar, W. (eds) (2002) *Building Virtual Communities*. Cambridge, Cambridge University Press.

Reybold, E., and Halx, M. (2012) Coming to Terms with the Meaning of Interdisciplinarity. *Journal of General Education*, 61, 4, 323–51.

Rhoades, G., and Sporn, B. (2002) Quality Assurance in Europe and the US. *HE*, 43, 3, 355–90.

Rice, E. (1991) The New American Scholar. *Metropolitan Universities*, 1, 4, 7–18.

Richardson, J. (1994) Cultural Specificity of Approaches to Studying in Higher Education. *HE*, 27, 4, 449–68.

Richardson, J. (1999) The Concepts and Methods of Phenomenographic Research. *RER*, 69, 1, 53–82.

Richardson, J. (2000) *Researching Student Learning*. Buckingham, Open University Press.

Richardson, J. (2011) Approaches to Studying, Conceptions of Learning and Learning Styles in Higher Education. *LID*, 21, 288–93.

Richardson, J., Morgan, A., and Woodley, A. (1999) Approaches to Studying in Distance Education. *HE*, 37, 1, 23–55.

Riesman, D. (1956) *Constraint and Variety in American Education*. Lincoln, NA: University of Nebraska.

Riordan, T. (2008) Disciplinary Expertise Revisited. *AHHE*, 7, 3, 262–75.

Roberts, G. (2003) Teaching Using the Web. *IS*, 31, 127–50.

Roberts, R. (2004) Managerialism in US Universities. *Critical Perspectives on Accounting*, 15, 4, 461–7.

Roberts, S. (2011) Traditional Practice for Non-traditional Students? *JFHE*, 35, 2, 183–99.

Robertson, J., and Bond, C. (2001) Experiences of the Relation between Teaching and Research. *HERD*, 20, 1, 5–19.

Robinson, C., and Hullinger, H. (2008) New Benchmarks in Higher Education. *JEB*, 84, 2, 101–9.

Robinson-Garcia, N., Torres-Salinas, D., Lopez-Cozar, E., and Herrera, F. (2014) An Insight into the Importance of National University Rankings in an International Context. *Scientometrics*, 101, 1309–24.

Rodriguez-Pomeda, J., and Casani, F. (2016) Legitimating the World-class University Concept through the Discourse of Elite Universities' Presidents. *HERD*, 35, 6, 1269–83.

Rodriguez-Pose, A., and Vilatla-Bufi, M. (2005) Education, Migration, and Job Satisfaction. *Journal of Economic Geography*, 5, 545–66.

Rogoff, B. (2003) *The Cultural Nature of Human Development*. Oxford, Oxford University Press.

Rogoff, B., and Lave, J. (eds) (1984) *Everyday Cognition*. Cambridge, MA: Harvard University Press.

Rome, E. de, Boud, D., and Genn, J. (1985) Changes in Academic Staff Perceptions of the Status of Teaching and Research. *HERD*, 4, 2, 131–43.

Rosado, D., and David, M. (2006) 'A Massive University or a University for the Masses?' *JEP*, 21, 3, 343–65.

Rose, D., Rose, M., Farrington, S., and Page, S. (2008) Scaffolding Academic Literacy with Indigenous Health Sciences Students. *JEAP*, 7, 165–79.

Rose, E., Le Heron, J., and Sofat, I. (2005) Student Understandings of Information System Design, Learning and Teaching. *Journal of Information Systems Education*, 16, 2, 183–95.

Rose-Redwood, C., and Rose-Redwood, R. (2013) Self-Segregation or Global Mixing? *JCSD*, 54, 4, 413–29.

Rosenblith, W. (1950) Auditory Masking and Fatigue. *Journal of the Acoustical Society of America*, 22, 6, 792–800.

Ross, P., Taylor, C., Hughes, C., Whitaker, N., Lutze-Mann, L., Kofod, M., and Tzioumis, V. (2010) Threshold Concepts in Learning Biology and Evolution. *Biology International*, 47, 47–54.

Rosser, A. (2016) Neo-Liberalism and the Politics of Higher Education Policy in Indonesia. *CE*, 52, 2, 109–35.

Rossi, F. (2010) Massification, Competition and Organizational Diversity in Higher Education. *SHE*, 35, 3, 277–300.

Roth, W.-M. (2007a) Emotion at Work. *MCA*, 14, 1–2, 40–63.

Roth, W.-M. (2007b) The Ethico-Moral Nature of Identity. *IJER*, 46, 83–93.

Roth, W.-M. (2012) Cultural-Historical Activity Theory. *Mathematics Education Research Journal*, 24, 87–104.

Roth, W.-M., and Lee, Y.-J. (2007) 'Vygotsky's Neglected Legacy'. *RER*, 77, 2, 186–232.

Roth, W.-M., and Lee, Y.-J. (2009) Cultural-Historical Activity Theory and Pedagogy. *Pedagogies*, 5, 1, 1–5.

Rothmann, J. (2016) The (de)Professionalisation of the Gay Male Academic Identity. *South African Review of Sociology*, 47, 4, 40–59.

Rovio-Johansson, A. (2013) An Application of Variation Theory of Learning in Higher Education. *IPHER*, 9, 261–79.

Rowbottom, D. (2007) Demystifying Threshold Concepts. *JPE*, 41, 2, 263–70.

Rowland, S., and Myatt, P. (2014) Getting Started in the Scholarship of Teaching and Learning. *Biochemistry and Molecular Biology Education*, 42, 1, 6–14.

Roxa, T., Olsson, T., and Martensson, K. (2008) Appropriate Use of Theory in the Scholarship of Teaching and Learning as a Strategy for Institutional Development. *AHHE*, 7, 3, 276–94.

Rubaii, N., and Bandeira, M. (2016) Comparative Analysis of Higher Education Quality Assurance in Colombia and Ecuador. *JCPA*, DOI:10.1080/13876988.2016.1199103.

Russell, D. (1997) Writing and Genre in Higher Education and Workplaces. *MCA*, 4, 4, 224–37.

Russell, E. (2015) The Internationalisation of Emerging Market Higher Education Providers. *International Journal of Business and Society*, 16, 2, 261–80.

Russell, J. (1958) An Example of Quality Control in Higher Education. *AAUP Bulletin*, 44, 3, 648–51.

Russell, J., Rosenthal, D., and Thomson, G. (2010) The International Student Experience. *HE*, 60, 2, 235–49.

Ryan, S., and Neumann, R. (2013) Interdisciplinarity in an Era of New Public Management. *SHE*, 38, 2, 192–206.

Ryle, A. (1969) *Student Casualties*. London: Allen Lane/The Penguin Press.

Saarinen, T. (2008) Persuasive Presuppositions in OECD and EU Higher Education Policy Documents. *Discourse Studies*, 10, 3, 341–59.

Sabri, D. (2011) What's Wrong with 'the Student Experience'? *DSCPE*, 32, 5, 657–67.

Sadler-Smith, E. (1996) Approaches to Studying. *ES*, 22, 3, 367–79.

Sadlo, G., and Richardson, J. (2003) Approaches to Studying and Perceptions of the Academic Environment in Students following Problem-based and Subject-based Curricula. *HERD*, 22, 3, 253–74.

Saele, R., Dahl, T., Sorlie, T., and Friborg, O. (2016) Relationships between Learning Approach, Procrastination and Academic Achievement amongst First-year University Students. *HE*, DOI 10.1007/s10734-016-0075-z.

Safon, V. (2013) What do Global University Rankings really Measure? *Scientometrics*, 97, 223–44.

Sahlin, K. (2012) The Interplay of Organising Models in Higher Education. pp. 198–221 in B. Stensaker, J. Valimaa and C. Sarrico (eds) *Managing Reform in Universities*. Basingstoke, Palgrave Macmillan.

Sahney, S. (2016) Use of Multiple Methodologies for developing a Customer-oriented Model of Total Quality Management in Higher Education. *IJEM*, 30, 3, 326–53.

Saka, Y., Southerland, S., and Brooks, J. (2009) Becoming a Member of a School Community while Working toward Science Education Reform. *SE*, 93, 996–1025.

Salaran, M. (2010) Research Productivity and Social Capital in Australian Higher Education. *HEQ*, 64, 2, 133–48.

Salcedo, H. (1988) Quality Indicators in Venezuelan Higher Education. *SEE*, 14, 1, 25–35.

Salehi, P., Rasdi, R., and Ahmad, A. (2015) Personal and Environmental Predictors of Academics' Work-to-Family Enrichment at Research Universities. *APER*, 24, 2, 379–88.

Saljo, R. (1997) Talk as Data and Practice. *HERD*, 16, 2, 173–90.

Salini, S., and Turri, M. (2016) How to measure Institutional Diversity in Higher Education using Revenue Data. *QQ*, 50, 1165–83.

Salisbury, M., Umbach, P., Paulsen, M., and Pascarella, E. (2009) Going Global. *ResHE*, 50, 119–43.

Salmi, J., and Saroyan, A. (2007) League Tables as Policy Instruments. *HEMP*, 19, 2, 31–68.

Salminen, A. (2003) New Public Management and Finnish Public Sector Organisations. pp. 55–69 in A. Amaral, L. Meek and I. Larsen (eds) *The Higher Education Managerial Revolution?* Dordrecht, Kluwer.

Sandberg, J. (1997) Are Phenomenographic Results Reliable? *HERD*, 16, 2, 203–12.

Sandri, O. (2013) Threshold Concepts, Systems and Learning for Sustainability. *EER*. DOI:10.1080/13504622.2012.753413. 13pp.

Sannino, A. (2011) Activity Theory as an Activist and Interventionist Theory. *TP*, 21, 5, 571–97.

Sannino, A., and Sutter, B. (2011) Cultural-Historical Activity Theory and Interventionist Methodology. *TP*, 21, 5, 557–70.

Santiago, R., and Carvalho, T. (2004) Effects of Managerialism on the Perceptions of Higher Education in Portugal. *HEP*, 17, 4, 427–44.

Santiago, R., and Carvalho, T. (2008) Academics in a New Work Environment. *HEQ*, 62, 3, 204–23.

Santiago, R., and Carvalho, T. (2012) Managerialism Rhetorics in Portuguese Higher Education. *Minerva*, 50, 511–32.

Santiago, R., Carvalho, T., Amaral, A., and Meek, L. (2006) Changing Patterns in the Middle Management of Higher Education Institutions. *HE*, 52, 2, 215–50.

Sanz-Menendez, L., Bordons, M., and Zulueta, A. (2001) Interdisciplinarity as a Multidimensional Concept. *RE*, 10, 1, 47–58.

Saroyan, A. (2014) Agency Matters. *IJAD*, 19, 1, 57–64.

Sarrico, C., Rosa, M., Teixeira, P., and Cardoso, M. (2010) Assessing Quality and Evaluating Performance in Higher Education. *Minerva*, 48, 35–54.

Sataoen, H. (2016) Transforming the 'Third Mission' in Norwegian Higher Education Institutions. *SJER*, DOI:10.1080/00313831.2016.1212253.

Saunders, D. (2015) They Do Not Buy It. *JMHE*, 25, 1, 5–28.

Sav, G. (2000) Institutional Funding and Managerial Differences in Racially Dual Higher Education Systems. *HEM*, 11, 3, 41–54.

Savin-Baden, M., McFarland, L., and Savin-Baden, J. (2008) Learning Spaces, Agency and Nations of Improvement. *LRE*, 6, 3, 211–27.

Scales, E. (1960) A Study of College Student Retention and Withdrawal. *JNE*, 29, 4, 438–44.

Scheja, M., and Pettersson, K. (2010) Transformation and Contextualisation. *HE*, 59, 2, 221–41.

Schellekens, A., Paas, F., and Merrienboer, J. van (2003) Flexibility in Higher Professional Education. *HE*, 45, 3, 281–305.

Schmeck, R., and Geisler-Brenstein, E. (1989) Individual Differences that affect the Way Students Approach Learning. *LID*, 1, 1, 85–124.

Schmidt, E. (2017) Quality Assurance Policies and Practices in Scandinavian Higher Education Systems. *JHEPM*, 39, 3, 247–65.

Schmitt, H. (1965) Teaching and Research. *JHE*, 36, 8, 419–27.

Schmoch, U., Fardoun, H., and Mashat, A. (2016) Establishing a World-Class University in Saudi Arabia. *Scientometrics*, 109, 1191–207.

Schomaker, R. (2015) Accreditation and Quality Assurance in the Egyptian Higher Education System. *QAE*, 23, 2, 149–65.

Schomburg, H. (2007) The Professional Success of Higher Education Graduates. *EJE*, 42, 1, 35–57.

Schomburg, H., and Teichler, U. (2006) *Higher Education and Graduate Employment in Europe*. Dordrecht, Springer.

Schuller, T., Baron, S., and Field, J. (2000) Social Capital. pp. 1–38 in S. Baron, J. Field and T. Schuller (eds) *Social Capital*. Oxford, Oxford University Press.

Schultz, R., and Stickler, W. (1965) Vertical Extension of Academic Programs in Institutions of Higher Education. *Educational Record*, Summer, 231–41.

Schultz, T. (1961) Investment in Human Capital. *American Economic Review*, 51, 1, 1–17.

Schummer, J. (2004) Multidisciplinarity, Interdisciplinarity and Research Collaboration in Nanoscience and Nanotechnology. *Scientometrics*, 59, 3, 425–65.

Schwartz, J. (2012) Faculty as Undergraduate Research Mentors for Students of Color. *SE*, 96, 3, 527–42.

Scott, P. (1995) *The Meanings of Mass Higher Education*. Buckingham, Open University Press.

Scott, P. (ed) (1998a) *The Globalization of Higher Education*. Buckingham, Open University Press.

Scott, P. (1998b) Massification, Internationalization and Globalization. pp. 108–29 in P. Scott (ed.) *The Globalization of Higher Education*. Buckingham, Open University Press.

Scott, P. (2005) Divergence or Convergence? pp. 53–66 in R. Barnett (ed.) *Reshaping the University*. Maidenhead, Open University Press.

Scouller, K. (1998) The Influence of Assessment Method on Students' Learning Approaches. *HE*, 35, 4, 453–72.

Scouller, K., Bonnano, H., Smith, L., and Krass, I. (2008) Student Experience and Tertiary Expectations. *SHE*, 33, 2, 167–78.

Scribner, S., and Cole, M. (1981) *The Psychology of Literacy*. Cambridge, MA, Harvard University Press.

Seeber, M., Cattaneo, M., Huisman, J., and Palerari, S. (2016) Why do Higher Education Institutions internationalize? *HE*, 72, 5, 685–702.

Segers, M., and Dochy, F. (1996) Quality Assurance in Higher Education. *SEE*, 22, 2, 115–37.

Seidman, A. (ed) (2012) *College Student Retention*. New York, Rowman and Littlefield, second edition.

Sellar, S., and Gale, T. (2011) Globalisation and Student Equity in Higher Education. *Cambridge Journal of Education*, 41, 1, 1–4.

Seloni, L. (2012) Academic Literacy Socialization of First Year Doctoral Students in US. *ESP*, 31, 47–59.

Semela, T. (2011) Breakneck Expansion and Quality Assurance in Ethiopian Higher Education. *HEP*, 24, 399–425.

Serow, R. (2000) Research and Teaching at a Research University. *HE*, 40, 4, 449–63.

Shah, M., Lewis, I., and Fitzgerald, R. (2011) The Renewal of Quality Assurance in Australian Higher Education. *QHE*, 17, 3, 265–78.

Shah, M., Nair, C., and Richardson, J. (2016) *Measuring and Enhancing the Student Experience*. Cambridge, Chandos.

Shah, M., and Richardson, J. (2015) Is the Enhancement of Student Experience a Strategic Priority in Australian Universities? *HERD*, DOI:10.1080/07294360.2015.1087385

Shahjahan, R., and Kezar, A. (2013) Beyond the 'National Container'. *EdR*, 42, 1, 20–9.

Shanahan, M., Foster, G., and Meyer, J. (2006) Operationalising a Threshold Concept in Economics. *IREE*, 5, 2, 29–57.

Shandas, V., and Brown, S. (2016) An Empirical Assessment of Interdisciplinarity. *IHE*, 41, 411–23.

Shapiro, H., Lee, C., Roth, N., Li, K., Cetinkaya-Rundel, M., and Canelas, D. (2017) Understanding the Massive Open Online Course (MOOC) Student Experience. *Computers and Education*, 110, 35–50.

Sharma, M., and McShane, K. (2008) A Methodological Framework for Understanding and Describing Discipline-based Scholarship of Teaching in Higher Education through Design-based Research. *HERD*, 27, 3, 257–70.

Sharp, S. (1995) The Quality of Teaching and Learning in Higher Education. *HEQ*, 49, 4, 301–15.

Sharrock, G. (2000) Why Students are not (just) Customers (and other reflections on *Life After George*). *JHEPM*, 22, 2, 149–64.

Shattock, M. (2003) *Managing Successful Universities*. Maidenhead, Open University Press.

Shen, K.-M., Lee, M.-H., Tsai, C.-C., and Chang, C.-Y. (2016) Undergraduate Students' Earth Science Learning. *IJSE*, 38, 9, 1527–47.

Shepherd, S. (2017) Managerialism. *SHE*, DOI:10.1080/03075079.2017.1281239.

Sheridan, V. (2011) A Holistic Approach to International Students, Institutional Habitus and Academic Literacies in an Irish Third Level Institution. *HE*, 62, 129–40.

Shields, R. (2013) Globalization and International Student Mobility. *CER*, 57, 4, 609–36.

Shin, J. (2011) Teaching and Research Nexuses across Faculty Career Stage, Ability and Affiliated Discipline in a South Korean Research University. *SHE*, 36, 4, 485–503.

Shin, J., Lee, S., and Kim, Y. (2013) Research Collaboration across Higher Education Systems. *SHE*, 38, 3, 425–40.

Shore, B., Pinker, S., and Bates, M. (1990) Research as a Model for University Teaching. *HE*, 19, 1, 21–35.

Shotton, H., Oosahwe, S., and Cintron, R. (2007) Stories of Success. *RevHE*, 31, 1, 81–107.

Shreeve, A. (2011) Joining the Dots. *HERD*, 30, 1, 63–74.

Shrestha, P. (2017) Investigating the Learning Transfer of Genre Features and Conceptual Knowledge from an Academic Literacy Course to Business Studies. *JEAP*, 25, 1–17.

Shultz, S., Scherman, A., and Marshall, L. (2000) Evaluation of a University-based Date Rape Prevention Program. *JCSD*, 41, 2, 193–201.

Silander, C., and Haake, U. (2016) Gold-diggers, Supporters and Inclusive Profilers. *SHE*, DOI:10.1080/03075079.2015.1130031.

Silver, H. (2003) Does a University Have a Culture? *SHE*, 28, 2, 157–69.

Simmons, J., Lowery-Hart, R., Wahl, S., and McBride, C. (2013) Understanding the African-American Student Experience in Higher Education through a Relational Dialectics Perspective. *ComE*, 62, 4, 376–94.

Simons, M., and Elen, J. (2007) The 'Research-Teaching Nexus' and 'Education through Research'. *SHE*, 32, 5, 617–31.

Simpson, A. (2015) The Surprising Persistence of Biglan's Classification Scheme. *SHE*, DOI:10.1080/03075079.2015.1111323.

Simpson, C., and Sommer, D. (2016) The Practice of Professional Doctorates. *JME*, 40, 5, 576–94.

Simpson, O. (2013) Student Retention in Distance Education. *OL*, 28, 2, 105–19.

Singell, L., and Waddell, G. (2010) Modeling Retention at a Large Public University. *ResHE*, 51, 546–72.

Skinner, B. (2017) Effective Teacher Talk. *ELT Journal*, 71, 2, 150–9.

Skolnik, M. (2010) Quality Assurance in Higher Education as a Political Process. *HEMP*, 22, 1, 67–86.

Skolnik, M. (2016) How do Quality Assurance Systems accommodate the differences between academic and applied higher education? *HE*, 71, 361–78.

Smeby, J.-C. (1996) Disciplinary Differences in University Teaching. *SHE*, 21, 1, 69–79.

Smeby, J.-C. (2006) *Professionalism in a Knowledge Society*. Oslo University College, Centre for the Study of Professions, Working Paper No. 7/2006, 20pp.

Smith, D., and Bocock, J. (1999) Participation and Progression in Mass Higher Education. *JEP*, 14, 3, 283–99.

Smith, J. (2017) Target-setting, Early-career Academic Identities and the Measurement Culture of UK Higher Education. *HERD*, 36, 3, 597–611.

Smith, L. (2009) Sinking in the Sand? *HERD*, 28, 5, 467–79.

Smolentseva, A. (2016) Universal Higher Education and Positional Advantage. *HE*, DOI 10.1007/s10734-016-0009-9.

Smyth, J. (1989) Collegiality as a Counter Discourse to the Intrusion of Corporate Management into Higher Education. *Journal of Tertiary Education Administration*, 11, 2, 143–55.

Snow, C. (1959) *The Two Cultures and the Scientific Revolution*. Cambridge, Cambridge University Press.

Snow, C. (1964) *The Two Cultures*. Cambridge, Cambridge University Press.

Sohail, M., Rajadurai, J., and Rahman, N. (2003) Managing Quality in Higher Education. *IJEM*, 17, 4/5, 141–6.

Somekh, B., and Nissen, M. (2011) Cultural-Historical Activity Theory and Action Research. *MCA*, 18, 2, 93–7.

Sonnemann, U. (1954) *Existence and Therapy*. New York, Grune and Stratton. Reprinted in 1999 by the Gestalt Legacy Press, New York.

Soo, K. (2013) Does Anyone use Information from University Rankings? *EE*, 21, 2, 176–90.

Soria, K., and Stebleton, M. (2012) First-generation Students' Academic Engagement and Retention. *THE*, 17, 6, 673–85.

Sortheix, F., Dietrich, J., Chow, A., Salmela-Aro, K. (2013) The Role of Career Values for Work Engagement during the Transition to Working Life. *JVB*, 83, 466–75.

Spady, W. (1970) Dropouts from Higher Education. *Interchange*, 1, 64–85.

Spady, W. (1971) Dropouts from Higher Education. *Interchange*, 2, 3, 38–62.

Srikanthan, G., and Dalrymple, J. (2007) A Conceptual Overview of a Holistic Model for Quality in Higher Education. *IJEM*, 21, 3, 173–93.

Srivastava, S. (2013) Threshold Concepts in Geographical Information Systems. *JGHE*. DOI:10.1080/03098265.2013.775569. 18pp.

St George, E. (2006) Positioning Higher Education for the Knowledge Based Economy. *HE*, 52, 3, 589–610.

Stacey, G., and Stickley, T. (2012) Recovery as a Threshold Concept in Mental Health Nurse Education. *Nurse Education Today*, 32, 534–9.

Staddon, E., and Standish, P. (2012) Improving the Student Experience. *JPE*, 46, 4, 631–48.

Stamoulas, A. (2006) Greece before the Bologna Process. *HEP*, 19, 433–45.

Stanley, L. (ed) (1997) *Knowing Feminisms*. London, Sage.

Stappenbelt, B. (2013) The Effectiveness of the Teaching-Research Nexus in Facilitating Student Learning. *EnE*, 8, 1, 111–21.

Steele, G. (2015) New Postgraduate Student Experience and Engagement in Human Communication Studies. *JFHE*, 39, 4, 498–533.

Steeples, C., Unsworth, C., Bryson, M., Goodyear, P., Riding, P., Fowell, S., Levy, P., and Duffy, C. (1996) Technological Support for Teaching and Learning. *CE*, 26, 1–3, 71–80.

Stein, S., and Andreotti, V. de (2016) Cash, Competition or Charity. *HE*, 72, 2, 225–39.

Steinberg, S. (1985) Human Capital. *Review of Black Political Economy*, summer, 67–74.

Steinhardt, I., Schneijderberg, C., Gotze, N., Baumann, J., and Krucken, G. (2016) Mapping the Quality Assurance of Teaching and Learning in Higher Education. *HE*, DOI 10.1007/s10734-016-0045-5.

Stella, A. (2006) Quality Assurance of Cross-Border Higher Education. *QHE*, 12, 3, 257–76.

Stensaker, B., and Maasen, P. (2015) A Conceptualisation of Available Trust-building Mechanisms for International Quality Assurance of Higher Education. *JHEPM*, 37, 1, 30–40.

Stensaker, B., and Norgard, J. (2001) Innovation and Isomorphism. *HE*, 42, 473–92.

Stephenson, S. (2017) Accounting Community of Practice Pedagogy. *AE*, 26, 1, 3–27.

Stetsenko, S., and Arievitch, I. (2004) The Self in Cultural-Historical Activity Theory. *TP*, 14, 4, 475–503.

Stich, A., and Reeves, T. (2016) Class, Capital and Competing Academic Discourse. *DSCPE*, 37, 1, 116–32.

Stiwne, E., and Jungert, T. (2010) Engineering Students' Experiences of Transition from Study to Work. *JEW*, 23, 5, 417–37.

Stoeber, J., Childs, J., Hayward, J., and Feast, A. (2011) Passion and Motivation for Studying. *EP*, 31, 4, 513–28.

Stoecker, J. (1993) The Biglan Classification Revisited. *ResHE*, 34, 4, 451–64.

Storen, A., and Wiers-Jenssen, J. (2016) Transition from Higher Education to Work. *TEM*, 22, 2, 134–48.

Storer, N. (1967) The Hard Sciences and the Soft. *Bulletin of the Medical Library Association*, 55, 1, 75–84.

Storer, N. (1972) Relations among Scientific Disciplines. pp. 229–68 in S. Nagi and R. Corwin (eds) *The Social Contexts of Research*. New York, Wiley.

Strauss, A., and Corbin, J. (1990) *Basics of Qualitative Research*. Thousand Oaks, CA, Sage.

Street, B. (1984) *Literacy in Theory and Practice*. Cambridge, Cambridge University Press.

Strengers, Y. (2014) Interdisciplinarity and Industry Collaboration in Doctoral Candidature. *SHE*, 39, 4, 546–59.

Stromquist, N., and Monkman, K. (eds) (2000) *Globalization and Education*. Lanham, MD, Rowman and Littlefield.

Stroude, A., Bellier-Teichman, T., Cantero, O., Dasoki, N., Kaeser, L., Ronca, M., and Morin, D. (2015) Mentoring for Women starting a PhD. *IJMCE*, 4, 1, 37–52.

Struyven, K., Dochy, F., Janssens, S., and Gielen, S. (2006) On the Dynamics of Students' Approaches to Learning. *LI*, 16, 279–94.

Stuart, M., Lido, C., Morgan, J., Solomon, L., and May, S. (2011) The Impact of Engagement with Extracurricular Activities on the Student Experience and Graduate Outcomes for Widening Participation Populations. *ALHE*, 12, 3, 203–15.

Stubb, J., Pyhältö, K., and Lonka, K. (2014) Conceptions of Research. *SHE*, 39, 2, 251–64.

Stukalova, I., Shiskhin, A., and Stukalova, A. (2015) Internationalization of Higher Education. *Economics and Sociology*, 8, 1, 275–86.

Sum, N.-L., and Jessop. B. (2013) Competitiveness, the Knowledge-based Economy and Higher Education. *JKE*, 4, 24–44.

Sun, H., and Richardson, J. (2012) Perceptions of Quality and Approaches to Studying in Higher Education. *HE*, 63, 3, 299–316.

Sutcliffe, W., and Pollock, J. (1992) Can the Total Quality Management Approach used in Industry be transferred to Institutions of Higher Education? *Vocational Aspect of Education*, 44, 1, 11–27.

Svensson, G., and Wood, G. (2007) Are University Students really Customers? *IJEM*, 21, 1, 17–28.

Svensson, L. (1977) On Qualitative Differences in Learning III. *BJEP*, 47, 3, 233–43.

Svensson, L. (1997) Theoretical Foundations of Phenomenography. *HERD*, 16, 2, 159–71.

Svensson, L. (2016) Towards an Integration of Research on Teaching and Learning. *SJER*, 60, 3, 272–85.

Svensson, L., and Wihlborg, M. (2010) Internationalising the Content of Higher Education. *HE*, 60, 6, 595–613.

Sweetland, S. (1996) Human Capital Theory. *RER*, 66, 3, 341–59.

Szreter, S. (2002) The State of Social Capital. *Theory and Society*, 31, 573–621.

Tan, D. (1986) The Assessment of Quality in Higher Education. *ResHE*, 24, 3, 223–85.

Tan, E. (2014) Human Capital Theory. *RER*, 84, 3, 411–55.

Tan, K., and Kek, S. (2004) Service Quality in Higher Education using an enhanced SERVQUAL Approach. *QHE*, 10, 1, 17–24.

Tan, K., and Prosser, M. (2004) Qualitatively Different Ways of Differentiating Student Achievement. *AEHE*, 29, 3, 267–83.

Tang, R., and John, S. (1999) The 'I' in Identity. *ESP*, 18, S23–S39.

Tapp, J. (2015) Framing the Curriculum for Participation. *THE*, 20, 7, 711–22.

Tapper, T., and Filippakou, O. (2009) The World-class League Tables and the Sustaining of International Reputations in Higher Education. *JHEPM*, 31, 1, 55–66.

Tapper, T., and Palfreyman, D. (1998) Continuity and Change in the Collegial Tradition. *HEQ*, 52, 2, 142–61.

Tapper, T., and Palfreyman, D. (2000) *Oxford and the Decline of the Collegiate Tradition*. London, Woburn Press.

Tapper, T., and Palfreyman, D. (2002) Understanding Collegiality. *TEM*, 8, 1, 47–63.

Tapper, T., and Salter, B. (1992) *Oxford, Cambridge and the Changing Idea of the University*. Buckingham, Open University Press.

Tardy, C. (2005) 'It's Like a Story'. *JEAP*, 4, 325–38.

Tari, J., and Dick, G. (2016) Trends in Quality Management Research in Higher Education Institutions. *Journal of Service Theory and Practice*, 26, 3, 273–96.

Tarrant, S., and Thiele, L. (2017) Enhancing and Promoting Interdisciplinarity in Higher Education. *Journal of Environmental Studies and Sciences*, 7, 355–60.

Tavares, O., and Cardoso, S. (2013) Enrolment Choices in Portuguese Higher Education. *HE*, 66, 3, 297–309.

Taylor, G. (1993) A Theory of Practice. *HERD*, 12, 1, 59–72.

Taylor, J. (2003) Institutional Diversity in UK Higher Education. *HEQ*, 57, 3, 266–93.

Taylor, J. (2007) The Teaching Research Nexus. *HE*, 54, 5, 867–84.

Teelken, C. (2012) Compliance or Pragmatism? *SHE*, 37, 3, 271–90.

Teelken, C., and Lomas, L. (2009) 'How to Strike the Right Balance between Quality Assurance and Quality Control in the Perceptions of Individual Lecturers'. *TEM*, 15, 3, 259–75.

Teichler, U. (1998) Massification. *TEM*, 4, 1, 17–27.

Teichler, U. (2004) The Changing Debate on Internationalisation of Higher Education. *HE*, 48, 1, 5–26.

Teichler, U. (2009) Internationalisation of Higher Education. *APER*, 10, 93–106.

Teichler, U. (2015) Academic Mobility and Migration. *EurR*, 23, S1, S6–S37.

Teixeira, P., Rocha, V., Biscaia, R., and Cardoso, M. (2012) Competition and Diversity in Higher Education. *HE*, 63, 3, 337–52.

Tennant, M., McMullen, C., and Krczynski, D. (eds) (2009) *Teaching, Learning and Research in Higher Education*. New York, Routledge.

Tessema, K. (2009) The Unfolding Trends and Consequences of Expanding Higher Education in Ethiopia. *HEQ*, 63, 1, 29–45.

Thomas, G., and James, D. (2006) Reinventing Grounded Theory. *BERJ*, 32, 6, 767–95.

Thomas, L. (2011) Do Pre-entry Interventions such as 'Aimhigher' impact on Student Retention and Success? *HEQ*, 65, 3, 230–50.

Thomas, R. (1973) Toward Quality in the Face of Quantity. *IRE*, 19, 4, 489–95.

Thompson, J., Conaway, E., and Dolan, E. (2015) Undergraduate Students' Development of Social, Cultural and Human Capital in a Networked Research Experience. *Cultural Studies of Science Education*, DOI 10.1007/s11422-014-9628-6.

Thorpe, M., and Godwin, S. (2006) Interaction and e-Learning. *SCE*, 28, 3, 203–21.

Tian, M., and Lowe, J. (2009) Existential Internationalisation and the Chinese Student Experience in English Universities. *Compare*, 39, 5, 659–76.

Tight, M. (2003) *Researching Higher Education*. Maidenhead, Open University Press.

Tight, M. (2004) Higher Education Research. *HERD*, 23, 4, 395–411.

Tight, M. (2006) Higher Education Research. *HER*, 38, 2, 42–59.

Tight, M. (2007) Bridging the Divide. *HE*, 53, 2, 235–53.

Tight, M. (2008) Higher Education Research as Tribe, Territory and/or Community. *HE*, 55, 5, 593–608.

Tight, M. (2009a) *The Development of Higher Education in the United Kingdom since 1945*. Maidenhead, Open University Press.

Tight, M. (2009b) The Structure of Academic Research. In A. Brew and L. Lucas (eds) *Academic Research and Researchers*. Maidenhead, Open University Press, 54–65.

Tight, M. (2011) Student Accommodation in Higher Education in the United Kingdom. *ORE*, 37, 1, 109–22.

Tight, M. (2012a) *Researching Higher Education*. Maidenhead, Open University Press, second edition.

Tight, M. (2012b) Higher Education Research 2000–10. *HERD*, 31, 5, 723–40.

Tight, M. (2012c) Levels of Analysis in Higher Education Research. *TEM*, 18, 3, 271–88.

Tight, M. (2013) Discipline and Methodology in Higher Education Research. *HERD*, 32, 1, 136–51.

Tight, M. (2014a) Collegiality and Managerialism. *TEM*, 20, 4, 294–306.

Tight, M. (2014b) Working in Separate Silos? *HE*, 68, 3, 379–95.

Tight, M. (2014c) Discipline and Theory in Higher Education Research. *RPE*, 29, 1, 93–110.

Tight, M. (2014d) Theory Development and Application in Higher Education Research. *IPHER*, 10, 249–67.

Tight, M. (2015a) Theory Development and Application in Higher Education. *EJHE*, 5, 2, 111–26.

Tight, M. (2015b) Theory Development and Application in Higher Education Research. *HEP*, 28, 4, 277–93.

Tight, M. (2015c) Theory Development and Application in Higher Education Research. *JEAH*, 47, 1, 84–99.

Tight, M. (2015d) Higher Education Research in the United Kingdom since 1945. In J. Case and J. Huisman (eds) *Researching Higher Education*. London, Routledge, 1–19.

Tight, M. (2015e) Research on Higher Education Policy and Institutional Management. In J. Huisman, M. Souto-Otero, D. Dill and H. de Boer (eds) *Palgrave International Handbook of Higher Education Policy and Governance*. Basingstoke, Palgrave Macmillan, 176–91.

Tight, M. (2016a) Phenomenography. *IJSRM*, 19, 3, 319–38.

Tight, M. (2016b) Examining the Research/Teaching Nexus. *EJHE*, 6, 4, 293–311.

Tight, M. (2018) Higher Education Journals. In P. Teixeira and J.-C. Shin (eds) *Encyclopedia of International Higher Education Systems and Institutions* (forthcoming).

Tight, M. (forthcoming a) Higher Education Journals: their characteristics and contribution. *HERD*.

Tight, M. (forthcoming b) Mass Higher Education and Massification. *HEP*.

Tight, M. (forthcoming c) Tracking the Scholarship of Teaching and Learning. *Policy Reviews in Higher Education*.

Tinto, V. (1975) Dropout from Higher Education. *RER*, 45, 1, 89–125.

Tinto, V. (1993) *Leaving College*. Chicago, IL, University of Chicago Press, 2nd edn.

Tinto, V. (2006) Research and Practice of Student Retention. *JCSR*, 8, 1, 1–19.

Tinto, V. (2012) *Completing College: Rethinking Institutional Action*. Chicago, IL, University of Chicago Press.

Tlili, A., and Obsiye, M. (2014) What is Coleman's Social Capital the Name of? *Critical Sociology*, 40, 4, 551–74.

Tofallis, C. (2012) A Different Approach to University Rankings. *HE*, 63, 1, 1–18.

Tomlinson, M. (2016) Students' Perceptions of Themselves as 'Consumers' of Higher Education. *BJSE*, DOI:10.1080/01425692.2015.1113856.

Tomusk, V. (2000) When East Meets West. *QHE*, 6, 3, 175–85.

Toren, N. (1991) The Nexus between Family and Work Roles of Academic Women in Israel. *Sex Roles*, 24, 11–12, 651–67.

Tormey, R. (2014) The Centre Cannot Hold. *THE*, 19, 1, 1–12.

Toth, Z., and Ludanyi, L. (2007) Combination of Phenomenography with Knowledge Space Theory to Study Students' Thinking Patterns in Describing an Atom. *Chemistry Education Research and Practice*, 8, 3, 327–36.

Toth-Cohen, S. (2008) Using Cultural-Historical Activity Theory to Study Clinical Reasoning in Context. *Scandinavian Journal of Occupational Therapy*, 15, 2, 82–94.

Toutkoushian, R., and Shafiq, M. (2010) A Conceptual Analysis of State Support for Higher Education. *ResHE*, 51, 1, 40–64.

Townley, G., Katz, J., Wandersman, A., Skiles, B., Schillaci, M., Timmerman, B., and Mousseau, T. (2013) Exploring the Role of Sense of Community in the Undergraduate Transfer Student Experience. *Journal of Community Psychology*, 41, 3, 277–90.

Trahar, S., and Hyland, F. (2011) Experiences and Perceptions of Internationalisation in Higher Education in the UK. *HERD*, 30, 5, 623–33.

Tranfield, D. (2002) Formulating the Nature of Management Research. *European Management Journal*, 20, 4, 378–82.

Trautwein, C., and Bosse, E. (2016) The First Year in Higher Education. *HE*, DOI 10.1007/s10734-016-0098-5.

Trede, F., Macklin, R., and Bridges, D. (2012) Professional Identity Development. *SHE*, 37, 3, 365–84.

Tribble, C., and Wingate, U. (2013) From Text to Corpus. *System*, 41, 307–21.

Tribe, J. (2010) Tribes, Territories and Networks in the Tourism Academy. *Annals of Tourism Research*, 37, 1, 7–33.

Trigwell, K. (2013) Evidence of the Impact of Scholarship of Teaching and Learning Purposes. *TLI*, 1, 1, 95–105.

Trigwell, K., and Prosser, M. (2004) Development and Use of the Approaches to Teaching Inventory. *EPR*, 16, 4, 409–24.

Trigwell, K., and Prosser, M. (2009) Using Phenomenography to Understand the Research-Teaching Nexus. *EC*, 13, 2, 325–38.

Trigwell, K., Prosser, M., and Ginns, P. (2005) Phenomenographic Pedagogy and a Revised Approaches to Teaching Inventory. *HERD*, 24, 4, 349–60.

Trotter, E., and Roberts, C. (2006) Enhancing the Early Student Experience. *HERD*, 25, 4, 371–86.

Trow, M. (1970) Reflections on the Transition from Mass to Universal Higher Education. *Daedalus*, 99, 1, 1–42.

Trow, M. (1973) *Problems in the Transition from Elite to Mass Higher Education.* Berkeley, CA, Carnegie Commission on Higher Education.

Trow, M. (1994) Managerialism and the Academic Profession. *HEP*, 7, 2, 11–18.

Trow, M. (1999) From Mass Higher Education to Universal Access. *Minerva*, 37, 303–28.

Trowler, P. (2009) Beyond Epistemological Essentialism. pp. 181–95 in C. Kreber (ed.) *The University and its Disciplines.* London, Routledge.

Trowler, P., Saunders, M. and Bamber, V. (eds) (2012) *Tribes and Territories in the 21st Century.* London, Routledge.

Trowler, P., and Wareham, T. (2008) *Tribes, Territories, Research and Teaching.* York, Higher Education Academy.

Trowler, V., and Trowler, P. (2010) *Student Engagement Evidence Summary.* York, Higher Education Academy.

Tsai, P.-S., Chai, C.-S., Hong, H.-Y., and Koh, H.-L. (2016) Students' Conceptions of and Approaches to Knowledge Building and its Relationship to Learning Outcomes. *Interactive Learning Environments*, DOI:10.1080/10494820.2016.1178653.

Tsouroufli, M. (2016) Gendered Pedagogic Identities and Academic Professionalism in Greek Medical Schools. *GE*, http://dx.doi.org/10.1080/09540253.2016.1262008.

Tucker, B. (2013) Student Evaluation to Improve the Student Learning Experience. *ERE*, 19, 7, 615–27.

Tummons, J. (2012) Theoretical Trajectories within Communities of Practice in Higher Education Research. *HERD*, 31, 3, 299–310.

Tummons, J. (2014) Learning Architectures and Communities of Practice in Higher Education. *IPHER*, 10, 121–39.

Turner, D. (2005) Benchmarking in Universities. *ORE*, 31, 3, 353–71.

Turner, J. (2012) Academic Literacies. *JEAP*, 11, 17–25.

Turner, R., Morrison, D., Cotton, D., Child, S., Stevens, S., Nash, P., and Kneale, P. (2017) Easing the Transition of First Year Undergraduates through an Immersive Induction Module. *THE*, DOI:10.1080/13562517.2017.1301906.

Ullah, R., Richardson, J., Malik, R., and Farooq, S. (2016) Perceptions of the Learning Environment, Learning Preferences and Approaches to Studying among Medical Students in Pakistan. *SEE*, 50, 1, 62–70.

Ulriksen, L., Holmegaard, H., and Madsen, L. (2016) Making Sense of Curriculum. *HE*, DOI 10.1007/s10734-016-0099-4.

Umakoshi, T. (1997) Internationalization of Japanese Higher Education in the 1980s and early 1990s. *HE*, 34, 3, 259–73.

Umbach, P., and Wawrzynski, M. (2005) Faculty do Matter. *ResHE*, 46, 2, 153–84.

Umemiya, N. (2008) Regional Quality Assurance Activity in Higher Education in Southeast Asia. *QHE*, 14, 3, 277–90.

Umino, T., and Benson, P. (2016) Communities of Practice in Study Abroad. *Modern Language Journal*, 100, 4, 757–74.

Urban, E., and Palmer, L. (2014) International Students as a Resource for Internationalization of Higher Education. *JSIE*, 18, 4, 305–24.

Usher, A., and Savino, M. (2007) A Global Survey of University Ranking and League Tables. *HEE*, 32, 1, 5–15.

Valadas, S., Almeida, L., and Araujo, A. (2016) The Mediating Effects of Approaches to Learning on the Academic Success of First-year College Students. *SJER*, DOI:10.1080/00313831.2016.1188146.

Välimaa, J. (1998) Culture and Identity in Higher Education Research. *HE*, 36, 2, 119–38.

Valimaa, J., and Hoffman, D. (2008) Knowledge Society Discourse and Higher Education. *HE*, 56, 2, 265–85.

Van Bragt, C., Bakx, A., Van der Sanden, J., and Croon, M. (2007) Students' Approaches to Learning when Entering Higher Education. *LID*, 17, 83–96.

Van Rossum, E. (1988) Students' Conceptions of Learning and Good Teaching in Dutch Higher Hotel Education. *Journal of Hospitality and Tourism Research*, 12, 2, 425–9.

Van Rossum, E., and Schenk, S. (1984) The Relationship between Learning Conception, Study Strategy and Learning Outcome. *BJEP*, 54, 1, 73–83.

Varpio, L., Aschenbrener, C., and Bates, J. (2017) Tackling Wicked Problems. *Medical Education*, 51, 353–65.

Varunki, M., Katajavuori, N., and Postareff, L. (2017) First-year Students' Approaches to Learning, and Factors related to Change or Stability in their Deep Approach during a Pharmacy Course. *SHE*, 42, 2, 331–53.

Venables, P. (1978) *Higher Education Developments*. London, Faber and Faber.

Vermetten, Y., Vermunt, J., and Lodewijks, H. (1999) A Longitudinal Perspective on Learning Strategies in Higher Education. *BJEP*, 69, 2, 221–42.

Vermunt, J. (1996) Metacognitive, Cognitive and Affective Aspects of Learning Styles and Strategies. *HE*, 31, 1, 25–50.

Vermunt, J., and Vermetten, Y. (2004) Patterns in Student Learning. *EPR*, 16, 4, 359–84.

Vidovich, L. (2002) Quality Assurance in Australian Higher Education. *HE*, 43, 391–408.

Vidovich, L., and Porter, P. (1999) Quality Policy in Australian Higher Education of the 1990s. *JEP*, 14, 6, 567–86.

Vilkinas, T., and Peters, M. (2014) Academic Governance provided by Academic Boards within the Australian Higher Education Sector. *JHEPM*, 36, 1, 15–28.

Virkkula, E. (2016) Communities of Practice in the Conservatory. *British Journal of Music Education*, 33, 1, 27–42.

Visser-Wijnveen, G., Van Driel, J., Van der Rijst, R., Verloop, N., and Visser, A. (2010) The Ideal Research-Teaching Nexus in the Eyes of Academics. *HERD*, 29, 2, 195–210.

Vorhaus, J. (2014) Education, Social Capital and the Accordion Effect. *JPE*, 48, 1, 28–47.

Vryonides, M. (2007) Social and Cultural Capital in Educational Research. *BERJ*, 33, 6, 867–85.

Vught, F. van (2008) Mission Diversity and Reputation in Higher Education. *HEl*, 21, 151–74.

Vught, F. van, and Westerheijden, D. (1994) Towards a General Model of Quality Assessment in Higher Education. *HE*, 28, 3, 355–71.

Vuori, J. (2013) Are Students Customers in Finnish Higher Education? *TEM*, 19, 2, 176–87.

Vygotsky, L. (1978) *Mind in Society*. Edited by M. Cole, J. John-Steiner, S. Scribner and E. Souberman. Cambridge, MA: Harvard University Press.

Walker, G. (2013) A Cognitive Approach to Threshold Concepts. *HE*, 65, 2, 247–63.

Walker, M. (1998) Academic Identities. *BJSE*, 19, 3, 335–54.

Walker, P. (2014) International Student Policies in UK Higher Education from Colonialism to the Coalition. *JSIE*, 18, 4, 325–44.

Walsh, E. (2000) Phenomenographic Analysis of Interview Transcripts. pp. 19–33 in J. Bowden and E. Walsh (eds) *Phenomenography*. Melbourne, RMIT University Press.

Wamboye, E., Adekola, A., and Sergi, B. (2015) Internationalisation of the Campus and Curriculum. *JHEPM*, 37, 4, 385–99.

Wan, C.-S., Yang, J.-T., Cheng, S.-Y., and Chiakai, S. (2013) A Longitudinal Study on Internship Effectiveness in Vocational Higher Education. *ER*, 65, 1, 36–55.

Wang, R.-J. (2003) From Elitism to Mass Higher Education in Taiwan. *HE*, 46, 3, 261–87.

Ward, H., and Selvester, P. (2012) Faculty Learning Communities. *ES*, 38, 1, 111–21.

Ward, S., and Meyer, J. (2010) Metalearning Capacity and Threshold Concept Engagement. *IETI*, 47, 4, 369–78.

Ware, A. (2015) The Great British Education 'Fraud' of the Twentieth and Twenty-first Centuries. *Political Quarterly*, 86, 4, 475–84.

Warhurst, R. (2008) Cigars on the Flight-deck. *SHE*, 33, 4, 453–67.

Warren Piper, D. (1994) *Are Professors Professional?* London, Jessica Kingsley.

Warshaw, J., and Hearn, J. (2014) Leveraging University Research to serve Economic Development. *JHEPM*, 36, 2, 196–211.

Watjatrakul, B. (2014) Factors Affecting Students' Intentions to Study at Universities adopting the 'Student-as-Customer' Concept. *IJEM*, 28, 6, 676–93.

Watson, C. (2011) Accountability, Transparency, Redundancy. *BERJ*, 37, 6, 955–71.

Watson, P. (2009) Regional Themes and Global Means in Supra-national Higher Education Policy. *HE*, 58, 419–38.

Watts, A. (1972) *Diversity and Choice in Higher Education*. London, Routledge and Kegan Paul.

Waworuntu, B., and Holsinger, D. (1989) The Research Productivity of Indonesian Professors of Higher Education. *HE*, 18, 2, 167–87.

Wawrzynski, M., Heck, A., and Remley, C. (2012) Student Engagement in South African Higher Education. *JCSD*, 53, 1, 106–23.

Weaver, D., Robbie, D., Kokonis, S., and Miceli, L. (2013) Collaborative Scholarship as a Means of improving both University Teaching Practice and Research Capacity. *IJAD*, 18, 3, 237–50.

Webb, G. (1997) Deconstructing Deep and Surface. *HE*, 33, 195–212.

Webb, S., Bathmaker, A.-M., Gale, T., Hodge, S., Parker S., and Rawolle, S. (2017) Higher Vocational Education and Social Mobility. *JVET*, 69, 1, 147–67.

Weert, E. de (1990) A Macro-analysis of Quality Assessment in Higher Education. *HE*, 19, 1, 57–72.

Weert, E. de (1999) Contours of the Emergent Knowledge Society. *HE*, 38, 1, 49–69.

Weiland, S. (1995) 'Belonging to Romanticism'. *RevHE*, 18, 3, 265–92.

Welle-Strand, A. (2000) Knowledge Production, Service and Quality. *QHE*, 6, 3, 219–30.

Wells, G. (2011) Integrating CHAT and Action Research. *MCA*, 18, 2, 161–80.

Wells, R. (2008) Social and Cultural Capital, Race and Ethnicity, and College Student Retention. *JCSR*, 10, 2, 103–28.

Welsh, J., and Dey, S. (2002) Quality Measurement and Quality Assurance in Higher Education. *QAE*, 10, 1, 17–25.

Wende, M. van der (2007) Internationalization of Higher Education in the OECD Countries. *JSIE*, 11, 3–4, 274–89.

Wendlandt, N., and Rochlen, A. (2008) Addressing the College-to-Work Transition. *JCD*, 35, 2, 151–65.

Wenger, E. (1998) *Communities of Practice*. Cambridge, Cambridge University Press.

Wenger, E. (2000) Communities of Practice and Social Learning Systems. *Organization*, 7, 2, 225–46.

Wenger, E. (2009) A Social Theory of Learning. pp. 209–18 in K. Illeris (ed.) *Contemporary Theories of Learning*. London, Routledge.

Wenger, E., McDermott, R., and Snyder, W. (2002) *Cultivating Communities of Practice*. Boston, MA, Harvard Business School Press.

Whitchurch, C., and Gordon, G. (2010) Diversifying Academic and Professional Identities in Higher Education. *TEM*, 16, 2, 129–44.

White, E., Roberts, A., Rees, M., and Read, M. (2014) An Exploration of the Development of Academic Identity in a School of Education. *Professional Development in Education*, 40, 1, 56–70.

White, J., and Lowenthal, P. (2011) Minority College Students and Tacit 'Codes of Power'. *RevHE*, 34, 2, 283–318.

White, N. (2007) 'The Customer is always Right?' *HE*, 54, 4, 593–604.

Whitley, R. (1984) *The Intellectual and Social Organization of the Sciences*. Oxford, Clarendon Press. Second edition published by Oxford University Press in 2000.

Wilcox, P., Winn, S., and Fauvie-Gauld, M. (2005) 'It was Nothing to do with the University, it was just the People'. *SHE*, 30, 6, 707–22.

Willcoxson, L., Cotter, J., and Joy, S. (2011) Beyond the First-year Experience. *SHE*, 36, 3, 331–52.

Wild, L., and Ebbers, L. (2002) Rethinking Student Retention in Community Colleges. *CCJRP*, 26, 503–19.

Williams, G. (1993) Total Quality Management in Higher Education. *HE*, 25, 3, 229–37.

Williams, G. (1997) The Market Route to Mass Higher Education. *HEP*, 10, 3–4, 275–89.

Williams, J., Davis, P., and Black, L. (2007) Sociocultural and Cultural-Historical Activity Theory Perspectives on Subjectivities and Learning in Schools and other Educational Contexts. *IJER*, 46, 1–7.

Williams, R. (1988) *Keywords*. London, Fontana (first edition 1976).

Williams, R., and Van Dyke, N. (2008) Reputation and Reality. *HE*, 56, 1, 1–28.

Willingham-McLain, L. (2015) Using a Scholarship of Teaching and Learning Approach to Award Faculty who Innovate. *IJAD*, 20, 1, 58–75.

Willis, T., and Taylor, A. (1999) Total Quality Management and Higher Education. *TQM*, 10, 7, 997–1007.

Wilton, L., Good, J., Moss-Racusin, C., and Sanchez, D. (2015) Communicating more than Diversity. *Cultural Diversity and Ethnic Minority Psychology*, 21, 3, 315–25.

Wimpenny, K., and Savin-Baden, M. (2013) Alienation, Agency and Authenticity. *THE*, 18, 3, 311–26.

Wimshurst, K. (2011) Applying Threshold Concepts Theory to an Unsettled Field. *SHE*, 36, 3, 301–14.

Winberg, C. (2008) Teaching Engineering/Engineering Teaching. *THE*, 13, 3, 353–67.

Wingate, U., and Tribble, C. (2012) The Best of Both Worlds? *SHE*, 37, 4, 481–95.

Winkel, M. van, van der Rijst, R., Poell, R., and van Driel, J. (2017) Identities of Research-active Academics in New Universities. *JFHE*, DOI:10.1080/0309877X.2017.1301407.

Winkler, E. (2017) Racism as a Threshold Concept. *REE*, http://dx.doi.org/10.1080/13613324.2017.1294564.

Winter, R. (2009) Academic Manager or Managed Academic? *JHEPM*, 31, 2, 121–31.

Wisker, G. (2007) Crossing Liminal Spaces. *Pedagogy: critical approaches to teaching literature, language, composition and culture*, 7, 3, 401–25.

Wisker, G., and Savin-Baden, M. (2009) Priceless Conceptual Thresholds. *LRE*, 7, 3, 235–47.

Wit, H. de (2011) Globalisation and Internationalisation of Higher Education. *Revista de Universidad y Sociedad del Conocimiento*, 8, 2, 241–8.

Woelert, P., and Millar, V. (2013) The 'Paradox of Interdisciplinarity' in Australian Research Governance. *HE*, 66, 6, 755–67.

Wojcieszek, J., Theaker, L., Ratcliff, M., MacPherson, L., and Boyd, J. (2014) Enhancing the First Year Student Experience through Academic and Professional Staff Collegiality. *IJFYHE*, 5, 1, 143–51.

Wolf-Wendel, L., Ward, K., and Kinzie, J. (2009) A Tangled Web of Terms. *JCSD*, 50, 4, 407–28.

Wolter, A., and Kerst, C. (2015) The 'Academization' of the German Qualification System. *RCIE*, 10, 4, 510–24.

Wood, P., and Cajkler, W. (2017) Lesson Study. *JFHE*, DOI:10.1080/03098 77X.2016.1261093.

Woodall, T., Hiller, A., and Resnick, S. (2014) Making Sense of Higher Education. *SHE*, 39, 1, 48–67.

Woodrow, J. (2006) Institutional Mission. *CHE*, 5, 4, 313–27.

Woolcock, M. (2010) The Rise and Routinization of Social Capital, 1988–2008. *Annual Review of Political Science*, 13, 469–87.

Wright, A. (2001) The Dalhousie Career Portfolio Programme. *QHE*, 7, 2, 149–59.

Wright, A., and Gilmore, A. (2012) Threshold Concepts and Conceptions. *JME*, 36, 5, 614–35.

Wright, P. (1989) Who Defines Quality in Higher Education? *HE*, 18, 2, 149–65.

Wyatt, J. (1977) 'Collegiality' During a Period of Rapid Change in Higher Education. *ORE*, 3, 2, 147–55.

Wyatt, L. (2011) Nontraditional Student Engagement. *Journal of Continuing Higher Education*, 59, 1, 10–20.

Yair, G. (2008) Can we Administer the Scholarship of Teaching? *HE*, 55, 4, 447–59.

Yan, Y., and Sendall, P. (2016) First Year Experience. *Journal of International Students*, 6, 1, 35–51.

Yang, R. (2000) Tensions Between the Global and the Local. *HE*, 39, 3, 319–37.

Yang, R. (2003) Globalisation and Higher Education Development. *IRE*, 49, 3–4, 269–91.

Yang, R., and Welch, A. (2012) A World-class University in China? *HE*, 63, 5, 645–66.

Yang, S., and Chen, S.-F. (2002) A Phenomenographic Approach to the Meaning of Death. *Death Studies*, 26, 143–75.

Yannuzzi, T., and Martin, D. (2014) Voice, Identity and the Organizing of Student Experience. *THE*, 19, 6, 709–20.

Yin, H., Lu, G., and Wang, W. (2014) Unmasking the Teaching Quality of Higher Education. *AEHE*, 39, 8, 949–70.

Ylijoki, O.-H. (2000) Disciplinary Cultures and the Moral Order of Studying. *HE*, 39, 3, 339–62.

Ylijoki, O.-H., and Ursin, J. (2013) The Construction of Academic Identity in the Changes of Finnish Higher Education. *SHE*, 38, 8, 1135–49.

Yokoyama, K. (2010) The Patterns of Change in Higher Education Institutions. *TEM*, 16, 1, 61–80.

Yonezawa, A. (2002) The Quality Assurance System and Market Forces in Japanese Higher Education. *HE*, 43, 1, 127–39.

Yonezawa, A., Nakatsui, I., and Kobayashi, T. (2002) University Rankings in Japan. *HEE*, 27, 4, 373–82.

Yorke, M. (2000) The Quality of the Student Experience. *QHE*, 6, 1, 61–75.

Yorke, M. (2013) Surveys of 'The Student Experience' and the Politics of Feedback. In S. Merry, M. Price, D. Carless, and M. Taras (eds) *Reconceptualising Feedback in Higher Education*. London, Routledge, 6–18.

Yorke, M. (2016) The Development and Initial Use of a Survey of Student 'Belongingness', Engagement and Self-confidence in UK Higher Education. *AEHE*, 41, 1, 154–66.

Yorke, M., and Longden, B. (2008) The First-Year Experience of Higher Education in the UK. York, Higher Education Academy.

Zaman, M. (2004) *Review of the Academic Evidence on the Relationship between Teaching and Research in Higher Education*. Nottingham, Department for Education and Skills, Research Report RR506.

Zepke, N. (2015) Student Engagement Research. *HERD*, 34, 6, 1311–23.

Zepke, N., and Leach, L. (2005) Integration and Adaptation. *ALHE*, 6, 1, 46–59.

Zepke, N., and Leach, L. (2010) Improving Student Engagement. *ALHE*, 11, 3, 167–77.

Zha, Q. (2011) China's Move to Mass Higher Education in a Comparative Perspective. *Compare*, 41, 6, 751–68.

Zhan, Y., and Wan, Z. (2016) Appreciated but Constrained. *THE*, 21, 6, 669–85.

Zhang, L., Bao, W., and Sun, L. (2016) Resources and Research Production in Higher Education. *ResHE*, 57, 869–91.

Zhang, X. (2007) Re-examining the Mission of the University in Mass Higher Education. *Frontiers of Education in China*, 2, 3, 378–93.

Zhang, Y., Gan, Y., and Cham, H. (2007) Perfectionism, Academic Burnout and Engagement among Chinese College Students. *Personality and Individual Differences*, 43, 1529–40.

Zhao, C.-M., and Kuh, G. (2004) Adding Value. *ResHE*, 45, 2, 115–38.

Zhao, C.-M., Kuh, G., and Carini, R. (2005) A Comparison of International Student and American Student Engagement in Effective Educational Practices. *JHE*, 76, 2, 209–31.

Zmas, A. (2015) Global Impacts of the Bologna Process. *Compare*, 45, 5, 727–47.

Zundans-Fraser, L., and Bain A. (2016) How do Institutional Practices for Course Design and Review address Areas of Need in Higher Education? *HERD*, 35, 4, 841–53.

Index